"I think I was saying 3–0 or 4–[...]
thinking there might be a bit o[...]
weather as it is at the moment[...]

D0130350

First Test, Third Day
Stuart G in Sydney: "You Poms never learn do you?" he scoffs.
"Before every Ashes series, you talk up your chances, and then we
thrash you."

Second Test, First Day
"Women do wear boxes, though they are a different shape to
men's as they have a different shaped pelvic bone," points out
Richard O'Hagan. "They refer to them as manhole covers."

Second Test, Second Day
Here's Richard Burgess. "When I saw Warney's haircut on the telly
last night, I was reminded of the time as a kid when the
neighbour's golden retriever had an operation and some of his
fur had to be shaved off."

Third Test, Second Day
"I hope you guys realise that I'm risking my very job just being
here?" wails James Holbrook from impending firedom. "New ICT
policy means I can only use t'internet for 5% of my working time.
Stuff the economy, I'm on here from 10.30 till I bunk off early at
four." The chance of finishing at four on a Friday. Bah! It's alright
for some.

Third Test, Fourth Day
At the moment it's like that time at school when you hear the girl
you fancy, fancies you. It couldn't possibly actually happen,
couldn't really be true. Could it? Rob Smyth

Fifth Test, First Day
"I'm enjoying your idiosyncratic coverage," says Michael Paterson.
"However, it poses me a problem. I work in the HR department at
Guardian headquarters. I formulate policy on matters such as
what constitutes excessive internet usage on company time. I
have spent so much time following your coverage today that I
will have to sack myself – obviously not until close of play."

Is it Cowardly to Pray for Rain?

MIKE ADAMSON
JAMES DART
SEAN INGLE
and
ROB SMYTH

ABACUS

GuardianBooks

ABACUS

First published in Great Britain as a paperback original
in October 2005 by Abacus

A CIP catalogue record for this book
is available from the British Library.

ISBN 0 349 11983 X

Typeset in Frutiger by M Rules
Printed and bound in Great Britain
by Clays Ltd, St Ives plc

Abacus
An imprint of
Time Warner Book Group UK
Brettenham House
Lancaster Place
London WC2E 7EN

www.twbg.co.uk

Contents

Fifth Test: The Oval, 8–12 September 2005   257

Preamble

Essentially the over-by-over should not work. It consists of one or two of our team sitting in the office watching a sporting event on a television set and describing it to the outside world on a rolling report. When audio streaming is now available on most computers, when televisions are increasingly apparent in public places, the idea that anyone would sit and refresh a computer screen as the best way to absorb a commentary just seems a bit daft. But it isn't. This summer our Ashes over-by-over coverage reached extraordinary heights – on the busiest days hundreds of thousands of readers logged on and joined in. Imagine our delight when, ahead of the fifth Test, an IT consultant appeared on the radio warning that workers 'clicking on internet cricket commentaries' would crash office systems. The informed and witty words of Rob Smyth, Sean Ingle, Mike Adamson and James Dart (with Barry Glendenning putting in an hour as twelfth man) spanned all sixty-one sessions played in the five Tests, and gathered our own barmy army of readers.

The written word can deliver more than a commentary on television or radio. You can visit a report in the afternoon and scan the morning's play to find the 'WICKET!' references without waiting for highlights and scoreboards, and you can read what it feels like to watch England squeak a crucial Test by two runs. It's all in the writing of course. 'Four Tests and more snakish twists and turns than Peter Mandelson on the Pepsi Max Big One' is how Sean Ingle opened his report on the final day of the fifth Test.

And then there is the audience. Every Ashes commentary attracted hundreds of email contributions – some witty and erudite, others unsuitable for family reading – covering everything from the migration of cricket coverage to satellite TV, to the rather alarming regularity of Rob Smyth's morning headaches.

At Guardian Unlimited we are all indebted to the reader power that enlivened our summer and we hope you enjoy our permanent record of those heady weeks. And if you enjoyed the over-by-over experience, you'll find online commentary on your other favourite sporting events at www.guardian.co.uk/sport.

Emily Bell
Editor-in-Chief
Guardian Unlimited

First Test

**Lord's,
21–24 July 2005**

First Day

The morning session

BY SEAN INGLE

Preamble: We've had the Twenty20 face-off, the NatWest Series, an additional (why?) one-day series also sponsored by NatWest, a Pietersen/Thorpe debate that's swung more ways than a tangled yo-yo and, earlier this week, the sort of trash usually spouted by bandana-wearing gangsta rappers from the streets, not Matthew Hoggard from Leeds, Yorkshire. Now, finally, it's day one of the first Test from Lord's. Game on!

Toss: Oh dear. A beaming Ricky Ponting calls heads – correctly – before announcing that Australia will bat first. Both sides line up as expected, with Jason Gillespie preferred to Michael Kasprowicz for the Aussies. "Is it only me that has been deflated before the series has even started by us losing the toss?" says John Dalby. "It was a crucial one to win and now the Aussies will be able to set the tone for the rest of the summer by finishing today on 360–3 and having the Test wrapped up in three days. After months of anticipation, I am truly miserable and it hasn't even begun."

1st over: Australia 9–0 (Langer 3, Hayden 6) Great start for Harmison, who gets Langer playing and missing with his first delivery, before whacking him on the elbow with his second. The bruise has already come up and it looks nasty. After a delay in play while Langer is given the all-clear from the Aussie physio, Harmison steams in . . . and lets him off the hook with one on his legs, which is steered away for three. Hayden then plays and misses, before scoring a lucky boundary off his thigh-pad. Eventually nine come off the over, which is a bit unfair considering Harmison produced three beauties.

2nd over: Australia 13–0 (Langer 7, Hayden 6) A decent-ish start from Hoggard, who gets Langer playing and missing again. He's also getting the ball to swing. "Is John Dalby actually Nasser Hussain operating under a pseudonym?" asks Ben Smith. "It's exactly that sort of attitude which has resulted in our failure for so many years."

3rd over: Australia 14–0 (Langer 7, Hayden 7) Solid over from Harmison finishes with one that nearly cuts Langer in half. Meanwhile your predictions are flooding in. "What's the betting that our initial enthusiasm will be slowly squeezed out of us as the Aussies rack up a big score by this afternoon, and that after two days in the field we will all be talking about the start of the football season instead?" predicts a cheery Paul Jaines.

4th over: Australia 18–0 (Langer 7, Hayden 11) England have bowled lots of decent deliveries here, but for scant reward. "Now we've lost the toss, I reckon the Aussies will score 400 and we'll lose this match and series by quite some margin," admits Mark Fournier, who I'm guessing is a Sisters of Mercy fan. "My gloomy prediction of 3–1 will be well on the way to fulfilment."

5th over: Australia 19–0 (Langer 8, Hayden 11) Harmison roughs Hayden up with a bouncer, and then follows it with a short one. He's fiery, but he's not getting much swing yet. "A 3–1 win, with the *Sun* using *The Empire Strikes Back* as the headline," predicts Alex from Leeds.

6th over: Australia 25–0 (Langer 13, Hayden 11) Hoggard is again as wild as his Heathcliffian hair. "England to win 4–0, the whitewash only being avoided by Australia after Jim Robinson collapses with a heart attack whilst standing at first slip in the second session of the third day of the fourth Test, and the game is stopped following a legal injunction by Toady," says Lee Rodwell. "Unfortunately, England's celebrations are cut short by the realisation that it was all just a dream. By Bouncer the dog."

7th over: Australia 26–0 (Langer 18, Hayden 11) This isn't looking good: after Harmison again makes Langer play and miss, he sends down a half-volley which is clouted through the covers and the scoreboard continues to tick over. "Pietersen is going to lose his head like Gazza in the 1991 Cup Final and get out for 12 and 0 in this Test. He will then burst into tears wearing plastic boobs and release a No. 2 hit single with Lindisfarne," claims Neil Ardiff.

WICKET! 8th over: Hayden b Hoggard 12 (Australia 35–1) Off the final delivery of another expensive over, Hoggard shocks everybody by finally finding his line, just on off stump. It jags back, going through bat and pad, before clattering into Hayden's stumps!

9th over: Australia 35–1(Langer 26, Ponting 0) Another decent over from Harmison, which is spoiled by a half-volley which Langer steers through the covers for four. "Are all you gloomers going to shut up now?" fires Ian Cheney. "Hayden gone so only nine more prolific batsmen to get through! Australia will be all out for 260 this innings with Warney being top scorer."

10th over: Australia 43–1 (Langer 26, Ponting 3) Pietersen drops Ponting! Hoggard gets one to move away, the Australian captain can't resist driving and England's new Boy Wonder, at gully, drops a very makeable diving catch. A huge let-off. "The all-time classic Bouncer the dog dream sequence episode of *Neighbours* is Australia's greatest (and possibly only) contribution to art culture," says Glen Sibley. "I stand to be corrected."

11th over: Australia 50–1 (Langer 31, Ponting 4) Harmison continues to take the fight to the Aussies: he's just nailed Ponting with a bouncer – the Aussie captain is bleeding from his left cheek and the physio is on again. After ten minutes' delay, Ponting brings up the 50 with a quick single.

12th over: Australia 51–1 (Langer 31, Ponting 5) Hoggard continues to frustrate: he's getting plenty of swing, but he's also continuing to drift down leg like Tom Jones in his 60s-seducing prime. "What price an 'Aussies Come to Harm' headline in the *Sun* tomorrow?" asks Jon Martin. "At least we know which Harmison has turned up. I'm feeling a lot more confident about the series now!"

WICKET! 13th over: Ponting c Strauss b Harmison 8 (Australia 55–2) Harmison looks like he's caught going-down-legitis, and allows Ponting to flick it off his pads for an easy boundary. But then he produces a real snorter, which Ponting can only fend to third slip, where Andrew Strauss takes a simple catch. "To widen Glen Sibley's Aussie Art culture I have three words," says Ravi Motha. "Men at Work."

14th over: Australia 66–2 (Langer 40, Martyn 2) Hoggard, apart from his wicket-taking delivery, continues to be poor. "The *Sun* headline tomorrow? What about 'Grievous Bodily Harmison'?" suggests Shane Firemaster.

WICKET! 15th over: Langer c Harmison b Flintoff 40 (Australia 66–3) Flintoff comes on for Harmison – and immediately strikes! He fires one in short and Langer can't resist the hook shot. However, it's quicker than he expects: it comes off the splice of his bat and loops high into the air and Harmison takes an easy catch at square leg.

WICKET! 16th over: Martyn c G Jones b S Jones 2 (Australia 66–4) Unbelievable: Simon Jones strikes with his first ball! Martyn tries to drive off the back foot, but it moves slightly and Geraint Jones snags a regulation catch behind the stumps. Apologies for all the exclamation marks, but what a start for England! "I really wish I worked with some Australians now," says Phil Butler, who surely speaks for the nation. "Not that I'm really working."

17th over: Australia 73–4 (Clarke 4, Katich 2) More fiery stuff from Flintoff, who's already bowling at 91.5mph, glaring at both Aussie batsmen, and peppering them with bouncers. If the Aussies thought this was going to be easy, they know different now. "Re: Aussie culture. What about Paul Hogan?" suggests Jonathan Riggall. "If it wasn't for him I'd still think that 'out back' was somewhere where me Dad lived in his shed."

18th over: Australia 78–4 (Clarke 4, Katich 6) Shot of the day from Katich! He steps into Jones's wide one and thumps it through the offside for four. "Re: antagonising Aussies. I'm going to Shepherd's Bush to watch the remainder of today's play," gloats Nicholas Read.

19th over: Australia 80–4 (Clarke 5, Katich 6) More hostile bowling from Flintoff, who turns Clarke around with the short stuff before nearly trapping him lbw. Just in time, Clarke manages to get bat on ball before pad. "I work with several Australians and have already done a celebratory tour of the office, much like the open-top bus trip taken by the England rugby team when they won RWC 2003," says James Peterson. "Except, of course, I am not wearing brown shoes with my blue suit."

20th over: Australia 81–4 (Clarke 6, Katich 6) Another huge appeal from Jones, who swings it back into Katich and flicks the back pad. Unfortunately his pad is millimetres outside off stump. Meanwhile the Aussies are firing back. "Settle down, chaps," says Evan Maloney. "It's a long summer."

21st over: Australia 83–4 (Clarke 7, Katich 6) With lunch just 10 minutes away, Clarke and Katich are content to watch and wait. Meanwhile, more debate regarding Aussie culture. "What about the Divinyls' 'I Touch Myself'? Not many songs about ladies doing That Kind Of Thing, and that's a fine example of the genre," says Louise Wright.

WICKET! 22nd over: Clarke lbw b S Jones 11 (Australia 87–5) Jones, like Hoggard before him, is alternating between ragged and brilliant. And after Clarke swats a loose one for four, Jones produces some extra pace, and catches him in front of his stumps. "How tedious – British people suggesting that Australians have no culture," says Cameron Haskell. "Err, besides oddball Germaine, there's Nick Cave, transnational DBC Pierre, Tim Winton, film-makers Fred Schepsi, Phillip Noyce, and all the good actresses going right now (Cate Blanchett, Naomi Watts and Nicole)."

23rd over: Australia 97–5 (Clarke 7, Gilchrist 8) Flintoff comes round the wicket to Gilchrist, who can't resist having a nibble and nearly goes for a duck. He then goes on to play a perfect cut stroke for four, and another that flies where fourth slip should be. England finish the morning with an eight-man slip cordon, before lunch is called. It's definitely their session, and they go off to a standing ovation.

Australia 97–5

The afternoon session

BY JAMES DART

Lunch break: The crowd are pumped, the OBO office is pumped and you're pumped too. "So, which tabloid is going to give it back to the Aussies with the 'Is That All You've Got?' headline?" asks Neil Kateley. "At least before having to be magnanimous in (narrow) defeat at the end of the series, naturally. But hey, let's enjoy this for as long as possible, eh?"

24th over: Australia 98–5 (Katich 7, Gilchrist 8) Jones resumes with the sky still somewhat overcast; good news for England's pace attack. A tidy opening over sees just one run come from Gilchrist's prod to silly mid-off. "I've just had a text from my friend Russell, who is at Lord's," explains Phil Roebuck. "He says the atmosphere is 'eclectic'. I think he means 'electric'."

25th over: Australia 100–5 (Katich 8, Gilchrist 8) Flintoff's still powering in after lunch, but his line is a little too much down the leg-side. "Frustrated from Tunbridge Wells here," starts a correspondent, who, for reasons that will soon become clear, we'll call "Laura". "All my friends are able to watch while at work (and rubbing my nose in it), while I am marooned up here without a television in sight – any suggestions from the OBO crew on how I can escape from the evil clutches of a global investment bank, and skive the afternoon off (suggestions on how to smuggle telly in here most welcome)?"

26th over: Australia 107–5 (Katich 12, Gilchrist 8) Katich punishes Jones for some short-pitched bowling, pulling him nonchalantly to the deep-fine-leg boundary. "Suggestion for Laura," mails a helpful and probably knowledgeable Roger Mortimer. "Sell your entire portfolio then accidentally buy some seriously overpriced stock with as much leverage as you can get your hands on, then watch the panic unfold. During said panic, creep out on all fours."

27th over: Australia 115–5 (Katich 12, Gilchrist 16) For the first time since lunch, Gilchrist is offered room to swing his arms from Flintoff, and he gratefully cuts, a little streakily, to the ropes. Nothing streaky next ball, mind, as he hammers Freddie through the covers again.

28th over: Australia 122–5 (Katich 12, Gilchrist 22) More impressive hitting from Gilchrist, who, as we all know, has the capability to turn a Test in a matter of hours. His latest boundary off Jones is pulled powerfully to square leg and England could seriously do with another wicket. Meanwhile, here's Nick Watson. "You might call this the understatement of the decade but Ponting's decision to bat first seems to have backfired somewhat. Of course I felt that it would at the time . . . even if I did predict 'these two will make a double hundred opening stand and Australia will win by an innings and 200 runs'. I just didn't want to tempt fate."

WICKET! 29th over: Gilchrist c G Jones b Flintoff 26 (Australia 126–6) Shocking footwork from Gilchrist as his flash outside off stump garners no more than a nick which Geraint Jones takes comfortably behind. Just what England needed and not what you expect from a player of Gilchrist's class.

29th over: Australia 128–6 (Katich 12, Warne 0) Out comes Shane Warne to the crease with Australia in real trouble.

30th over: Australia 137–6 (Katich 16, Warne 5) More of a hopeful pull, with his eye off the ball, from Warne as Australia register another boundary. But Gilchrist's fall has clearly given both Flintoff and Jones an extra yard of pace.

31st over: Australia 146–6 (Katich 16, Warne 14) Flintoff gives Warne the stare after some head-height action spears off the legspinner's bat, over the slips, and to the boundary. Warne makes the Lancashire man even madder after the next ball, rising to meet a wide short-length delivery with a crisp clatter through point. "Ricky Ponting's decision to bat first certainly has backfired," fumes Justin Horton. "I had a bet, nine quid at 7–1, on Australia winning the toss and putting England in. Ponting cost me seventy quid. Mind you I'm far too civilised to be glad that Harmison hit him on the head."

32nd over: Australia 155–6 (Katich 16, Warne 23) It's taken just over seven overs for Australia to rattle up their last 50 runs; with Warne cracking Jones over mid-off to bring up the 150. "Laura – can't you contrive a reason to visit the trader's floor?" wonders Andy Williams. "Surely they've got tellies galore?"

33rd over: Australia 158–6 (Katich 18, Warne 24) Harmison returns to the attack and the move almost pays immediate dividends. A rising delivery to Warne strikes the splice of the bat, spiralling towards Andrew Strauss at gully. The batsman leaps to take the catch, but can only get a hand on the ball, failing to cling on to what would have been a spectacular take. "I happen to know that Nick Watson (28th over) is on holiday with his fiancée," snitches Tom Newman. "What on earth is he doing sitting indoors sending in emails to the OBO – about cricket, for heaven's sake? I give the marriage a month tops."

34th over: Australia 163–6 (Katich 22, Warne 25) Cracking shot through extra cover from Katich, who is quietly going about his business at the crease without any major scares. "Surely Laura could spend a paltry amount of what I'm sure is a massively inflated salary on a pocket-sized TV?" suggests self-confessed IT geek Chris Amstrong.

35th over: Australia 168–6 (Katich 22, Warne 26) Four extras as Harmison strays a little too far down leg, while Warne chalks up another single. Meanwhile, here's Andy Killeen. "Ponting's decision to bat first does look arrogant and misguided, but let's not get carried away. In the ODIs the bowlers of both sides looked in better form than their batting colleagues. I want to see solid knocks from our top three before I relax."

36th over: Australia 175–6 (Katich 27, Warne 27) The cloud breaks as sunshine bathes Lord's for the first time this afternoon. Vaughan will know that the next 10 overs will be crucial; he can't afford Warne and Katich to still be there, hauling Australia back into the game.

Drinks break: Australia 175–6 (Katich 27, Warne 27) "How typically English," says Andrew Goldsby. "We encounter a girl who not only likes cricket but we all presume makes good money and what do we do? Run her down as much as possible. Madness." Hear, hear, Andrew.

WICKET! 37th over: Warne b Harmison 28 (Australia 175–7) Warne edges across his crease once too often, leaving his leg stump exposed. Harmison ruthlessly uproots it, sending Warne back to the pavilion and bringing Brett Lee to the crease. "While I deplore the over-use of exclamation marks nearly as much as I abhor inappropriate apostraphes, I do feel that the dispatch of an Australian batsman by England during an Ashes Test is surely sufficient grounds for exclamation," said Eddie Cochrane, mere moments before the wicket. Hopefully this has been good enough for you, Eddie! Eh?!

WICKET! 37th over: Katich c G Jones b Harmison 27 (Australia 178–8) A short-length Harmison delivery is the worst ball to try and make things happen from. Katich's mistimed pull goes skywards behind the stumps, Geraint Jones steadies himself to take a simple catch.

38th over: Australia 178–8 (Lee 3, Gillespie 0) Flintoff gets an immediate opportunity to get into Gillespie with some short-pitched action. Here's Trevor Pearce, quick to jump on to a name riff: "Can I be the 100th [14th, actually] person in the last minute to say that I hope your use of exclamation marks in your 37th over didn't give your correspondent the Summertime Blues? C'mon! (Everybody)."

39th over: Australia 178–8 (Lee 3, Gillespie 0) Lee attempts to guide Harmison behind square, but only picks out the crazily coiffed Pietersen in the gully. It is an easy chance, right into his body, but he still puts it down.

WICKET! 39th over: Lee c G Jones b Harmison 3 (Australia 178–9) Pietersen will be feeling a whole deal better now as Lee survives just one ball longer. He tickles Harmison with an edge off his glove that drifts down leg-side, where Geraint Jones takes a superb catch low to his left. Time to call Mr McGrath . . .

39th over: Australia 182–9 (Gillespie 0, McGrath 4) . . . and Glenn arrives in style, hammering Harmison to the midwicket boundary.

40th over: Australia 190–9 (Gillespie 1, McGrath 10) Frustration for Flintoff as McGrath catches a thick edge that flies over the despairing dive of Strauss. "What on earth is the point of getting the *Guardian* if you can't be mean about merchant bankers?" asks Phil Smith.

WICKET! 41st over: Gillespie lbw b Harmison 1 (Australia 190 all out) A 'five-fer' for Harmison as he traps Gillespie right in front of middle and leg. No dispute from the umpire, and England have skittled Australia for just 190. The challenge has been laid down . . .

England batsmen getting–their–pads–on time: Sorry readers, but we'll be having none of this "Stonefish, Donald Fisher, Dame Edna . . . boys . . . onehelluva . . .beating" on here, I'm afraid. Anthony Walker can get away with this, though: "Well done to the plucky Australians for getting beyond the 40th over in their first innings – a feat (just) beyond the mighty Bangladesh earlier in the season . . ."

England first innings

1st over: England 4–0 (Trescothick 4, Strauss 0) McGrath is right on his line immediately, giving Trescothick plenty to think about right from the off. "Heavens. Why so many nasty comments about Australian culture (or lack thereof) during the first session?" wonders Douglas Wilson, "Culturally Impoverished in Sydney". "Are all your English readers following OBO whilst re-reading *Ulysses*? We're letting you win at the cricket – what else do you want?"

2nd over: England 8–0 (Trescothick 4, Strauss 0) Lee's fired up – too fired up – as Strauss tries to duck a bouncer that clips him on the shoulder and flies over the slip cordon for four leg byes. Meanwhile, Kieran Taylor chirps: "Do the Aussies realise that they can have more than 50 overs to bat today? The much-derided NatWest Challenge is looking like a stroke of genius now. As the high priest of Oz rock Stefan Dennis once sang, 'Don't It Make You Feel Good?' Yes I do."

3rd over: England 8–0 (Trescothick 4, Strauss 0) A maiden from McGrath. Daniel Ashley writes: "I cannot get 'I Touch Myself' out of my head after someone mentioned it during the first innings hours ago. Bah!" It's "Don't It Make You Feel Good?" by Stefan Dennis, for me, Daniel. Bah!

4th over: England 9–0 (Trescothick 4, Strauss 1) "Not out" is the call from Rudi Koertzen as Lee, Gilchrist and the Australian team launch a concerted vocal appeal after the ball clips Strauss on the shirt and flies to the wicket keeper. Television replays show the umpire was spot-on.

5th over: England 10–0 (Trescothick 4, Strauss 2) McGrath's cranking the pressure up on the England pair, as they look to see off as much of his opening spell as possible. "Try singing 'Don't It Make You Feel Good?' with feeling but without the trademark Dennis glowering scowl," challenges Tim Down. "I think you'll find it's impossible, even if you manage not to clench your fist at the same time."

6th over: England 10–0 (Trescothick 4, Strauss 2) The England openers still can't shake the shackles Lee and McGrath are imposing upon them. Very few cheap deliveries from the pair, which is what you expect. "What absolute pomposity from Douglas Wilson," blasts Dale Sharpe. "Letting us win? Can't they just admit that they played awful? You wait, if England do win the Ashes I bet the old Aussie line of 'Well we only have 20 million people, you'd expect England to win' will be put out." And that, my friends, is tea.

Australia 190; England 10–0

The evening session

BY MIKE ADAMSON

Tea break: With only 47 overs bowled so far today, it's going to be a long evening session. Long enough, dare I say it, for England's batsmen in the warm Lord's sunshine to overtake the measly Australian total of 190 (apologies if that puts a hex on them). There's no disputing England have won the morning session and afternoon session, so unless the Aussies can do something this evening, they'll surely be staring defeat in the face.

WICKET! 7th over: Trescothick c Langer b McGrath 4 (England 10–1) Well that didn't take long. McGrath notches his 500th Test wicket with the very first ball of the session. Trescothick played at a full and straight one, but only managed to edge it to Justin Langer at third slip for an easy catch. Expect the Aussies to turn the screw now.

WICKET! 7th over: Strauss c Warne b McGrath 2 (England 11–2) And there's No. 501. An almost identical dismissal, except this time the nick was thinner and travelled to the safe hands of Shane Warne at first slip. We should've known it was too good to last.

8th over: England 13–2 (Vaughan 3, Bell 0) Vaughan tries to pull a Lee delivery which was too full for the shot, but gets just enough on it to bring up two runs. England appear very nervous here, not surprisingly. "I used to play cricket at Keynsham Town Cricket Club (where Marcus Trescothick learnt his trade)," says Daniel Smith, innocently enough. "Whilst playing for the Under-11s I once had a fight with his cousin, Neil Trescothick, as his off-spin was annoying the hell out of me in the nets. In retrospect I may have over-reacted – could you put out a national apology to the Trescothick family for my behaviour?" Anyone else ever had a run-in with one of our star cricketers, or their relatives?

9th over: England 14–2 (Vaughan 3, Bell 1) Bell leaves one which went very close to his off stump, and receives a mouthful from McGrath for his trouble. Then it's Vaughan's turn to let one by his stumps with more confidence than those Englishmen watching. "I can't believe you would tempt fate like that and have the gall to think that a bracketed 'apologies if that puts a hex on them' will suffice," says an angry Luke Shiach. "I hold you responsible for the Ashes whitewash that will doubtless follow." I am truly sorry.

10th over: England 14–2 (Vaughan 3, Bell 1) A maiden for Lee, who is bowling a good line and with real pace – consistently around the 92mph mark. Bell is struggling to get a bat on it, which I suppose is at least better than edging one. As you can sense, the optimism generated earlier is slowly seeping away.

11th over: England 14–2 (Vaughan 3, Bell 1) More of the same from McGrath. Those accusations of him being past his best are looking a little fanciful now.

12th over: England 18–2 (Vaughan 3, Bell 5) Bell proves his limbo-dancing ability by ducking under a brutal bodyline bouncer from Lee before proving his batting ability with an immaculate cover drive. That pushes his Test average up to 301, which isn't too shabby.

WICKET! 13th over: Vaughan b McGrath 3 (England 18–3) What happened to this wonderful batting surface we were promised? A good-length McGrath delivery just died as it hit the pitch, creeping under the England captain's bat and striking off stump about half a foot up. Now it's up to the two Ashes debutants to steady the ship. "How many do we need to avoid the follow-on?" asks Neil Strange. Thankfully, we can't follow on.

13th over: England 18–3 (Bell 5, Pietersen 0) Kevin Pietersen negotiates his first few balls in Test cricket comfortably, but it's the Aussies who are singing now. "As we like to say at the G – 'Ooh a Glenn McGrath, ooh a Glenn McGrath . . . I saaaayy!!'" So says Jacob Murray-White in Melbourne.

14th over: England 19–3 (Bell 6, Pietersen 0) A run! For Ian Bell. The less said about the rest of the over, the better from an England point of view. "Back when Steve Harmison was a slip of a lad playing for Ashington as an Under-17, I thrashed him to all parts of the ground one Friday night," says Chris Bone. "First ball dug in and over point it went for a one-bounce four! More of the same followed as we cantered home by eight wickets. 'Thanks for the net,' I chirped as I left the field. His response is unprintable on a family website."

WICKET! 15th over: Bell b McGrath 6 (England 19–4) These updates are becoming depressingly repetitive. McGrath picks up his fourth wicket with a beautiful delivery which clipped the top of Bell's off stump after a slight inside edge.

16th over: England 21–4 (Pietersen 2, Flintoff 0) KP scores his first runs with a prod through the off-side. "Without wishing to say I told you so, does anyone else wish we'd picked Graeme Thorpe?" writes Jim Price and countless others. "Prove me wrong, Pietersen, please prove me wrong."

WICKET! 17th over: Flintoff b McGrath 0 (England 21–5) Dear, dear, dear. McGrath beats the bat again with a ball that kept low and hits an England batsman's off stump for a third time this afternoon. The good news is it's meant to rain on Saturday and Sunday.

17th over: England 25–5 (Pietersen 2, G Jones 4) A glorious square cut puts four in Geraint Jones's column, which almost makes him England's top scorer.

18th over: England 25–5 (Pietersen 2, G Jones 4) Gillespie is into the attack, which *might* not be the worst thing for England. Lewis Murdoch observes wisely: "At least we can't revert to the days of middle order collapses if the top of the order fail to provide something to collapse from. Harmison must be wondering why he bothers."

19th over: England 25–5 (Pietersen 2, G Jones 4) Yet another maiden for McGrath whose figures are now 5 for 11 off 10 overs. "Not a run-in as such," says Greg Chivers, "but Geoff Boycott and I tried to stare each other out on Wakefield Westgate station once. He won. I was only 13 and he was a patient Test match opener. In hindsight it was no competition really, was it?" Nope.

20th over: England 29–5 (Pietersen 6, G Jones 4) Shot! Pietersen decides to take advantage of the fact Gillespie is bowling, and sends the ball hurtling through the covers with a back-foot drive. "Mike," begins Danny Edmunds sternly, "how does it raining on Saturday and Sunday help us? At this rate it'll be over tomorrow."

21st over: England 34–5 (Pietersen 6, G Jones 9) Another cracking square cut by Jones, who then works the ball into the leg-side for a single. "At what point do we decide to bring on Vikram Solanki?" asks John Hall.

22nd over: England 39–5 (Pietersen 6, G Jones 13) Jones strokes another Gillespie delivery for four through the off-side. "Maybe this is just a cunning plan by England to ensure McGrath keeps on bowling believing he has got us where he wants us and has almost finished us off, and then straining too hard and bowling too long suffers a stress fracture, and is no longer able to play for the rest of the series," says Nick Watson breathlessly.

23rd over: England 40–5 (Pietersen 7, G Jones 13) McGrath works his way through another over, keeping the ball on a tight line and length. If Ponting had a heart, he would give the creaking paceman a rest, and the English batsmen a chance, now. "Now I'm not saying it's entirely your fault, but things were going a lot better until you turned up!" says John Gibbons. It's OK, John, I take full responsibility.

24th over: England 44–5 (Pietersen 8, G Jones 16) Runs galore for England – well, four of them, as Pietersen nicks a single and then Jones nervously guides (give him the benefit of the doubt) the ball between the slips and gully for two (and another I didn't see).

25th over: England 48–5 (Pietersen 8, G Jones 20) Just as I was about to write how impressive Jones is looking, McGrath fizzes one straight through the wicketkeeper/batsman. McGrath has now bowled 13 overs on the spin, hence Raminder Dhendsa's questions: "Surely Glenn McGrath has bowled his allocation now? When does the bits and pieces fifth bowler come on?"

26th over: England 49–5 (Pietersen 9, G Jones 20) The cracks on the pitch are still causing England some bother. This time Gillespie gets one to shoot up, but Jones manages to fend it off with his arm. "Geraint is made for this situation," says Mostyn Lewis with eerie confidence. "I'm expecting at least 80 from the man, backed up by 40s from KP and Wheelie-Bin, with a cameo run-a-ball 30 from M-O-M Harmison. And we've got a 40–run first-innings lead." Hmmm.

27th over: England 49–5 (Pietersen 9, G Jones 20) At long last McGrath leaves the attack, but there's not much respite for England as he's replaced by Lee. "I am going out for a drink with some Aussie friends this evening, something a couple of brief hours ago I was really looking forward to," says James Parker. "Now all my best (and rarely used) taunts are worthless." Now what taunts would they be?

28th over: England 53–5 (Pietersen 9, G Jones 24) A close shave for Jones who comes agonisingly close to nicking a McGrath-esque Gillespie delivery, before he brings up England's half-century in style with yet another square cut.

29th over: England 64–5 (Pietersen 15, G Jones 29) "A lovely, measured shot from Pietersen." Those were the words of Mark Nicholas, and I'm not one to argue. In fact, I will repeat them, but substitute Pietersen's name out for Jones: a lovely, measured shot from Jones. This is more like it.

30th over: England 68–5 (Pietersen 19, G Jones 29) It's Pietersen's turn again to play a glorious – well, good – shot, flicking the ball through midwicket for four. These two are starting to free their arms after digging in when they first entered the fray.

31st over: England 68–5 (Pietersen 19, G Jones 29) Another decent if unspectacular over from Lee brings a maiden. Ponting must surely be thinking about drafting Warne into the attack soon. "Can we please drop Tres, open with Vaughan and then get Thorpe in as well?" asks Tim Golby, forgetting that we (the readers and the OBO commentator) don't actually have that much power over selection. "There's as much chance of Tres getting runs this summer as there is of me getting the office honey to agree to a date."

32nd over: England 76–5 (Pietersen 27, G Jones 29) Gillespie again commits the cardinal sin when bowling to Pietersen of drifting towards leg stump. The ball, of course, disappears to the boundary to bring up the 50 partnership. As does the next ball.

33rd over: England 79–5 (Pietersen 27, G Jones 30) The Australian pacemen begin to look a little weary.

34th over: England 79–5 (Pietersen 27, G Jones 30) Warne finally enters the action, and his first ball leads to a big shriek from those around the batsmen after it thuds into Pietersen's pad. Not out.

WICKET! 35th over: G Jones c Gilchrist b Lee 30 (England 79–6) Jones's courageous knock is ended by a snorter from Lee which is spooned up into the air off the top of his bat and falls into Gilchrist's hands.

35th over: England 88–6 (Pietersen 27, Giles 8) Giles somehow emerges from a fierce over from Lee with eight to his name after surviving a quick yorker, a threatening bouncer, an edge through the slips to the boundary, nudging the ball in the air to short leg off a no-ball, and then stroking another yorker through mid-on for four. And breathe.

36th over: England 90–6 (Pietersen 28, Giles 9) Pietersen and Giles struggle through another Warne over, picking up a single each.

WICKET! 37th over: Giles hit wicket b Lee 11 (England 92–7) Lee bowls the last over of the day, and it's typically brutal, short-pitched fare. The King of Spain deals admirably with it, until he steps back and tramples all over his own stumps. A sad end to a most dramatic day.

Australia 190; England 92–7

Second Day

The morning session

BY JAMES DART

Preamble: After a dramatic first day can England again turn the tide?

38th over: England 93–7 (Pietersen 29, Hoggard 0) Shane Warne opens the attack with Pietersen facing and it only takes two balls for the home fans to have their hearts in their mouths; a loud shout as the ball clips Pietersen on the pads and the batsman is quite fortunate to escape.

39th over: England 98–7 (Pietersen 34, Hoggard 0) Glenn McGrath's first delivery is a real comedy effort. Pietersen backs off, complaining about his line of sight, but the bowler is still in mid-flow and his ball chases the Hampshire man down leg-side, forcing him into some hasty movement. Pietersen responds with a clip through gully for four. "Is it just because it's Lord's, but why is no-one asking hard questions about the state of the pitch?" wonders Tom Hopkins. "If 17 wickets went down on day one of a county game the ECB would be popping in for a look, so why not here?"

40th over: England 98–7 (Pietersen 34, Hoggard 0) Pietersen clearly has confidence in Hoggard's stoic approach, which the Yorkshireman displays in fending off a Warne maiden. "Let's have optimism," says Raminder Dhendsa. "Pietersen clearly has the ability to score quickly and I think yesterday proved he has the temperament. Hoggard and Jones can both bat a bit, even Harmison occasionally looks like he knows what he's doing with the willow. I think another 50–60 runs would put England right in this match."

41st over: England 101–7 (Pietersen 36, Hoggard 0) Up comes the 100 for England, taking precisely one ball longer than the entire Australian innings. "Did you hear Beefy's prediction overnight?" asks Richard Clarke. Can't say I did, Richard – celeb parties and all that. "He said: 'It could go either way.' Stunning and insightful as ever."

WICKET! 42nd over: Hoggard c Hayden b Warne 0 (England 101–8) Attempting to cut Warne away on the off-side, Hoggard catches a thick edge to Matthew Hayden at slip, who juggles with the ball before taking it with a despairing reach as he goes to ground.

42nd over: England 101–8 (Pietersen 36, Harmison 0) It could well be time for Pietersen to start slogging – easier said than done with McGrath in the attack. Meanwhile, this from Denby Dale: "If Super Kev Pietersen guides us to 150 I'll go awag around the office kissing everyone, especially the post girl!" Lucky lady.

43rd over: England 116–8 (Pietersen 51, Harmison 0) Watch out post girl, here comes Denby. Fourteen runs in three balls and Pietersen is raising his bat for a debut Test fifty. "A most exciting day ahead," beams Alex Cooke. "Will Simon Jones run out KP? Or should that be when will Simon Jones run out KP?" They'll have to get to No. 11 first, Alex. Oh.

44th over: England 122–8 (Pietersen 57, Harmison 0) Up go the npower six posters around the ground as Pietersen smashes Warne into an upper tier.

WICKET! 44th over: Pietersen c Martyn b Warne 57 (England 122–9) Pietersen looks to repeat his previous-ball hammering of Warne and looks to have pulled it off, only for Martyn to make up a good 25 yards and take a diving catch right on the rope. Fantastic stuff, if not for England.

44th over: England 124–9 (Harmison 1, S Jones 1) "How about some lies and deception today?" pleads Peter Dillon. "For example, tell us that England are doing well, with Pietersen and Hoggard both on double centuries. We'll be none the wiser until we all get home from work, and then we won't care anyway because it's the weekend."

45th over: England 128–9 (Harmison 1, S Jones 5) Cracking stroke through mid-off from Jones, who gets through McGrath's over quite competently. "What's the betting the sweatiest folk at Lord's today are the ECB bean-counters?" says Richard Crone. "Imagine if it's all over by tonight, having to refund three days' worth of tickets for the biggest money-earner since the Herberts were last here."

46th over: England 141–9 (Harmison 3, S Jones 14) Brett Lee's introduction brings even more pace to the attack, but it also provides England with two useful no-balls; they'll take anything right about now as they move within 49 of Australia's total.

47th over: England 148–9 (Harmison 5, S Jones 19) Every run counts, much like a cricket variation on the old Paul Daniels gameshow. Jones has a good old swing of the bat, edging it high over the slips to the third man boundary. Not that he was aiming there, mind.

48th over: England 155–9 (Harmison 11, S Jones 20) Lee's last over didn't impress Ricky Ponting much; he brings Warne back on. It doesn't make an immediate difference, however, as Harmison times him straight over the long-on fielder for four. "Is Denby (42nd over) going to still kiss one and all now England have got to 150 as he pronounced earlier?" queries Ravi Motha. We can only hope, Ravi . . . for the post girl's sake, at least.

WICKET! 50th over: Harmison c Martyn b Lee 11 (England 155 all out) A vital final-wicket partnership of 33 comes to an end as Harmison's mistimed loft to mid-off gives fielder Martyn a much easier catch than the one he produced to remove Pietersen earlier.

Graham Thorpe news snap: A career of 100 matches has just come to a formal conclusion after the left-hander confirmed his retirement from Test cricket, with immediate effect. After the batting debut of Pietersen, perhaps his loss won't be felt too strongly.

Australia second innings

1st over: Australia 2–0 (Langer 1, Hayden 1) Harmison comes steaming in, but Australia comfortably negotiate the over without any of the painful knocks they sustained yesterday. Here's Gareth Radford with a plea for your help: "My team for Saturday is currently two short of players due to a stag night and a prior appointment with Spearmint Rhinos, erm, dancing parlour. So, I'm on the look-out for two willing cricketers tomorrow to play in Southsea, Hampshire; we are a pub cricket team so any standard." Oh, and here's the amorous Denby Dale: "Thanks Super Kev for turning this day into an unexpected beauty. I may be some time . . ."

2nd over: Australia 9–0 (Langer 5, Hayden 4) "Why has it suddenly been announced play must be finished by 6pm?" demands Steve Castle. "I drove home furiously last night to catch the remaining 15 overs, probably triggering several speed cameras in the process. Imagine my chagrin when play suddenly ended after the King of Spain was dismissed. Lunacy!" Purely TV reasons, Steve. Can't afford to eat into *The Simpsons* and, more importantly, *Hollyoaks*, apparently.

3rd over: Australia 9–0 (Langer 5, Hayden 4) A maiden from Harmison with some good-line bowling, keeping Hayden on the back foot. He even beats the outside edge on one occasion, but fails to pick up the crucial nick. "Can I ask Gareth Radford just how low-standard players he is really willing to accept?" asks Richard Clarke. "The last time I played cricket (2 yrs ago) I didn't bat or bowl and dropped a catch. My friend Richard would also like to play but is a complete malco. Neither of us have any kit." Here's Joe Neate: "Gareth, seeing as you're playing tomorrow and based in Hampshire, just give Pietersen and Warne a call, they should be free by then."

4th over: Australia 14–0 (Langer 6, Hayden 8) "This is Thorpe's way of highlighting the fact that he could have put the current England openers to shame," says Dan Fawbert Mills. "If I was Thorpe, I too would be disgusted with everything that I saw yesterday. There needs to be a clear-out of the 'old boys club' in English cricket. Forget the middle order, they do better than the lazy opening batsmen who seem to be secured a place in the side, whatever their form or performance on the pitch."

5th over: Australia 14–0 (Langer 6, Hayden 8) Another maiden from Harmison. While the pitch isn't doing a great deal at the moment, he's keeping the tourists from breaking out early into a powerful opening stand. "If the BBC can cancel *Neighbours* for two weeks over Wimbledon, then surely Channel 4 can let us see some cricket," harrumphs Ed Fuller. "I don't want to see cheating Jake bag Becca anyway; he deserves that about as much as Gillespie deserves to be in the Aussie bowling attack!!"

WICKET! 6th over: Langer run out (Pietersen) 6 (Australia 18–1) The latest scampered single attempt finds Pietersen at silly mid-on. His pinpoint throw strikes the base of the stumps with Langer about 12 inches short. Just what England needed. Here's Sean Clayton: "Re. Richard Clarke. 'The last time I played cricket (2 yrs ago) I didn't bat or bowl and dropped a catch.' That definitely sounds like Rikki Clarke hiding behind a 'Richard' disguise from the looks of it." But we could have some help from Andy Green: "I live in Southsea and used to play for Devon U-19s. I am an overweight all-rounder (in more ways than one), but mainly concentrate on fast bowling, well medium fast . . . not as fast as I was, maybe a fast medium . . . actually can I just bat?"

6th over: Australia 19–1 (Hayden 11, Ponting 0) The Australian skipper, sporting a plaster over the reported stitches he picked up from a Harmison bouncer yesterday, arrives to join Hayden at the crease.

7th over: Australia 21–1 (Hayden 11, Ponting 2) Harmison manages to find the McGrath delivery that accounted for both Michael Vaughan and Andy Flintoff, but it's just off target and Ponting survives, a very relieved batsman.

8th over: Australia 25–1 (Hayden 12, Ponting 5) Crazy running from Australia again, forcing a third run and earning a viewing from the third umpire. "Dan Fawbert Mills (fourth over) is talking rubbish," says Richard Preston. "The England selectors are finally giving players the chance to play themselves back into form and have recognised the need to maintain a squad of regular players."

9th over: Australia 32–1 (Hayden 19, Ponting 5) Better play from Hayden with a lovely four down the ground off Flintoff. "It's not Pietersen replacing Thorpe that's so much the worry," says Grace Pickering. "It's the fact that there is not a single batsman in our top order who can play defensively – they all seek to dominate the bowling. How much could we have done with a Thorpe innings yesterday/today? A partnership of him with KP/Fred/GO Jones could have sorted us right out."

10th over: Australia 37–1 (Hayden 24, Ponting 5) Harmison loses his line, giving Hayden room outside off stump which he uses to crash the ball to the extra-cover boundary.

11th over: Australia 41–1 (Hayden 28, Ponting 5) A lovely tug down leg-side from Hayden, albeit to a poor Jones delivery, flies to the ropes for four, prompting Mike Atherton to exclaim: "He's a good puller!" Much like the "love rat" Jake, methinks. "Mr Preston (8th over) is correct," says Matt Kwan. "A team must have a core group of players. How ridiculous would it be if Ponting or Vaughan had a rough patch and was dropped?"

12th over: Australia 42–1 (Hayden 28, Ponting 6) Just the one run from the over as Ponting scuttles through; there will probably be one more over to come before lunch.

13th over: Australia 47–1 (Hayden 32, Ponting 7) Hayden really has his eye in as he pulls Jones away to square leg for four, nudging Australia towards 50. "Are *Guardian* readers watching *Hollyoaks*?" asks Tim Dunn. "It's a stupid show and all of us should aim a bit higher. Dopy 'Becca' would not exactly understand things like Steve Bell, would she?" Not if she keeps getting it on with student Justin, Tim. Or at least that's what someone tells me. Anyway, that's lunch.

Australia 190 and 47–1; England 155

The afternoon session

BY SEAN INGLE

Preamble: The skies are darkening over Lord's. If there are any mystics who happen to be England fans reading this, now might be time to cock your legs in strange directions, mumble incoherently, and pray for rain.

13th over: Australia 50–1 (Hayden 34, Ponting 8) Flintoff produces some extra pace and bounce and tempts Hayden into a slog – which turns out to be a horrible top edge which flies high into the clouds, says hello to the passing EasyJet, and drops just short of third man.

14th over: Australia 54–1 (Hayden 34, Ponting 12) Simon Jones opens with a loose one on leg stump, which gifts Ponting an easy boundary. After that he's solid, if unthreatening. "I can't be the only one who is receiving a torrent of abusive texts from Aussie mates in return for some – admittedly – over-zealous early texting re: the Australian Test team's demise yesterday," says Paul Harrison. "Could you broadcast a simple 'yes OK, we can see the score' on behalf of us all?"

WICKET! 15th over: Hayden b Flintoff 34 (Australia 54–2) Flintoff strikes! He produces one that stays low, and Hayden – on the front foot – pulls it on to his stumps.

16th over: Australia 59–2 (Ponting 15, Martyn 0) Huge lbw appeal from Jones! But eagle-eyed umpire, Aleem Dar, spots that Ponting got some bat as well as pad to one that cut back. "In the olden days of Radio 4's *Test Match Special* much time was devoted to discussing the merits of cakes sent in by listeners," points out Steve Page. "This tradition should be revived in the modern internet OBO era." Good idea, Steve: please send them to GU Sport. Prizes and mentions to the best. Oh, and we're big fans of Konditor & Cook.

17th over: Australia 61–2 (Ponting 17, Martyn 2) Tidy over from Flintoff, just two off it. "Paul Harrison (over 14) might like to try mentioning the words 'Jonny' and 'Wilkinson' to his chums from Captain Cook's Mistake," suggests David Larrington. "I find it often has the desired effect . . ."

18th over: Australia 67–2 (Ponting 22, Martyn 2) Jones is suffering from Devon Malcolm-itis: every over since lunch he's produced four or five hostile deliveries and then, when the Aussies are looking nervous, he bowls one or two down leg and the pressure is released.

19th over: Australia 67–2 (Ponting 22, Martyn 2) Martyn's watchful, and Freddie's line is tighter than a supermodel's belt. Maiden.

20th over: Australia 70–2 (Ponting 22, Martyn 5) England need wickets. They nearly got one there – first Jones almost attracted the edge with one that eased away, then he produced an inswinger which nearly cut Martyn in half.

21st over: Australia 76–2 (Ponting 26, Martyn 5) Another big Flintoff appeal – but umpire Rudi Koertzen has a message for England: not out. "'Captain Cook's Mistake' was responsible for shipping out all the good cricketers from England 200 years ago," says Mark Cooke. "Now they're having to be shipped in."

22nd over: Australia 78–2 (Ponting 27, Martyn 6) Jones continues. His line is better, but he appears to be tiring. Perhaps it's time for Harmison?

23rd over: Australia 84–2 (Ponting 32, Martyn 6) Flintoff is getting more movement now, and, after producing a swinger that hits Martyn in the, er, swingers, he gets one to jag back sharply and has a decent lbw appeal. "Talking of cakes (over 16) – any chance of a Delia-style appearance from David Graveney?" asks Matthew Croxall. "Barmy Army! Where are you?! Let's be 'avin you!"

24th over: Australia 87–2 (Ponting 33, Martyn 6) Hoggard replaces Jones, and immediately launches into England's 55th lbw appeal of the day, after Ponting swings and misses. "I still find it ironic that 220 years on Australians choose to come back to England for a life behind bars," says James Peterson.

25th over: Australia 92–2 (Ponting 40, Martyn 6) Slowly, steadily, confidently, the Australians are easing towards establishing a 150 lead. There's nothing flashy going on at the moment – just lots of ones and twos.

26th over: Australia 95–2 (Ponting 41, Martyn 8) Swings and roundabouts: Hoggard isn't drifting down leg-side like he was yesterday, but he's not getting any swing either. Drinks.

27th over: Australia 100–2 (Ponting 40, Martyn 12) Harmison replaces Flintoff, but the runs keep coming as Martyn lofts him through third man for four to bring up the 100.

WICKET! 28th over: Ponting c sub b Hoggard 42 (Australia 100–3) Hoggard strikes! Two deliveries after another huge lbw appeal Ponting throws his wicket away, jabbing to sub James Hildreth of Somerset at point.

28th over: Australia 104–3 (Martyn 12, Clarke 4) Clarke gets off the mark with a punch through midwicket.

29th over: Australia 108–3 (Martyn 12, Clarke 4) Harmison produces a delivery that's wilder than Motley Crue in their 80s cock-rock-tastic prime, and watches as it flies high and wide of Geraint Jones's glove and races for four byes. "One for the geeks out there – when was the last Test in which no Australian player reached 50?" asks Jamie Reeman. "First correct answer wins Ricky Ponting's signed plaster."

30th over: Australia 109–3 (Martyn 12, Clarke 4) Hoggard continues to Martyn. The Australian No. 4's normal instinct is to attack, but so far he's scored just 12 from 45 balls.

31st over: Australia 112–3 (Martyn 14, Clarke 5) Martyn bravely risks two to Hoggard, who steams in like Goughy attacking a plateful of pies, before throwing just high of the stumps. Martyn is in by inches. "Anyone else think the timing of Thorpe's announcement was strange?" asks Raminder Dhendsa. "What if one of the middle order gets injured? Surely Thorpe would have been first reserve." Agree completely, Raminder.

32nd over: Australia 114–3 (Martyn 15, Clarke 6) Hoggard is all honest Yorkshire grit and graft, but isn't finding much swing. Australia now lead by 149. "The last Test in which no Australian player reached 50 was probably the latest Sri Lanka v. West Indies Test," reckons Ben Dimmack. "Not many Aussies in either team there."

33rd over: Australia 114–3 (Martyn 15, Clarke 6) After forcing Martyn to take evasive action with two nasty bouncers, Harmison nearly tempts him with one that leaves the bat. Maiden.

34th over: Australia 126–3 (Martyn 19, Clarke 13) "Not sure if this is an urban myth or not, but Ian Fleming named James Bond's nemesis, Blofeld, after Henry Blofeld's father," suggests John Osbourne. "Apparently they were at Eton together and didn't get on." Mmm, anyone know whether this is true?

35th over: Australia 127–3 (Martyn 19, Clarke 14) Harmison's continuing to bowl well – in the high 80s, and with lots of fierce inswing. "I think Thorpe retired after one of England's more emphatic collapses just to accentuate what a mistake dropping him was," reckons Jimmy Ainsworth. "Why was it always Thorpe v. Pietersen for a place? What about Bell? Knocking 160 against Bangladesh is akin to stealing a kid's tricycle – easy to do, strangely satisfying at the time, but leaves you with an empty feeling for weeks. Not that I'm speaking from experience, you understand."

36th over: Australia 130–3 (Martyn 19, Clarke 17) Great news for the seven Ashley Giles fans who've written in asking when he's going to get a bowl. He's on at the Nursery end. He's bowling round the wicket, to a defensive field, but the Aussies still manage to nibble three runs off that over. "Yes, it was Blowers' Dad," says Matthew Cobb (and 334 others). "He said so on *Desert Island Discs* last year."

37th over: Australia 132–3 (Martyn 19, Clarke 19) Harmison continues to probe, with scant reward. He's certainly been the pick of the England bowlers this afternoon. "I've cast a quick eye over the stats from the past decade, and I reckon that the last match in which no Aussie got a 50 was against England at the Oval in 1997," says Josh M. "Top scorer was Blewett with 47."

38th over: Australia 139–3 (Martyn 24, Clarke 21) Not the greatest start from Giles, who drops one short and is clouted for four.

39th over: Australia 140–3 (Martyn 24, Clarke 21) Oh dear, oh dear, oh dear. Simon Jones replaces Harmison and immediately he gets his reward . . . or rather he doesn't as Clarke's drive is spilt by Pietersen in the covers. That's the third catch he's dropped this Test – and probably the easiest. Tea.

Australia 190 and 140–3; England 155

The evening session

BY JAMES DART

Preamble: I notice that GU Towers is bereft of cake deliveries at the moment, so it looks like the only ones in this OBO will be those both teams are munching through at the moment during tea. Well, that's probably more of a myth; I'm not sure exactly what counts as tea fodder for cricketers these days.

40th over: Australia 140–3 (Martyn 24, Clarke 21) Ashley Giles kicks things off from the Nursery End with a tidy maiden.

41st over: Australia 140–3 (Martyn 24, Clarke 21) A good start to the session from England, but neither Australian batsman is looking under serious threat of losing his wicket. "Speaking of cakes, in our small company of only 23 people, there happens to be two birthdays, so we are just at the business end of our second set of cakes," mocks Ben Walton. "Yummy!" Bah!

42nd over: Australia 148–3 (Martyn 24, Clarke 29) Michael Clarke is targeting the King of Spain as he slogs Giles into the open space at deep midwicket. "A stirring fifty in the face of adversity; three dropped catches; a run-out; and the worst haircut on show. Is it fair to say that this Ashes series is just a sidenote to Kevin Pietersen's over-sized personality?" ponders Stuart Youngs.

43rd over: Australia 153–3 (Martyn 25, Clarke 34) A stirring stroke to the long-off boundary from Clarke as Australia pass the 150–mark. Meanwhile, here's Kevin Lynch, potentially the OBO saviour: "A girly corner of the office here get a load of cakes in every Friday and always have plenty left over as their eyes are invariably too big for their bellies. We normally move in and hoover up about now, but I'd be happy to bike some over were you to print this nonsense!" Consider it printed, Kevin.

44th over: Australia 157–3 (Martyn 25, Clarke 35) Sloppy work down the leg-side by wicket-keeper Geraint Jones as a Giles delivery slips through his gloves. Here's Toni Garcia: "Me and a few of the girls have tickets for August 5. We've decided cricket is the great untapped male market; anyone up for looking after five 25–year-old girls on that day?" My inbox is bracing itself, Toni.

45th over: Australia 170–3 (Martyn 37, Clarke 35) Nice footwork from Steve Harmison prevents a boundary off Simon Jones's bowling, but his line is drifting down leg far too frequently – and it's got Geoff Boycott fuming.

46th over: Australia 178–3 (Martyn 40, Clarke 40) Giles can't find his line, nor his length, and as for actually spinning it, well . . . Not a good sign, this – his six overs have cost 28.

47th over: Australia 184–3 (Martyn 41, Clarke 45) Vaughan is facing some serious thinking, tinkering around with his fielders in a bid to stop this burgeoning stand. More worryingly though, Kevin Lynch has been turned, becoming what Aussies term a 'caketaker' or something: "Toni Garcia may very well have just gazumped your cakes if they can secure me a ticket for accompanying five 25–year-old girls to some cricket match or whatever it is . . ." And Ed

Barnard would like to offer his, ahem, services: "Five 25–year-old women? At a Test match? With me in the same ground? With my reputation?"

48th over: Australia 188–3 (Martyn 44, Clarke 46) Giles continues to plough a somewhat ineffective furrow as Australia comfortably work him around for a flurry of singles. "Further to your musings about whether or not the cricketers will have enjoyed cakes for tea, I questioned a colleague who is a member of the MCC," says Tony Spratt. "He reckons that the fielding team will have a cuppa and a banana or two each, current batsmen and those who have yet to bat will have something similar, and batsmen who are already out will stuff themselves stupid. In this professional age, he says, cakes are unlikely to figure largely in the diets of the players. So probably not, then."

49th over: Australia 188–3 (Martyn 44, Clarke 46) A maiden from Flintoff, but Martyn and Clarke are both looking good for comfortable half-centuries. "Me and my four 25–year-old mates also have tickets for Edgbaston on August 5," beams the lucky Chris Hawes. "I am sure they will all happily look after Toni and her friends. However, she should be warned that we will possibly not be at our most attractive as we may well be in nun's uniforms." Meanwhile, Steven Randell adds: "I find it disgraceful that Toni should make such overtures via this medium. I hate it when women treat me as a piece of meat. I'll be there on the 7th though, so if she wants to hang around for a couple of days I'll make it worth her while."

50th over: Australia 202–3 (Martyn 49, Clarke 54) The Clarke fifty comes up with a whip to the deep midwicket boundary off Giles. Here's a cautionary tale from Justin Newland: "Toni must promise not to behave like the last girl I took to the cricket. I thought I was on to an absolute winner with her, until she got fidgety about 45 mins into the first innings. 'What's wrong?' I asked, 'you not enjoying it?' 'When's half-time?' she replied."

51st over: Australia 205–3 (Martyn 49, Clarke 57) Australia are quickly taking total charge; the last 50 came from just 47 balls. "Just to reply to Chris Hawes," begins the returning Toni Garcia. "If you are going in fancy dress, we may just do the same. Nurses' uniforms anyone?"

52nd over: Australia 211–3 (Martyn 50, Clarke 62) Giles just isn't getting enough out of this Lord's wicket to justify his continuation in the attack. "We have a motto at our cricket club – average cricketers, good boozers," notes Jim Lewis. "As the standard of England's fielding has been village to say the least, they could adopt our motto. Who do you think would win the Ashes if it came down to boozing? My money's on Freddie drinking the Aussies under the table!" Not if David Boon got a shock recall, I reckon.

53rd over: Australia 213–3 (Martyn 52, Clarke 62) The Australian pair have now extended their side's lead to 248. And, ahead of his next over, Darren Downs asks: "What is the point of Ashley Giles?" Answers on a postcard, please.

54th over: Australia 221–3 (Martyn 52, Clarke 70) Now, we're not saying England are getting desperate, but Ian Bell's just been brought into the attack. "The big question now is when and at what score do the Aussies declare, I suppose," says a deflated James Huxtable. After England's first innings, that might not be too far away.

55th over: Australia 223–3 (Martyn 53, Clarke 71) Richard Jones is first to reach us in our great Ashley Giles quiz: "What's the point of Ashley Giles? To make me feel better about myself." But Jim Lewis responds: "What Darren Downs doesn't realise is that Ashley Giles is the King of Spain. . . I believe he'll call his fleet up and send the Aussies back whence they came. The Armada is on its way!"

56th over: Australia 230–3 (Martyn 53, Clarke 78) Hoggard is brought back to liven up a wavering attack. How England must be regretting Pietersen's drop of Clarke earlier in the innings. "Now that Thorpe has announced his retirement, maybe Ashley is there for his batting prowess (only Pietersen of the first six scored more runs)," observes Philip Hadfield.

57th over: Australia 243–3 (Martyn 61, Clarke 83) More top-drawer batting from Clarke, timing Flintoff to the cover boundary with ease. Louise Wright jumps into the Giles debate: "He's using up some of the European forename mountain and avoiding wasting the scarcer surname supply by employing two male first names as a whole name. Similar sterling work is done by David James, Nick Ross and George Michael. He should be held up as an example to us all."

58th over: Australia 247–3 (Martyn 61, Clarke 87) In a topical nod to this evening's athletics, this match is running away faster than Asafa Powell. Apologies for the crow-barring, but it is, readers, it really is.

59th over: Australia 251–3 (Martyn 65, Clarke 87) Back comes Harmison in a bid to break this 151–run fourth-wicket stand. "The man is a legend and should not be criticised," shouts Matthew Smith, taking to his Giles-themed soapbox. "Last summer's 31 wickets were no flash in the pan. On this note, myself and several friends will be attending the Old Trafford Test and are learning the words to the Spanish national anthem to celebrate England's favourite Spanish monarch. LONG LIVE THE KING!"

60th over: Australia 252–3 (Martyn 65, Clarke 88) A momentary lapse from Martyn, who goes fishing outside off stump and only just fails to nick Hoggard to Jones behind the stumps. "I take it as uninterrupted coverage of England's pasting continues that Kevin Lynch has reneged on his offer (43rd over) and no pastries have as yet showed up at GU Towers?" notes the observant Colm Gilmore. You're telling me.

61st over: Australia 253–3 (Martyn 65, Clarke 89) "Why can't we be a bit more upbeat?" asks the very upbeat Nick Watson. "True world-beaters would be saying to themselves, let's get these two out quickly, and skittle the rest out for less than 50, and we can win the match, rather than messing around waiting for the Aussies to declare. If you are beaten psychologically you are beaten physically and vice versa. Mind over matter and all that . . ." I'll do my best, Nick. Harmison's latest over has the Australians at sixes and sevens as Clarke only musters one single. That over could prove pivotal, what with the moral victory England took from it.

WICKET! 62nd over: Clarke b Hoggard 91 (Australia 255–4) A frustrated Clarke heads back to the pavilion after catching a nasty inside edge from an outside-off-stump Hoggard delivery and finding the timber. An important moment for England to break the 155–run stand and hope remains if they can prise a couple more wickets tonight.

WICKET! 63rd over: Martyn lbw b Harmison 65 (Australia 255–5) What were we saying about the momentum possibly shifting? Harmison roars in with the first ball of his over and traps Martyn on the back foot.

63rd over: Australia 260–5 (Katich 4, Gilchrist 1) The Lord's crowd make themselves heard for the first time in a good few hours as Harmison and Adam Gilchrist square off. "Hurrah!" beams Alex Cooke. "Could you ask Nick Watson to send in a few more 'upbeat' predictions? If it worked once, it could work again . . ." Meanwhile, Mark Fournier notes: "Is Matthew (over 59) quite sure the Spanish national anthem has any words? I was under the impression it didn't. I too shall be at Old Trafford and shall enjoy his futile efforts immensely."

64th over: Australia 260–5 (Katich 4, Gilchrist 1) At least the arrival of a new pair of batsmen at the crease has taken Australia out of their stride for a brief moment, with Flintoff producing a maiden.

65th over: Australia 262–5 (Katich 5, Gilchrist 2) Nothing too dramatic from Gilchrist just yet, fending off some testing Harmison deliveries. "If you want cake, I think you'll have to try and attract an older, mumsier readership," notes Caspar Salmon. "Your young readers do not strike me as bakers. If the OBO featured whimsical commentary about gardens, and birdspotting instead of witty references to *Hollyoaks*, I'm almost certain you would find Chocolate Sachetortes streaming through the doors of GU Towers."

66th over: Australia 269–5 (Katich 9, Gilchrist 5) Glancing out of GU Towers makes one recognise just how many types of birds there are around the city of London. Floating high above the people below . . . Nope, sorry Caspar, can't do it, cakes or no cakes.

67th over: Australia 270–5 (Katich 9, Gilchrist 6) Another good over from Harmison, conceding just a single to Gilchrist. "Does the Spanish national anthem have words?" asks Paul Lakin, rhetorically. "In true *Guardian* style the answer is maybe: 'There are no official words for the Spanish anthem. José María Pemán (1897–1981) and Eduardo Marquina (1879–1946) have written, unofficially, different words.' Yes, I am quite bored, since you ask."

WICKET! 68th over: Gilchrist b Flintoff 10 (Australia 274–6) A huge wicket for Flintoff and England! The all-rounder manages to get the ball to nip back at Gilchrist, staying a little low and clipping the inside edge and striking the stumps. The lead is still 309, but England are giving themselves a chance.

69th over: Australia 278–6 (Katich 10, Warne 1) A loud shout for lbw from Harmison and the England fielders, who, much like Stella, have well and truly got their groove back. The ball strikes Warne a little high up on the pads, though, and the King of Spin survives.

70th over: Australia 279–6 (Katich 10, Warne 2) "I've just seen some TV pictures of Ricky Ponting and his plaster," says Francis Smith. "He looks a bit like that Nelly chap, don't you think?" Not really, Francis, but I've got an image of Ponting rapping away . . .

WICKET! 70th over: Warne c Giles b Harmison 10 (Australia 279–7) That's the point of Ashley Giles, sitting in the gully, waiting for Harmison to get one to rise on Warne and clip the top of the bat and provide him with a simple catch. For the second day running, play ends with a wicket.

Australia 190 and 279–7; England 155

Third Day

The morning session

BY SEAN INGLE

Preamble: Let's be honest here – England are up against it. The weather, alas, probably won't save them: the skies are only John Major grey, and about as threatening as meeting the former PM in a dark alley.

71st over: Australia 283–7 (Katich 10, Lee 4) Harmison's first ball is a beauty, but Lee's thick edge flies past slip for four. Meanwhile Ian Roberts writes: "Can I be first on the board to say that our local deli, here in Columbus, Ohio, has eight flavours of Walkers Crisps." You can, Ian, although in truth there's not much competition.

72nd over: Australia 285–7 (Katich 12, Lee 4) Flintoff's first over loosens the limbs, but doesn't threaten. "I'm just thinking about the turnaround in Durban last year," says Stefan Hopewell, whose surname seems partiularly apt. "Skittled out for 139 in the first innings, no one was expecting a good batting performance in the second. Tresco and Strauss then share a stand of 273, and England finish on 570–7. We can do it again!" Let's hope so, Stefan.

73rd over: Australia 286–7 (Katich 12, Lee 5) More good stuff from Harmison, who hurts Lee with a lifter that rattles into his fingers. "I'll be sat at work until the close of play, but I truly believe we can get 350 so fingers crossed the bowlers do their duty once more and the batsmen follow suit," says Stefan Ludewig. "C'mon England!"

74th over: Australia 289–7 (Katich 12, Lee 8) Another near-miss for England, as Lee gets a bottom edge which skids down towards fine leg. Meanwhile Mr Swathi wants to know: "When they spend tons of money on the ugly media centre, why can't they increase the total number of seats in the ground?" Fair point, Mr Swathi, but I must stick up for the media centre. For a start, members of the media get free cake at tea-time – and they don't skimp on the quality either.

WICKET! 75th over: Lee run out (Giles) 8 (Australia 289–8) What a throw from Ashley Giles! Harmison whacks it into Lee's fingers – again – there's hesitation among the batsmen before they decide to set off on a quick single to point. But Giles is too quick, and takes out middle stump with a direct hit!

76th over: Australia 298–8 (Katich 17, Gillespie 4) Nearly another wicket as Katich goes for an outrageous front-foot pull outside off stump. His shot lobs high into the air before landing short of Harmison at deep midwicket. "They may get free cake in the media centre, but that's not much use to you in Farringdon, though, eh?" says Joe Sanderson. "Or me in work, I suppose." True, Joe, true. Sadly.

77th over: Australia 298–8 (Katich 17, Gillespie 4) Harmison peppers Gillespie, who holds on. Australia now lead by 333.

78th over: Australia 310–8 (Katich 29, Gillespie 4) Brilliant from Katich! He brings up the 300 with an uppercut over fourth slip and then, next ball, cuts Flintoff through point for another boundary. And to make things worse, he then nibbles one fine for his third four in a row.

79th over: Australia 314–8 (Katich 29, Gillespie 8) Australia now lead by 349. England's highest score to win a Test match is 332, so they'll need a record score to win this.

80th over: Australia 317–8 (Katich 32, Gillespie 8) Hoggard replaces Flintoff, but the runs continue to flow. Meanwhile this from Stuart G in Sydney: "You Poms never learn, do you?" he scoffs. "Before every Ashes series, you talk up your chances, and then we thrash you."

81st over: Australia 322–8 (Katich 37, Gillespie 8) Harmison takes the new ball . . . but Katich immediately pulls him for four! A single off the third ball leaves Gillespie to see out the last three deliveries but he proves up to the task, even if the last one thuds painfully into his belly.

82nd over: Australia 326–8 (Katich 41, Gillespie 8) Not a great over from Hoggard, who doesn't threaten and twice sees Katich cut him through deep square leg for two.

83rd over: Australia 326–8 (Katich 41, Gillespie 8) Harmison's roughing up of Gillespie continues, with one that smacks him in the, er, crown jewels. Maiden.

84th over: Australia 329–8 (Katich 42, Gillespie 8) We've seen four overs with the new ball and the pitch has done nothing untoward, which should encourage England. They still have to get Australia out, mind, and there's little sign of that happening.

85th over: Australia 329–8 (Katich 42, Gillespie 8) A wide one from Harmison stays at ankle height, otherwise it's a quiet over. Maiden. "Anyone agree that Harmison should try a Brett Lee beamer on McGrath when he comes in to keep him out of the second innings?" suggests Stefan Hopewell.

86th over: Australia 329–8 (Katich 42, Gillespie 8) At long, long, last Hoggard gets some movement off the seam: it darts away from Gillespie, who plays and misses.

87th over: Australia 332–8 (Katich 44, Gillespie 9) Flintoff replaces Harmison, but this quiet period continues. Just three runs off the over, one from a shocking misfield off Simon Jones. "Anyone else experiencing vague feelings of depression?" asks a sombre Dean Smith.

88th over: Australia 333–8 (Katich 45, Gillespie 9) Geraint Jones drops a sitter! Simon Jones comes on for the ineffective Hoggard and he immediately gets some movement. Gillespie gets an edge and G Jones, who strangely goes at it with one glove, puts him down.

89th over: Australia 336–8 (Katich 47, Gillespie 9) Flintoff continues but so, sadly, do the runs. "Unlike you people in the UK, we in Turkey are getting the Sky broadcast of the game. It's live, but noticeable absentees from the commentary box are Davids Lloyd and Gower – possibly everyone's favourite pairing. Conspiracy theories anyone?" writes Wayne Trotman in Izmir.

WICKET! 90th over: Gillespie b S Jones 13 (Australia 341–9) Jones strikes! A superb 90mph delivery moves away and uproots Gillespie's stump.

91st over: Australia 350–9 (Katich 55, McGrath 2) Katich brings up his 50 with a single off his legs. "Sorry to be tedious, but is Wayne Trotman of Izmir (over 89) any relation to Dan Trotman, one of my second-year Zoology students at Manchester University?" asks Matthew Cobb. Well, Wayne?

92nd over: Australia 356–9 (Katich 56, McGrath 6) Oh dear, oh dear. Now McGrath's just hit Jones for a boundary, off his legs. Jones replies with a snorter, which McGrath misses, and G Jones worryingly drops.

93rd over: Australia 357–9 (Katich 57, McGrath 6) After Katich takes a single, McGrath confidently survives the rest of Flintoff's over. "Re: Aussie Stuart G's email – Surely unutterable smugness has some physical form, and surely Stuart G will choke on it," suggests Richard N of Queensland.

94th over: Australia 359–9 (Katich 58, McGrath 7) Again Katich takes a single off the first ball of the over, again England can't trouble McGrath.

95th over: Australia 364–9 (Katich 59, McGrath 10) Ashley Giles on for Flintoff. Like the rest of the Australian batsman, McGrath has no problems in dealing with the King of Spin/Spain. "As far as I am aware, Dan is no relation of mine," says Wayne Trotman in answer to Matthew Cobb in over 91. "Anyway, since he shares the illustrious surname, Dan certainly deserves fine grades; does he get them, though?"

96th over: Australia 366–9 (Katich 60, McGrath 10) Jones tries to bounce out McGrath, but he confidently steps under it, before a leg bye takes the Australian lead to over 400. This partnership is now worth 25.

97th over: Australia 372–9 (Katich 66, McGrath 10) Shot from Katich! Giles strays outside off stump and Katich eases him through the covers for four. That's lunch, with the Australians leading by 407 runs.

Australia 190 and 372–9; England 155

The afternoon session

BY SEAN INGLE

Preamble: Australia lead by 407. Worse still, the weather still looks reasonable. Speaking of which, Mike Hughes from Canada wants to know: "Has anyone been spotted doing a Rain Dance in the vicinity? If so, I hope they're more successful than our current first eleven." No such luck, Mike.

98th over: Australia 376–9 (Katich 66, McGrath 14) Rubbish. Another easy catch dropped, this time from the normally reliable Flintoff at second slip, after McGrath had edged Jones's outswinger. It sums up England's day.

99th over: Australia 380–9 (Katich 67, McGrath 16) More fielding woes. Geraint Jones, who was superb in the one-dayers, fumbles again and McGrath is able to escape Harmison.

100th over: Australia 380–9 (Katich 67, McGrath 20) Oh dear, oh dear. A Jones bouncer hits McGrath's glove and loops towards Geraint Jones. He scrambles towards it, gets into position to take an easy catch, and then drops it. Incredible miss.

WICKET! 101st over: Katich c S Jones b Harmison 67 (Australia 384 all out) Katich goes, after uppercutting Harmison to third man. And, what do you know, Simon Jones – who's watched four catches go down off his bowling, holds it. England need 420 to win.

England second innings

1st over: England 1–0 (Trescothick 1, Strauss 0) McGrath to Trescothick, who jabs one away to get England off the mark. Their plan is simple: see off the new ball, get forward to the bowlers and get off to a good start. If they can do that, who knows?

2nd over: England 1–0 (Trescothick 1, Strauss 0) Hostile start from Lee. "How's about this?" suggests Peter Starking. "Test cricket has become a much quicker game in the last few years. Therefore teams batting last are getting much longer and much better pitches to chase on and so it should follow that the record for the biggest chase should be broken soon in the modern era. Add in the fact, as Hoggard says, that McGrath is old and almost certainly too tired to bowl and some blind optimism and we've practically won already."

3rd over: England 2–0 (Trescothick 1, Strauss 1) After Strauss gets off the mark with a roll off his pads, Trescothick – who displays no footwork, naturally – edges McGrath. Fortunately it drops just short of second slip.

4th over: England 3–0 (Trescothick 1, Strauss 2) Trescothick is struggling: he's just been hit twice on the shoulder by two skiddy Lee bouncers, both times having taken his eyes off the ball. "What's with all the doom and gloom?" asks Sean Moore from New York. "You know they're going to make it – three half-centuries and a century (Bell?) from the top six, with only Flintoff (40s) and Trescothick (30s) missing the 50. Jones and Giles will chip in with 70 between them. Another 30 from the tail-enders. Spooky eh?" Or wildly optimistic. You decide.

5th over: England 4–0 (Trescothick 1, Strauss 3) Strauss works McGrath off his legs for another single. He has to be careful though: the delivery before hit the outside edge.

6th over: England 8–0 (Trescothick 1, Strauss 7) Lee continues to probe; Strauss continues to resist, before hitting a perfect cover drive for four. The pitch is showing no demons so far (over-by-over reporter touches desk, sadly it's not wood).

7th over: England 9–0 (Trescothick 2, Strauss 7) McGrath goes round the wicket to Trescothick, which suggests England's openers have done something right.

8th over: England 9–0 (Trescothick 2, Strauss 7) Lee continues to huff and puff, but Trescothick is equal to the task. Maiden. Meanwhile the Glenn McGrath backlash has started. "Why is everyone raving about McGrath?" splutters Stefan Hopewell. "Harmison got better bowling figures in the first innings." But McGrath does have 500–odd Test wickets . . .

9th over: England 12–0 (Trescothick 2, Strauss 10) Strauss steers into double figures. The Australian bowling has been tight, but the pitch looks decent, and both openers seem comfortable at the moment (famous last words, etc).

10th over: England 16–0 (Trescothick 6, Strauss 10) Fastest ball of the Test so far – a 95mph howitzer from Lee. "I'm trapped in the deep south of the USA where no one knows nor cares about Ashes," sighs Steve Lamport. "Yesterday I was assumed to be an Australian in a restaurant again. Should I boycott every establishment in which this happens and risk starvation or continue to try and form a local cricket league from re-educated restaurant workers?" Suggestions, anyone?

11th over: England 18–0 (Trescothick 6, Strauss 12) The attrition continues: McGrath continues to tease and tempt, England continue to resist.

12th over: England 23–0 (Trescothick 6, Strauss 17) A change in bowling as Gillespie replaces Lee – and he immediately gets the treatment from Strauss who pulls him away for four. He's a bit lucky with a bottom edge that just misses his leg stump, mind. Drinks.

13th over: England 27–0 (Trescothick 6, Strauss 21) A nasty delivery from McGrath has Strauss driving and missing. My, that was close. "Re: Steve in 10th over. Americans might take up cricket if we start a rumour baseball was invented by the French," suggests Matt Morrow.

14th over: England 31–0 (Trescothick 10, Strauss 21) Shot from Trescothick! He doesn't have to bludgeon it, he just times it through the covers and it races away for four.

15th over: England 37–0 (Trescothick 16, Strauss 21) Another nice boundary from Trescothick, who plays McGrath with soft hands down to third man for four. "Coming up to midnight and I'm off to bed now (looking after two-year-old twins makes one rather tired)," says Brendan Jones from Sydney. "But my non-prediction, for what it's worth, is that tonight England at stumps will be either 184–1 or 134 all out." Let's hope it's the former, Brendan.

16th over: England 39–0 (Trescothick 16, Strauss 21) Two no-balls in a row from Gillespie sends the Lord's crowd into boozy, post-lunch cheers. "As a long-time follower of the *Guardian*'s live sport coverage, I've just discovered online TMS," says Jon Moxon. "Makes a great combination. I haven't seen or heard live cricket for 10 years, being in Japan."

17th over: England 43–0 (Trescothick 16, Strauss 25) Lee replaces

McGrath and two deliveries into the over the pitch, for the first time this innings, misbehaves itself. Fortunately it goes under Strauss's bat, and wide of the stumps.

18th over: England 44–0 (Trescothick 17, Strauss 25) Better from Gillespie, who's pitching the ball on off stump and getting it to move away. He seems to have found his rhythm and his pace (he's now up to 84–5mph). "Japan is not the best place to be following the cricket from," admits Gus Williams, "but we do get the pleasure of regular earthquakes to make up for it. Praise be to my neighbour's wireless connection, which means my laptop doesn't have to leave my side and I don't have to miss a ball."

19th over: England 50–0 (Trescothick 23, Strauss 26) An eventful over. Trescothick guides Lee through the covers for four – to which Lee retaliates with a 93mph bouncer. Then Trescothick gets an edge, with soft hands, which flies through the slips for another couple.

20th over: England 55–0 (Trescothick 27, Strauss 26) Warne on for Gillespie. The initial signs are ominous: there are two HUGE lbw appeals as Trescothick pads up without playing a shot (the second looked plum). Umpire Aleem Dar says no, however. "The problem with Matt's suggestion (13th over) is that the French will start to believe they did invent baseball," says Steve Lamport. "If it becomes their national sport then it's a short step to the entire EU taking up the game. It's best we keep it contained in a controlled environment – like an incurable disease."

21st over: England 64–0 (Trescothick 31, Strauss 31) Lee fires a 93mph bouncer at Strauss and then gives him some verbals for good measure. Strauss smiles back and then clips him past gully for four.

22nd over: England 65–0 (Trescothick 31, Strauss 32) Another huge lbw appeal from Warne, last ball before tea. Replays show that was definitely out – but umpire Dar thought (wrongly) that Trescothick got some bat on it. That's tea.

Australia 190 and 384; England 155 and 65–0

The evening session

BY SEAN INGLE

Preamble: It was Australia's morning, but England's afternoon. Michael Vaughan's side need another good session this evening. Meanwhile Anton Lawrence wants to know why we would want the Americans to play cricket. "They would just make the game shorter, and have substitutes and daft expressions like 'Power Play'. Oh."

23rd over: England 71–0 (Trescothick 32, Strauss 33) Lee starts us off again, and England immediately attack. After Strauss picks up a single, Trescothick gets four leg byes past deep fine leg for four before adding a single of his own. "Has anybody written in with the idea of setting up a company called jamodu to benefit from the free advertising every time the television shows the npower advert on the pitch upside down?" asks Keith Meldrum.

24th over: England 72–0 (Trescothick 33, Strauss 33) Another huge lbw appeal from Warne! It's certainly going to hit middle stump, but Strauss got the tiniest of inside edges.

25th over: England 72–0 (Trescothick 33, Strauss 33) "So what will you do when tomorrow's predicted rain arrives, especially if there's no cake to type about?" asks Lindsay Chapman. "I might even feel sorry for you, and send you some Hobnobs or something."

26th over: England 76–0 (Trescothick 33, Strauss 37) Worrying signs for England – Strauss is not picking the flipper at all. He tries a premeditated sweep, misses it, and is grateful that it squirms past his stumps.

WICKET! 27th over: Strauss c and b Lee 37 (England 80–1) Brilliant from Lee, whose bouncer has Strauss all over the place. He gets an edge, which goes high into the air and Lee – who has to make a full sprint – takes a superb diving catch. Although, looking at the replays, he might have grounded that.

28th over: England 94–1 (Trescothick 44, Vaughan 4) "Would you really eat cake sent in by readers?" asks Trevor Holden. "Does anyone remember a *Private Eye* cartoon from decades ago? A mad scientist rubs his hands gleefully as the radio cricket commentator pegs it on the air after eating a sent-in cake!"

29th over: England 94–1 (Trescothick 44, Vaughan 4) McGrath comes back for Lee. "If Australia were so keen on having a gentleman's agreement on catches then why are they appealing for lbws that are missing by a gazillion miles?" fumes Daniel Howdon. "And why has Lee just claimed a catch that he clearly grassed? And why do fools fall in love?"

WICKET! 30th over: Trescothick c Hayden b Warne 44 (England 96–2) Oh dear, oh dear – Warne, who's been getting enormous spin, strikes. He gets one that slides away from Trescothick, takes the edge and Hayden takes a sharp catch. England are in trouble now, and there's no sign of that rain we were promised.

31st over: England 98–2 (Vaughan 4, Bell 2) McGrath continues to Bell, who – rather luckily – gets a bottom edge behind square. Cue more sledging from McGrath. "I just wanted to pass on some good news to John Moxon and Gus Williams," says Michael Jones. "I recently managed to find a couple of places showing the cricket live in Tokyo. In Shinjuku the Clubhouse has full coverage and in Roppongi Paddy Foleys is showing it."

32nd over: England 101–2 (Vaughan 4, Bell 5) Bell brings up the hundred, using his feet to Warne, before guiding him through the covers.

33rd over: England 104–2 (Vaughan 4, Bell 8) Drinks. Meanwhile, some England fans out there are still hopeful. "Wouldn't it be nice if England used the masses of time at their disposal to grind out a painstakingly slow but irrepressible victory and really make Australians eat a wholesome slice of humble pie (or cake for that matter) for a change?" suggests Nick Watson.

WICKET! 34th over: Bell lbw Warne 8 (England 104–3) Warne strikes again! Bell leaves a straight one, which hits his pads in front of middle stump. Pietersen comes in and cuts Warne for four.

35rd over: England 111–3 (Vaughan 4, Pietersen 7) A couple of runs off that over, but the expectant buzz has certainly gone out of this Lord's crowd. "I don't suppose anyone knows of a place to watch the cricket in Boston. I'm stuck at Harvard and desperately need to find new ways of avoiding working on my dissertation on the syntax of Native American languages," says Ben Braithwaite. "I have also been constantly called an Australian."

36th over: England 111–3 (Vaughan 4, Pietersen 7) Vaughan drives stupidly at one that's turning and is grateful that it falls just short of gully. England need to grit this out. "Pass on my thanks to Michael Jones," says Jon Moxon. "Sadly I'm in Saga (tell him not to laugh). Saga Cricket Club was Kyushu champion in 1999 though. We had a useful side – in spite of my being a part of it."

WICKET! 37th over: Vaughan b Lee 4 (England 112–4) Vaughan goes! It's almost an identikit dismissal to how McGrath got him in the first innings, but while it did stay a bit low, Vaughan didn't play down the right line (like Thursday then). England are in deep, deep trouble now.

38th over: England 117–4 (Pietersen 10, Flintoff 3) Warne continues to Flintoff who, like Strauss and Bell before him, isn't looking comfortable.

39th over: England 118–4 (Pietersen 10, Flintoff 3) Lee is gnarling and growling at Flintoff, as well as digging it in short. Freddie is mostly content to defend, but when he flicks one off his ribs he only just misses leg gully.

WICKET! 40th over: Flintoff c Gilchrist b Warne 3 (England 118–5) Another one bites the dust. Warne produces a quicker one, Flintoff tries to cut him but it's on him quicker than he thinks, and Gilchrist takes a very fine catch behind the stumps. How England could've done with Graham Thorpe here, eh?

41st over: England 124–5 (Pietersen 17, G Jones 0) Lee produces a full toss that's virtually a beamer. It hits Pietersen's legs, right in front of middle stump, but umpire Koertzen takes pity on England's boy wonder. "I'm not one to resort to cheap insults, but there's an uncanny resemblance between Brett Lee and Beavis from *Beavis and Butthead*," says Sean Chambers, who earns a spotters' badge.

42nd over: England 130–5 (Pietersen 23, Jones 0) Pietersen's going out in a blaze of glory: he's just slogged Warne over midwicket for four.

43rd over: England 140–5 (Pietersen 32, G Jones 0) Six from Pietersen! What a shot – it flew miles over midwicket, into the second tier, and even Lee is forced to smile. Three more off the over takes England towards 150. They only need another 280 to win this . . .

44th over: England 144–5 (Pietersen 36, G Jones 0) What a shot from Pietersen! He steps into Warne's leg-break and flat bats it for four. Incredible.

45th over: England 148–5 (Pietersen 36, G Jones 4) Gillespie replaces Lee, but the runs continue to come as Jones flicks him through deep backward square for four.

46th over: England 150–5 (Pietersen 37, G Jones 5) It's starting to rain at Lord's. Now all we need are some biblical storms, or Pietersen to continue playing like Botham à la Headingley 1981.

47th over: England 152–5 (Pietersen 41, G Jones 6) The rain is definitely getting heavier at Lord's (and it's lashing down in Guardian Towers in Farringdon). Meanwhile the drunken England fans are asking Gillespie, "Where's your caravan?"

48th over: England 156–5 (Pietersen 42, G Jones 6) With Warne coming round the wicket, and Pietersen content to pad up, scoring has slowed. "England finally make an opening stand on a deadish wicket, and then Vaughan, Bell and Flintoff go for less than a Gillespie partnership – sad or pathetic?" asks John Burnes. Both, John, both.

Rain has stopped play: That's it for the night.

Australia 190 and 384; England 155 and 156–5

Fourth Day

The morning session

BY MIKE ADAMSON

10.15am Good morning everyone. The good news is it's raining outside, and it looks fairly set, which suggests England could hold out for a long period today. The bad news is that once the two teams finally do emerge on to the pitch, Australia only need five more wickets for victory.

10.30am It has actually stopped raining here in Farringdon, but not at Lord's apparently where light drizzle still reigns.

10.55am Mark Nicholas has just confirmed that the weather is expected to brighten up this afternoon, though more showers are predicted for tomorrow. How depressing it is, though, that after all the hype and excitement about a more competitive Test series, we're banking on the rain to prevent England losing.

11.30am Mark Nicholas returns to inform us that it's still raining. And then he's off again to be replaced by *The Newlyweds*, which is going to result in some rapid-fire channel-flicking in this office.

Midday Still no signs of any cricket bats or people dressed in white on the TV, I'm afraid, merely some *Friends* – it's "The One with the Nanny" for those interested.

12.40pm It's still raining at Lord's, and the general consensus is that it will remain raining until about 4pm. "I thought I'd send my apologies," says Lindsay Chapman. "Yesterday I promised that I'd send some Hobnobs to the poor soul covering OBO today, to cheer them up during the downpour. Having seen yesterday's highlights, though, I've spent the morning putting the finishing touches to my 'Read for England' hat. Then I realised that I'd much rather he continued to be available for Notts to help them to a long overdue Championship win. Still battling with my conscience, so the Hobnobs are on hold." Get those Hobnobs in, Lindsay. No excuses.

1pm "Stupid rain! I hate it!" writes Charlie Gidney. "Because of the weather, I'm now going to have to watch the German Grand Prix. Do you know how boring the next two hours are going to be? Grr." I am only too aware of this, Charlie.

1.30pm "Here's some lap-by-lap coverage for you in the absence of cricket," writes Chris Heeley.

"Lap one: some cars are following each other in a circle. Lap two: they're not ordinary cars you understand – people have unbelievably spent their lives and millions of pounds making sure they can follow each other in a circle really really fast. Lap three: the pointless waste of precious fuel reserves continues."

2.10pm "What I'm really missing about the cricket is Gilchrist's nauseatingly nasal whine of 'Nice one Shane", every time Warne bowls a ball," says Sean Chambers. "I wonder if you can get it as a ringtone." At least it would be an improvement on that stupid frog.

2.40pm IT HAS STOPPED RAINING! At least it has stopped raining in Farringdon. And in central London according to my correspondent Monica Kendall.

3pm The covers have been removed, the umbrellas are down, the players are out on the field warming up, and an inspection is due at 3.15pm. The suggestion is that play will hopefully commence at around 4pm.

3.43pm The players are walking out to the wicket. Let play begin.

49th over: England 156–5 (Pietersen 42, G Jones 6) The first shot of the day, an easy forward defensive from Geraint Jones, is met by huge cheers from the surprisingly large crowd.

50th over: England 157–5 (Pietersen 43, G Jones 6) As expected Shane Warne is straight into the attack. Kevin Pietersen scores the first run of the day with a drive to point. But then Warne turns the next ball about three feet past Jones's bat – how are you meant to play that?

WICKET! 51st over: G Jones c Gillespie b McGrath 6 (England 158–6)
A terribly poor shot from Jones. In trying to pull a delivery which
was too full for the stroke, he looped the ball into the waiting
hands of Gillespie for a simple catch at mid-on. Not what was
required in this situation.

WICKET! 51st over: Giles c Hayden b McGrath 0 (England 158–7)
Giles survives his first ball, but edges his second to the gleeful
Hayden at gully. This is pretty pathetic from England.

52nd over: England 159–7 (Pietersen 45, Hoggard 0) The players
have gone off again, and the England fans, obviously not too
bothered about the lack of entertainment, are singing and dancing
in the rain, delighted that the weather could yet save their team. It
seems this will just be a brief stoppage, though. "I'm so glad you all
enjoyed the first two sessions of the Test so much," mocks Jacob
Murray-White in Melbourne. "It makes this so much more
enjoyable."

53rd over: England 159–7 (Pietersen 46, Hoggard 0) Pietersen takes
a single off McGrath's second ball, leaving Hoggard to face the man
who he said was over the hill. McGrath unsurprisingly bounces him
with the next two balls, both of which the Hog evades.

54th over: England 161–7 (Pietersen 47, Hoggard 0) Warne is trying
everything against Pietersen, but KP is happy just to block his
friend's bowling and pick up a single.

WICKET! 55th over: Hoggard lbw b McGrath 0 (England 164–8)
McGrath traps Hoggard plumb in front of his stumps, hitting him in
line with off stump just below the knee. "I am an ex-pat Brit who
moved to the Middle East because of the chronic illness of optimism
among British sports fans," says Haim Ben Shalom. "How did
anyone ever think this Ashes would be different from the eight
before it? Are we really this stupid?"

WICKET! 56th over: Harmison lbw b Warne 0 (England 167–9)
Warne gifts Pietersen his 50 with a rank long-hop which he pulls
through midwicket, but then Harmison, lasting one ball less than
Giles, fails to pick the slider and becomes Warne's fourth victim of
the innings. England aren't putting up too much resistance here.

57th over: England 168–9 (Pietersen 52, S Jones 0) McGrath finds
the inside edge of Pietersen's bat, but the ball lands six inches short

of Gilchrist. "So, what can England offer Graham Thorpe to get him to play?" wonders Richard Simpson. "Make Ian Bell wash his car and cut his lawn for the rest of the summer?"

58th over: England 180–9 (Pietersen 64, S Jones 0) Pietersen decides he's had enough of this and clobbers the first ball of the over against the spin and into the stand on the on-side. A huge hit. Next ball he goes after Warne again but has to modify his shot and picks up two to long-on. Then he strokes it to mid-off but rejects the single. The next ball generates laughter all round as Warne bowls a 70mph bouncer which Gilchrist takes above his head. Then Pietersen smacks the last ball of the over back over Warne's head for a one-bounce four. Quite an eventful over all in all.

WICKET! 59th over: S Jones c Warne b McGrath 0 (England 180 all out) Jones edges McGrath's first ball to first slip, where Warne does the honourable thing of taking the catch and ending the match. The Aussies must be wondering quite what all the fuss was about with this England team.

Australia 190 and 384; England 155 and 180

Australia won by 239 runs

Second Test

Edgbaston,
4–7 August 2005

First Day

The morning session

BY SEAN INGLE

Preamble: Just when England needed a break, they've got one: during practice this morning Glenn McGrath crocked his ankle and is out of the second Test. Meanwhile Michael Vaughan has lost the toss – again – and Ricky Ponting has put England in on what looks a classic green-top. This could be a very interesting morning . . .

1st over: England 1–0 (Trescothick 0, Strauss 0) Here we go, Brett Lee to Trescothick . . . and the first ball is a horrendous wide, which ends up going to second slip. Cue huge cheers from the Edgbaston crowd.

2nd over: England 5–0 (Trescothick 0, Strauss 4) Gillespie, who's slicked on half a tub of soul-glow judging by the grease on his hair, takes the new ball. Like Lee, he doesn't make the greatest of starts, and Strauss opens his account with a low dab through third man for four. "I reckon McGrath has chucked a sickie," suggests Matthew Huntingdon. "Just look at his figures at Edgbaston: six wickets at an average of 41.7!"

3rd over: England 17–0 (Trescothick 12, Strauss 4) Lee pitches wide again first ball, but this time Trescothick crashes him through the covers for four. He repeats the trick twice more to leave Lee scratching his blond highlights in frustration. "How are the *Guardian* journalists backing Ashley Giles for this match?" asks Peter Lovell. "I'm doing it in the only way I know how and putting money on him to be man of the match. A couple of quid at 40–1 and if it comes in I'm going to send him the lot." Any suggestions?

4th over: England 17–0 (Trescothick 12, Strauss 4) Strauss nervously edges at a Gillespie outswinger, it flies low to Warne at first slip . . . and he does a Pietersen and drops it! "Everyone shut up," fumes Adam Nutley, possibly while chucking his toys out of the pram. "All this gloating over McGrath's misfortune will come back to bite us on the arse. Remember what happened in the last Test when everybody wrote him off?"

5th over: England 22–0 (Trescothick 16, Strauss 4) So far this pitch looks about as dangerous as Jason Donavon's left hook. "Glenn McGrath might have a poor average at this ground, but what about Harmison?" argues Ewan Dunnett. "Looking at his figures – I think he checks in at 77 per wicket."

6th over: England 27–0 (Trescothick 16, Strauss 9) Strauss, who's looked the more tentative of England's openers, produces the shot of the morning, slapping a delivery on a length through point for four. "I've resolved not to shave until Giles takes a 5–for in the Ashes, or he retires," says David Horn. "By 2007 I should have a fine, streaming, facial adornment." And look like David Bellamy.

7th over: England 27–0 (Trescothick 16, Strauss 9) Lee, all Beavis and Butthead snarl, has at last found his line, but there's very little swing or seam. Maiden. "I thought I'd do England a favour and get in early with the doomsaying," says David Smith. "I bet we're all out for less than 150. There. Now we're the underdogs, we have a chance of bravely clawing out an unlikely result in the face of insurmountable odds."

8th over: England 36–0 (Trescothick 21, Strauss 13) Trescothick's moving his feet – really! – and crashes yet another boundary to move into the 20s. England are (famous last words alert) looking set fair. "I am a little confused by all the rule changes of late. Can McGrath join in this Test later on as a super sub?" asks Joff Harvey.

9th over: England 42–0 (Trescothick 25, Strauss 13) Brett Lee's first bouncer of the morning nearly takes Trescothick's head off. The retaliation comes thick and fast, as Tresco plunders yet another four. "The *Guardian* has lacked a paranoid firebrand columnist since Julie Burchill's departure," Kieran Morgan writes. "Why not show your support for Ashley by offering him a weekly opinion slot in Weekend?"

10th over: England 44–0 (Trescothick 27, Strauss 13) Gillespie is desperately trying to get something out of the wicket, but the ball is swinging less than your grandfather's hips at a disco and the pitch is flatter than week-old lemonade.

11th over: England 50–0 (Trescothick 28, Strauss 17) Shot from Strauss, who rocks back on his heels and clouts a classic square cut for four to bring up the 50. Not the greatest of starts for new bowler Michael Kasprowicz.

12th over: England 54–0 (Trescothick 32, Strauss 17) "Why is it when England lose, we all turn on the King of Spain?" splutters Stephen Smith. "It's a bit of a cliché now, surely? It's a bit harsh to blame a defeat on a guy who bowled 11 overs, when Hoggard was as lumbering as ever and Vaughan forgot how to use a bat."

13th over: England 55–0 (Trescothick 32, Strauss 17) Yet more luck for England as Trescothick slaps a Kasprowicz outswinger straight to Matthew Hayden at gully . . . only for the umpire to call "No-ball!". "As the wicket is soft, the ball will make indentations. If the weather warms up the pitch will harden and produce variable bounce," says Charles Downes. "Batting first sounds like a good toss to lose now!" Couldn't agree more, Charles.

14th over: England 60–0 (Trescothick 32, Strauss 22) Another change in the bowling, as the MC announces: "From the Pavilion End, Shane Warne." You wouldn't expect lots of spin from this pitch, and so far there isn't – Strauss watches for a while and then smashes him down the ground for four.

15th over: England 60–0 (Trescothick 32, Strauss 22) Kasprowicz continues with metronomic accuracy, and Trescothick is content to watch. Maiden.

16th over: England 68–0 (Trescothick 32, Strauss 30) Strauss, who was completely bamboozled by Warne at Lord's, is now smashing him this way and that. Great stuff! Meanwhile Jon Ingram wants to know: "When was the last time Warne bowled as early as the 14th over of a first innings for Australia?" Anyone?

17th over: England 68–0 (Trescothick 32, Strauss 30) Kasprowicz has yet to get anything out of a pitch that's slower than a Viennese Waltz. "Given how flat the wicket sounds, I think England should bat for all five days, tire the Australians and then win at Old Trafford," suggests Pranay Sanklecha.

18th over: England 77–0 (Trescothick 39, Strauss 31) Trescothick charges down the ground and smashes Warne for six. Shot! "Warne has once before bowled within the first 15 overs of a Test match," says Dom Hastings. "It was early in his career – and Mark Taylor had promised if he got five wickets by lunch on the first day, he would happily share his captain's plate of cheeseburgers and nachos with him at lunch. *Wisden* remarks that Warne had to settle for a cheese and pickle sandwich."

19th over: England 86–0 (Trescothick 47, Strauss 32) Runs! Runs! Runs! "I know it is early on the first day, but when was the last time an Australian captain won the toss, sent in the opposition, and won the Test match (playing Bangladesh or Zimbabwe doesn't count)?" asks Drew Wagner. "I think Steve Waugh said that 99 times out of 100 he would immediately elect to bat first, the other 1% he would think about sending the opposition in, and then after two seconds of consideration would decide to bat anyway."

20th over: England 86–0 (Trescothick 47, Strauss 32) Better from Warne, and Strauss is content to block. Maiden. "Blame Giles for the first Test?" splutters Tom Willoughby. "Too damn right – Warne is turning the ball square and the King of Spain bowls 11 for 45 odd. Not even Johnnie Cochrane could defend that one."

21st over: England 86–0 (Trescothick 47, Strauss 32) Another maiden. "Quick point. The Viennese waltz is actually very fast indeed, it's the English waltz that's as slow as the Edgbaston wicket," says Ben Usher (and six others).

22nd over: England 95–0 (Trescothick 50, Strauss 39) Paul Meek, a Kiwi in Australia, writes: "If Trescothick and Strauss can make batting look this easy, I kind of fear what the Aussie innings will be like – I reckon Nathan Astle's quickest double-century record will be knocked off in half the time by Adam Gilchrist."

23rd over: England 103–0 (Trescothick 50, Strauss 47) Shot! Glorious cover drive from Strauss! And, just for good measure, he repeats the trick next ball to bring up the 100 partnership – the first by England's openers against Australia for eight years. "If ever there was a time for a flat-track bully it's now," suggests Mark Pennington. "If we let the Aussies have McGrath as a super sub, can we have Graeme Hick?"

24rd over: England 110–0 (Trescothick 56, Strauss 47) Warne is trying everything at the moment – there was even a rare sighting of his flipper that over – but to no avail. "Can you please pass on a message to all the Aussies out there?" asks Colin Moors. "This kind of score is what you'll have to look forward to when Warne and McGrath finally call it a day. Welcome to the real world."

25th over: England 112–0 (Trescothick 57, Strauss 48) Lee comes on for Kasprowicz, but England play him comfortably. "Utter tosh from Drew Wagner (over 19) sadly," writes my over-by-over colleague Rob Smyth, adjusting his anorak. "Waugh was a disciple of bowling first: he did it 11 times, and they won all 11."

WICKET! 26th over: Strauss b Warne 48 (England 112–1) Warne strikes! He pushes a quicker one through and, as Strauss tries a cross-bat cut, it darts back viciously and bowls him. Meanwhile more stick for Drew Wagner. "It was WG Grace who said when you win the toss, you bat etc," fumes Graham Bartlett. "It's bad enough we give them the Ashes for nearly 20 years without people rewriting the game's rich tapestry of stories and putting them in Aussie mouths!"

27th over: England 132–1 (Trescothick 77, Vaughan 1) Brilliant from Trescothick, who lofts Lee wide of gully for four, then uppercuts him over deep third man for six, square drives him for another boundary and (keep up at the back) cuts him for four. Lunch. "Just read Colin Moors' comments. Tell that turkey that unless they come up with a new brainwashing machine which transforms weak-minded poms into arrogant world beaters, you will only ever be making up the numbers, mate. You are a nation built on greatness which has turned into a nation of weak-minded nobodies who accept losing as the norm," says Brad Callaghan, who I'm guessing is Australian.

England 132–1

The afternoon session

BY MIKE ADAMSON

Preamble: While England fans may be slightly excited by what has undoubtedly been an encouraging start, I should warn readers that England had done equally well when I entered the OBO hot seat on the Thursday of the first Test, only to then lose seven wickets for 89 runs.

28th over: England 135–1 (Trescothick 77, Vaughan 4) A fairly quiet first over from Jason Gillespie after lunch. "It is my melancholy duty to announce that for the first time in my life I have bet on England to win a cricket match," says Jacob Murray-White in Melbourne. "I couldn't resist and I thought I may need some solace." See how quickly these Aussies turn?

29th over: England 146–1 (Trescothick 77, Vaughan 14) The Eric Hollies Stand erupts as Michael Clarke quite unnecessarily shies at the stumps only to concede four overthrows. Then Vaughan hints he may be coming into some form with a gorgeous cover drive which bisects the fielders. Cue chants of "Easy, easy, easy."

30th over: England 155–1 (Trescothick 82, Vaughan 18) Tresco brings up his highest-ever Test score against Australia by flicking the ball off his hips for four. Then Vaughan smacks a glorious square cut to the boundary. This is rather impressive fare.

31st over: England 162–1 (Trescothick 88, Vaughan 18) "Good start by England, but with even the great Warnester himself not being able to turn one, what on earth is the thinking behind Giles's selection?" wonders Glen Sibley.

32nd over: England 162–1 (Trescothick 88, Vaughan 18) What's this? A Jason Gillespie maiden? As improbable as it may seem, it is actually true. "Could the mighty OBO-ers help me with some suitably disrespectful jibes I can put in my brother's 40th birthday card?" asks Eddie Kerridge. Well?

WICKET! 33rd over: Trescothick c Gilchrist b Kasprowicz 90 (England 164–2) Having pushed his way into the nervous nineties, Trescothick plays a loose shot outside off stump and nicks one to Gilchrist for a regulation catch.

WICKET! 33rd over: Bell c Gilchrist b Kasprowicz 6 (England 170–3) Having confidently cracked one past point for four, Bell edges the next ball to Gilchrist for another easy catch, prompting my colleague Barry Glendenning to ask whether the Warwickshire man is actually a batsman.

34th over: England 171–3 (Vaughan 18, Pietersen 0) After the drama of the last over, the game settles down again with, remarkably, another tight Gillespie over. Daniel Herman writes in: "Eddie Kerridge might like to try: 'Happy 40th birthday! The Government Actuary's Department estimates that you have 42.8 years left to live!'" Cruel, but not as cruel as some which may not be printed here. Shame on you.

35th over: England 183–3 (Vaughan 23, Pietersen 5) Kevin Pietersen accelerates to a strike rate of 400 after one ball thanks to a nicely timed on-drive which races to the rope. "As I am fairly new to cricket, can someone please explain to me the point of Bell?" asks Kaye Smith.

36th over: England 185–3 (Vaughan 24, Pietersen 5) Warne is back into the attack. "Surely all your readers are missing the real implications of England's good start," writes Adrian Harte. "An England win would seriously boost Ireland's chances of World Cup success in 2007. Another abject defeat would potentially lead to wholesale changes including a first cap for Ed Joyce, thus making this year's leading run-scorer ineligible for Ireland duty."

WICKET! 37th over: Vaughan c Lee b Gillespie 24 (England 187–4) Gillespie dug one in short (a predictable tactic given Vaughan's dodgy elbow) and Vaughan was slow on it with his attempted pull shot, slicing the ball to Lee at long leg. "Trescothick, Bell gone . . . look, Mike, maybe best if you take the afternoon off before we have a repeat of Lord's?" says Jared McGeechan.

38th over: England 191–4 (Pietersen 7, Flintoff 4) England are feeling the heat now. Flintoff is nearly out for a duck when his mistimed drive just goes over the head of mid-off. "Could I suggest 'Happy birthday, you're older than Ashley Giles's bowling average' for Eddie Kerridge?" says Andy Smith.

39th over: England 193–4 (Pietersen 9, Flintoff 4) "To answer Kaye Smith, the point of a bell is so that, when cycling, people know you're coming up behind them," says Ben Hendy unhelpfully. "Oh, wait, no, I see, the point of Bell, not a bell. No, no idea then."

40th over: England 197–4 (Pietersen 10, Flintoff 7) A loud appeal from Warne against Flintoff, for lbw this time, is met by another emphatic "Not out" from Billy Bowden.

41st over: England 201–4 (Pietersen 14, Flintoff 7) "Clearly, this mini-collapse has all been planned in advance," thinks Alex Holland. "They're just setting the stage for Giles to come in and score a double century, silencing the critics and winning the man of the match award. He'll follow that up with a seven-for and a six-for, with Simon Jones picking up the remainder, winning back his girlfriend as a result. Then Thorpe will give David Graveney a hug."

42nd over: England 211–4 (Pietersen 14, Flintoff 17) Flintoff is in a fair amount of trouble against Warne, failing to pick each of Warne's variations. First he played inside the one that turns a couple of feet, then he plays outside the one that goes straight on. Then Warne lets Flintoff off the hook with one ball he can read – the full-toss, which is duly dispatched over the infield. Then he takes one giant stride down the pitch and launches the final ball of the over for six over mid-on. What was I writing at the start of the over?

43rd over: England 221–4 (Pietersen 24, Flintoff 17) Pietersen has picked up where he left off at Lord's, here playing a classic back-foot cover drive for four runs, then a short-of-length ball on the up through the off-side for another two. And then the pick of the bunch, a wristy drive past mid-on, to which any words I write here will not do justice.

44th over: England 227–4 (Pietersen 24, Flintoff 23) Billy Bowden's got his slow-motion arm-extension working again, reacting to an effortless Andrew Flintoff swipe to cow corner. It's Warne's turn to shake his head. These two have put on 40 runs in just 42 balls.

45th over: England 236–4 (Pietersen 29, Flintoff 27) Yet another boundary and it's Pietersen's turn this time, cutting Gillespie (his delivery, not his hair) through the gully area. And then Flintoff joins in the fun, pulling Gillespie powerfully over midwicket.

46th over: England 240–4 (Pietersen 31, Flintoff 29) "Let's not forget that Bell's average is still pretty Bradman-esque," remarks Kevin Lynch. "Although while we discuss this Pietersen's strike rate is going through the roof. I'm predicting an England stroll to victory some time on Sunday afternoon." How fickle we all are.

47th over: England 242–4 (Pietersen 32, Flintoff 30) Flintoff has a lucky escape when an inside edge just evades his leg stump. Lee, back into the attack, smiles ruefully – he looks pumped up for this spell. "In the *Evening Standard* last night, it was claimed that the King of Spain is cricket's favourite misprint," says Billy Luckhurst. "This is surely overlooking my school cricket tour where my friend, whose surname is Spinks, had the P replaced with a T on the back of his tour shirt, by accident of course." Of course.

48th over: England 244–4 (Pietersen 33, Flintoff 31) Pietersen only has one thing on his mind here, and that's to attack. However, this approach almost proves his undoing as he fails to spot Warne's slider and is agonisingly close to edging the ball to Gilchrist. "Can someone explain what's going on with Warne's shoes?" asks Ben Colclough. "They're like platforms with spats. Is he wearing flares as well?"

49th over: England 255–4 (Pietersen 33, Flintoff 42) Flintoff almost goes the way of Vaughan, trying to hook Lee but top-edging the ball to long-leg. Then Lee produces another pacy bouncer, Flintoff closes his eyes à la Botham in '81, and thrashes the ball into the stand.

50th over: England 263–4 (Pietersen 34, Flintoff 49) Geoffrey Boycott was just espousing the virtues of defensive batting when Flintoff planted Warne down the ground into the sightscreen for his fourth six. Flintoff has faced only 44 balls for his 49 runs.

51st over: England 265–4 (Pietersen 35, Flintoff 49) Flintoff is almost out yet again when he notices that Lee has bowled a slower ball at the last nanosecond and tries to pull his bat out of the way too late. The ball fell just out of the reach of the grasping extra cover.

52nd over: England 274–4 (Pietersen 39, Flintoff 54) The "Easy, easy" chants are sounded again, first in response to Andrew Flintoff's fifty, then to another Pietersen controlled slog for four. "This may be the kiss of death," says Ian Cheney, "but isn't this what we've all been waiting for – The Fred and Kevin Show! Let's see if they can bring on 300 between them in as many balls!" I thought I had exclusive rights on the kiss of death.

53rd over: England 288–4 (Pietersen 39, Flintoff 68) Another huge over. First Flintoff continues his Botham impression with another hook for six, then guides one down to the vacant third-man boundary, and lastly lets fly square of the wicket. That's the 100 partnership and it's taken just 96 balls.

54th over: England 289–4 (Pietersen 40, Flintoff 68) Clearly concerned by the mountain of runs that England are piling up, Warne confers with Ponting after every ball to ensure this is the last over Australia must bowl before tea. And with the Aussie bowling around the wicket into the rough, Flintoff is content to let the ball hit his front pad and block the over out.

England 289–4

The evening session

BY SEAN INGLE

Preamble: It's been an incredible day so far, but the suspicion remains that England need these two to kick on – especially as Australia could easily make 600 on a pitch that's flatter than a supermodel on a lettuce diet. "Serious question for everyone if I may – what is the highest first-day score of a Test match?" asks Dom Hastings. Well?

WICKET! 55th over: Flintoff c Gilchrist b Gillespie 68 (England 290–5) Oh dear, oh dear, oh dear. Gillespie gets one to move away, Flintoff slashes at it, and Gilchrist takes an easy catch behind the stumps. "I've always wondered – do the teams actually drink tea at tea?" asks William Church. "Surely they lay a brew on as an option?" They do, William – but (boring fact alert) most players will have water or a sports drink.

56th over: England 292–5 (Pietersen 42, G Jones 1) Pietersen continues to come out punching, but he nearly gives Kasprowicz a caught and bowled. "What do players drink at tea? Judging by Flintoff's shot to get out, I'm thinking scrumpy," suggests Tom Chivers.

57th over: England 292–5 (Pietersen 42, G Jones 1) There's none of

Flintoff's *Sturm und Drang* romanticism from Geraint Jones, who's content to block Gillespie's over. Maiden.

WICKET! 58th over: G Jones c Gilchrist b Kasprowicz 0 (England 293–6) Kasprowicz gets some extra bounce which seems to startle Jones, as he can only fend it to Gilchrist. Giles immediately gets off the mark with a four through gully. "Don't know if this is the answer to Dom Hastings's question (preamble), but Australia ended the first day of the third Test in 1930 on 3 for 458," says Stefan Hopewell. "Don Bradman scored 309 runs on the first day, which is still a record for one day of a Test match."

59th over: England 299–6 (Pietersen 44, Giles 5) England badly need Giles, who averages 20 in Test cricket, to stick around for a while. Let's hope a well-timed sledge doesn't put him off. "So they don't all sit around delicately drinking Earl Grey from a china tea-set?!" sighs Lee Kelly. "No cake?! No scones?! My illusions are shattered!"

60th over: England 306–6 (Pietersen 44, Giles 9) A HUGE slice of luck there for Ashley Giles who edges Kasprowicz, only to watch it drop between second slip and gully. Meanwhile, the number of emails slagging off Geraint Jones has already reached double figures.

61st over: England 310–6 (Pietersen 45, Giles 15) Great shot from the *Guardian*'s Ashley Giles (yes, we're sticking by him for now) through deep cover, takes him on to 15. Meanwhile Denby Dale has a poser: "What are batsmen known as in ladies' cricket? Is it batswoman, batsperson or, simply, batter?"

62nd over: England 316–6 (Pietersen 46, Giles 19) Something strange is going on here: Giles is continuing to attack, while Pietersen seems to be settling into an anchor role. Another Gilo boundary briefly stops the crowd's Mexican wave (they greet it with widespread four signals). "I may be a broken record on this, but I find it hard to believe that Thorpe would be doing anything other than occupying the crease now had he been selected ahead of Bell," says Stuart Roberts.

63rd over: England 328–6 (Pietersen 58, Giles 19) Pietersen brings up his fifty with a controlled slog (if that's not an oxymoron) through mid-on, before smashing on through the covers and the gully for two more fours. Brilliant stuff.

64th over: England 336–6 (Pietersen 63, Giles 19) Warne comes back and immediately has two huge appeals for lbw against the *Guardian*'s Ashley Giles. Both looked absolutely plum, but umpire Bowden isn't having any of it.

65th over: England 341–6 (Pietersen 63, Giles 23) Giles takes on the bouncer, and sends it between two fielders for four. "I might have missed the boat on the whole tea discussion, but surely you should mention Jack Russell, who drank 20 cups a day and had the habit of re-using his tea-bag, hanging it on a nail above the kettle, ready for the next time," says Will Fiennes. "In the final Test against Australia at The Oval in 1989, Russell apparently used the same bag through all five days of the match, which equates to something close to 100 cups. I'm geek enough to have copied that out when I read it in the paper."

WICKET! 66th over: Giles lbw Warne 23 (England 342–7) Giles, having survived three lives, finally goes! Warne's delivery pitches on his boot, in front of middle stump, and after a moment's deliberation umpire Bowden waggles his finger.

WICKET! 67th over: Pietersen c Katich b Lee 71 (England 348–8) Now Pietersen goes! After slogging Lee for six, he tries to repeat the trick, but mistimes it straight to Katich at deep midwicket. "Not only did Jack Russell drink 20 cups of tea a day, but he also ate nothing but baked beans during an entire tour of the sub-continent and he was universally recognised to be the best gloveman of his generation," says Ben Mimmack. "It's high time the England management made the relevant changes to Geraint Jones's diet before the next Test."

68th over: England 353–8 (Hoggard 4, Harmison 3) Loud cheers from the Edgbaston crowd as Hoggard and Harmison add some singles, to take Warne's figures to 100 off 20 overs. Warne's comeback? A regal bow of the head. "In response to Denby Dale's poser: 'What are batsmen known as in ladies' cricket? Is it batswoman, batsperson or, simply, batter?' The answer is – easy wickets!' says Scott Beattie, who'd better be wearing a crash helmet.

69th over: England 367–8 (Hoggard 4, Harmison 13) Harmison takes on Lee – and top edges him over Michael Kasprowicz at fine leg for six! Next ball, he pulls Lee through midwicket for four. Incredible stuff. Meanwhile Gareth Williams wants to know whether Denby Dale (over 61) "is where they film *Last of the Summer Wine*?" Well, Denby?

WICKET! 70th over: Harmison b Warne 17 (England 375–9) The ball after Harmison charges down the pitch and smashes Warne straight over his head for four, Warne gets him with the slider. "Re: women cricketers – do they wear boxes?" asks Henry Scowcroft.

71st over: England 377–9 (Hoggard 6, S Jones 1) Hoggard keeps the scoreboard ticking with a flick down to third man, before Jones gets off the mark with swipe to deep cover. "It beggars belief that none of these batsmen have gone on to make a big hundred," says P Ervoe, speaking for many readers. "If Harmison doesn't extract some life out of this pitch tomorrow we will be likely to concede a first-innings deficit of 200."

72nd over: England 383–9 (Hoggard 6, S Jones 7) Warne continues to Jones. He's got plenty of rough patches to work with and has Jones playing and missing for fun. "Women do wear boxes, though they are a different shape to men's as they have a different shaped pelvic bone," points out Richard O'Hagan. "They refer to them as manhole covers."

73rd over: England 384–9 (Hoggard 7, S Jones 7) "My parents deserve a good shoeing for naming me after a town in West Yorkshire which is only famous for it's Millennium Pie," says Denby Dale. "Oh, and *Last of the Summer Wine* is filmed in Holmfirth."

74th over: England 384–9 (Hoggard 7, S Jones 7) Warne continues to probe and tease, Hoggard to stoically defend. Maiden.

75th over: England 386–9 (Hoggard 7, S Jones 8) For the first time today, we're seeing a "normal" Test match, with the batsmen watchful and the bowlers teasing and tempting. Just the two off that over. Meanwhile Mike Peacock is proud to admit that: "Ex-women's cricket captain Rachel Heyhoe-Flint once signed my brother's box."

76th over: England 387–9 (Hoggard 8, S Jones 8) England's obdurate defence to Warne continues, as does the suspicion that the Aussies will fancy their chances on this pitch. "Perhaps the best way to defeat the Aussies, is to not let Mike Adamson near the OBOs?" asks Jascha Elliot.

77th over: England 389–9 (Hoggard 8, S Jones 9) Gillespie nearly gets Jones with a slower one which just misses the bails. Otherwise the blockade continues. "Now that's more like it, England," says Johnny Sultoon. "Hoggy adopting a nice gritty strike rate of 20–odd. We may as well promote him to No. 4 and groom him as the new Thorpe."

78th over: England 392–9 (Hoggard 12, S Jones 8) Warne continues to flick his wrist this way and that, and Hoggard continues to practise his defensive shot. Until he cover-drives Warne for four off the last ball of the over. "Wouldn't it be wise to declare now and have 10 overs at them this evening?" suggests Richard Clarke. Surely England need every run they can get, Richard?

79th over: England 405–9 (Hoggard 15, S Jones 18) Shot from Jones! He leans back and smashes Gillespie straight down the ground for six. Two balls later, a similar straight drive just evades Langer in the deep and brings up the 400.

WICKET! 80th over: Hoggard lbw b Warne 16 (England 407 all out) The slider strikes again. Hoggard tries to slog-sweep Warne, misses, and umpire Bowden has an easy lbw decision to make. "Perhaps England should have taken note of Geoff Boycott, who was espousing the benefits of defence earlier? It's all very well going at five an over but we needed to score at least 500," says Lee Wilkey. "In fact, let's get rid of Bell and bring back Boycs."

England 407

Australia first innings

The batsmen walk on to the pitch . . . and it starts to rain. That's it for the day.

Second Day

The morning session

BY ROB SMYTH

Preamble: England scored fast enough to win a game yesterday, but they also scored fast enough to lose one, and the delirium surrounding their exhilarating slogathon obscures the fact that, at best, 407 is a par score. The first session today is crucial. It's a bit overcast, which should be good for England, and maybe Matthew Hoggard will break the habit of a lifetime and do something significant in an Ashes Test.

WICKET! Hayden c Strauss b Hoggard 0 (Australia 0–1) Told you Hoggard was rubbish: he bowls a borderline half-volley first ball, and Hayden drives it straight to short extra cover! The first golden duck of his career.

2nd over: Australia 4–1 (Langer 0, Ponting 4) Blimey, that should have been 0 for 2. Ponting plays tip and run into the off-side, and would have been run out by a direct hit from Pietersen. Instead he gets four overthrows. "Read somewhere yesterday (possibly here) that this pitch is ideally suited to flat-track bullies," says Cai Evans. "In view of this, I can't help thinking that a Matthew Hayden ton is on the cards today. (Hope I'm spectacularly wrong, naturally)." You are, Cai. Now do one.

3rd over: Australia 6–1 (Langer 0, Ponting 6) "I don't suppose there's any chance that Shane Warne tripped over a pie this morning, ruling himself out of the Test and the rest of the series?!" chuckles Matthew Huntington in the mistaken assumption that he's hilarious and not in any way a David Brent clone.

4th over: Australia 16–1 (Langer 0, Ponting 14) Ponting looks like he really means business – a leg-stump half-volley from Hoggard is tucked away to square leg with the minimum of fuss. Later in the over, Ponting slams another wretched delivery through extra cover off the back foot.

5th over: Australia 23–1 (Langer 3, Ponting 18) Langer's getting roughed up big-time by Harmison here: another short one nails him just under the ribcage. Then Ponting clips another swaggering four. "Donnie Darko is just what England need right now," says Lee Kelly. "He can go back in time and arrange for a jet engine to fall on Bell."

6th over: Australia 29–1 (Langer 8, Ponting 18) Langer, relieved to be away from the Harmison hammer, has a kitchen-sink drive at a wide one from Hoggard and skews it over the top for four. Here's Richard Burgess. "When I saw Warney's haircut on the telly last night, I was reminded of the time as a kid when the neighbour's golden retriever had an operation and some of his fur had to be shaved off."

7th over: Australia 39–1 (Langer 9, Ponting 26) Ponting is doing an Azharuddin Lord's 1990 here – he swivel-pulls Harmison for another princely boundary; then he check-pulls another. It looks like we're in for another run-fest.

8th over: Australia 44–1 (Langer 10, Ponting 29) More leg-stump dross from Hoggard is worked away by Ponting for three more. Here's Richard Clarke. "Bell: performed well against a poor West Indian line-up, did what was expected of him against Bangladesh and had three poor innings against Australia (at no point getting out through overly careless batting). This may sound silly but he looked assured facing his first two balls yesterday." It sounds sillier than you could ever know, pal.

9th over: Australia 50–1 (Langer 14, Ponting 30) The pitch has definitely lost the little zing it had early on; Langer clunks a pull off Harmison for four through mid-on, a pretty streaky shot.

10th over: Australia 50–1 (Langer 14, Ponting 30) Simon Jones rightly replaces the ineffectual Hoggard, and England's fields are already fairly defensive. A maiden.

11th over: Australia 52–1 (Langer 15, Ponting 31) Another peach from Harmison kicks and jags *that* far past Langer's outside edge – he has bowled very well this morning on a pitch which, essentially, has little in it for him. "Help," says Joe Shooman. "My nephew's eight on Sunday and I don't know what to buy him. He likes football." A Lars Von Trier box set? The Bauhaus back collection?

12th over: Australia 52–1 (Langer 15, Ponting 31) Jones, bowling to only two slips, beats Ponting's outside edge with a ball that wobbled like a jelly that has Gareth Keenan's stapler in it. Another maiden and, to my right, Barry Glendenning is almost crying with laughter. Two minutes later I find out why: Martin Jol has a brother whose name is Cock.

13th over: Australia 61–1 (Langer 16, Ponting 39) The Harmison bouncer doesn't get up, and Ponting drags an effortless pull for four. He looks in ominously good touch; later in the over he clips a poor delivery for four more.

14th over: Australia 74–1 (Langer 17, Ponting 51) Geoff Boycott is outchuntering me, his gripe being that England have fed Ponting's leg-side strength early on. It's a fair point, but he's not exactly a one-trick pony, as he shows with a tremendous drive through mid-off. "Why doesn't Joe Shooman buy his nephew a Brighton & Hove Albion shirt with "OWEN" on the back of it?" says Martin White. "It might start a few rumours?" Nah – he's married.

15th over: Australia 75–1 (Langer 18, Ponting 51) Freddie into the attack, and a testing, disciplined over to Ponting outside off stump.

16th over: Australia 80–1 (Langer 19, Ponting 55) "Hello Rob Smith," says Andrew Pinkham. " When will the King of Spain be on?" Right now, and Ponting sweeps him deliciously for four.

17th over: Australia 82–1 (Langer 20, Ponting 56) Another good over from Flintoff, but England need a wicket before lunch as Australia are looking really snug here. Ponting, of course, would have been run out by a direct hit on 0. Gah!

18th over: Australia 87–1 (Langer 20, Ponting 61) The King of Spain story, for those who have been in California for the last four years: Ashley Giles had some benefit mugs with 'The King of Spin' printed on them. Only some spanner put 'The King of Spain' on them. Cue no hilarity whatsoever and an increasingly tiresome story.

Meanwhile, Giles feeds Ponting a nice half-volley that is belted through the covers for four. That's your fault, Dave Houghton.

19th over: Australia 87–1 (Langer 20, Ponting 61) England's increasing desperation manifests itself in a ludicriously optimistic lbw appeal against Ponting for a ball that hit him outside off, was going over, and took the inside edge.

WICKET! 20th over: Ponting c Vaughan b Giles 61 (Australia 88–2) My colleague Ashley Giles strikes in his third over! Ponting tried a lazy sweep and merely top-edged it to Vaughan at short fine-leg. Was it the slider? Was it the quicker one? Who cares! The end of a spectacularly good innings, and the England fielders are going absolutely ballistic.

21st over: Australia 92–2 (Langer 22, Martyn 3) Martyn flips Flintoff lazily to leg, but there is a spring in England's step again. All hail Gilo.

22nd over: Australia 98–2 (Langer 24, Martyn 8) Justin Langer is called "one short" despite clearly putting his bat over the line. Let's hope England win by one run, eh? "Did you get out of the wrong side of bed this morning, Smyth?" asks Jim Whibley. "You seem to be in an awfully cantankerous mood. Most comments so far this morning are being treated with complete disdain; I expect this to get similar treatment." I thought I was chipper.

23rd over: Australia 108–2 (Langer 25, Martyn 16) Gah! Two escapes for Martyn: first he edges Flintoff tantalisingly between slips and gully for four, and then he gloves a brutish delivery just wide of the diving Jones down the leg-side. Splendid stuff from Freddie.

24th over: Australia 114–2 (Langer 27, Martyn 16) Nearly lunch, and it'll be orange Lucozade all round for me. Meanwhile, Langer fresh-airs a big yahoo at Giles, and the ball sneaks between Geraint Jones's legs for four. That was a very useful over. "It's miserable where I work," says Adrian James. "A place called Swanley on the M25, and the weather is not too good either. I don't think there is a place in England that has more chavs and carnies. Does anyone else out there work in similarly depressing towns?" A little place I grew up in that I like to call Sittingbourne is even better.

WICKET! 25th over: Martyn run out (Vaughan) 20 (Australia 118–3) That's another one! Michael Vaughan hits the stumps direct from mid-on with a magnificent piece of fielding after some terrible running from Martyn, who was almost dawdling towards the crease at the bowler's end. What a wicket to get off the last ball before lunch! That's cheered me up no end.

England 407; Australia 118–3

The afternoon session

BY SEAN INGLE

Preamble: A huge session, this, obviously. Can England take another couple of wickets to take a grip on this game? And how will Ashley Giles cope with Michael Clarke, who biffed and bashed him all over Lord's?

26th over: Australia 128–3 (Langer 27, Clarke 10) After Langer sees out the last ball of Flintoff's over, the shaven-headed Jones steams in with punkish vigour. He produces one absolute jaffer – which swings and misses Clarke's bat by millimetres.

27th over: Australia 130–3 (Langer 28, Clarke 10) Harmison on for Flintoff. He's yet to build up a full head of steam, but Langer treats him with respect. "See if you can get a song going round the press box, and, fingers crossed, round the rest of the stadium too: 'We all love the King of Spain, singing Viva Espana!'" suggests Simon Kiely, who seems under the impression that I'm actually at Edgbaston rather than in my Farringdon bunker.

28th over: Australia 135–3 (Langer 32, Clarke 11) Another patchy Jones over; Langer takes advantage with a clipped boundary off his legs.

29th over: Australia 141–3 (Langer 33, Clarke 16) Clarke is looking smoother than an Italian stallion's pitter-patter. "A group of us are heading up to Old Trafford next week, and we are keen to take up Shane Warne's challenge to make up a song about him which makes him laugh – has anyone got any ideas?" asks Andy Pickford. Well?

30th over: Australia 142–3 (Langer 34, Clarke 16) Jones is getting some movement off the pitch here. He's also still straying on to leg, but only one run that over.

31st over: Australia 145–3 (Langer 36, Clarke 17) Some bounce from Harmison, but there's more easy singles out there than on Faliraki High Street.

32nd over: Australia 148–3 (Langer 36, Clarke 18) A change in approach from Jones, who is deliberately bowling outside off stump to a predominately off-side field.

33rd over: Australia 150–3 (Langer 39, Clarke 18) What about something like England are going to win the Ashes," suggests Nathan Davis. "That should make him laugh."

34th over: Australia 155–3 (Langer 40, Clarke 22) Jones continues his policy of bowling two foot outside off stump, only this time Clarke goes after him and pulls him brilliantly through midwicket.

35th over: Australia 156–3 (Langer 41, Clarke 22) Ashley Giles comes back and immediately launches into a huge lbw appeal against Langer after getting the ball to spin (note to readers: this is not a misprint). It only moved an inch, mind, and umpire Bowden correctly rules not out.

36th over: Australia 162–3 (Langer 46, Clarke 23) Langer moves steadily towards his half-century with another four off Jones, who's looking tired. "Over on TMS Aggers has been boasting about how he's got rid of his moles from his lawn," says Matthew Cobb. "How about you, Sean – do you have any trouble with moles?" I don't have a lawn, Matthew, yet alone several acres of land.

37th over: Australia 166–3 (Langer 48, Clarke 25) The nibble-and-nurdle cricket continues. "A while ago The Oval sang 'Check him out now, the fat boy bowler,' to the tune of Fatboy Slim's little ditty, while watching Warne get tonked for 20 in one over by Sourav Ganguly," says Jon Quinn. "What about that?"

38th over: Australia 173–3 (Langer 52, Clarke 28) Hoggard returns, and Langer helps himself to a half-century. "I'm going to the Ashes tomorrow with about 10 friends," says Ben Morrison. "I've never been to a cricket match in my life. I'm mostly after tips on what to shout out to avoid looking like an amateur." Probably best avoid "Nice off-break, Gilo."

39th over: Australia 178–3 (Langer 53, Clarke 32) Nice change of pace from Giles nearly gets Clarke. "Regarding the King of Spain and his much-vaunted crockery, did these pieces ever actually go on sale?" asks Dan Atkinson. "A quick scan of eBay shows no luck. Do any of your other readers have a King of Spain cup and, if so, would they accept a fair and gentlemanly price for one?"

40th over: Australia 179–3 (Langer 54, Clarke 32) Better from Hoggard, just the one off the over. Alex Holland has this tip for newbie Test-watchers: "Dress as a schoolgirl, a Viking or a nun, or at the very least, don't wear yellow. Action is only required when any number on the scoreboard hits either 50 or 100. You should then cheer/jeer loudly, depending on whether it's Us or Them. Do that, keep up the Mexican waves, and no one will look twice at you."

41st over: Australia 180–3 (Langer 55, Clarke 32) England are bottling up the Aussies here – but can they get a wicket?

42nd over: Australia 182–3 (Langer 56, Clarke 33) England keep up the pressure – just two off that over. Meanwhile as Kieran Mongon points out, you can pick up Ashley Giles, King of Spain mugs at thecricketshop.co.uk. "Incidentally, this is the first page that your lazier readers would have come to had they bothered to Google 'Ashley Giles king of Spain'."

43rd over: Australia 189–3 (Langer 57, Clarke 39) Shot! Clarke, who's one of the best players of spin in the world, uses his feet superbly before punching Giles for four through midwicket. More runs follow, and the Aussies relieve the pressure.

44th over: Australia 193–3 (Langer 61, Clarke 40) Textbook cover drive from Langer! The Australians are playing the sort of cricket England should've done yesterday: they're not getting sucked into a macho-man contest. "Ben must not, under any circumstances fall asleep, unless he wishes to be the object of ridicule," points out Karl Wills.

WICKET! 45th over: Clarke c G Jones b Giles 40 (Australia 193–4) The King is alive, long live the King! The *Guardian*'s Ashley Giles pushes a quicker one through (62mph compared to the usual 52mph), Clarke gets a nibble, and Jones takes a very fine catch behind the stumps. "My, your over-by-over coverage is popular," says Neil Smith. "The Cricketshop website has crashed."

46th over: Australia 195–4 (Langer 62, Katich 0) Flintoff comes back into the attack and nearly gets Katich first ball – his edge falls just short of Strauss at third slip. Meanwhile Gemma Harris is unhappy. "Does anyone else think that it's truly unfair than a non-cricket lover manages to get tickets to an Ashes Test?" she splutters. "The ECB should make all ticket applicants take a quiz and allocation should be based on results. That way only professional cricket watchers get to fill the grounds."

47th over: Australia 200–4 (Langer 63, Katich 0) There's a spring in Giles's step now and, incredibly, he's even getting plenty of turn. One delivery was almost Warnesque. "Giles taking wickets, Jones holding catches, are you sure you are watching Australia play and not a re-run of the Windies series?" asks a bemused Andrew James.

48th over: Australia 202–4 (Langer 64, Katich 0) Another steady-as-she goes over from Flintoff, who's hitting the pitch hard but not getting much out of it.

49th over: Australia 207–4 (Langer 65, Katich 4) Giles continues to tease and probe, and is unlucky when Katich thick-edges him through third man for four. "Great idea that by Gemma Hayes," scoffs Jon Cardy. "That way, when all you 'professional cricket watchers' have grown old and died, the stands can be filled with empty seats. Well thought out, that one."

WICKET! 50th over: Katich c G Jones b Flintoff 4 (Australia 208–5) Flintoff strikes! He's been bowling round the wicket to Katich, but comes back over. Immediately Katich fends him faintly to Geraint Jones, who takes a routine diving catch.

51st over: Australia 216–5 (Langer 70, Gilchrist 4) England are really applying the squeeze here – another wicket and they'll be into the tail. Meanwhile this from Paul Ward. "Why on earth do cricketers shout 'catch it' when the ball flies in the direction of a fielder?" he wonders. "Are fielders too stupid to realise what to do with the red object coming towards them?"

52nd over: Australia 218–5 (Langer 71, Gilchrist 5) A snorter from Flintoff, who gets a 90mph howitzer to move away from Gilchrist and nearly takes the edge. "The mug sold by the Cricket Shop looks to be junk," says Dave Barnett. "It's a 2005 version. The inscription reads, "One Is The King Of Spin, The Other Is The King Of Spain!"

(there would have been more exclamation marks if there was room). This is the cricketing equivalent of buying a Diana – Princess of Hearts commemorative plate from the back of the *Daily Mail*. How can I get hold of the original ones?" Anyone?

53rd over: Australia 219–5 (Langer 72, Gilchrist 5) Langer takes a single, but otherwise the Aussies are content to block. That's tea. It's been an enthralling session.

England 407; Australia 219–5

The evening session

BY ROB SMYTH

Preamble It's been another belting day's play at Edgbaston and, wonderful to relate, England are on top. Marginally. Australia are 219 for 5, 188 runs behind, with Andrew Flintoff and my respected colleague Ashley Giles the pick of the England attack.

Thank you! To the girl from *Guardian* ad planning who has just bought some rice krispies-style cake for the OBO team. "You're like our Test Match Special," she said, which makes me feel like Henry Blofeld. And yes, I am much happier now.

The King of Spain: the truth "Sorry to be a killjoy," says Dominic Smith, "but I seem to remember an article saying that while the media had portrayed the King of Spain thing as a total disaster in which a hapless Warwickshire Club Shop employee ordered ten million 'Spain' mugs, in fact there were only about 10 ever made before the problem was spotted and corrected. So I think Dave Barnett will be unlucky in his search." How much would *they* sell for on eBay?

54th over: Australia 226–5 (Langer 77, Gilchrist 6) Here we go then, and this session should be a cracker. Langer kicks it off by pulling Flintoff beautifully for four.

55th over: Australia 229–5 (Langer 78, Gilchrist 8) Gilo to Gilly, which is brave. A quiet over as the sunny summer vibes wash over my receding pate.

56th over: Australia 236–5 (Langer 78, Gilchrist 14) Flintoff is switching over and around the wicket to Gilchrist – he's one of the few bowlers who has the discipline to maintain his line and length while doing that. Gilchrist nonetheless drives a good-length delivery through extra cover for four.

57th over: Australia 240–5 (Langer 78, Gilchrist 14) Langer is sizing up Giles with increasingly malevolent intent, but it's a high-risk business at the moment. No, really. "Cricket," says James Kilk. "Hello Rob Smyth, you are my hero. From James Kilk."

58th over: Australia 246–5 (Langer 79, Gilchrist 19) Fuller from Flintoff, and Gilchrist simply slams him down the ground for four. Beautiful shot. "I've got a better idea," says David Brooks. "At a given moment why don't you shout 'Hands in the air if you love hip hop' and then we'll all do it. I have visions of entire openplan offices coming to a halt whilst their workers sit there with their hands in the air. Also, then we can identify fellow OBO readers, the guy next to me might be reading this, but like me, he's going to great lengths not to be observed. Those not in the know will be confused."

59th over: Australia 250–5 (Langer 80, Gilchrist 21) Nip and tuck again. This is such an important session in the context of the game, the series, and my forthcoming night on the tiles.

60th over: Australia 254–5 (Langer 81, Gilchrist 24) Jones comes on for Flintoff, and that's it. "Smyth. Raise the banter levels. The emails you use are dry," says Dom Hastings, having just sent this rib-tickling cracker.

61st over: Australia 255–5 (Langer 81, Gilchrist 24) It's all gone pretty quiet, with Langer in particular playing a totally Boycottian innings, something which nobody else has done on what remains an essentially easy-paced pitch. I'm getting bored now as the prospect of the pub looms; someone send some amusing emails, for eff's sake.

WICKET! 62nd over: Langer lbw b S Jones 82 (Australia 262–6) "What a swinger," yelps Mark Nicholas, and with good reason – an absolutely storming full inswinger from Simon Jones traps Langer in front. It was just clipping leg, and that's a massive wicket for England.

62nd over: Australia 262–6 (Gilchrist 24, Warne 0) "What do you call a man standing in a cemetery wearing two raincoats?" sniggers Andrew Miller. "Max Bygraves."

63rd over: Australia 267–6 (Gilchrist 25, Warne 4) Warne has a comedy charge at Giles – no really, it was hilarious – and scuffs a hoick on to his boot. Then he gets him away through cover for four.

64th over: Australia 272–6 (Gilchrist 27, Warne 8) Jones beats Warne outside off with a boomeranging peach. As it were. And then he does it again – excellent bowling. "Do any of your readers happen to know if the Seven Stars at the back of Grays Inn is any good?" says Russell A Taylor. "Was probably going to sink a few jars there this evening. You're all more than welcome to join . . ." Sure, Russ, I'd love to sack off a raucous loserboys' night out in Soho to come meet you. Will you be the one at the bar on your own supping a Carling top while studiously reading a graphic novel?

WICKET! 65th over: Warne b Giles 8 (Australia 273–7) The greatest spin bowler in history bowls Shane Warne. Ugh. Warne came flying down the wicket, missed the mother of all hoicks, and the ball just carried on to clatter into the stumps. Three for Gilo, and advantage England.

65th over: Australia 273–7 (Gilchrist 28, Lee 0) Here's Tom Dawkins. "Two snowmen sat in a field, one says to the other, 'can you smell carrots?' Do I win a T-shirt?" Get out.

66th over: Australia 278–7 (Gilchrist 27, Lee 4) Dropped catch! Well, technically. Jones squared Lee with another jaffa and Flintoff, plunging low to his right, just got fingertips on the way down. A technical chance, in the way that Jim Davidson is technically a comedian. Lee's response is to larrup a square cut for four.

67th over: Australia 282–7 (Gilchrist 31, Lee 6) For a frightening split second then I thought Gilo had unveiled his doosra. In fact it was his stock ball – it didn't turn – and though Brett Lee was plumb in front, it pitched outside leg. "Let's get this Aussie innings over by tonight, I've got a gig in Soho tomorrow and I'm nervous enough about that," says Stacy Squibb. "Besides which the guy opposite me is nervously watching your commentary and not doing any work!! If it all goes pear-shaped though, have you got room for a girl to join your raucous lads' night? I'm good at carrying pints." Jeez, we have some popular OBO readers out there, eh? Drinks.

WICKET! 68th over: Lee c Flintoff b S Jones 6 (Australia 282–8)
That'll do! First ball after the drinks break, and Simon Jones strikes.
Another good delivery, moving away, and Lee edges it straight into
the big bucket hands of Flintoff at second slip. England are in
danger of getting a big lead here.

68th over: Australia 284–8 (Gilchrist 32, Gillespie 1) Gillespie is *that*
close to going first ball to a real grubber; he got his bat on it at the
very last minute. "You've got a girl, who's also a singer for a band,
offering to buy you pints for the evening and you are turning her
down?" says Wesley Ball. "No wonder you are so crabby. Clearly
deeply frustrated at some level."

69th over: Australia 285–8 (Gilchrist 33, Gillespie 1) Here's Jamie
Reeman. "Stacy Squibb? I'm beginning to think that some of the
names on here are made up. Regards, Cock Jol."

70th over: Australia 290–8 (Gilchrist 38, Gillespie 1) Gilchrist blazes
a drive off Jones wide of slip for four. Yes I know the Social is not in
Soho, we're going there later. Jeez.

71st over: Australia 291–8 (Gilchrist 39, Gillespie 1) Gilchrist takes a
single off Giles's first ball. And nothing else happens. "Enthralled as
I am by the social arrangements of readers 'lucky' enough to be in
the London area, can you run a thread that's a bit more inclusive?"
says Matt Lincoln. "By the way, is anyone up for a drink in central
Aberdeen tonight?"

72nd over: Australia 296–8 (Gilchrist 39, Gillespie 5) Gillespie is a
hugely improved batsman – here he thwacks Jones through cover
for four off the back foot. Surely it's Harmy time? Even Hammer
time would do.

73rd over: Australia 299–8 (Gilchrist 42, Gillespie 5) "I'm losing
patience with Ingle and Smyth," says Hannah Quarmby. "I try and
converse and nothing! Pah to banter! Stick it! I'm off to the pub."
Bye, then. Don't wait up.

74th over: Australia 301–8 (Gilchrist 43, Gillespie 6) Freddie's on,
and England's lead is down to two figures. Nearly. Gillespie is a very,
very good defensive batsman. Insert your own if-he-starts-bowling-
properly-he-could-be-an-all-rounder gag (sic) here. "I've just logged

on to GuardianDating.Com and there's some cricket commentary going on," titters Rex. "What's happened?"

75th over: Australia 307–8 (Gilchrist 48, Gillespie 7) More probing from Giles; more defence from Gillespie; more pangs for a pint from Smyth. "What's pink and fluffy?" says Matty Joyce. "Pink fluff." This is the standard you people have set.

WICKET! 76th over: Gillespie lbw b Flintoff 7 (Australia 308–9) A boomeranging yorker from the brilliant Flintoff traps Gillespie lbw, but it was almost certainly going down leg. It swung an absolute mile, and Gillespie's steadfast 37–ball innings is over.

WICKET! 76th over: Kasprowicz lbw b Flintoff 0 (Australia 308 all out) Carbon copy from Flintoff, who will be on a hat-trick in the second innings. That was an absolute jaffa. Flintoff ends with 3 for 52, and England lead by 99. Come on!

England second innings

1st over: England 4–0 (Trescothick 4, Strauss 0) What a cracking statement of intent: Lee's first ball is full and wide, and Trescothick times it superbly through extra cover for four.

2nd over: England 6–0 (Trescothick 5, Strauss 1) Emails have dried up dramatically; you'd almost think it was 5.30pm on a Friday and everyone was nursing their first pint. "Come on England," says Stuart Youngs, who isn't. "This is the most homesick I've been in the year that I've been out of the country. However, if it means that for 16 years I was the jinx that prevented England turning over the Aussies then for the good of the nation I'll stick it out Stateside."

3rd over: England 11–0 (Trescothick 10, Strauss 1) Brainless stuff from Brett Lee – full and in the slot again, and Trescothick clatters it through the covers for four. Meanwhile, as Rory MacQueen has pointed out, this is the first time England have had a first-innings lead in an Ashes Test since the glory days of Edgbaston '97.

4th over: England 16–0 (Trescothick 10, Strauss 5) England will be happy enough to see out tonight without losing a wicket; Australia, for their part, look like they want to get off the pitch and regroup – their body language is pretty poor.

5th over: England 20–0 (Trescothick 14, Strauss 5) Not many overs left – three, probably, as this farcical new ICC rule means play must finish at six regardless. Means I can go to the pub at six regardless, you say? What a sensible new innovation from the ICC.

6th over: England 25–0 (lead by 124; Trescothick 18, Strauss 6) Kasprowicz is on already – I'm predicting that Jason Gillespie will never play Test cricket again; get me – but it makes no odds: Trescothick larrups a square cut for four. England look very, very comfortable just now.

WICKET! 7th over: Strauss b Warne 6 (England 25–1) Oh. My. Goodness. Shane Warne comes on, and his second ball turns an absolute mile – and bowls Strauss middle stump behind his legs! Extraordinary stuff. A truly remarkable piece of bowling. Meanwhile, Hoggard survives the last four balls, despite a ring of about 400 Aussies surrounding the bat. A stunning end to another stunning day in a stunning match – if only the same adjective could describe this commentary.

Australia 308; England 407 and 25–1

Third Day

The morning session

BY ROB SMYTH

Preamble Morning. I have quite the headache. "Smyth," begins my lovely sometime colleague Georgina Turner. "I trust you're sat at your desk looking and feeling suitably shambolic." Damn straight.

8th over: England 25–1 (Trescothick 19, Hoggard 0) A quiet first over from Brett Lee – a maiden. "Morning," says Mark Pearson. "Am I the first?" The first, the last, the only. Is it time to go home yet?

9th over: England 25–1 (Trescothick 19, Hoggard 0) You know you're at Edgbaston when Matthew Hoggard gets virtually a standing ovation for a forward defensive. An awkwardly played maiden as Warne probes mischievously on and around off stump and my hangover probes malevolently on and around my outsized cranium.

10th over: England 26–1 (Trescothick 20, Hoggard 0) "I have no sympathy," says Lee Johnson, like I asked for some with my self-pitying whining. "I was working until 11. But I managed to tell my girlfriend the origins of the King of Spain this morning, naked in bed with a cuppa. She laughed so much that hot tea went everywhere. No sex for a week I think."

11th over: England 27–1 (Trescothick 21, Hoggard 0) Warne goes over the wicket to Trescothick, bowling well wide of off stump, and immediately causes problems. I'd imagine Warne will bowl virtually all day at one end, and it should be a cracking contest.

WICKET! 12th over: Trescothick c Gilchrist b Lee 21 (England 27–2)

Oh dear. Short and wide from Lee, and Trescothick, fiddling outside off stump with a half-arsed cut shot, snicks through to Gilchrist. It won't surprise you that there was no foot movement.

WICKET! 12th over: Vaughan b Lee 1 (England 29–3) Bloody hell: Lee has knocked Vaughan over straight away. It jagged back, and maybe kept a fraction low, but Vaughan was neither back nor forward – like with his dismissal by Glenn McGrath at Lord's – and his horror series continues. Game on, and how.

13th over: England 29–3 (Hoggard 1, Bell 0) Maiden from Warne, and some majestic commentary from Benaud and Boycott, who have explained Vaughan's myriad technical flaws in an instant. It's almost enough to make a man forget his raging hangover.

WICKET! 14th over: Hoggard c Hayden b Lee 1 (England 31–4) Another one for Brett Lee, albeit the gimme of Hoggard, who simply carved straight to Hayden at gully. It's KP time. "So how much did you drink?" asks Ben Osguthorpe, who really shouldn't be expecting me to correctly type such an awkward surname at this hour. "Is it enough to brag about or was it just a few Bacardi Breezers like a big girl?" Not sure – it gets hazy after the 44th pint. Or was it the fourth?

14th over: England 31–4 (Bell 1, Pietersen 0) An enormous shout first ball as Pietersen shaped to fend off a short ball as Gilchrist took it down the leg-side. Billy Bowden said no; replays said maybe. I think he gloved that.

15th over: England 31–4 (Bell 1, Pietersen 0) There's more banter than a night out with the OBO losers as Warne probes away at Bell, his humiliating first-Test dismissal fresh in everyone's memory. A maiden.

16th over: England 32–4 (Bell 1, Pietersen 1) Lively stuff from Lee, who hits Pietersen and then beats his attempted flap through the covers. "Do others wonder how Gilchrist's militant sportsmanship tallies with yelping 'catch it' every time ball touches bat?" asks Richard in Queensland. The only thing I'm wondering at the moment is whether a hungover lunchtime KFC will cure me or make me puke.

17th over: England 44–4 (Bell 1, Pietersen 13) Crisis, what crisis?

Pietersen gets down on one knee and whaps Warne miles over midwicket for six – a simply magnificent shot. And then he does it again: same shot, same result. "A lunchtime KFC will certainly cure you by making you puke," says Lee Johnson. "It's as simple as that." Nice.

18th over: England 47–4 (Bell 4, Pietersen 13) "I thought that I would let you know about this," says Matthew Gibson. "I'm not sure that the thought of jumping up and down would be that good for a hangover though: www.worldjumpday.org." Ouch. Even cutting and pasting that hurts.

19th over: England 47–4 (Bell 4, Pietersen 13) A maiden from Warne to Bell, and here's Simeon Everett, whose name is clearly made up. "Should I go to watch the Newcastle v Yeading friendly this afternoon or go home to watch the cricket?" I'm sorry, I thought that was a rhetorical question.

20th over: England 57–4 (Bell 11, Pietersen 14) Bell hits his first boundary, guiding Lee to the vacant third-man area. Back in today's episode of One Man And His Hangover, I feel almost human again, and am tentatively contemplating a lunchtime range-finder. "World jump day?" chuckles Luciano Howard. "Why did they tell Michael Vaughan that? Ho hum." For those of you who aren't sad enough to watch the cricket on telly AND read the OBO, Vaughan did a really odd and entirely unnecessary jump at just about the time Brett Lee sent his off stump flying.

21st over: England 61–4 (Bell 15, Pietersen 14) Bell works a Warne full toss away for four, and English cricket's oddest couple since I had a dream about me and Charles Colville bonding over a warm Heineken and a game of Stratego have restored some order after that tortured start to the morning.

22nd over: England 63–4 (Bell 15, Pietersen 16) Jason Gillespie comes on, and very little happens. "Rob just cos I want a mention," begins Andy Bradshaw. "I'm so sad that I'm watching the TV, listening to TMS and following you lot on the OBO. Can anyone 'top' that in the sadness stakes?" If anyone can top it, they might want to top themselves while they're at it.

23rd over: England 66–4 (Bell 18, Pietersen 16) Here's Michael Kane. "I learned a long time ago that hangovers go in peaks and troughs (like an oscilliscope for the mental state). At certain times of the day, you will feel magnificent remembering all the times of last night when your jokes WERE funny and oh how sophisticated you were! Other times will be full of self loathing and deep shudders at the time you spilled your drink over the table or leered terribly at the barmaids. You really just have to go with the flow. Oh and don't eat fast food." In the afternoon session: Michael Kane's guide to meeting pretty young ladies. Talking of which, you'll be underwhelmed to know that Smyth got back on the horse last night after a fallow period that felt like four years but was probably longer, and I'd like the record to show that it was me who pulled away. Honest.

24th over: England 68–4 (Bell 20, Pietersen 16) An encouraging sign of some uneven bounce there, as Gillespie beats Bell's attempted force. And I'm boring myself. "Dear Rob," says Julien Lesage. "Thought I'd send this again cos you may have missed its brilliance first time round." Is that what they're calling the delete button these days?

WICKET! 25th over: Pietersen c Gilchrist b Warne 20 (England 72–5) Pietersen missed a sweep and the ball hit thigh, chest and elbow – and possibly glove, though I suspect not and Pietersen was furious – before being very smartly taken by Gilchrist. That was a big, big wicket, if extremely fortunate but then Pietersen should have been given out caught off the glove first ball and it all evens itself out and I think it's time to end this sentence now. The end.

26th over: England 74–5 (Bell 21, Flintoff 1) Gillespie beats Flintoff with a fine leg-cutter. England's lead is 173 now, and blimey this is tense. That was a marvellous take from Gilchrist, one-handed and low as the ball pinballed around. It was very similar to Graeme Hick's dismissal on the final morning at Brisbane in 1994, with only one difference: Hick hit it.

WICKET! 27 th over: Bell c Gilchrist b Warne 21 (England 75–6) Dear me. A majestic piece of bowling from Warne, spitting furiously out of the rough and across Bell, whose forward defensive merely produced the thinnest edge on the way through to Gilchrist.

27th over: England 75–6 (Flintoff 2, G Jones 0) "Pub joke," promises Neil Stork-Brett. "An Englishman, an Irishman and a Kiwi walk into a pub. The Englishman has a chicken under his arm, the Irishman has a frog sitting on his head and the Kiwi is leading a horse. The barman looks up and says 'Is this some kind of joke?'"

28th over: England 82–6 (Flintoff 7, G Jones 2) Gillespie, who really is staggeringly innocuous for a once borderline-great bowler, overpitches and is flipped deliciously through midwicket by Flintoff. Shot son!

29th over: England 83–6 (Flintoff 8, G Jones 2) Bad news: I'm still here, and will be all day. And Freddie has pulled up lame – he's having his shoulder gingerly massaged by a buxom blonde (OK, a balding physio) after jerking something while square-cutting Warne. This doesn't look good.

30th over: England 85–6 (Flintoff 9, G Jones 3) A thoroughly inept piece of cricket – Geraint Jones clunked a miserable drive straight back at Jason Gillespie, who dropped an absolute dolly.

31st over: England 87–6 (Flintoff 10, G Jones 3) Cheating Aussie fuggers – apparently Bell didn't hit his either! "Big fat hairy (insert your own euphemism here)," says Dan Jones. "Publish that you fugger." I really need a range-finding pint Jonesy; if anyone's in Farringdon I'll be the one nursing a Hurlimann in the Betsey Trotwood in ten blissful minutes' time.

32nd over: England 89–6 (Flintoff 10, G Jones 3) England are playing for lunch now, and so am I. Email. Mick Swales. Cut-and-paste job. "My fiancee has chosen this crucial Saturday of the summer to hold a wedding pow-wow with various females of our families in my front room. I'm hiding in the study listening to TMS and reading OBO. I always find chicken fried rice is a good hangover cure."

33rd over: England 95–6 (Flintoff 16, G Jones 3) That's lunch – England lead by 194, and I'm off. See you in half an hour.

England 407 & 95–6; Australia 308

The afternoon session

BY ROB SMYTH

Preamble: Hup. Here we go again, then.

WICKET! 34th over: G Jones c Ponting b Lee 9 (England 101–7) Geraint Jones falls to an absolute snorter from Brett Lee in the first over after lunch. A big wicket, and you can't really blame Geraint Jones there.

34th over: England 101–7 (Flintoff 18, Giles 0) It's hard to know what England need here – a lead of 300 (201 in the second innings) is a minimum, I'd have thought. "Post-lunchtime pint joke," says John Jordan. "A sausage goes into a pub and asks for a pint of bitter. The barman says, 'Sorry mate – we don't serve food'." Ugh.

35th over: England 102–7 (Flintoff 19, Giles 0) "Go Rob!" exclaims the BBC's Julia Blyth. "Get back on that horse! Tongue those randoms! And comfort yourself with this: the only thing wrong with her is she clearly has a lower lung capacity than you, and her pulling away was merely a subtle sign that she was very impressed with your fitness levels. Or: stop whinging, at least you're getting some, huh?" That, chaps, was a booty call.

36th over: England 110–7 (Flintoff 26, Giles 0) Flintoff opens his injured shoulder and slices a meaty drive off Lee over the top of the cordon for four. He's now England's top scorer, which is a sorry state of affairs when he has less runs than I have years.

37th over: England 111–7 (Flintoff 26, Giles 1) A quiet over from Warne to Giles, as my mind wanders to the Pine Barrens episode of *The Sopranos*. "Only ever had a dress on once, mate," says Tony Greig to Geoff Boycott. I left it there.

38th over: England 114–7 (Flintoff 28, Giles 2) The lead is now 213, which is not really enough given that Australia will begin their chase on a third- rather than a fifth-day pitch. "Girls recognise booty calls too FYI," says Kirstin Smith. Not when I'm sending them they don't. Besides, I meant Ms Blyth was calling the boys to alleviate her frustration. I mean, she might not be that way inclined but then she wouldn't be emailing me if she was as that's clearly all anyone's after.

39th over: England 114–7 (Flintoff 28, Giles 2) A maiden from Warne to Giles.

40th over: England 118–7 (Flintoff 29, Giles 6) Giles just about manages to squeeze out a reverse-swinger from Lee before it does some Shaolin on his off stump. "Why," thunders Paul Smith, punching a nearby wall. "Why when we get 400 do we say 'imagine what the Aussies will do?' or when Giles gets one to turn do we go 'imagine what Warne will do?' But when someone as mediocre as Lee gets a few wickets through invariable bounce do we not say 'imagine what Harmison will do'? Declare now, Vaughany lad."

41st over: England 119–7 (Flintoff 29, Giles 6) The Geraint Jones debate is hotting up. His runs have certainly dried up of late – his average is dropping through the 20s faster than, erm, a drunken student's trousers – but I still don't think batting Chris Read at No. 7 is an option; only if England dropped a bowler, with Flintoff down to No. 7, could it work realistically.

42nd over: England 124–7 (Flintoff 31, Giles 8) In terms of scores, and increasing uneven bounce, this game is following a very similar pattern to the Trent Bridge Test of 2003. That said, that was a much spicier pitch than this. The end result would do quite nicely though.

43rd over: England 127–7 (Flintoff 34, Giles 8) Channel 4 have gone to the gee-gees, so I have very little to say.

44th over: England 131–7 (Flintoff 38, Giles 8) Michael Kasprowicz gets his first bowl of the innings/day/lifetime/whatever, and Flintoff pulls his second ball emphatically for four. Anyone got anything to share with the nation? Or the four people who are reading this?

WICKET! 45th over: Giles c Hayden b Warne 8 (England 131–8) Warne's leg-spinner was pitched perfectly on leg stump and ripped across to take the edge of Giles's forward prod. Matthew Hayden at slip completed a textbook leggie's dismissal.

WICKET! 45th over: Harmison b Warne 0 (England 131–9) Shane Warne is on a hat-trick after fooling Steve Harmison with the slider. Warne has 5 for 39 after a regal performance, and England are in trouble.

45th over: England 135–9 (Flintoff 38, S Jones 4) Simon Jones survives the hat-trick ball, and whaps his second through extra-cover for four. Nice.

46th over: England 155–9 (Flintoff 51, S Jones 8) Twenty off the over! Freddie may well have engaged the long handle: first ball he misses a charging yahoo at Kasprowicz; second ball he drives imperiously for six over midwicket, and the fourth goes even further to bring up a cracking and very brave half-century. Shot! When he then takes a single, Jones edges a booming drive wide of second slip for four. Here's Julia Blyth. "I'd love to say that I'm not a desperate fanboy, but no one would believe me and hey, it's not even true. So there's that. And with England wickets tumbling faster than my self-esteem, who cares!"

47th over: England 156–9 (Flintoff 52, S Jones 8) Respectful stuff from Flintoff, who takes a single off Warne's fourth ball and allows Jones to play out the over.

48th over: England 161–9 (Flintoff 53, S Jones 12) Amazing stuff – Brett Lee bowls to Flintoff with all nine fielders on the boundary. He takes a single off the third ball, and then Jones drives Lee inside-out over extra cover for four!

49th over: England 162–9 (Flintoff 54, S Jones 12) "I'm in Poland nursing a nasty cocktail hangover," says Matt Legault. "Shocking how such small drinks can cause so much carnage."

50th over: England 180–9 (Flintoff 71, S Jones 12) What a shot from Andrew Flintoff! Lee's first ball came on nicely and he drove it back over his head absolutely magnificently, right over the stands. That was absolutely stunning – as was Michael Clarke's attempt to stop the next ball going for four. And the next ball? Flintoff clubs it over long-on again! Then he takes a single off the fourth ball. The next ball is a corker, full and straight and it knocks Jones off his feet while pinning him plumb in front – stone dead, knocking middle back about 30 yards. Gone and forgotten! And Billy Bowden says not out!

51st over: England 181–9 (Flintoff 72, S Jones 12) Clever stuff from Warne, who pins Flintoff on the defensive by bowling well outside leg stump: it's simply too risky to take Warne out of the rough.

52nd over: England 182–9 (Flintoff 73, S Jones 12) Same again – Flintoff takes a single off the fourth ball, and Jones survives.

WICKET! 53rd over: Flintoff b Warne 73 (England 182 all out) That's that: Flintoff misses a heave at Warne and is bowled – Warne has 599 Test wickets, and 6 for 46 today, Australia have to chase 282 to win, and Flintoff's magnificent innings is over. See you after tea.

England 407 and 182; Australia 308

The evening session

BY ROB SMYTH

Preamble: England 1 Australia 1. England 0 Australia 2. The difference is immense – an anti-climax for the rest of the series, or one big climax – and this innings is absolutely titanic. Nice touch from Warne, incidentally, who shouted after Flintoff as he walked off to say 'Well played, Freddie.' The Aussies are very good like that.

1st over: Australia 0–0 (target 282; Langer 0, Hayden 0) A fiery first over from Harmison, and a fiery response from Justin Langer – who goes after pretty much everything. In spite of all that, it's a maiden.

2nd over: Australia 4–0 (Langer 0, Hayden 4) Really interesting field for Hayden, similar to the one in the first innings: one slip, three men on the drive on the off-side and one on the drive on the leg. So he edges one low to third man to get off the mark, and off a pair.

3rd over: Australia 10–0 (Langer 5, Hayden 5) They're off to the effing racing! Like anyone gives a flying flip!

4th over: Australia 20–0 (Langer 14, Hayden 6) Langer drives Hoggard through the covers with ominous assurance, and then fiddles another boundary to third man. Good start for the Aussies.

5th over: Australia 20–0 (Langer 14, Hayden 6) A maiden from Harmison to Langer, and England already look just slightly flat.

6th over: Australia 22–0 (Langer 14, Hayden 8) Hayden swings and misses at a length ball from Hoggard. "*TMS* are discussing the merits of 'US retro punk band Green Day'," says Matthew Cobb. "What is the world coming to? Has someone slipped something into Blofeld's tea?" Are you serious? How the hell did they get on to them?

7th over: Australia 23–0 (Langer 15, Hayden 8) Australia look a bit too comfortable for comfort here, and I reckon Flintoff – shoulder permitting – and Giles will be on pretty soon. "Michael Vaughan is thinking to himself. 'Thank God you aren't "Just-in", cos if you stayed any "Langer", Steve's gonna "Harm-U, Son"'!!!" says Andrew Miller, the same Andrew Miller whose excellent, erudite work you read every day on cricinfo. "Good grief." Quite.

8th over: Australia 30–0 (Langer 17, Hayden 13) Here's Gilo, as predicted, and Langer bat-pads his first ball just past the diving Ian Bell at short leg. My colleague wanted to be respected as an important player in English cricket: he certainly is now, because if he doesn't bowl well here England have got problems. There is a lot of rough, four left-handers in the top seven, and one of them – Hayden – has just clubbed Giles back over his head for four. Shot.

9th over: Australia 33–0 (Langer 18, Hayden 14) I really need a drink now – I stupidly failed to realise they took tea (when I was going to nip out for a swift range-finder) when England were out, so now I'm stuck.

10th over: Australia 37–0 (Langer 18, Hayden 18) I don't like the look of this at all – England need the force of the Flintoff personality to try and get them a wicket from somewhere.

11th over: Australia 40–0 (Langer 21, Hayden 18) Harmison comes around the wicket, but Australia continue to make ominously serene progress. "Why aren't you guardianistas rotating the commentary strike??" asks Dominic Humphrey. "Hayden, Strauss, Vaughan Williams, it's music to my eyes." Professional curiosity – what did you have for lunch? Was it mushroom-based?

12th over: Australia 47–0 (Langer 28, Hayden 18) England are struggling big-time now.

WICKET! 13th over: Langer b Flintoff 28 (Australia 47–1) Frederick Flintoff, I want your children. Langer survived the hat-trick ball but not the second, elbowing a lifter back on to his stumps. Pure, bewildering force of personality took that wicket. This man is an absolute legend.

WICKET! 13th over: Ponting c G Jones b Flintoff 0 (Australia 48–2) I have shivers all over my spine – this is unfathomably good cricket from Flintoff; in this case a snorting, full-length leg-cutter that

Ponting, who had already survived two big shouts for lbw, could only nick through to Jones. What an over!

14th over: Australia 48–2 (target 282; Hayden 18, Martyn 0) Maiden from Jones to Hayden. Phew.

15th over: Australia 49–2 (Hayden 18, Martyn 1) Flintoff really is working up a serious pace – consistently just shy of 90mph. Hayden just digs out a superb yorker, and here's Charlie Talbot. "Sorry to hear you missed a drink. You'll no doubt be delighted to know I not only managed a half-time drink, I even got to see the wicket as well on a small badly-tuned TV in the bar."

16th over: Australia 53–2 (Hayden 18, Martyn 5) Jones is bowling well wide of off stump at Martyn, trying to tempt him into chasing one. He doesn't, but he does check-drive a swinging half-volley gracefully through the covers for four.

17th over: Australia 65–2 (Hayden 19, Martyn 14) Another good over from Flintoff, in which Martyn, feeling away from his body, edges to third man for four. Then he flips the next ball away to fine leg for four more. Anybody still out there? Send some emails. Please.

18th over: Australia 67–2 (Hayden 20, Martyn 15) There should be 90 minutes' more play tonight, and England will hope to pick up at least one more wicket, maybe a couple. Maybe eight.

19th over: Australia 68–2 (Hayden 21, Martyn 15) Flintoff bowls very well. I write lots about it. Computer crashes. I can't be arsed to write it again. "Hey mate, sorry you're feeling lonely out there," says Giorgio Gaglia. "If that's of any comfort your commentary is wicked, I'm Italian and I hated cricket but you got me addicted!"

20th over: Australia 70–2 (Hayden 23, Martyn 15) Harmison returns, but he's definitely lacking a bit of zing. "I feel for you," says Chaka Khan, or was it Andy Winter. "I'm doing some online coverage for Gillingham v. Colchester to very few, in fact probably no readers. Hoping to catch the last hour or so of the Test on TV. Or I might stick with your over-by-overs. Haven't decided yet. By the way, it's 1–0 to Colchester at the moment."

21st over: Australia 72–2 (Hayden 23, Martyn 15) It's all gone a bit quiet: this is Flintoff's fifth over, and I think the Aussies are happy just to see him off. "It is 4.40 in the afternoon and you are still hungover," frowns Mike Landers. "You must be getting old, fella." In my twenties. Next. "Why not quit the lager and try something a bit more suitable for your ageing frame? Like sherry."

22nd over: Australia 74–2 (Hayden 23, Martyn 16) I'm flagging now, to be brutally honest. "How's the tumbleweed with you?" says Max Fordham. "I'm sharing the office with an ex-Afghan rebel and a miserable Welshman who was Cerys Matthews's boyfriend when they were both six."

WICKET! 23rd over: Hayden c Trescothick b S Jones 31 (Australia 82–3) Hayden falls – caught brilliantly, two-handed, by Trescothick at slip as he flashed at an outswinger. That's another huge breakthrough for England. Come on!

23rd over: Australia 82–3 (target 282; Martyn 16, Clarke 0) This is a sensational game – every time you think the momentum is shifting it, erm, shifts again. "Detroit just hit a homer, if you are interested (which I'm not)," says Julia Renton. Eh?

24th over: Australia 95–3 (Martyn 21, Clarke 4) Four byes well down the leg-side from Harmison, who is well off the pace here. I'd be tempted to give Hoggard a go at Clarke early, even though his bowling has been pretty shoddy in this series so far.

25th over: Australia 103–3 (Martyn 28, Clarke 5) It was obvious England would replace Harmison, but Vaughan has chosen to do so with Ashley Giles. If England can just nick one more out tonight, they'll be happy; if Australia end on, say, 145 for 3, it'll be a nervy night's sleep. Well, except for me, as I intend to blast myself out with about 10 pints of Stella, so that's nice.

WICKET! 26th over: Martyn c Bell b Hoggard 28 (Australia 107–4) Another one gone! Matthew Hoggard returns, and his first ball is flicked absent-mindedly towards midwicket, where Ian Bell takes a sprawling catch. A bit of a poor stroke from Martyn, but who gives a stuff?!

26th over: Australia 115–4 (target 282; Clarke 9, Katich 8) What a shot first ball! Hoggard steamed in, oozing intent, and Katich just timed him sumptuously through the covers. Later in the over, he chops an attempted cut low to third man for four more. And then he under-edges just short of Geraint Jones. Oof. Here's Marc Kelly.

"Does anyone else feel that Hoggard wouldn't look too out of place sitting astride a combine harvester, floppy straw hat on his head, shouting 'Get orf me land' to some poor Aussie?"

27th over: Australia 123–4 (Clarke 17, Katich 8) Get Gilo off. Now. Clarke has him in his pocket at the moment.

28th over: Australia 125–4 (Clarke 18, Katich 9) Two runs off that Hoggard over, and nearly time for a beer.

29th over: Australia 130–4 (Clarke 19, Katich 13) An excellent cut shot from Katich brings him four more off Giles.

30th over: Australia 132–4 (Clarke 20, Katich 14) It's time for Freddie. If England can just winkle one more out tonight they will be firmly in charge. Two off Flintoff's first over. "Don't go for beer!" screams Lindsay Chapman. "I'm another one stuck in the office, attempting to write up my doctoral thesis. Your OBO and Freddie-the-hero's antics are the only thing keeping me going. Don't taunt me with beer, I've already had to cancel my plans for tonight, possibly costing me a friend. Not sure the letters after my name will be worth it. We may be few, but we neeeeed you. (Feel better now?)"

WICKET! 31st over: Katich c Trescothick b Giles 16 (Australia 134–5) I missed a wicket 'cause I went for a loo break, but who cares! England are absolutely on top now: Giles has dismissed Katich, taken by a juggling Trescothick at slip as he carved at a ball that didn't turn. He played *for* turn, which is a dangerous assumption when Gilo is bowling.

32nd over: Australia 134–5 (target 282; Clarke 20, Gilchrist 0) A very lively maiden from Flintoff to Clarke.

WICKET! 33rd over: Gilchrist c Flintoff b Giles 1 (Australia 136–6) Gilo has done it again! Gilchrist couldn't resist having a pop, but with the ball coming out of the rough he could only skew an attempted drive to Freddie Flintoff at mid-on. What a day this has been!

33rd over: Australia 136–6 (target 282; Clarke 20, Gillespie 0) Australia have sent in a nightwatchman for Shane Warne in Jason Gillespie. I know the game isn't over, but it's really difficult to resist the urge to shout GET IN!!!!!!!!!!!

WICKET! 34th over: Gillespie b Flintoff 0 (Australia 137–7) The cherry on the icing on the defining day of Andrew Flintoff's career – a marvellous inswinging yorker that pinned Gillespie stone dead in front. The Edgbaston crowd is going wild.

34th over: Australia 139–7 (target 282; Clarke 23, Warne 1) I'd just like to point out that the only reason I'll be drinking Stella is because I'm going to a Stella Screen showing of *Donnie Darko*, so I'm guessing it won't be free Heineken chasers all round. That said, the way this has gone I'd nail a pint of warm White Lightning just now.

35th over: Australia 140–7 (Clarke 24, Warne 1) England have taken the extra half-hour in a bid to finish it all tonight. Nothing doing in that Giles over, apart from some comedy timewasting from Shane Warne.

36th over: Australia 144–7 (Clarke 25, Warne 4) An inside-edge from Warne negates another massive shout for lbw from Flintoff; good decision from Billy Bowden.

37th over: Australia 144–7 (Clarke 25, Warne 4) Another pretty good maiden from Giles to Warne, who misses with a windy woof to leg.

38th over: Australia 146–7 (Clarke 27, Warne 4) "I bet you wanted that extra half-hour like billio," says Becky Ashley. "Are you tempted just to make up the next eight overs and scarper off for your Stella?" Sorry, who are you? This is the cleaner – the bloke who was sat here forgot to turn his computer off.

39th over: Australia 158–7 (Clarke 27, Warne 16) Warne lifts Giles brilliantly over square leg for six, and then repeats the shot next ball; they only need another 124, you know . . .

40th over: Australia 165–7 (Clarke 29, Warne 16) Clarke digs out a really good, reverse-swinging yorker from Flintoff, and the two have an exchange of words that probably wasn't a discussion of who the best OBO writer is. They're still having words now. Three more overs to go.

41st over: Australia 169–7 (Clarke 29, Warne 16) That was astonishing – Warne straight drove Harmison back to the bowler and sauntered out of his crease, bat dangling in the air like that broad's leg in *The Graduate* ads, and Harmison's shy at the stumps missed by *that* much. Bizarre.

42nd over: Australia 174–7 (Clarke 30, Warne 20) I'm getting a Trinidad 1998 feeling here. Surely Australia can't win this, with Michael Clarke playing Carl Hooper and Shane Warne playing David Williams. One over left today, and that's the end of Andrew Flintoff's truly immense contribution for the day.

WICKET! 43rd over: Clarke b Harmison 30 (Australia 175–8) Absolutely magnificent stuff from Stephen Harmison – a wonderful slower ball that bowled Michael Clarke neck and crop. He didn't have a clue what was going on and, from the last ball of a truly bewildering day's play, England have surely sealed this match. I'll be back for the last rites tomorrow.

Australia 308 and 175–8; England 407 and 182

Fourth Day

The morning session

BY ROB SMYTH

Preamble: Morning.

44th over: Australia 177–8 (target 282; Warne 20, Lee 2) "If it gets to 60 or 70 needed . . ." says Sean Ingle, sat opposite me, but in my hungover state – it makes yesterday's hangover feel like an epiphany – I have absolutely no worries about England here, mate.

45th over: Australia 179–8 (Warne 21, Lee 2) Freddie's first over passes without incident, save for an lbw shout against Warne that got caught in the throat. Too high.

46th over: Australia 182–8 (Warne 24, Lee 2) Anyone out there? Back at the cricket, Warne misses an almighty mow at a cracking away-swinger from Harmison.

47th over: Australia 187–8 (Warne 25, Lee 2) It's been a pretty quiet start so far – three no-balls in that Flintoff over, but not a lot else – and Australia's requirement is down to two figures. "Now, please," says Heathers. "Aggers just said that England fans want to see a tight match with Australia out there for a while. This is not so. I want it to be over before I'm hungry enough to make breakfast. I'm making pancakes." Oof. The mere thought of eating anything at the moment is enough to make me feel ill.

48th over: Australia 198–8 (Warne 30, Lee 10) Warne crunches Harmison square on the off-side for four – a very good shot, but I'm far too ill to think this might be the start of a horrendous Australian victory march. Lee then shoulders a Harmison snorter tantalisingly over the slips, and then clips him nicely for four. 84

to win. "I was wondering if anyone knew the significance of the "23" pendant that Warne wears?" asks Bev Swainston.

49th over: Australia 207–8 (Warne 36, Lee 11) Warne back-cuts Flintoff for four more. I'm not worried. Yet.

50th over: Australia 216–8 (Warne 41, Lee 15) Warne fends an unfathomably good lifter from Harmison over first slip for four, and I'm officially nervous: 66 to win after Brett Lee smears Harmison through mid-off for fur. Four. Whatever.

51st over: Australia 220–8 (Warne 42, Lee 18) I'm starting to get hacked off now to be honest: the pitch is doing nothing and these Aussies look far too comfortable. We've only got one slip in! "Hi again Rob, how was last night?" asks Katy Robinson. I have no idea, but I fear there were seedy joints involved. "I'd like your readers to know about something called google: Warne will lead Hampshire with the number 23 on his back, a number worn in the past by the likes of David Beckham and Michael Jordan, but do not be misled. He explains: 'When I first played for St Kilda Aussie Rules football club back in '88 I was given the squad number 23. When Australia first started putting squad numbers on cricket shirts, I wanted to stick with my old footie number, and it's supposed to be my lucky number at roulette'."

52nd over: Australia 220–8 (Warne 42, Lee 18) If there was a sofa at GU I'd be behind it: Giles is on, and it's getting very tense. A maiden, and a good one, with Lee looking for every opportunity to free his arms and welt one into Coventry.

WICKET! 53rd over: Warne hit wicket b Flintoff 42 (Australia 220–9) Freddie does it again, albeit in bizarre circumstances. Flintoff speared a swinging yorker in towards Shane Warne's leg stump, it missed by quite a way, but Warne did a Cruyff turn on his off stump and sent it flying. You couldn't make it up, and luckily you don't have to. Priceless slapstick.

53rd over: Australia 226–9 (target 282; Lee 22, Kasprowicz 1) Lee carves a no-ball to third man for four.

54th over: Australia 227–9 (Lee 22, Kasprowicz 1) One off Giles's over, and Flintoff will have first dibs on Kasprowicz now.

55th over: Australia 236–9 (Lee 24, Kasprowicz 5) Big shout from

Flintoff first ball; at the time I thought Kasprowicz got outside the line, but I'm not so sure having seen the replay. Then Lee cuts agonisingly over the slips, and Kasprowicz – who is walking miles across his stumps before Flintoff bowls – clips for four.

56th over: Australia 249–9 (Lee 29, Kasprowicz 13) OK, I'm nervous again – Lee dances down and blasts Giles high over midwicket for four. A really good shot – as was Kasprowicz's smack down the ground for four more – and 33 to win. This is getting right on my wick. "How's the head now Rob?" says Suzy Byrne. "Potters off to kitchen to turn on the frying pan and put on the sausages." You what?

57th over: Australia 252–9 (Lee 31, Kasprowicz 15) The tension is absolutely brutal – so far, Australia have added 115 since the loss of the seventh wicket.

57.1 overs: Australia 252–9 (Lee 31, Kasprowicz 15) Losing this game just does not bear thinking about, so we're going ball-by-ball to describe the miserable last rites of England's Ashes campaign. Giles to Lee – dot ball.

57.2 overs: Australia 252–9 (target 282; Lee 31, Kasprowicz 15) And another.

57.3 overs: Australia 253–9 (target 282; Lee 32, Kasprowicz 15) Lee drives for one.

57.4 overs: Australia 254–9 (target 282; Lee 32, Kasprowicz 16) Kasprowicz sweeps for one. Help!

57.5 overs: Australia 254–9 (target 282; Lee 32, Kasprowicz 16) Dot ball.

58 overs: Australia 255–9 (target 282; Lee 33, Kasprowicz 16) A single, and Giles is looking very innocuous.

58.1 overs: Australia 256–9 (target 282; Lee 34, Kasprowicz 16) Flintoff has been replaced by Harmison, and some bloated lug in the crowd has his hand pensively clutching his chins. A single.

58.2 overs: Australia 258–9 (target 282; Lee 34, Kasprowicz 18) Kasper chips in the air for two. This is torture.

58.3 overs: Australia 262–9 (target 282; Lee 34, Kasprowicz 18) Four byes down the leg-side! Dear me, that was shocking keeping from Jones.

58.4 overs: Australia 262–9 (target 282; Lee 34, Kasprowicz 18) Dot ball.

58.5 overs: Australia 262–9 (target 282; Lee 34, Kasprowicz 18) And another.

59 overs: Australia 262–9 (target 282; Lee 34, Kasprowicz 18) And again.

59.1 overs: Australia 262–9 (target 282; Lee 34, Kasprowicz 18) This is awful – the pitch is doing nothing and I think Australia will win this. Flintoff replaces Giles, so this is it now – England's two big hitters on to finish it one way or the other. I really need the loo as well. Lee has a huge yahoo and misses.

59.2 overs: Australia 262–9 (target 282; Lee 34, Kasprowicz 18) Lee gets in behind the line of a short one.

59.3 overs: Australia 262–9 (target 282; Lee 34, Kasprowicz 18) Another short one fended down well.

59.4 overs: Australia 262–9 (target 282; Lee 34, Kasprowicz 18) Lee throws the bat down in pain after being pinned by a short one. That hit him right on the glove and, frankly, that looked bleedin' painful. Lee is getting treatment. But he looks like he'll be OK.

59.5 overs: Australia 262–9 (target 282; Lee 34, Kasprowicz 18) Dot ball.

60 overs: Australia 263–9 (target 282; Lee 34, Kasprowicz 18) A leg bye, and it's down to 19. This is horrible.

60.1 overs: Australia 267–9 (target 282; Lee 38, Kasprowicz 18) Oh dear – Brett Lee inside-edges Harmison to fine leg for four!

60.2 overs: Australia 267–9 (target 282; Lee 38, Kasprowicz 18) Dot ball.

60.3 overs: Australia 267–9 (target 282; Lee 38, Kasprowicz 18) Lee just digs out a very good full delivery.

60.4 overs: Australia 267–9 (target 282; Lee 38, Kasprowicz 18) Lee chases a wide one and misses. I can't take this any more.

60.5 overs: Australia 267–9 (target 282; Lee 38, Kasprowicz 18)
Driven to gully on the bounce.

61 overs: Australia 267–9 (target 282; Lee 38, Kasprowicz 18) Lee is beaten by a beauty.

61.1 overs: Australia 268–9 (target 282; Lee 38, Kasprowicz 19)
Dropped! Kasprowicz steered Flintoff to third man, and Jones, diving forward, grassed a gettable chance diving forward.

61.2 overs: Australia 273–9 (target 282; Lee 38, Kasprowicz 19) A no-ball screams away for four byes down the leg-side. This isn't funny any more.

61.3 overs: Australia 274–9 (target 282; Lee 39, Kasprowicz 19) A single.

61.4 overs: Australia 275–9 (target 282; Lee 39, Kasprowicz 20) A single. Eight to win.

61.5 overs: Australia 276–9 (target 282; Lee 40, Kasprowicz 20)
Another single, and Australia are coasting here.

62 overs: Australia 276–9 (target 282; Lee 40, Kasprowicz 20) Dot ball.

62.1 overs: Australia 277–9 (target 282; Lee 41, Kasprowicz 20) Six to win, and I'm not enjoying this one bit. Lee takes a single off Harmison.

62.2 overs: Australia 277–9 (target 282; Lee 41, Kasprowicz 20) Dot ball down the leg-side – and Jones even stopped this one.

62.3 overs: Australia 277–9 (target 282; Lee 41, Kasprowicz 20)
Superb yorker is squeezed out by Kasprowicz.

62.4 overs: Australia 277–9 (target 282; Lee 41, Kasprowicz 20)
Down the leg-side.

62.5 overs: Australia 277–9 (target 282; Lee 41, Kasprowicz 20) Left alone outside off.

63 overs: Australia 277–9 (target 282; Lee 41, Kasprowicz 20) Dot ball, and it's over to Freddie.

63.1 overs: Australia 277–9 (target 282; Lee 41, Kasprowicz 20) Lee ducks under a bouncer.

63.2 overs: Australia 277–9 (target 282; Lee 41, Kasprowicz 20) Left alone outside off.

63.3 overs: Australia 277–9 (target 282; Lee 41, Kasprowicz 20) Lee ducks under another bouncer.

63.4 overs: Australia 277–9 (target 282; Lee 41, Kasprowicz 20) And another.

63.5 overs: Australia 277–9 (target 282; Lee 41, Kasprowicz 20) A swing and a miss. This is astonishing stuff.

64 overs: Australia 278–9 (target 282; Lee 42, Kasprowicz 20) A single. A boundary will win this now, and Sean Ingle and I are reaching for the Prozac.

64.1 overs: Australia 279–9 (target 282; Lee 43, Kasprowicz 20) A single for Lee off Harmison.

64.2 overs: Australia 279–9 (target 282; Lee 43, Kasprowicz 20) Back defensive from Kasprowicz, and I still need the loo. Maybe I'll hold it for now.

ENGLAND HAVE WON BY 2 RUNS! THEY'VE WON! GET IN! An absolute brute of a lifter from Harmison; Kasprowicz gloved it from somewhere under his nose, and Jones – Geraint Butterfingers Flippin' Jones – took a cracking low catch to his left. A remarkable end to one of the all-time great Test matches, and some top-class stuff from the Aussies: the whole team are on the pitch shaking hands generously. Brett Lee finishes on 43 not out – a wonderful innings – and the pulse rates of Messrs Smyth and Ingle are returning to something resembling normalcy. Unbelievable stuff, and I have an appointment with the loo.

Australia 308 and 279; England 407 and 182

Third Test

Old Trafford,
11–15 August 2005

First Day

The morning session

BY JAMES DART

Preamble: The big team news? It's bad for an unchanged England: both Glenn McGrath and Lee have been named in the Aussies' XI. But there is some good news for Michael Vaughan: he's won the toss and elected to bat. Mind, Ricky Ponting got it completely wrong when he won the toss at Edgbaston. . .

1st over: England 4–0 (Trescothick 4, Strauss 0) Unsurprisingly, the ball is handed to McGrath, who is back to his old tricks immediately. First delivery is right on target, just past the edge, and the second strikes the top of Trescothick's bat and loops fortunately over the slips for four. Third beats the outside edge, fourth right on the money, fifth beats the edge again and sixth is just a little wide. Meanwhile, without wanting to dampen a nation's fervour, does anyone feel, a little like me, that England were a tad lucky to win the second Test?

2nd over: England 6–0 (Trescothick 4, Strauss 2) Brett Lee is already at his snorting 90mph-pace best. Meanwhile my MediaGuardian.co.uk colleague, Stephen Brook, has draped a large Aussie flag next to my desk. Let's see how long it stays there, eh?

3rd over: England 17–0 (Trescothick 13, Strauss 3) That's more like the run-rate we're accustomed to, as Trescothick plunders the attack with some flowing strokes. "The second Test was only close because your colleague Mike Adamson was providing the OBO," says Keith Bowman. Erm, guess who's handling the evening session tonight, Keith?

4th over: England 17–0 (Trescothick 13, Strauss 3) Great pace early in the day from Lee, and Strauss gets an edge that falls just short of third slip. "England would not have won had Warne not trodden on his own wicket," claims Michael Brunstrom. "But I wouldn't have had it any other way. His face! I've got it on video."

5th over: England 18–0 (Trescothick 14, Strauss 3) "How on earth were England lucky to win the last Test?" blasts Andrew Moore. "They outplayed Australia for most of the game and were unlucky not to wrap it up long before Kasprowicz was out." McGrath keeps it on his tried-and-tested line throughout the over, and without much foot movement Tresco edges behind. Adam Gilchrist goes to his left, but puts the one-handed chance down. He really should have taken it, Geraint Jones fans.

6th over: England 19–0 (Trescothick 15, Strauss 3) Beavis and Butthead Lee continues to menace England's openers, writes Sean Ingle (who's temporarily covering for James Dart, whose computer has crashed for the third time today). Strauss survives, but he doesn't look convincing.

7th over: England 24–0 (Trescothick 17, Strauss 6) Sorry readers, back in the hot seat. "I was telling my father-in-law that Freddie had hit more sixes in the second Test than anyone had ever hit in an Ashes Test before, including Botham," explains Toby Chapman. "Unimpressed he claimed that the boundaries these days aren't as big as they were in his day. Can this be true?"

8th over: England 24–0 (Trescothick 17, Strauss 6) An audible 'clunk' echoes around Old Trafford as Strauss gets smashed on the helmet by a pearler of a Lee bouncer. In a nice show of sportsmanship the Aussies rush in to check him out. Meanwhile, here's some advice to deal with a certain member of the Media section, from Paul Medcraft: "May I suggest folding the flag your colleague has left for you so that only its upper left quadrant can be seen."

9th over: England 26–0 (Trescothick 18, Strauss 6) Better from Trescothick, who survives the over and picks up two runs in the process. "The boundaries are not as big as they were, it's true," beams an informed Neil Ardiff. "There has to be a bigger gap between the rope and the spectators in case of pitch invasions. Heaven forbid there might be an Erika Roe moment."

WICKET! 10th over: Strauss b Lee 6 (England 26–1) A beauty of a slower ball from Lee completely deceives Strauss, who is bowled for the third innings on the trot. That's 150 wickets in Test cricket for Lee, who has shown no sign of his injury in this opening spell.

11th over: England 29–1 (Trescothick 18, Vaughan 2) The pressure really is on Vaughan now for a substantial innings; just 32 runs have come from his four stays at the crease so far in this series. "Brett Lee spends two nights in a British hospital and comes out firing on all cylinders – what's all this about MRSA?" wonders Richard Hayden.

12th over: England 39–1 (Trescothick 18, Vaughan 12) Two timely boundaries, albeit not overly convincing, from Vaughan in Jason Gillespie's first over. "Why not just go ahead and chop up the blue bit with the stars from Stephen's flag and make lots of little hankies for him to sob into when we win?" hoo-hah's James Houston.

13th over: England 40–1 (Trescothick 19, Vaughan 12) "At what point can we stop talking about cricket and start chatting about the genius that was last night's *Lost*?" wonders Cassie Smith. Just after I've finished this over, Cassie, which sees Trescothick nudge a quick single into the off-side. Polar bears? Jungle monsters? Handcuffed female cons?

14th over: England 44–1 (Trescothick 19, Vaughan 12) More wicketkeeping shenanigans from Gilchrist, who's 'having a Jones' as the cruel might suggest, letting a swinging Gillespie delivery squirm underneath his body and off for four.

15th over: England 49–1 (Trescothick 19, Vaughan 17) The rare sight of four runs, actually all run, as Vaughan clips McGrath towards the cover ropes.

16th over: England 58–1 (Trescothick 23, Vaughan 22) Vaughan is playing nicely at the moment, possibly as well as he's done so far in the series. Back to *Lost*, which seems to be dividing you right down the middle. James Millington harrumphs: "The first series has finished here in NZ and I can tell you the ending isn't worth watching the whole bloody series for." But Ben Morgan contends: "It was awesome! I'm taking bets on which one they eat first."

17th over: England 65–1 (Trescothick 27, Vaughan 25) The returning Lee replaces McGrath, whose first spell after injury doesn't appear to be showing any visible after-effects. *"Lost* – perfect setting for beach cricket,"* suggests Hugh Strickland. Pitch looks overly sandy (not enough sea-hardened surface) for my liking, Hugh, and far too slanted. It'd put Lord's to shame.

18th over: England 67–1 (Trescothick 28, Vaughan 26) At last a false shot from Vaughan, whose fish outside off stump to Gillespie just misses the edge. "Does anyone think the fat guy in *Lost* bears an uncanny resemblance to Robert Key?" snorts Giles Harding, with a gag that I'm surprised hadn't arrived earlier.

19th over: England 70–1 (Trescothick 30, Vaughan 26) Alex Holland has high hopes of cricket breaking out in *Lost*: "There's plenty of bamboo for the stumps. I reckon the mysterious guy who plays backgammon would be a cracking umpire, to boot. How can one fashion an appropriate ball from desert island materials?"

20th over: England 75–1 (Trescothick 30, Vaughan 30) Mixed performance from Gillespie, who beats Vaughan with a cracker moments after seeing the England skipper blast him to the cover boundary. "Robert Key is currently to be found starring in that car advert where the kids act like middle-aged salary men," chirps a helpful Charlie Tinsley. "He's the fat one." Leave it there, Charlie – we don't want another Richard Bacon-Magic Numbers moment.

21st over: England 79–1 (Trescothick 34, Vaughan 30) After some short-pitched bowling, Trescothick finally gets one from Lee at a fuller length, and a little wide, enabling him to drive just behind square for a fourth boundary of his innings. So far, as *Lost* cricket ball suggestions, we've got polar bear dung and this from Huw Neill: "You could fashion one out of a nail file, some superglue and said coconut. You would need a tweezer to tease out the hairs on one side to get the necessary swing in those humid conditions though."

22nd over: England 88–1 (Trescothick 34, Vaughan 39) Cracking strokes from Vaughan, whose flowing bat has taken him to 39 from 38 balls. "I hate to spoil everyone's fun but *Lost* is an American production so it will be baseball, American football and all the other English imitation sports they play over there," says spoiler Daniel Kelly. "The only cricket in *Lost* will be an insect."

23rd over: England 93–1 (Trescothick 35, Vaughan 41) Both of

England's batsmen are closing in on their half-centuries with assurance. Here's Tom Willoughby: "Re: *Lost* – give them a couple of years on that desert island and they'll all bear a resemblance to Jason Gillespie."

24th over: England 93–1 (Trescothick 35, Vaughan 41) Vaughan chases Gillespie's rising delivery outside off stump, but his flash just fails to nick an edge. Dom Smith asks: "I read the other day that Stuart MacGill is married to a *Neighbours* actress. We've been trying to decide which one. So far our shortlist is Plain Jane the Super Brain or one of the twins." We can help, Dom. Rachel Friend, who played nanny Bronwyn Davies, love interest (wife) of Henry Ramsay, is indeed married to Mr MacGill.

25th over: England 93–1 (Trescothick 35, Vaughan 41) Another maiden and that's lunch. No sign of Shane Warne yet, which has surprised some, but I'm sure we'll see him soon after he's had a feed.

England 93–1

The afternoon session

BY SEAN INGLE

26th over: England 94–1 (Trescothick 36, Vaughan 41) As the Old Trafford crowd launches into its first boozy chant of "Ing-er-land, Ing-er-land", Gillespie bowls a decentish over.

27th over: England 105–1 (Trescothick 46, Vaughan 41) Listen to those Heineken-fuelled roars! Trescothick firmly pushes at one from McGrath, which goes straight down the ground for four. Does anyone else think Kevin Pietersen's new blue rinse is a touch too close to James Anderson circa 2003? And we all know what happened to him . . .

28th over: England 113–1 (Trescothick 50, Vaughan 43) Gillespie looks even less likely to get a wicket than Hans Blix was to find an Iraqi WMD. "I'm bloody starving, but I'm sticking around to hear Warne's first ball," says Andrew Jolly, who's surely a distant relative of Mike Gatting. "He's promised to do something special, but he'd better get a move on, cause my blood sugar level's getting low."

29th over: England 120–1 (Trescothick 50, Vaughan 49)
Unbelievable escape for Michael Vaughan. First he edges a wide one to slip, only for Gilchrist to drop a high one. Then next ball, he's bowled through the gate – only for umpire Bucknor to rule a no-ball. Finally, to top things off, he swats McGrath away to move to 49. Quite incredible stuff. "Having sampled a few sherberts at the Edgbaston Test I reckon it's probably Carlsberg or Red Stripe-fuelled roars," says Simon Porter (and others).

30th over: England 123–1 (Trescothick 51, Vaughan 50) A single brings up Vaughan's fifty. "What did happen to James Anderson?" asks Stephen Smith. "He wasn't that bad a bowler, and he couldn't do much worse than Hoggard has this summer." He's still at Lancashire, Stephen, where he's sinking like a stone.

31th over: England 123–1 (Trescothick 51, Vaughan 50) Maiden. "After what's just happened to Vaughan I've thrown some money on England taking the series, this has got to be ours," cries Paul Murphy. Steady, Paul, steady.

32nd over: England 126–1 (Trescothick 51, Vaughan 53) Shot from Vaughan through midwicket! "Is this the same James Anderson who your colleague, Andy Wilson, described as going through an 'encouraging resurgence' on Tuesday, having followed a 5–for with a 3 for 27 against Northants?" asks Alex Holland (and others).

33rd over: England 130–1 (Trescothick 52, Vaughan 54) Great duel this between Vaughan and McGrath, who nearly gets the England captain with an 86mph yorker. The two exchange words – something like "Nice delivery, Glenn," I imagine.

34th over: England 132–1 (Trescothick 52, Vaughan 56) At last, the Aussies turn to Warne. His first ball is a beaut – not quite a ball of the century, but Vaughan is certainly surprised by the spin and only just blocks.

35th over: England 142–1 (Trescothick 52, Vaughan 66) Shot of the day from Vaughan! He jumps on a decentish McGrath outswinger and clobbers him through point for another boundary. "Compare Anderson's stats with England hero Matthew Hoggard – who has taken, er, 20 wickets at 36.6 in Division Two this season, a good 14 places below Jimmy," says Will Scott.

36th over: England 149–1 (Trescothick 56, Vaughan 67) Bad news for Ian Bell and Andy Strauss: Warne's just got one to spin from middle to nine inches outside off. Trescothick retaliates with a bludgeoning boundary through long-on.

37th over: England 149–1 (Trescothick 56, Vaughan 67) Lee replaces McGrath and immediately is back to top speed, firing in a succession of 90mph howitzers. Maiden. "Thanks for the commentary," Vinay Aravind writes, "but please guard against Carpal Tunnel Syndrome with all this typing you're doing!" Don't worry, Vinay, I'm rotating my wrists like a German techno fan to a particularly catchy beat.

38th over: England 151–1 (Trescothick 58, Vaughan 67) Drinks. Meanwhile this from Chris Mason. "We need to research the effect colouring your hair has on sporting performance," he says. "To be honest, I don't like Pietersen's chances in this game with that appalling blue streak."

39th over: England 156–1 (Trescothick 62, Vaughan 70) Lee is bowling murderously quick here: a 91mph bouncer nearly takes Vaughan's head off. But after the England captain nibbles a single, Trescothick hunts a wide one and crashes it through the covers for four. Meanwhile Gavin Wallace wants to know: "Do you think Andy Caddick would be able to bowl faster if he plastered his ears against his head?" A no-brainer, surely, Gavin?

40th over: England 160–1 (Trescothick 62, Vaughan 74) Anything Trescothick can do, Vaughan can match: Warne drops one short and is biffed to the boundary through gully. "The impact of hair colouring on sporting performance is a tricky one," says Neil Forshaw. "Abel Xavier certainly backs claims that it has a negative effect, but Gazza was sublime with the peroxide look."

41st over: England 162–1 (Trescothick 63, Vaughan 74) Lee is grunting and growling away, but this pitch looks as tricky as a GCSE media studies exam.

WICKET! 42nd over: Trescothick c Gilchrist b Warne 63 (England 162–2) Warne's 600th Test wicket is one of his strangest: Trescothick sweeps at a short one, which clips his bat, hits Gilchrist's knee and rolls into the Aussie vice-captain's gloves. At the end of the over, the Old Trafford crowd gives him a standing ovation. "Does Gillespie dye his hair?" ponders Charlie Rowlands. "He looks suspiciously grey at the roots."

43rd over: England 166–2 (Vaughan 79, Bell 0) Quiet over from Lee. "Who could forget Dan Petrescu and his merry men letting a victory over England and a bottle of peroxide go to their heads before getting ceremonially dumped out of France 98 by Croatia," asks Alastair Judge (and others).

44th over: England 167–2 (Vaughan 79, Bell 1) Bell gets off the mark with a single to Warne. "This has no relevance to anything that's gone before, but I just wanted to let it be known that Scarlett Johansson accidentally touched my backside while sitting next to me at the Groucho on Saturday night," says Jascha Elliot. "Can any OBO readers beat that for a sad attempt to bask in the reflected glory of a celebrity?"

45th over: England 173–2 (Vaughan 85, Bell 1) Andrew Steed wants to know: "Does anyone in their right mind think that Bell is going to score more than 10 runs in this innings?" Why not, Andrew?

46th over: England 173–2 (Vaughan 85, Bell 1) Warne is getting bounce as well as turn now. Bell holds on. Meanwhile Chris Blunt says he sat once sat next to Arthur Smith in the Sports Bar in Berlin. "We were watching the 1997 FA Cup Final on an Italian satellite feed. Is that any good?" What do you think, Chris?

47th over: England 175–2 (Vaughan 87, Bell 1) Katich (number of Test wickets: 11) replaces Lee. His over is interrupted by a topless male streaker, but otherwise is fairly decent. "Alastair McKenzie like totally looked at me while babbling into his mobile phone opposite the Assembly Rooms in Edinburgh the other evening," says Siobhan Kavanagh. "Oh for heaven's sake, he was Archie in *Monarch of the Glen* – get with it people."

48th over: England 175–2 (Vaughan 87, Bell 2) Warne continues to tie up England's batsmen – which begs the question, why wasn't he on earlier? "I snogged a girl who'd snogged the drummer out of Shed Seven," writes Timothy J Golby. "Somehow we managed to keep our tryst out of the papers, but that paparazzi lot are parasites."

49th over: England 185–2 (Vaughan 88, Bell 10) Katich serves up a juicy full toss to the hithertho diffident Bell, who smashes him straight down the ground for four. "I see Jascha Elliot's Scarlet Johansson encounter and raise her my experience on Tuesday night, when I played poker with none other than Dr Raj Persaud of Richard and Judy fame," says Chris Clough. "Needless to say, I didn't win."

50th over: England 185–2 (Vaughan 88, Bell 10) Maiden. "I filmed Franz Ferdinand before they were famous at a gig in Sheffield," says Matt Risby. "I have the tapes in which they discuss Eel-Skin shoes for over 30 minutes. Rock and roll eh?"

51st over: England 186–2 (Vaughan 89, Bell 10) Katich's chinamen are surprisingly effective. Just one single for Vaughan. "I am reliably informed (by my mother, the source of all wisdom) that Seamus Heaney has used our loo. Howzat?" says Alex Cooke.

52nd over: England 193–2 (Vaughan 92, Bell 14) Bell is rewarded for his graft and fight with a boundary through midwicket. Warne's response? One that darts sideways and nearly takes the edge.

53rd over: England 194–2 (Vaughan 93, Bell 14) Vaughan edges closer to a Test hundred with another run. "I used to regularly chat with Brett Lee during the last Ashes series in the Bondi Hotel," says Shane in London. "I actually made him admit Vaughan would've made the Aussie team when the big debate was that no Pom could better their opposite number!"

54th over: England 195–2 (Vaughan 94, Bell 14) A great session for England ends with another Vaughan single. Tea.

England 195–2

The evening session

BY MIKE ADAMSON

Preamble: Here is an email my colleague James Dart received this morning from James Peterson: "In the nicest gentlemanly-English-cricket-playing way, wouldn't it be wise to rest Mike Adamson from the OBO – simply because he seems to preside over the worst sessions for England?" I would've happily taken that fiver you offered, James, and headed to the pub, but Sean Ingle has taken the editorial decision to land me in the hot seat and initiate the rapid demise of English cricket.

55th over: England 200–2 (Vaughan 95, Bell 17) McGrath can't stop Vaughan picking up two singles and Bell stroking the ball through the off-side for three to bring up the 200. "Why don't we re-open the debate on which members of the England squad would get into the Aussie side today?" says Tom Huddart. "My money goes on Flintoff, Pietersen and Harmison making it straight away, with Trescothick and Vaughan threatening to break into the batting top three. Come to mention it, why don't we throw it the other way. Which Aussies would make it into the England squad? Or am I getting a little carried away? I suppose Warne might get Giles's spot." Gilchrist might have a small claim as well.

56th over: England 204–2 (Vaughan 99, Bell 17) Vaughan moves to 99 thanks to a juicy full toss from Warne and some lazy work from McGrath on the boundary. "Sorry to totally blow everyone out of the water," says Jamie Reeman, continuing your tales of brushes with celebrity, "but I appeared with Ian Botham on the *Saturday Morning Picture Show* in 1986 with him teaching me how to bat. We ended the show hitting tennis balls at Frank Sidebottom. Beat that."

57th over: England 209–2 (Vaughan 102, Bell 18) Bell picks up a single to square leg to give Vaughan four balls with which to bring up his century. But he only needs one, slightly mistiming a drive to mid-off which ends up wide of mid-off. Who cares how he managed it, the bare fact is that he's the first player in the series to have reached three figures.

58th over: England 210–2 (Vaughan 103, Bell 18) Shane Warne races through another over bowling around the wicket. "Former Ireland, Man City and Everton star Terry Phelan once pointed out to me that a copy of FHM had the choice of four different covers when I was working in WH Smith," writes David Edwards. "This was not much of a surprise to me given that the magazine had 'Special Edition – 4 different covers' written in fairly large letters across it, but you can't expect that much from a man who had to go on international duty with Jason McAteer."

59th over: England 211–2 (Vaughan 104, Bell 18) McGrath has nobody to blame but himself after putting down a simple catch after tricking Bell with his slower ball. Meanwhile, Michael Howard says: "Jon Pertwee, of *Doctor Who* and *Wurzel Gummidge* fame, lived in the house two doors down from me. Not when we lived there though. Of course, the leader of the Tories shares his name with me, and last but certainly not least I work with the esteemed sports reporter Sean Ingle's girlfriend's father!! Howzat?" Not out.

60th over: England 215–2 (Vaughan 108, Bell 18) Warne is continuing with his round-the-wicket approach, but he releases the pressure he has been applying by dragging one short, which Vaughan pulls to the rope on the leg-side. "When I was living in Budapest in 2002 I was walking drunkenly across the Gellert Bridge at 4.30 in the morning and bumped into Eddie Murphy. He was shooting *I-Spy*. Terrible film." So says Heath Greene, film critic.

61st over: England 215–2 (Vaughan 108, Bell 18) Another lucky escape for Bell as he once again fails to pick McGrath's slower ball. After giving the bowler some catching practice in the previous over, Bell this time tries to test out the cover's fielding, but the ball lands just short.

62nd over: England 217–2 (Vaughan 110, Bell 18) A quiet over until Warne again pulls one short to Vaughan, who seems happy to wait for the bad ball and put it away. Two runs this time. "Vaughnie would've sneezed and pulled a muscle on 99 if you were cursed, perhaps it has been lifted," says Julian Tuddenham, who I fancy may be an Australian trying to tempt fate.

63rd over: England 217–2 (Vaughan 110, Bell 18) Bell isn't enjoying himself too much against McGrath. The one time McGrath pitches one short of a length outside off stump, Bell has a wild swipe at it, the intended destination being a man in row Q. He missed.

64th over: England 221–2 (Vaughan 113, Bell 18) After Vaughan picks off another bad Warne ball – not often one has the chance to write that phrase – the spin king returns to an over-the-wicket approach. "Who does Jamie Reeman think he is?" asks a furious Graeme King. "*The Saturday Morning Picture Show?* Try *Going Live* with Philip Schofield and Sarah Greene back in 1992. I was a competition winner, on the show with Sandy Toksvig and Mike McShane, Right Said Fred miming to 'Deeply Dippy' and Harry

Enfield not being very funny. Now that is a true 15 minutes of fame, not to say 1h 45m of fame, just before *Football Focus* on a Saturday morning. Reeman, you're dreaming."

65th over: England 231–2 (Vaughan 123, Bell 18) Australian desperation is growing exponentially: Gillespie is back into the attack. And Vaughan scores 10 off the first three balls. Great scenes. "I can tell English morale is improving," says Alex Holland, "as no one has said, 'If we can score so many runs on this pitch, think of what the Aussies will do'."

66th over: England 231–2 (Vaughan 123, Bell 18) After the waywardness of Gillespie, Warne is back to his consistent best, bowling a maiden to Bell.

67th over: England 239–2 (Vaughan 131, Bell 18) Gillespie strays on to leg stump three times in a row and is punished as you might expect by Vaughan. This particular Gillespie spell may not last too long. "I'll see Graeme King's *Going Live* and I'll raise him winning 'Two Peas in a Pod' on *Mark & Lard* on my birthday some years ago. As it was my birthday Lard gave me a special 'biggidy-biggidy-bong' as well. I thrashed the woman I was playing and all I won was a £10 record token!"

68th over: England 241–2 (Vaughan 131, Bell 20) Big cheers from the crowd for Bell, who scores his first run for 12 overs – make that two runs – when Warne over-pitches one. "On Monday I played tennis in Prague," says John Edwards innocently enough. "On the court next to us was none other than Mrs Smicer! She was pretty good too." Do you mean at tennis, John?

69th over: England 252–2 (Vaughan 137, Bell 25) I'm sure Jason Gillespie used to be a darn good bowler. Yet again Gillespie bowls it down leg-side, and yet again Vaughan smacks it through midwicket to add four to the quickly growing total. Then Gillespie almost rams my words back down my throat by sending through a quicker delivery which Bell inside-edges past the stumps for another four. Drinks.

70th over: England 258–2 (Vaughan 142, Bell 25) I don't know what was in the Australians' drinks during the break, but first Warne bowls a short and wide no-ball which Vaughan drills through point, then he finds Vaughan's outside edge but Hayden puts down a fourth drop of the day at slip. It went quickly to him, but he should've clung on to it.

71st over: England 272–2 (Vaughan 156, Bell 25) "Easy, easy, easy." So sing the Old Trafford crowd. Three more classic boundaries for Vaughan off Gillespie's first three balls. Without meaning to gloat, it's great to see the Aussies in such turmoil. Gillespie has bowled 15 overs for 87 runs. Oh, and no wickets.

72nd over: England 275–2 (Vaughan 156, Bell 28) Ian Bell is doing a useful job for his captain here, occupying the crease at one end while he builds his confidence and allowing Vaughan to play freely at the other. "At the Edgbaston Test there was much discussion, led by me, of whether Pietersen wears a thong," says Andrew Ratcliffe rather worryingly. "He seems to enjoy wearing figure-hugging semi-transparent trousers and there was little sign of vpl. I concluded that either a thong or skimpy briefs were his underwear of choice. I'd be interested to hear whether anyone can definitively confirm or deny this." Anyone brave enough?

73rd over: England 283–2 (Vaughan 163, Bell 29) Gillespie has been belatedly kicked out of the attack and part-time left-arm chinaman Simon Katich drafted back in. He can't stop the flow of runs, though. Vaughan takes two steps down the track and plants the ball firmly over midwicket, bisecting the fielders on the boundary.

74th over: England 287–2 (Vaughan 166, Bell 30) Another half-chance for Matthew Hayden at slip as a Bell edge lands at the big man's left foot. "The reason your jinx is no longer working is because everyone now knows about it," writes Natasha Dickinson prematurely. "It's like telling people what you wish for, it cancels the magic." There's over an hour to go yet, Natasha.

WICKET! 75th over: Vaughan c McGrath b Katich 166 (England 290–3) That was the only way Vaughan was going to get out today: a juicy full toss which could have been dispatched anywhere, but was pulled straight to McGrath at cow corner. A fine innings, though.

76th over: England 291–3 (Bell 33, Pietersen 1) Pietersen gets off the mark after a (possibly) friendly welcome from Warne, with a nudge to the on-side. "It's nearly 5pm – have you been doing as suggested earlier and giving us a rosy story instead to hide your usual bad influence on the team, or is the score really 286–2 with Captain Fantastic racking up the runs?" asks a suspicious David Hibell. Well it was, David, but I thought it was time for a wicket to make the story plausible.

77th over: England 296–3 (Bell 34, Pietersen 5) "I think Andrew Ratcliffe (72nd over) should get back to the Trinny & Susannah section of the BBC website," says Neil Taylor. "Talk to the hand, or some other such Americanism."

78th over: England 299–3 (Bell 34, Pietersen 8) Expressing typical confidence, Pietersen goes after a flighted Warne ball with a huge swing, and ends up almost falling over thanks to an air shot. Warne has a little chuckle to himself. "I like to think Pietersen abstains from any form of underwear at all, including jock-strap and box, in keeping with his extremely confident manner," writes Simon Molony.

79th over: England 305–3 (Bell 35, Pietersen 13) The 300 draws a huge roar from some 20,000 or so beer-fuelled Mancunians, handed to England on a plate as it was by a Brett Lee loosener. "Mike, I think that Natasha is the new jinx," says Martyn Gaunt (cf over 74). "Don't display any more of her mails just in case, it's not worth the risk. Also, should a wicket follow this mail, ban me too!"

80th over: England 307–3 (Bell 36, Pietersen 14) Pietersen again takes on Warne, clips the ball straight at short leg, but Langer is unable to hold on to the quickly moving ball. England have had a large slice of luck today, but to their credit they've taken full advantage. Mat Thomas writes, clearly looking for a HONK: "What are the odds of KP going nuts in the last hour?"

81st over: England 315–3 (Bell 41, Pietersen 17) The new ball is due, but Australia aren't taking it because they obviously think Warne can snare Pietersen at some stage. What it does mean is that Lee is bowling with an 80–over-old ball and not extracting the same bounce and speed as he could do. The upshot? Bell's first boundary for 12 overs, cut through the off-side. "Will Pietersen overtake Bell before the end of play?" asks Craig Finbow. Not with shots like that.

82nd over: England 315–3 (Bell 41, Pietersen 17) A maiden for Warne, with Bell wisely keeping Pietersen away from the danger end.

83rd over: England 315–3 (Bell 41, Pietersen 17) Ponting throws the ball to Katich in an obvious attempt to lure Pietersen into a false sense of security and a similar dismissal to Vaughan's. It doesn't work, though, as the power-hitter reluctantly puts his defensive technique on display. "Garth Crooks once mistook me for a member of the hotel staff and asked me where the press room was in the Radisson when Rio Ferdinand was being banned by the FA for his missed drugs test," says Neil Cullingford. "His question was surprisingly to the point actually."

84th over: England 319–3 (Bell 45, Pietersen 17) A sweetly timed and placed shot down the ground from Bell, who is waking up to the fact that he has the ability to play at this level.

85th over: England 325–3 (Bell 50, Pietersen 18) Katich gifts Bell four more runs with a high full toss outside off stump. Bell duly obliges, and then brings up his first half-century against Australia with an easy single. "Seeing as we're going so well, is now a good time to discuss when we should declare?" says Alastair McCulloch. "I reckon we should try to get to 700 by about 5pm tomorrow, then bowl them out twice in two days and win by an innings in the humiliating style the Aussies used to."

86th over: England 331–3 (Bell 55, Pietersen 19) Bell's confidence is growing. Probably his finest shot of the day is a front-foot drive off Warne which flies past extra cover. Neil Taylor says: "Does anyone else think that Vaughan's managed to swap breakfasts with the Aussie team this morning? Even Mogadon-scoring-rate Bell looks comfortable playing the supporting role."

WICKET! 87th over: Pietersen c sub b Lee 28 (England 333–4) Australia hand Brett Lee the new ball, and he strikes immediately by banging the ball in short and fast. Pietersen attempts a hook but it doesn't come out of the meat of the bat and the ball lands in the safe hands of substitute fielder Brad Hogg.

88th over: England 341–4 (Bell 59, Hoggard 4) The doughty Matthew Hoggard is the man sent in to act as nightwatchman. "It's going to be a draw, isn't it?" says Joshua Hardie rhetorically, not pausing to let me say "no". "England 467 all out, they reply with 523, we struggle to 296 and they are 117 for 3 on Monday night. I can see it." So it would seem.

WICKET! 89th over: Hoggard b Lee 4 (England 341–5) Brett Lee steams in for the last over of the day in the hope of taking Hoggard's wicket, achieving his aim with the final ball of the day which clips the top of the batsman's off stump.

England 341–5

Second Day

The morning session

BY SEAN INGLE

Preamble: So what will it be, then? A healthy total of 500, squeezing the Australians' cojones till they squeak? Or another textbook example of the English batting collapse? Having lost two wickets late last night England need to push on here – and they should do on a pitch that's tamer than Shakespeare's Shrew.

90th over: England 341–5 (Bell 59, Flintoff 0) McGrath starts at three-quarter pace (think Dominic Cork, but more accurate); until a 77mph snorter has Bell playing and missing. "This is no way meant to be offensive," says Nick Coombes. Yes, Nick. "But when you were a youth were you teased that your first initial and surname together form Single?" Never, although there was the odd rendition of "Ingle Bells" at Christmas. And Sean-off Shotgun.

91st over: England 345–5 (Bell 59, Flintoff 4) A hearty roar from the Old Trafford crowd as Flintoff's prod through third man speeds to the boundary. Speaking of Freddie, this from Andrew Lewis. "If Flintoff scores 44 or more today, or is not out for 11 or more, he will have a higher batting than bowling average, the mark of a class all-rounder. What a stat, eh?" I'm sure there are better stats around, Andrew, surely?

92nd over: England 346–5 (Bell 59, Flintoff 5) Strange. It seems to be a deliberate McGrath policy to drop six or seven miles off his pace. Most of the deliveries that over were just 77mph – but they pitch on a sixpence and Flintoff is rightly content to watch.

WICKET! 93rd over: Bell c Gilchrist b Lee 59 (England 350–6) Lee bangs in a 91mph snorter and Bell, trying a rather frantic hook shot, gets a thin nick. Umpire Steve Bucknor waits and waits . . . and waits some more, before finally raising his finger. By the way, we're not having a schoolnames riff – an awful lot of you, after all, seem to have gone to school with a Mike Hunt.

94th over: England 354–6 (Flintoff 9, G Jones 4) With a lusty, almost Conan the Barbarianesque swing of his blade, Flintoff crashes a boundary through backward point. "Here's a stat for you: Simon Jones has a batting average of 51 for the series. Simon Jones!" says Ned Morgan. Hmm, not exactly *Freakanomics*, is it?

95th over: England 358–6 (Flintoff 9, G Jones 8) Another low edge through third man, another boundary, another I've-had-one-too-many-pickled-onions grimace from Brett Lee. "How about 8% of the population of Worcestershire is over 75," says Piers Canodas. "Er, I'll get my coat."

96th over: England 358–6 (Flintoff 9, G Jones 8) Flintoff is still taking no chances against McGrath. Maiden. "Talking of *Freakanomics* – I'm reading it at the moment and did you know the Americans chomp their way through $1bn of chewing gum every year?" says Alex Gibson. "Beat that!"

97th over: England 361–6 (Flintoff 10, G Jones 8) Apart from two no-balls that over, Lee is bowling brilliantly. "If Jones manages 8 not out today, he'll have the series' highest batting average," says Csaba Abrahall. "Although Glenn McGrath's current series average is infinity, which is probably even higher and could only be topped – if my school playground memories serve me correctly – by infinity and one."

98th over: England 366–6 (Flintoff 14, G Jones 8) Another controlled edge through third man, another boundary, this time from Flintoff. McGrath comes back: first with a bouncer that Flintoff nearly edges and then a quicker one that Freddie nearly cuts on to his stumps. "I didn't learn much from three years of studying a BSC in Cell and Molecular Biology, but I do know this," says Jon Sexton. "1mg of Botchalism is enough to wipe out the worldwide population of guinea pigs."

99th over: England 367–6 (Flintoff 14, G Jones 8) Twice Lee tries to bounce Flintoff out, twice he plays a high forward defensive. "Quite believably 13% of Americans believe Joan of Arc was the wife of Noah," says Dave Collins, continuing this strange stats riff. "It must be true because I read it in *Zoo*!"

100th over: England 369–6 (Flintoff 15, G Jones 11) McGrath continues to look as threatening as a dead dingo, and England add a couple of easy singles. "One thing John Sexton didn't learn is how to spell Botulism," says Ben Mimmack (and about 197 others). "Besides I think he means Botulinum Toxin, since Botulism is the illness caused by the poisoning. Yes I am a geek."

101st over: England 374–6 (Flintoff 15, G Jones 15) Jones is looking as comfortable as he's looked all series out there: Lee twice over-pitches and Jones strokes him away. "The Americans chomp their way through $1bn of chewing gum every year? I reckon that's what the Aussie slips cordon gets through in a day," reckons Andrew Jolly. Meanwhile it's started to rain at Old Trafford.

102nd over: England 375–6 (Flintoff 16, G Jones 15) A change in the bowling: Shane Warne for Glenn McGrath. And, surprise, surprise, Jones is in trouble from the off – he tries to charge down the track, ends up in no man's land, but just manages to get a bat on it. "Botulinum Toxin is most commonly found in cans of tuna that have been dented in the packing process," says Sally Barrett. "Reckon it's worth a warning. I too am a geek."

103rd over: England 376–6 (Flintoff 18, G Jones 15) The rain continues, and so does Lee. And his barrage of bouncers nearly pays off as Flintoff, finally unable to restrain himself, swings wildly and misses a nick by millimetres. Meanwhile it's lashing now, forcing the players to dash off.

11.35am update: The rain has stopped, so play should start again fairly sharpish. More readers' thoughts: "Forget Guinea Pig genocide, 1mg of Botulinum Toxin (botox) is enough to render five million Anne Robinsons completely expressionless," says Dr Giles Harding.

11.43am update: Play is about to start. Meanwhile this from Helen Young. "Can Sally Barrett (over 102) confirm if the Botulinum Toxin is found in any dented cans, or just tuna?"

103rd over: England 382–6 (Flintoff 18, G Jones 20) Brett Lee returns with a full-toss loosener and is smashed down the ground for four.

He then follows it up with a bouncer that's called a wide. Cue ironic cheers. "You may not be aware but in government departments no one does any work on Friday and most offices are deserted by 2.30pm," says Richard Clarke. "Consequently, the OBO team can rest assured they are not throwing sand in the over-oiled mechanism of the civil service."

104th over: England 388–6 (Flintoff 18, G Jones 25) First ball, Bowden turns down Warne's huge lbw appeal, and second ball Warne nearly gets one to slide under Jones's bat. Jones's response? A crashing four straight down the ground.

105th over: England 401–6 (Flintoff 25, G Jones 31) Lee's struggling with his run-up in these wet conditions and is biffed to the boundary by both Flintoff and Jones. Great stuff! "Say the average salary is £22,000, that works out at about £10 per hour. Say people spend an hour-and-a-half a day on OBO, and there's 100,000 of them, that's a total cost to the economy of £1.63m. £8.1m for the Test and £40.5m for the series. I wouldn't hold your breath for the honours list," says Olly Jenkins.

106th over: England 411–6 (Flintoff 34, G Jones 32) Warne continues, but now he's getting the treatment too! Meanwhile Sally Barrett is back. "The chemical make-up of tuna makes it a particularly vulnerable safe-haven for botulinum. However, any dented cans are at risk of harbouring bacteria." So now you know.

107th over: England 419–6 (Flintoff 39, G Jones 34) Ponting reverts to that trundler par excellence, Jason Gillespie, but he's meat and drink for Flintoff, who pulls him for another boundary. "Keeping an eye on the OBO actually increases the productivity in my company," says Hugo Hutchinson. "We are publishing an autobiography of Flintoff and a book on leadership by Vaughan, so it's only fair that we keep an eye on how our authors are doing out at the crease."

108th over: England 423–6 (Flintoff 42, G Jones 35) Another Warne over is greeted by joyous chants of "We're going to win 4–1" from the England fans. "Suddenly those 10p reductions on dented cans don't seem quite the bargain they used to," says Netto shopper Craig Easterbrook.

109th over: England 432–6 (Flintoff 46, G Jones 40) Langer, sweeping on the boundary, has a simple stop to make – but he slips comically and can only watch as it rolls for four. "We should deliberately dent cans and sell them to the Japanese as the new macho food," suggests Dr Tom Charnock. "Eat tuna with a 1 in 25,000 chance of a gruesome death!"

WICKET! 110th over: Flintoff c Langer b Warne 46 (England 433–7) Flintoff tries to hit Warne out of the ground, but he slightly mishits it, and sends it straight down long-on's throat. Huge break there for the Aussies, who've been looking pretty demoralised.

111th over: England 434–7 (G Jones 42, Giles 0) Giles survives a pumped-up Warne. Meanwhile this from Paul Walters. "While Olly Jenkins's analysis provides a good start, it fails to consider the counterfactual, ie, it assumes that the 90 minutes assigned to OBO would have been used productively," he suggests. "Arguably OBO viewing may just displace the hour-and-a-half that would have been spent making tea, talking to a colleague etc. In fact, seeing as you have to be at your desk to enjoy OBO, you may be doing productive things like answering the phone. Therefore, OBO could be contributing to national income, even before you consider the value added of the internet, computer and power companies, and not to mention the 'halo effect' that the success of cricket has on wider economic activity."

WICKET! 112th over: G Jones b Gillespie 42 (England 434–8) Dear oh dear. Gillespie gets one to dart back and takes out Jones's off stump. Suddenly, in two minutes, all of England's good work this morning goes up in smoke. That's lunch.

England 434–8

The afternoon session

BY JAMES DART

Preamble: After England's latest end-of-session collapse, Ashley Giles and Steve Harmison are trudging out to the crease, looking to dodge the showers and lift this hefty first-innings total beyond 450.

112th over: England 437–8 (Giles 0, Harmison 3) Nickelback lead singer Chad Kroeger gets the action back under way, but new batsman Harmison quickly cracks him for three through cover. "In terms of loss of productivity to the UK economy, I have Cricinfo up for the ball-by-ball, Guardian for the over-by-over and BBC as a back-up in case either crashes," explains Jack. "By the time I have read all three, effectively I will have watched each ball about three times, so for an eight-hour-day's play, that is 24 hours' time lost. Multiply that by one million of your listeners – one million days = 2,700 years or 39 complete lifetimes of an adult man. Scary."

WICKET! 112th over: Giles c Hayden b Warne 0 (England 438–9) The master spinner ends the England spinner's short stay at the crease as he gets the ball to turn, catch a thickish edge, and give Matthew Hayden an easy catch at slip.

113th over: England 444–9 (Harmison 10, S Jones 0) Crucial runs from a swinging Harmison, who cracks Kroeg, sorry, Gillespie (force of habit) over mid-off for two runs and then over mid-on for four. Meanwhile, Bert Warriner mails in: "My cricket-novice girlfriend has asked me why Shane Warne is wearing sunscreen on his face and I've suggested that it could be due to sponsorship, habit or a desire for the easy availability of grease. Does anyone know which it is or have any better ideas?"

WICKET! 113th over: S Jones b Warne 0 (England 444 all out) A fourth wicket (No. 603) for Warne, who completely deceives Jones's attempted slog to beat his defences all ends up and crash into the stumps. Considering England were 433–6, the total is a little disappointing. But Michael Vaughan would have taken this yesterday morning.

Australia first innings

1st over: Australia 2–0 (Langer 2, Hayden 0) A good line from Harmison gets the pressure on to Justin Langer immediately, but a forceful prod through extra cover picks up two. Meanwhile, here's a tale of treachery and redemption from Robert Myers. "Had a little wander over to the BBC over-by-over coverage (I know, I know, but she looked so attractive after six pints and it didn't mean anything). The quality of their coverage is OK, but the comments from the crowd are awful – 1201: Gavin emails to say: 'Warne against Flintoff is like Barney Rubble and Fred Flintstone going at it!' I mean, sincerely, you wouldn't let drivel like that get out on your site, would you? I promise I won't stray again if you'll take me back." Talk to the hand, uh-huh, girlfriend, click of the fingers, etc and so on.

2nd over: Australia 3–0 (Langer 2, Hayden 0) Matthew Hoggard begins arguably his most important innings so far this series and within two deliveries has Hayden in a cold sweat. Swinging back into the left-hander, Hayden is beaten and the ball raps him on the pads. Umpire Billy Bowden shakes his head, but Hawkeye claims it would have struck the edge of leg stump. A tough decision all round.

3rd over: Australia 9–0 (Langer 2, Hayden 6) Four for Hayden, but it was a less-than-convincing, mistimed stroke. "Why all this fuss about the cost to the economy?" demands Ben King. "I'm more bothered by the fact that if it wasn't for the constant refreshing of the *Guardian*, I'd go mad with boredom and my work wouldn't be fooled into thinking I'm working. I'm sure I'm not the only one. At least this way I can scrape another week's wages before my employer realises I'm not actually doing anything worthwhile." Are you working on the BBC commentary, Ben?

4th over: Australia 17–0 (Langer 10, Hayden 6) "I swear that yesterday the cricinfo commentator compared a juicy full toss from Katich to a KitKat – he said the ball was covered in chocolate and wrapped in silver foil," exclaims Richard Clarke. "Not like you OBO guys – you have bare journalistic talent." Bare being the word, Richard, especially after seeing Langer crack two real Curly Wurlys to the cover ropes off Hoggard, left reeling like a discarded Aero wrapper.

5th over: Australia 26–0 (Langer 15, Hayden 10) "I hope you guys realise that I'm risking my very job just being here?" wails James Holbrook from impending firedom. "New ICT policy means I can only use t'internet for 5% of my working time. Stuff the economy, I'm on here from 10.30 til I bunk off early at four." The chance of finishing at four on a Friday. Bah! It's alright for some.

6th over: Australia 30–0 (Langer 15, Hayden 14) Hayden opens the face and runs Hoggard through third man for four as the Aussies continue their solid start. "Surely Curly Wurlys are not a good description for what were presumably bad balls – that would imply they swung lots and were delicious," suggests Tom Carver. "Might a Wham bar be better?"

7th over: Australia 31–0 (Langer 16, Hayden 14) Looked like being a maiden from Andy Flintoff before Langer nicked a single last ball. England went for the run-out but hit the stumps way too late.

8th over: Australia 36–0 (Langer 21, Hayden 14) "James, if you want to bunk off early on a Friday (or even a Thursday!) why don't you become a Heathrow baggage handler!" honks Chris Maiden.

9th over: Australia 37–0 (Langer 22, Hayden 14) General sightscreen shenanigans from the groundstaff, who have got themselves into Langer's line of sight. They quickly hide behind a wall, but the eagle-eyed Aussie can still see them. "Could you please show a sterner hand with all this talk of chocolate-flavoured deliveries," pleads Ben Lowing. "It'll get out of hand and the next thing we'll know is that Mike Gatting will have made an international comeback. Stop it before it's too late for us all . . ." Lucky Flintoff didn't bowl a Yorkie then.

10th over: Australia 37–0 (Langer 22, Hayden 14) Fine over from Hoggard, who beats the outside edge of Langer with a pearler. Maiden. It's Friday afternoon all right. "If Aussie cricketers were animals, my first choice would put Phil Daniels lookalike Langer down as a vole!" hollers Andy Morris in hangover-induced surreal mode.

11th over: Australia 41–0 (Langer 22, Hayden 18) Shot of the innings from Hayden, who climbs all over Flintoff's short and wide delivery to thump him to the cover boundary. "On the animal tip, does anyone else think Ian Bell has a certain lupine look to him?" wonders Nicholas Evans. Meanwhile, here's Rupert Smith: "Re 8th over: I think the Aussie fielders are Heathrow baggage handlers; look at all the things they've droppped!" Honk.

Drinks break: "I hate to state the obvious but Ponting is clearly half gerbil," beams Gemma Harris. "GO Jones would be more of a hamster." And Kevin Plummer adds: "I know he's not strictly an animal, but Adam Gilchrist bears a striking resemblance to

Gollum/Smeagle from *Lord of the Rings*. I think it may have something to do with his strange face-size to head-size ratio."

12th over: Australia 44–0 (Langer 25, Hayden 18) Three more runs to Langer as the sound of boozed-up fans springs out from the stands; it's the Australians, along with the WG Grace-a-like that Channel 4 have employed this summer. Changing tack: "Whatever happed to Alex Tudor?" ponders Barry White. "His brother dated my ex-friend."

13th over: Australia 52–0 (Langer 26, Hayden 25) "While Flintoff and Jones came together this morning at a tense period for England, you would have expected Vaughan to be watching his men's progress intently from the balcony," says Will Hersey. "But what was England's captain doing? TV pics showed him with his head buried in the *Daily Star*. Quality." Or not.

14th over: Australia 52–0 (Langer 26, Hayden 25) A maiden from new bowler Simon Jones. "I didn't know Barry White had an interest in cricket!" sniggers Ceri Price. "Maybe he was a secret fan and sometime player . . . can you imagine the Walrus of Love out there in front of the stumps? Hmm . . . I guess there's already Shane Warne, though . . ."

15th over: Australia 58–0 (Langer 31, Hayden 25) Another boundary from Langer, who guides Flintoff through the field at gully. Any clamour for Giles to get an early introduction into the attack?

WICKET! 16th over: Langer c Bell b Giles 31 (Australia 58–1) Honestly, I didn't wait until Giles began this over to write that last entry. The King of Spain almost delivers at first with a massive appeal for an edge behind. Bowden shakes his head, but my colleague Mike Adamson claims he'd have given it. There's no denying it one ball later, mind, as Langer clips it to Ian Bell at forward short leg, who takes a fantastic diving one-handed catch.

17th over: Australia 60–1 (Hayden 26, Ponting 1) "Alex Tudor can currently be found playing for Essex seconds," says Kieran Blackburn, the first person to actually mail in some information about the former England man, instead of noting the questioner's "amusing" Barry White name.

18th over: Australia 66–1 (Hayden 31, Ponting 2) A good tidy over from Giles is spoilt by Hayden cracking a full toss outside off stump to the extra-cover boundary. "Tudor can also be found commentating on Radio Five cricket every now and then, when Gatting, Gooch, Stewart et al have something better to do," says Alex Walter.

19th over: Australia 67–1 (Hayden 32, Ponting 2) The run-rate has slowed right down after Giles's strike. "As someone who's fairly new to this cricket lark (I know, I know, a bit like football fans who only watch internationals) can anyone tell me why bowlers appear to rarely make international captains?" asks Mark Douglas. "Is it their sullen, unpredictable manner perhaps?"

20th over: Australia 73–1 (Hayden 33, Ponting 7) Hayden is perhaps a little overly keen to try and work Giles away down the leg-side and would have been relieved to have handed his partner the strike after a tough couple of deliveries. Ponting takes his cue and times Giles to the extra-cover boundary in style.

And that is tea – Australia 73–1 (Hayden 33, Ponting 7): Back to the pavilion for some mid-afternoon munchies. The wicket of Langer was a crucial strike for England, who were just starting to struggle in the field. I'm off for some mid-afternoon munchies of my own.

England 444; Australia 73–1

The evening session

BY MIKE ADAMSON

Preamble: England need some wickets. Soon.

WICKET! 21st over: Ponting c Bell b S Jones 7 (Australia 73–2) That'll do nicely. The Adamson curse is broken. First ball of the session leaps on Ponting, flies off the shoulder of his bat and loops to Ian Bell at point. A great start.

22nd over: Australia 75–2 (Hayden 34, Martyn 1) A good, tight start to the session from Ashley Giles, conceding just two singles. He even manages to turn one (only a few inches, but it's a start). "Your jinx thing," begins Tom Chivers. "As far as I can tell it's only worked its dubious magic on the English batsmen so far. Now that England are in the field, will that mean they're getting slogged for 20 an over, or could it possibly always work against the batting side? What are your thoughts? Aussies all out for 85, anyone?"

23rd over: Australia 81–2 (Hayden 34, Martyn 1) Simon Jones bowls one slightly down the leg-side, which his namesake at wicketkeeper elects to let go under his body for four byes. Anyone who says his keeping has improved needs their eyes testing. "I'm currently researching the long history of rubbish adverts involving England cricketers," says Charles Heymann. "Vaughan's current radio ads for 'Asda mums' is a particularly unwelcome addition, as is Lamb and Botham's lame double act for British meat. Can anyone else recall others?" Anyone?

WICKET! 24th over: Hayden lbw b Giles 34 (Australia 82–3) Don't stand there shaking your head, Hayden. Get back to the pavilion. That was what Ashley Giles and umpire Billy Bowden should have said after the Australian was hit on the pad in line with the off stump (though it was close) by another spinner from the King of Spain. With Michael Clarke unlikely to bat because of his back injury, the tourists might now be looking anxiously at the follow-on target.

25th over: Australia 90–3 (Katich 7, Martyn 3) A fantastic piece of fielding at second slip from Flintoff, but only to prevent four runs rather than claim another wicket. "Botham's uninspiring Shredded Wheat ads for a starter," chips in Stephen Hakansson. "He doesn't even look healthy after walking from Land's End to John o'Groats."

26th over: Australia 94–3 (Katich 11, Martyn 3) Another big shout for lbw from Ashley Giles and his pals, but Billy Bowden shakes his head this time as the ball wasn't doing enough. "How about the one with Graham Gooch advertising the hair loss remedy?" says Andrew Pooley. "I think it was only in newspapers and magazines, but was nevertheless truly awful." It certainly was.

27th over: Australia 94–3 (Katich 11, Martyn 3) A maiden from Jones, bowling a probing line in the so-called "corridor of uncertainty". "You just referred to 'another spinner from the King of Spain'," writes Stuart Youngs, who claims to have a cricket team named after him. "This in itself implies that more than one has already spun. How many is he up to in the game and for your anoraks out there what is the most amount of deliveries that Gilo has ever managed to spin in a Test? I'm guessing nine." That could be generous, I think.

28th over: Australia 98–3 (Katich 14, Martyn 4) The last couple of overs have been rather quiet, so let's just take a moment to enjoy the fact that we are level in an Ashes series with Australia, and have the upper hand in this Test . . . Now back to the emails: "I went to the Great British Beer Festival last week," writes Peter Coyne, "and the programme included a painfully cringe-making one-page ad with Freddie Flintoff casually propping up the bar with some cask ale or other."

29th over: Australia 109–3 (Katich 14, Martyn 15) Martyn brings up the Australia hundred with an excellent cut shot. And then adds another four with a drive square of the wicket. "Is it me, or is Rob Key not a walking advert for the complete Ginsters catalogue?" asks Charlie Wilson.

30th over: Australia 113–3 (Katich 15, Martyn 18) An outstanding sprawling stop on the boundary from Andrew Flintoff halts proceedings for a minute while the third umpire has a look at the replay, and decides to award Australia just three runs. Good work, big fella. "I think Bob Willis should do an advert for the Samaritans," says Paul Edginton, "as his commentaries must be responsible for a fair portion of the people who phone them."

31st over: Australia 113–3 (Katich 15, Martyn 18) Flintoff is rewarded for his fine fielding by being given a bowl, and responds by turning in a maiden. For those who are asking, the follow-on target in Test cricket is worked out by subtracting 200 from the total, and adding one. Therefore Australia need to score 245. "There's no better feeling than waking up in Florida to sun, 30–degree heat, a swimming pool, OBO reports of the King of Spain turning a delivery and the news that the Aussies are fearing the follow-on," writes Andrew Ward, who confesses to be ignoring the sun, 30–degree heat and swimming pool on holiday to follow the OBO.

32nd over: Australia 115–3 (Katich 17, Martyn 18) Gilo turns another one (that's three) which strikes Katich's pad and induces another big, but fruitless, appeal. "So Stuart Youngs has a cricket team named after him," says Julian Coleman bitterly. "And a royal house. And a half-decent bitter. All I get is a poxy mustard. And they can't even spell that right. Life's not fair."

WICKET! 33rd over: Katich b Flintoff 17 (Australia 115–4) Katich chooses to leave the first ball after the drinks break, which proves to be a big mistake as Flintoff gets one to swing back into the left-hander and uproot the off stump. "Don't be doing down Iberian Royalty," orders Nick Evans. "Gilo has the straight one and the quicker straight one. That bloke Warne has only got two up his sleeve as well, and he does all right."

34th over: Australia 120–4 (Martyn 19, Gilchrist 4) Gilchrist is promoted to No. 6 in the absence of Michael Clarke. And, incidentally, he's moved to four without me noticing. "Mike," says Lyndon Hills. "You write that the follow-on target is worked out by subtracting 200 from the total, and adding one. So why not just subtract 199?" Hmmm, I suppose you could do that.

35th over: Australia 129–4 (Martyn 20, Gilchrist 12) Adam Gilchrist edges one to second slip. Unfortunately, Marcus Trescothick, standing in as captain for Michael Vaughan who's gone off for a pit-stop, has elected not to have a second slip for some reason, so the batsman picks up four. "Julian Coleman also has a range of camping gas stoves named after him," says Thomas De Vecchi helpfully. "Surely walkers and mountaineers have praised his name on many occasions in cold, wet and remote locations."

WICKET! 36th over: Martyn b Giles 20 (Australia 129–5) Anything Shane Warne can do, the King of Spain can do, er, almost as well. Martyn is clean bowled by one which pitched in the rough outside leg stump and turned (that's four) a good couple of feet.

37th over: Australia 132–5 (Gilchrist 14, Warne 1) Bell drops Gilchrist. Flintoff is again causing the Australian a great deal of trouble, as he has done all series. Meanwhile, my colleague James Dart has labelled Giles's delivery in the previous over "the ball of the century", bearing in mind that Warne's ball to Gatting at Old Trafford in 1993 was, obviously, in the last century. "Messrs Youngs & Coleman should think themselves honoured," writes Malcolm Dunn. "I'm named after a defunct old man's clothes shop (nice caps though)."

38th over: Australia 135–5 (Gilchrist 15, Warne 2) An incredibly quick over from Giles yields two runs. "We are witnessing the end of the Australian dynasty," says Dominic Rowles. "It will be like when Kennedy was shot; where were you when England finished the Aussie upstarts. Drinking a cup of tea, avoiding real work in my case."

39th over: Australia 139–5 (Gilchrist 15, Warne 6) Channel 4 have just produced an interesting statistic, which is that Australia haven't been forced to follow on for 17 years (1988, Karachi, v Pakistan for those anoraks among you). Warne moves Australia four runs closer to maintaining that record with a streaky shot through cover. "Looks like we took a wicket with the first ball after the tea-break," says Daniel Ashley, "and then again with the first ball after the drinks break. I think we need another break of some sort. Any ideas from the army of OBO readers?" It has to be a streaker, I suppose. Any volunteers (not that I am encouraging that kind of thing)?

40th over: Australia 142–5 (Gilchrist 17, Warne 7) Another false shot from Gilchrist trying to drive Giles down the ground. His dragged inside edge just misses the stumps. "I have a small town near Paisley where Old Firm footie players live and the city with the highest obesity rate in America both named after me. Also, my name is featured in the tagline for a space-based Hollywood blockbuster. Despite all this, people still spell my name Huston. Perhaps printing my name in your OBO will increase its profile sufficiently so people learn to spell it. Here's hoping." So says James Hus. . . sorry, James Houston.

41st over: Australia 144–5 (Gilchrist 18, Warne 7) Gilchrist calls a reluctant Warne through for a single after stroking the ball out to the sweeper on the cover boundary. Reluctant because Flintoff is giving Warne a good going-over with some fierce short stuff. "I've just discovered that I've got an Australian seamer called Shane named after me," says Jon Harwood. "Now that's depressing."

42nd over: Australia 148–5 (Gilchrist 22, Warne 7) Another head-in-hands moment. Giles tempts Gilchrist to go after him by tossing one up, the batsman obliges but mistimes the shot and only just clears the man waiting for that very shot. "Let's hope England choose not to make Australia follow on," says Alun Parsons. "Do we want to be facing Warne in the fourth innings chasing, say, 100? Let's try to get 500–odd ahead."

43rd over: Australia 152–5 (Gilchrist 22, Warne 11) Steve Harmison is brought back into the attack and his first ball is met by an aggressive stroke down the ground by Warne. "I think I've just upset the NHS's patient records system in Southwark by over-zealously refreshing Internet Explorer," says Justin McLintock. "It'll be OK?" Let's hope so, Justin.

44th over: Australia 156–5 (Gilchrist 22, Warne 12) Tense moments as Steve Bucknor calls for the third umpire after a run-out appeal. Warne is relieved to see the words "not out" flash up on the big screen. "Don't talk to me about family names," says Chris Armstrong. "One of my uncles landed on the moon, the other reckoned he could play a trumpet. I'm an IT geek, can you imagine the disappointment my parents are feeling?" Your cousin's quite a good cyclist as well, isn't he?

Drinks break: Here's your break, Daniel Ashley (over 39). Will it lead to another break-through?

45th over: Australia 162–5 (Gilchrist 23, Warne 17) A good over from Harmison, but he's still wicketless in this innings. And then, to rub it in, Warne cracks the last ball of the over past point for four. "Jon Harwood should consider himself fortunate not to be one vowel away from a celebrity butler," says Paul Birrell. "I have to make the same joke every time someone asks me for my full name. It's hell."

46th over: Australia 163–5 (Gilchrist 24, Warne 17) Giles turns another one a long way out of the footmarks, forcing Warne to play and miss, but the ball misses the off stump by millimetres. "It never ceases to amaze me how England fans are unable to contain themselves when something goes their way, however briefly," Fintan Gleeson says. "It also never ceases to amuse me when things inevitably go wrong, as it will. The Aussies are certainties for the Ashes. England fans should be force-fed all the arrogant nonsense they are currently polluting the commentary with." It's only fair to give the Australians a chance to reply, isn't it?

47th over: Australia 177–5 (Gilchrist 29, Warne 21) Short and wide: not where you want to be bowling to Gilchrist, Mr Harmison. "Are you kidding me?" asks Stuart Youngs. Not intentionally, Stuart. "Chris Armstrong writes in and we're talking about moon landings and Tour de France victors? I think the fact that his namesake was a perennially over-rated striker is the real news."

48th over: Australia 182–5 (Gilchrist 30, Warne 25) A lovely shot from Warne, tracking Giles and then planting him into the stand via one bounce off the grass.

WICKET! 49th over: Gilchrist c G Jones b S Jones 30 (Australia 182–6) The Joneses have teamed up to dismiss Gilchrist. Simon Jones's first ball back into the attack seams away from the batsman, finds his outside edge and provides a regulation catch for Geraint Jones.

50th over: Australia 190–6 (Warne 34, Clarke 2) The new batsman is Michael Clarke, who has Matthew Hayden as his runner due to a back injury. Which gets me thinking: does anyone know if there's been an occasion when both batsmen have had a runner, so that all the runs have actually been performed off the square?

51st over: Australia 196–6 (Warne 35, Clarke 7) Clarke doesn't look impeded by his injury as he strokes the ball elegantly past mid-off for three. "I'd like to thank Fintan Gleeson for his most worthy sentiments on over 46," says Richard House, and I can detect a note of sarcasm in his voice. "Should any OBO readers meet him in the pub tonight, kindly buy him a drink on my behalf. He'll need one."

52nd over: Australia 196–6 (Warne 35, Clarke 7) Giles really is bowling very well, extracting both turn and bounce from a dry pitch. "In one of Fred Trueman's books he tells a very funny story when two tail-enders in a county game both had runners," says Damian Hocking. "In the ensuing confusion a run-out occurred with all four batsman at the one end."

WICKET! 53rd over: Clarke c Flintoff b S Jones 7 (Australia 197–7) Simon Jones's slower ball proves Clarke's undoing as his attempted slog is mistimed and falls to the ecstatic Flintoff.

54th over: Australia 206–7 (Warne 43, Gillespie 2) Shane Warne is commanding respect here, carrying the fight to England almost single-handedly. He follows up a huge six off Ashley Giles with a single to long-off to retain the strike.

55th over: Australia 209–7 (Warne 44, Gillespie 4) Another testing over from Flintoff, but the tail-enders are providing strong resistance. "Talking of arrogance I read in several places Australian predictions of a 3–0 or 4–0 series win, with only the weather preventing Australia winning 5–0," said Alun Parsons. "My experience of life is that there's no such thing as a certainty. Let's hope pride comes before a fall for Fintan Gleeson."

56th over: Australia 210–7 (Warne 45, Gillespie 4) The fielders crowd the batsman in the last over of the day in the hope of obtaining one final wicket, but Gillespie sees it through. It's been another good day for England, who walk off to a standing ovation from the Old Trafford crowd.

Australia 210–7; England 444

Third Day

The morning session

BY ROB SMYTH

Preamble – rain stopped play: Morning all. It's a beautiful day: England might – just might – be within sniffing distance of the Ashes, United are on at 12.15, Smyth is back on the horse, and the sun is shining over Farringdon. If not Old Trafford, where it's pelting down.

An email, which admittedly isn't funny but it is informative and what more can you want? "Hello Rob," says Matthew Cobb. "From [trendy] Chorlton, just down the road from Old Trafford, I can report that it has just stopped raining, and the West is starting to look lighter. It is blustery and very damp. Could easily rain again by 10.30."

10.30am Like a particularly zealous stripper's thong, the covers are coming off, and it looks good for play at around approximately 11:12:34. So.

Inspection due at 11am . . . as I wrestle with, on the one hand, wanting England to get as much time as possible to nail these sub-standard Aussies and, on the other, quite like the idea of it pouring down so I can go and watch Everton v. United at 12.15. I'm a bad man.

Another email as Mark Nicholas speculates that play will begin at about 12.30 "You sound like a bad man," says Katy Robinson. "You also sound quite cute! I imagine you look like Damien Martyn. Am I right?" Not so much warm as Siberian. I'm thinking Damien Martyn meets Dennis Pennis meets Arjen Robben meets

Seth Cohen meets Chris Evans. But I'm not ginger, before you think that; *strawberry* blond.

It's effing raining And heavily, too. Here's an email to cool the cockles while I go and do something else. "Oh dear," begins Barnaby. "Katy Robinson sounds like the kind of woman who only picks men she thinks she can tame. Bad but cute? Why do women do that? Still, at least we now know where her interest in horses comes from."

11.25am "Now without trying to sound harsh," lies James Green, " I am of the view that strawberry blond is almost worse than being ginger! You see if you were ginger at least people would make fun of you but as a strawberry blond no one knows what to say: do we make fun of you for being blond or ginger?!" No, you bow down at my strawberry blond feet.

In response to Barnaby, by the omnipresent Katy Robinson "Oops Barnaby – did I hit a nerve?! Are you good but cute? You're wrong, anyway as my ideal man would be one of the current Aussie team: from what I can see, they come already tamed. As for horses, my interest peaked at My Little Pony, I'm afraid, and I quickly swapped Apple Jack for Action Man anyway." I can send you each other's email addresses if you really really really wanna zig-a-zig-ahhhhhh.

11.42am Lunch is at 12, with no immediate prospect of play thereafter. With every minute the need for England to enforce the follow-on – if they have the chance – becomes greater. If these substandard Australians get away from here at 1–1, and GD McGrath is fully fit for Trent Bridge, the pendulum may swing again.

That's lunch I'm off. Thanks for keeping me entertained during the inaction.

Australia 210–7; England 444

The afternoon session

BY ROB SMYTH

Preamble: No play this morning, and no prospect of any this afternoon, but my good mood persists. Although not very clearly, clearly. "Hello," says Rachel Hayes, "you sound desperately in need of cheering up. *Deadwood* season one might do it, but only in the sense of 'Thank God I don't live there' . . . PS A mate of mine claims to have strawberry blond hair. As I say to him, a man saying this sounds a bit weedy, and anyway, it's just a pale ginger colour when you get down to it. Deal with it!" Nature beat me to the punch, chino.

Who says it's grim up north? "Should've posted my emails then, you twonk," says Leeds fan Steve Churnin. "As it is, the blows to my confidence as a result of non-publication have stopped me emailing. Or have they? (clearly not). Actually do you mind just making the cricket scores up? I'm pretty bored here."

GIRLS ALOUD ARE ON CD:UK!! No word of a lie.

I'm off to do the football As it looks like there's no prospect of play. If there is, I'm up a certain creek sans paddle. Until then, follow Everton v. United on guardian.co.uk/football, should you be that way inclined.

BAH! I can't do the football as I can't get effing Premiership effing Plus. Great. And yes, it is still raining in Manchester. Probably. I don't actually know this as Channel 4 have the effing gee-gees on.

12.50pm The absolute earliest there'll be play is 2.00. I'm off for some lunch. Toot toot.

1.51pm It's still raining, by the bucketload. I suspect we won't get any play today. None. Zip. Beggar all. Those sub-standard Aussies may get off the hook here.

2.10pm A brief break to talk some cricket. Overnight I didn't think the follow-on was too important, but now the little passage of play when this game resumes is absolutely crucial: England simply *must* enforce the follow-on. Australia need 35 runs, England three wickets. It'll be a huge boost to these sub-standard Aussies to get out of this one alive.

That's tea Effectively. The inspection is planned for 3.30, so I'd have thought the earliest we'll get play – if at all – is 4.30. So I'm off until 3.30. See you then.

Australia 214–7; England 444

The evening session

BY ROB SMYTH

Preamble: Afternoon chinos. Anyone out there? My email still isn't working you say? Strawberry blond? Ah.

2.56pm Australia have had four runs added to their total because of – heaven forbid – a cock-up from Steve Bucknor yesterday. So 31 to avoid the follow-on if play ever resumes.

The covers are off That's what it says here and I'm sticking to it. Play will resume, erm, quite soon hopefully – the umpires are inspecting at 3.30. Meanwhile, I wore flip-flops to work today – sun was shining, weather was sweet, yeah – but it's now pouring down. I look and feel like a prize prat.

Play will start at 4pm It looks pretty good at Old Trafford – fairly bright, and play can go on potentially until 7pm (there are 38 overs left). Great for England, a sickener for my planned night out, but on balance probably the right decision from the big man above.

57th over: Australia 215–7 (need 245 to avoid follow–on; Warne 46, Gillespie 4) It's slippy and sloshy out there, and Harmison almost goes rear-over-bristol when trying to field Warne's slice to Jones's third ball of the day.

58th over: Australia 216–7 (Warne 47, Gillespie 4) Another single to Warne, then five balls of solid defence from Gillespie. You could barely get a more contrasting pair of lower-order batsmen than these.

59th over: Australia 224–7 (Warne 49, Gillespie 5) Gah! Warne pops one up tantalisingly and it lands just short of cover. The next ball is a bouncer that booms over the head and outstretched arm of the pint-sized Geraint Jones for five wides. "Are your emails working?"

asks James Green. Hup. "Am I talking to myself?" Yup. "Does God have it in for all of English sport?" Nup. "What colour will KP have his hair for the Fourth Test? My guess is it won't be strawberry blond . . ." Shuddup.

60th over: Australia 225–7 (Warne 50, Gillespie 5) Warne, who leads the table for most Test runs without a hundred (he hilariously holed out on 99 back in the day) completes a really good, responsible fifty – amazing what he can do when he doesn't try to welly every ball out of the ground. Here's Dan Hart: "Channel 4 think to take the follow-on, Radio 4 say to not take it. Who's right, and what's the official *Guardian* stance should England bowl them out in time?" Just say no. Don't give these sub-standard Aussies a sniff.

61st over: Australia 227–7 (Warne 50, Gillespie 5) Flintoff on for Jones, and a bat-wobbling maiden – well, it would have been but for a no-ball, and the yorker that Warne chipped for one, and those six sixes that I just made up – to his love-in partner Warne. "Keep rambling," demands Lindsay Chapman, like a female Paulie Walnuts in the Pine Barrens episode of *The Sopranos*.

62nd over: Australia 231–7 (Warne 55, Gillespie 5) Warne makes space to bullet Giles down the ground for four, but there's a twist: Giles *just* couldn't lay a finger on the ball as it flew past, hitting the stumps with Gillespie out of his ground. If Giles got a touch on that – and I think he did with his fingertip, looking at the replay – Gillespie was gone. But like an episode of *Two Pints of Lager* . . . there's worse to follow: Geraint Jones misses a frankly straightforward stumping chance next ball as Warne gives Giles the charge and misses a big roundhouse hoick.

63rd over: Australia 233–7 (Warne 55, Gillespie 7) Gillespie may not be able to bowl a fat bloke downhill at the moment, but he looks very snugly ensconced in dead-bat mode: he has seven off 33 balls now.

64th over: Australia 245–7 (needed 245 to avoid follow–on and effing well got it; Warne 67, Gillespie 7) Two more to Warne, and I don't think there's much danger of England enforcing the follow-on here – especially after Warne bashes Giles over mid-on for a brilliant one-bounce four. Marvellous batting from Warne, and if Giles continues he'll get his first Test hundred today, I think. Or maybe tomorrow: from nowhere, the rain has started teeming down and the players have pegged it off.

An email "This care in the community thing with Geraint Jones as a wicketkeeper has surely run its course by now?" says Mike Atkinson, whose pitiful grasp of grammar is redeemed by a vaguely amusing email. "And now Warne rubs his nose in it, the follow-on is saved and it's raining. Marvellous." You're having a nervous breakdown, aren't you?

Most of the spectators have done one But in the name of professionalism, and in case anyone important logs on, I'm staying till the bitter end. Which should be quite soon: it doesn't look good. Like you losers care: the only email I've had in the last 10 minutes is from 'Free Pizza Party'. Will Summer be there?

They're coming back on! Maybe. It's a lovely evening in Manchester, and the umpires hope to inspect at 5.50pm. And I want to go home.

Play to resume at 6.10pm FOR SIX EFFING OVERS! I COULD HAVE HAD SIX EFFING PINTS BY NOW!

65th over: Australia 246–7 (Warne 67, Gillespie 7) Flintoff starts with an attempted yorker, and Gillespie cocks forward with his beloved smothering defensive stroke. He remains as strokeless as a mangy cat with beer breath for the rest of a probing over, save a little deflection to fine leg off the last ball.

66th over: Australia 246–7 (Warne 67, Gillespie 7) The Ashley Giles story continues with an umbrella of close-in fielders on the off-side for Gillespie. A maiden, and I think I have an alcohol problem as I'm absolutely gaspin'.

67th over: Australia 254–7 (Warne 69, Gillespie 7) Geraint Jones drops Warne off an absolute sitter! Straightforward nick, and Jones just fumbled it. Frankly that looked embarrassing, but he won't have been helped one little bit by the blinding glare of the evening sun right in his eyeline. Nonetheless, a three-course meal for his critics to dine out on.

68th over: Australia 260–7 (Warne 74, Gillespie 7) Giles into the rough to Warne, who dances down the track and clubs it back over Giles's head for four more. Brutal, bold, brilliant.

69th over: Australia 261–7 (Warne 75, Gillespie 7) The penultimate over of the day is nicely bowled by Flintoff, but Gillespie plays killjoy with the deadest of dead bats.

70th over: Australia 264–7 (trail by 180; Warne 78, Gillespie 7) That's it; I'm off to get hammered. It's been . . . well, it's been pretty non-existent, but a pleasure nonetheless. See you back here tomorrow morning for Shane Warne's first Test century.

Australia 261–7; England 444

Fourth Day

The morning session

BY ROB SMYTH

Preamble: Morning one, morning one. Welcome to another massive day in this barnstorming series. There are huge patches of rough developing now, so if Australia get to within 100 of England, it could be a very interesting match. These Aussies may be sub-standard, but I wouldn't write them off just yet – especially with the remarkable Mr Warne at the very peak of his magical powers.

Today's riff A Britpop special. In a frankly humbling development, it's exactly 10 years since a young, lithe, centre-partinged Smyth rushed to Parrott Records in Canterbury in his lunchtime to buy 'Roll With It' (but not Country House; Oasis always did the better B-sides back in the day, and I always empathised with the Manc skanks). It was the zenith of Britpop, and it brings a tear to the eye. So, today, favourite Britpop memories – Northern Uproar? Louise Wener looking staggeringly attractive (and very cold) on that Lamacq-presented Britpop Now programme? Those ironic pink 'Take That Love You' T-shirts? *Select* magazine? Bluetonic? The chorus on 'Daydreamer'? Ooh I'm getting all warm and nostalgic now. I could almost drink a warm can of Carling.

71st over: Australia 268–7 (Warne 80, Gillespie 8) Frederico Flintoff starts the day with a no-ball and then Gillespie edges just short of slip, as debate rages as to who should bowl at the other end. Meanwhile, two questions: does anyone know if the P&P in Fulham is any good as I'm going there tonight? And any recommendations for my now-finally-working iTunes?

72nd over: Australia 270–7 (Warne 81, Gillespie 9) It is Harmison, and no alarms for Australia so far, as the trickle of emails eat into my already fragile sense of self-worth. "Canterbury????" chuckles Brian Wellings. "Was that you I saw then, ten years ago, lying unconscious outside the Three Tuns in Watling Street, clutching a warm Carling in one hand and bag of indie singles in the other?" Depends – was I wearing a pink Take That Love You T-shirt? Did I look like Damon Albarn? Someone told me I did once, back in the Britpop day. I don't any more, though our hairlines have remained close friends.

73rd over: Australia 276–7 (Warne 82, Gillespie 12) More Rackemannesque (Sydney '91, anyway) defence from Gillespie, who I wish would just rack off. This is becoming a seriously irritating partnership, and what's more alarming still is that England just don't look like taking a wicket. As for Warne's hundred, he seems determined to get 'em in singles. (Insert your own seriously unfunny lame gag here.)

74th over: Australia 278–7 (Warne 83, Gillespie 12) England are basically waiting for the new ball here – only one slip for Harmison to Warne, who chinese cuts for another single. Seventeen to go, and I hope he gets them because he has played beautifully. Then I hope he twangs a swinger during an unorthodox, borderline depraved and stupidly over-zealous celebration, is unable to bowl in the second innings, and England romp to victory by 244 runs.

75th over: Australia 279–7 (Warne 84, Gillespie 12) Flintoff. Gillespie. Maiden. Thanks, incidentally, for all your iTunes recommendations – they were all rubbish. "Britpop was dire with hindsight wasn't it?" says Olly Winkles, relieving himself all over my nostalgic parade. "Except for the wonderful Dodgy of course. *Free Peace Sweet* was the soundtrack to my post-A-Level summer, and is possibly the worst-named album in history." Dodgy?! Very droll. They were rubbish and they had a fat comedy drummer, so . . . Meanwhile, that's a good riff: worst album name ever. Two nominations: Sugar – *File Under Easy Listening*; and Smashing Pumpkins – *Mellon Collie and the Infinite Sadness*.

76th over: Australia 283–7 (Warne 86, Gillespie 13) England just haven't been at it this morning – this pair have added 82 now – though hopefully they can clean up with the second new ball in four overs' time. "Morning!!!" says Phil Hackett. "Your updates are a godsend as I'm in work without a telly." Me too; it's a bummer hah?

WICKET! 77th over: Warne c Giles b S Jones 90 (Australia 287–8) Simon Jones comes into the attack, and Warne cuts his first ball up and over for four. Shot! Then he falls next ball, hooking straight to Giles on the squareleg fence. I may well be the only Englishman who is sad at that outcome – it was a wonderful innings, and Warne deserved his first Test hundred. "Easy winner," says Dom Booth, in reference to the Worst Album Titles . . . Ever!!!!! "*Now Phats what i Small music* by those comedy house muppets Phats & Small. Another in a similar ilk: *A Salt with a dealy Pepper*. Nice."

78th over: Australia 291–8 (Gillespie 17, Lee 0) Now that Warne's gone, it's safe for Gilo to come out from behind the sofa: his second ball is chipped tantalisingly over the blundering Hoggard at mid-off by Gillespie.

79th over: Australia 291–8 (Gillespie 17, Lee 0) Only a big inside-edge saves Brett Lee from being cleaned up by a Jones swinger. "I'm sort of distraught about that," says Cricinfo's Andrew Miller. "Been reduced to a right messed-up bundle of emotions this summer!" Darn tootin'. Two English cricket writers. Feeling sympathy. For Shane Warne. Fat cocky bleached-blond quintessential Aussie Shane Warne. When he gets himself out. In the nineties. What the fugg?

80th over: Australia 293–8 (Gillespie 18, Lee 1) "Nice coverage," says Ian Robinson, beginning with the now obligatory sycophantic lie to ensure publication, and ignoring the fact I've just had Jones batting for Australia for the last four overs. "My fave Britpop moment came when Blur played Brixton on the rollercoaster tour with Jesus & Mary Chain, My Bloody Valentine and Dinosaur Jnr. As their set reached a psyched-out climax, a very fresh-faced Damon pulled his trousers and pants down and just stood with his genitalia exposed to all and sundry. A rather limp claim to fame but hey. And before you ask, it was a fair size." Chino, I know how big the Brixton Academy is – I used to live there.

WICKET! 81st over: Lee c Trescothick b S Jones 1 (Australia 293–9) The new cherry is due, but Vaughan – in my opinion correctly, though Michael Slater disagrees and what does he know – decides to give Simon Jones one more over, maybe two, with the old ball. And in a rare development, I'm spot on: Jones moves one away nicely, Lee edges, and Trescothick takes a lovely diving, two-handed catch at slip to give Jones a richly deserved five-for, his first in Tests in England. Good bowling, good captaincy, even better commentary I'm sure you'll all disagree.

81st over: Australia 293–9 (Gillespie 18, McGrath 0) "The point about Warne is that you're not alone," says Matthew Cobb. "As CMJ pointed out on *TMS*: the whole of the (real) Old Trafford crowd rightly gave him a standing ovation. You don't get that in footy." Wrong! United fans gave Ronaldo a standing ovation after his hat-trick for Real Madrid at OT in 2003, so . . . That said, there's been a really heart-warming chivalry about this series. Now I hope we bash the bejeesus out of these sub-standard convicts.

82nd over: Australia 294–9 (Gillespie 19, McGrath 0) That wicket also took Jones's Test average below 30, which is a fair effort. Meanwhile, anyone remember Popsicle? I only have one album of theirs – I can't even remember what it's called – but it's utterly brilliant.

83rd over: Australia 294–9 (Gillespie 19, McGrath 0) Jones beats Gillespie's attempted force with a climbing, kicking rip-snorter of an off-cutter. Maiden, and drinks. "Good morning from Chicago, Illinois," chirps Ben Ogden. "It's 5am." No it's not. "I'm watching live via the web, and your OBO coverage is far more enthralling than the 'action' I paid $100 for . . . BTW, the worst album title ever? How about REO Speedwagon's *You can Tune a piano but you can't Tuna fish* . . . or have I just aged myself?" You're making these up now aren't you?

84th over: Australia 296–9 (Gillespie 20, McGrath 1) Harmison comes on, though still with only one slip!

WICKET! 85th over: Gillespie lbw b S Jones 26 (Australia 302 all out) Jason Gillespie – stonewaller, only ever defends, boring as a jam with Travis and that fat fella from Keane. Just pulled Jones imperiously in front of square for six was that? Blimey. England's response is to take the new ball immediately, and Jones pins Gillespie in front – Hawkeye had it going *that* far over the top – with a fine off-cutter to finish with Test-best figures of 6 for 53. England's lead is a healthy 142.

England second innings

1st over: England 2–0 (led by 142 on first innings; Trescothick 1, Strauss 1) These sub-standard Aussies are even copying our field placing now: McGrath has an absurd mid-off for Trescothick, just as Hoggard has had for Hayden. "Here's one for the Britpop debate," says Joe Stead. "What was Echobelly's famous song? After having found the album gathering dust last week we listened to it and couldn't recognise any of the songs. Was there an at least slightly attractive singer that might explain this, can't remember that either." Blimey, anything else, Joe? Want me to wash your swingers while I'm here? Echobelly: yes, and yes. Famous song was the impossibly chipper "Great Things". ("King of the Kerb" did well too.) Singer was Sonia Aurora-Madan, or some such.

2nd over: England 4–0 (Trescothick 1, Strauss 2) Déjà vu as Lee's bouncer pins Strauss flush on the grille – and draws blood under his ear – as he pulls away from a hook shot. Oof. "My nomination would go to the horribly named *The Unauthorised Biography of Reinhold Messner* by the otherwise magnificent Ben Folds Five," says Ben Hendy. "God knows why they went for that mouthful."

3rd over: England 4–0 (Trescothick 1, Strauss 2) Strauss edges McGrath a fraction short of Ponting at second slip, and England might be happy just to get to lunch without losing any wickets.

4th over: England 11–0 (Trescothick 8, Strauss 2) Really lively stuff from Brett Lee, peaking at about 94mph; when he finally pitches one up, Trescothick slashes airily and leaden-footedly for four behind point.

5th over: England 14–0 (Trescothick 10, Strauss 2) McGrath beats Trescothick with a jaffa, albeit off a no-ball. "Britpop honeys," pants Ian Roberts. "The girl from Salad". Good call. What was her name again? Didn't she present on MTV? Where is she now? Would she like to have coffee?

6th over: England 23–0 (Trescothick 10, Strauss 10) Lee has Strauss exactly where he wants him right now, but sadly a regulation, dangling-bat edge flies at waist height right between those good friends Warne and Ponting at first and second slip. There's a real sense that Strauss has done something to offend the Aussies –

Warne has had words all series, Lee's having angry words now – though heaven knows what as he's about as inoffensive as they come.

7th over: England 25–0 (Trescothick 12, Strauss 10) "Come on, Warney, get us going here," drawls Adam Gilchrist, and that sums it up. Never in his illustrious career has Warne oozed such talismanic qualities as now. Australia are all leaning on his shoulders, looking for the inspiration to drag themselves back into this game.

8th over: England 26–0 (Trescothick 12, Strauss 11) "Salad singer," says David Mainwaring. "Marijne van der Vlugt! Blimey!" Right, enough of the perving – we have a cricket match on this afternoon. England lead by 168, and I'm off for a spot of lunch.

Australia 302; England 444 and 26–0

The afternoon session

BY ROB SMYTH

Preamble: Here we go again then.

9th over: England 32–0 (Trescothick 16, Strauss 13) Quiet first over from McGrath after lunch, as I privately and then publicly lament the unfulfilled promise of last night's outing.

10th over: England 41–0 (Trescothick 25, Strauss 13) Trescothick greets Lee with a crunching cut stroke for four, and then slams a pull imperiously through midwicket for another. England lead by 183; should they declare now against these sub-standard Aussies?

11th over: England 42–0 (Trescothick 27, Strauss 12) It is pretty bizarre that Warne isn't bowling – I'm sure he will be soon – and his inexplicable exclusion from the attack until half-way through the afternoon session on the first day takes on more sinister connotations in the context of the alleged contretemps between Warne and Ponting at Edgbaston.

12th over: England 47–0 (Trescothick 27, Strauss 16) Strauss absolutely clatters a short, wide delivery from Brett Lee over the top for four. Cracking shot. "Well," begins a sympathetic Glenn Perry, "it's your own fault for wearing those flip-flops out at night-time, Rob." Fashion comes at a price.

13th over: England 52–0 (Trescothick 31, Strauss 16) Tresco is playing really nicely here (usually the cue for a flat-footed waft); there he times McGrath deliciously to the midwicket fence.

14th over: England 59–0 (Trescothick 36, Strauss 17) Trescothick steers Lee deliberately over the slips for four to take England's lead to 200, and Australia are under the hammer here all right. The non-use of Warne is bewildering.

15th over: England 64–0 (Trescothick 41, Strauss 17) Warne comes on at last, and Trescothick makes an impressive statement of intent by smearing his first ball over midwicket for four. It might end in tears, but who cares: England need fast runs, and whether they lost one wicket or 10 is an irrelevance. Unless they're bowled out for 64 of course.

WICKET! 16th over: Trescothick b McGrath 41 (England 64–1) After 10 days of Frank Spencerish slapstick, Glenn McGrath was due some luck, and he got some there. Trescothick played an orthodox defensive stroke, but as he set off to look for a quick single, the ball bounced up and then looped on to the top of his stumps. The end of a good innings.

16th over: England 66–1 (Strauss 17, Vaughan 1) Vaughan leans into his second ball outside off like a chav on a dancefloor and is only denied a boundary by a cracking diving stop from specialist gully fielder Matthew Hayden.

17th over: England 70–1 (Strauss 17, Vaughan 5) Nice shot from Vaughan, who works Warne through midwicket for his first boundary.

18th over: England 71–1 (Strauss 18, Vaughan 5) McGrath trots in gently around the wicket and beats Strauss with the ease of a man conducting an experiment on a dying ant (which is admittedly only dying because he's just stamped on it) just to kill five minutes.

19th over: England 72–1 (Strauss 19, Vaughan 5) Strauss is playing Warne immaculately from the non-striker's end here. No emails for ages, so . . .

20th over: England 77–1 (Strauss 22, Vaughan 7) Lovely shot from Strauss, clipping McGrath through midwicket for three more.

21st over: England 78–1 (led by 142 on first innings; Strauss 23, Vaughan 7) Cat and mouse at the moment, as England try to milk Warne without taking too many risks at this stage. They nearly lose a wicket anyway, Vaughan chipping to mid-off where Brad Hodge takes a diving catch on the bounce.

22nd over: England 85–1 (lead by 227 now; Strauss 25, Vaughan 12) A moment to sum up Jason Gillespie's tour. Vaughan went up and over off McGrath, and Gillespie, running round at third man, fumbled an absolutely routine take over the boundary. That was the work of a broken man.

23rd over: England 86–1 (Strauss 26, Vaughan 12) Warne beats Strauss with a cracker that rips back out of the rough and also keeps a fraction low.

24th over: England 91–1 (Strauss 31, Vaughan 12) A rollocking pull from Strauss off McGrath brings him his most convincing boundary of the day. "Your efforts are being appreciated here by me in Tokyo, though you may be amazed how few people are interested, in a city of 28 million," says Simon Collins. "Are we really going to beat the Aussies?" I fear we might, you know, though even if we win this game (as we should), it'd be very dangerous to write them off. For a start, I don't think the Jason Gillespie buffet will be on show in the next Test. At the moment it's like that time at school when you hear the girl you fancy fancies you. It couldn't possibly actually happen, couldn't really be true. Could it?

25th over: England 93–1 (Strauss 34, Vaughan 12) There's still an element of the learner driver about Strauss's attempts to play Warne, but here he forces nicely through the covers for two.

WICKET! 26th over: Vaughan c sub (Hodge) b Lee 14 (England 97–2) Still no sign of Gillespie, as Lee replaces McGrath, but the decision is justified with the wicket of Michael Vaughan. Lee dug it in, and Vaughan just helped it on its way down to fine leg, where Brad Hodge judged an awkward chance superbly.

26th over: England 99–2 (led by 142 on first innings; Strauss 36, Bell 1)

27th over: England 100–2 (Strauss 36, Bell 2) Here's Matthew Innes. "You might want to replace 'led by' with 'lead by'. Also, your quips about your drinking have me rolling about on the floor. You're such a funny guy! Keep it up! I wish I was your friend." Yeah, wish I was your friend too, pal. England LED by 142 on first innings; they now LEAD by 142 + whatever their second-innings score is.

28th over: England 102–2 (Strauss 37, Bell 3) Bell survives in bizarre circumstances. A short ball from Lee beat his attempted pull stroke to nail him in the breadbasket before flying back, hitting leg stump pretty hard – and not dislodging the bails. "Why don't they put Freddie & Pietersen in to score some quick runs?" says Dom Booth. "With the prospect of a bit of rain and quick runs needed it seems silly not to?" Nah – plenty of time yet, and we're not immune from defeat yet anyway.

29th over: England 104–2 (Strauss 38, Bell 4) It's all pretty quiet at the moment, and England must be careful not to lose too much momentum here: only five runs off the last three overs. "What's it like working on a Sunday?" says Ben Yeoh. "Or is watching England in the lead so unusual, it's not like work at all? Where/what's the most unusual place/times you've had to work?" Probably during the last Ashes series – sat in the *Wisden* offices on my own all night, although I was allowed to work at home for the Christmas/New Year Tests and, erm, fell asleep for about three hours during the first day of the Sydney Test. Shocker.

30th over: England 105–2 (led by 142 on first innings; Strauss 38, Bell 5)

31st over: England 105–2 (Strauss 38, Bell 5) England are definitely starting to stagnate here: six runs from the last five overs now. Bell is in first gear, as you'd expect of a new batsman, while Strauss hasn't got out of second gear all innings, or indeed all series.

32nd over: England 115–2 (Strauss 46, Bell 7) England lead by 250 now, having led by 142 on first innings, and Strauss celebrates by hooking Lee beautifully for six.

33rd over: England 115–2 (Strauss 46, Bell 7) Warne squares Bell up with an absolute beauty, catching him plumb in front in the process. But the ball pitched well outside leg.

34th over: England 119–2 (Strauss 48, Bell 8) Bell hooks Lee airily but safely over square leg. Not a particularly good shot. In fact, a rubbish one. England lead by 261.

35th over: England 128–2 (led by 142 on first innings; Strauss 57, Bell 8) Strauss moves to his first Test fifty against Australia with an emphatic slog-sweep off Warne; he's still nowhere near his fluent best, but this performance represents a firm step in the right direction. Sufficiently empowered, he dances down to drive Warne through midwicket for four. Shot! And that's tea.

Australia 302; England 444 and 128–2

The evening session

BY ROB SMYTH

Preamble: England lead by 270, there are 48 overs left, and all is well. The worry, however, is that Australia will get offered the light sooner rather than later when they get asked to bat again, so depending on the weather it might be worth England batting on well past 400 so they can post ultra-attacking fields tomorrow. But in an ideal world they'd want to bat for, say, 25 more overs to bash another 130 and then have 20 overs at these sub-standard Aussies tonight.

36th over: England 132–2 (first–innings lead: 142; Strauss 61, Bell 8) Gillespie gets his first bowl of the innings, and Strauss rocks back to slam him over point for four. "Alright Rob," says Tom Crane. "Am I the only one who finds the 'betfair blokes' really annoying? It's bad enough having to live with ad breaks in the cricket but those two goons really get on my wick!" To be fair, the 'I bet you have a bet in the next five seconds' ad made me snigger the first time I saw it. By the 144th it had me contemplating self-harm with a blunt pencil, but I suppose you can't have everything.

37th over: England 132–2 (Strauss 61, Bell 8) Maiden from Warne to Bell, who needs to get his skates on here, risks or no risks: he currently has eight from 37 balls.

38th over: England 134–2 (Strauss 63, Bell 8) Gillespie gets an official warning from Billy Bowden, I suspect for his Nickelback haircut but it might have been for running on the pitch.

39th over: England 137–2 (Strauss 65, Bell 9) Warne turns one ball an absolute mile across Strauss and past leg stump; this all bodes well for Gilo getting stuck into the four left-handers in the Aussie top six tomorrow.

40th over: England 139–2 (Strauss 65, Bell 10) Ian Bell has moved into selfish territory now: 10 off 41 balls just is not acceptable in the context of the match. In fact it's reprehensible, particularly with KP and Freddie twiddling bats, thumbs and who knows what else in the dressing-room.

41st over: England 140–2 (Strauss 66, Bell 10) Make that 10 off 44 balls for Bell, the man who said "I've got all the shots" in a recent interview in SPIN magazine. Maybe you'd care to share a couple with us then?

42nd over: England 142–2 (Strauss 67, Bell 11) I've seen more urgency in that weird dream I had the other night in which Hetty Wainthrop and Hilda Ogden had a fantasy mud wrestle. Two off the over, and that's 14 off six overs since tea.

43rd over: England 156–2 (Strauss 73, Bell 15) The slug Olympics continue, with one off Gillespie's ove- hang on, Strauss has wellied him over extra cover for four. That's more like it. Chuck in a rash of no-balls and a decent Bell push for three, and England take 14 from the over. "I hate to obsess about Gillespie's hair, but he OBVIOUSLY dyes it," says Dom Booth. "You could see less prominent roots on a badger!"

44th over: England 166–2 (Strauss 74, Bell 25) Gilchrist's excellent chance misses with a missed stumping. Bell came down the wicket to Warne, missed completely and was well out of the ground as the ball kicked past Gilchrist for four runs (even though Bell almost certainly didn't hit it). Later in the over Bell gets away with a choked club over midwicket. Four more.

45th over: England 179–2 (Strauss 76, Bell 36) McGrath replaces Gillespie, and Bell cover-drives him exquisitely for four; not once, but twice. Thirteen off the over, and England lead by 321. "What was the spat between Warne and Ponting you referred to in Over

11?" says Alex Porritt. Apparently – and they have since denied it – the two had a big ding-dong over Ponting's decision to bowl first at Edgbaston (and thus depriving Warne of the chance to clean England up on a fourth-innings pitch).

46th over: England 180–2 (first–innings lead: 142; Strauss 77, Bell 36) These sub-standard Aussies really are struggling: Warne decides to do a bit of timewasting, then he beats Bell with an absolute peach. "This carping on about Bell is pathetic," thunders David Armitage. "What's wrong in a fellow playing himself in, and then going for his shots?" Er, plenty if these sub-standard Aussies end up eight down at the close tomorrow, like South Africa were in the second Test last winter.

47th over: England 185–2 (Strauss 80, Bell 37) England are in overs 25–40 mode: the two finishers are at the crease, when what we really want to see is the two punishers. Someone slog one up in the air! "I see from the ecb website that Geraint Jones is due to be answering emails sent to the Team Blackberry," says Lindsay Chapman. "Is it worth us emailing en masse and asking if he thinks he should still be in the team?" I couldn't possibly encourage such behaviour. But it *is* a free country.

48th over: England 198–2 (Strauss 85, Bell 45) I've seen many things in my life and now I've just seen Ian Bell hit Glenn McGrath for a straight six. It was a delightful shot: he picked the slower ball, and just sweet-spotted over long-off. Simple. The charge is on, and McGrath looks like a man whose wife has just swapped his Smiths vinyl collection for an Usher CD.

49th over: England 202–2 (Strauss 88, Bell 46) Gilchrist misses another alarmingly straightforward stumping as Bell misses a charge at Warne. This is priceless comedy! "The strangest thing about this Test is how ordinary the Australians are looking," says Paul Meek. "This is the superteam of the decade, and they just have not set the pace of the match at all. I think it is the first time since Kim Hughes that the Australian team looks so disorganised. A changing of the Test cricketing guard?"

50th over: England 204–2 (Strauss 89, Bell 46) Bell would have been run out by a direct hit from the bowler McGrath. He wasn't. "Some humble pie with your coffee, Mr Smyth?" says Rob Smith. "Or maybe a straight six off McGrath?" Er, yeah, I take it you lot were the ones calling for Bell to be dropped this time last week. All I said is that he should get his skates on, and he has. Next!

51st over: England 213–2 (Strauss 98, Bell 46) Just to improve their already close friendship, Strauss brings out the reverse sweep against Warne. Then, next ball, he hoicks a long-hop miles into the crowd at square leg for six. Shot!

52nd over: England 219–2 (Strauss 103, Bell 46) That's Strauss's century – he rocks back to pull McGrath superbly for four. Given that he was cracked in the face by Brett Lee early doors, and that he has been out of nick, that is a really fine innings.

53rd over: England 223–2 (Strauss 106, Bell 48) To clarify, there are 30 overs left after this. The lead is 365, and it's a shame we haven't had the chance to see KP administer some bish-bosh.

WICKET! 54th over: Strauss c Martyn b McGrath 106 (England 224–3) Andrew Strauss pulls McGrath towards deep square leg, where Damien Martyn takes the catch diving forward. Brett Lee even ran up to shake Strauss's hand on the way off. Awwww.

WICKET! 54th over: Pietersen lbw b McGrath 0 (England 225–4) We've seen this before: Kevin Pietersen misses a full bunger first ball and is plumb in front. It was ingeniously bowled from McGrath, from around the wicket, and Pietersen just didn't see it at all.

54th over: England 226–4 (first–innings lead: 142; Bell 50, Flintoff 0) A second half-century of the match for Bell, who really has paced his innings perfectly – I said that all along. It took 81 balls, and contained four whole boundaries. Then Gilchrist drops Flintoff, a very awkward one-handed chance diving forward. Amazingly, that's Gilchrist's 87th missed catch or stumping in this match.

56th over: England 234–4 (Bell 56, Flintoff 2) The lead is 376, and England will surely declare once it hits 400. "What's with all the eulogising about Warne?" moans Ed Collington. "The other day you said he was the only joy of this series, and today you were disappointed he didn't get his ton. Bin the Fosters and sup up a London Pride, you Aussie-fixated turncoat."

57th over: England 236–4 (Bell 57, Flintoff 2) Flintoff is looking to open his shoulders, but nothing doing against Warne.

58th over: England 241–4 (first–innings lead: 142; Bell 59, Flintoff 4)

59th over: England 248–4 (Bell 61, Flintoff 4) Only 25 runs in the last seven overs, which is a bit sluggish at a time when England should be going at six and more an over, even allowing for the presence of a new batsman. Four byes from Warne, with McGrath hobbling comically after the ball, don't do England any harm, and the lead is approaching the magical 400. Ten to go.

WICKET! 60th over: Flintoff b McGrath 4 (England 248–5) Flintoff finally does open his shoulders, and has his stumps splayed as he misses a smear across the line. Unselfish stuff from Freddie although, given that he got four off 18 balls, he might as well have done that to his first ball.

60th over: England 259–5 (Bell 61, G Jones 10) Blistering running from Geraint Jones brings up the 250, who then pulls McGrath thrillingly through square leg. A declaration must be due very soon – England's lead is over 400 now.

61st over: England 264–5 (Bell 65, G Jones 11) "What time can play go on until tonight?" says Katy Robinson. 6.30. "Why haven't England declared yet?" Er, they're about to.

WICKET! 62nd over: Bell c Katich b McGrath 65 (England 264–6) A five-for for McGrath, as Bell holes out at long-off. I thought that might prompt the declaration, but then I thought I'd be married with kids by the time I hit 29. I suppose England just want to be completely certain on what is still a decent pitch. I have no such excuse.

62nd over: England 280–6 declared (lead by 422; G Jones 27, Giles 0) What a shot from Geraint Jones! McGrath went around the wicket, and Jones sweet-spotted him gloriously over midwicket for six. Then he dumps the next one over Gilchrist's head for four! And then he smites six more! This has been a sparkling cameo from Jones: 27 off 13 balls, and Michael Vaughan calls time there. Australia will need a world-record 423 to win.

Australia second innings

1st over: Australia 0–0 (chasing 423; Langer 0, Hayden 0) Play will finish at 6.30pm tonight, then there are a maximum of 108 overs tomorrow. Harmison starts with a maiden: lively and kicking off the pitch.

2nd over: Australia 6–0 (Langer 4, Hayden 1) The light is closing in as Hoggard bowls a pretty anodyne over – no sign of significant or indeed insignificant swing, and Langer crashes him past point for four. I really think Vaughan should have given the new ball to Freddie here.

3rd over: Australia 7–0 (Langer 4, Hayden 2) One off Harmison's over, and Gilo is coming on already.

4th over: Australia 8–0 (Langer 4, Hayden 3) Michael Vaughan must have been told he can't bowl his quicks because of the light, as he's loosening up himself. Giles's first over passes off without incident and, if you're listening Fate, I really can't see Australia losing a wicket tonight.

5th over: Australia 9–0 (Langer 4, Hayden 4) If you'd told me four weeks ago that Michael Vaughan would come on second change for the fifth over of an Australian innings with England in with a major chance of going 2–1 up, I'd have punched you right in the kisser for being so stupid.

6th over: Australia 9–0 (Langer 4, Hayden 4) Maiden from Giles to Hayden.

7th over: Australia 10–0 (Langer 5, Hayden 4) One off Vaughan's second over.

8th over: Australia 15–0 (Langer 10, Hayden 4) Classy shot from Langer, crunched through extra cover for four when Giles over-pitches.

9th over: Australia 19–0 (Langer 14, Hayden 4) Justin Langer survives a big shout for lbw from Vaughan: he padded up to the Vaughan arm ball and, though it would have been a brave decision to give it out, Hawkeye had it hitting off stump.

10th over: Australia 24–0 (Langer 14, Hayden 5) That's it for the day.

Australia will need 399 tomorrow, England 10 wickets, and there should be 108 overs in which it will be decided. It should be immense, and I hope you all enjoy it.

Australia 302 and 24–0; England 444 and 280–6 dec

Fifth Day

The morning session

BY SEAN INGLE

Preamble: The maths is simple. Australia, who ended an enthralling fourth day on 24–0, need another 399 in a maximum of 108 overs to win. England just need 10 wickets. Simple, eh? Oh.

Here we go . . . It's a sell-out at Old Trafford, and 10,000 frustrated Mancunians have been turned away at the gates. The England team walk out to huge applause before going into an American Football-style huddle. "In order to head problems off before they begin, does anyone know if it's possible to damage a computer by clicking on 'refresh' too frequently?" asks a nervous Phil Berry. Well?

11th over: Australia 25–0 (Langer 14, Hayden 5) As huge cries of "Ing-er-land" roll around Old Trafford, Harmison steadies himself and bowls. It's a decent first over – including a slanter which has Hayden playing and missing. Just one run from it, a no-ball. "Whenever England need a wicket, I go to the desktop scorecard and click F5 like a madman for ten minutes," says David Nuge. "So far it's worked about seven times out of ten."

WICKET! 12th over: Langer c G Jones b Hoggard 14 (Australia 25–1) Hoggard strikes first ball. It's a classic outswinger which has Langer nibbling outside off stump – and not even Geraint Jones will drop that one! "I found in the Edgbaston Test that whenever my girlfriend stopped watching we took wickets," says Andy Smith. "She's at work today and can't watch. Wahey, victory is assured." Steady Andy . . .

13th over: Australia 28–1 (Hayden 6, Ponting 1) Harmison continues to probe outside off stump at around 85mph, Hayden continues to leave. "In my capacity as a professional software engineer, I can confirm that constantly refreshing a webpage doesn't hurt your computer," says Stephen Smith, probably in between mouthfuls of cheesy Doritos and games of Warhammer 40,000.

14th over: Australia 32–1 (Hayden 6, Ponting 5) Encouraging news for England: Hoggard is getting some movement off the seam. One moves too much, however, and Ponting's easy prod through midwicket brings up a boundary. "I took David Nuge's advice and pressed F5 manically, and do you know what?" says J Fitzgerald (and others). "Sound advice my son!" Meanwhile Peter Thompson says: "On the last day of the Edgbaston Test, I made the ultimate sacrifice of leaving the room when Australia needed six to win. On the 'going to the toilet in the pub to enable your team to score a goal' principle, I, personally, induced the England victory. My contribution is yet to be officially acknowledged."

15th over: Australia 39–1 (Hayden 11, Ponting 7) Harmison is still yet to reach full pace, or to threaten, and the Aussies make hay. Perhaps it's time for Flintoff? "I am sat here with two laptops on the go (one work, one cricket) and I feel like Rick Wakeman," says Graeme Stewart. "Maybe a 20–minute keyboard solo will help me finish my document but it won't help with the F5–ing, will it?"

16th over: Australia 44–1 (Hayden 15, Ponting 7) You'd expect the Australian batsman to be a model of defensive obduracy, but Hayden's still playing his natural game, hooking a Hoggard no-ball for four. Meanwhile hundreds of you reckon going to the toilet helps bring England a wicket – maybe a nationwide 11am loo break will do the trick?

17th over: Australia 47–1 (Hayden 15, Ponting 10) Very early in the day, the *Guardian*'s Ashley Giles replaces Harmison. I'm not convinced by this tactic. Still, it's a good first over – Ponting is nearly stumped (his back foot was in by millimetres) before he edges uncertainly through third slip.

18th over: Australia 51–1 (Hayden 15, Ponting 14) Hoggard's bowling very straight to Ponting, hoping for some outswing or an lbw decision. But the Australian captain is equal to the task. "You might point out to flustered F5–pressers that the Mozilla Firefox browser has a downloadable extension that enables you to refresh automatically every five seconds or five minutes or whatever you tell it, thereby leaving your fingers free for more important tasks such as writing this email," says Bob Barton.

19th over: Australia 52–1 (Hayden 16, Ponting 14) Spin for Ashley Giles! And it surprises Ponting by fizzing from leg to off like a freshly opened 7–Up. "Maybe Graeme Stewart (over 15) could attach an angle-poise lamp to his cricket laptop through the USB port and wave his hand through the beam to refresh in a kind of Jean-Michel Jarre Rendez-vous Moss-Side kind of way," suggests Gavin Digby, not unreasonably.

20th over: Australia 65–1 (Hayden 21, Ponting 21) A big cheer as Flintoff replaces Hoggard – and another one as Ponting pulls Freddie for six. Flintoff shakes his head and then comes back two balls later with a beauty which Hayden nicks to third slip. But England only have two slips and the chance is gone. "Your readers' advice sounds like it comes from the Natural Law party," splutters Nick Watson. "Maybe we should all start yogic flying to empower our bowlers with the nation's strength?"

21st over: Australia 67–1 (Hayden 22, Ponting 22) Good stuff from Giles, who's getting bounce as well as some turn.

22nd over: Australia 67–1 (Hayden 22, Ponting 22) Maiden. "Why not use the desktop scorecard," says Iain King." It's updated automatically as well so no need to wear out your keyboard or download dodgy apps. A great productivity aid (or at least it would be if I didn't just sit here staring at it waiting for it to update . . .)."

23rd over: Australia 71–1 (Hayden 22, Ponting 26) Ponting goes for a suicidal single before deciding better of it a third of the way down. Giles tries for the run-out, but the Australian captain just makes it back. "I'm sitting in an office of the only 35 people in the entire country totally oblivious to what is happening at Old Trafford – cue much embarrassment when I punched the air when Hoggard struck," says Charles Heymann. "Any advice for keeping up any pretence of work?"

24th over: Australia 80–1 (Hayden 29, Ponting 27) Flintoff again gets Hayden to edge, again it flies through where third slip should be. Michael Vaughan has a first, second and fourth slip – but surely England shouldn't be worrying about saving the singles here?

25th over: Australia 87–1 (Hayden 35, Ponting 27) Australia on the charge! The ball after Hayden pads up – Ashley Giles's big appeal deserved more from umpire Bucknor – he lofts an enormous six over deep midwicket. "It beats me why no one's talking about the statistical possibility of an Aussie win," says Dennis Marshall from Colorado. "With 80–odd overs, four an over will do it. And that's about what they're scoring at this morning."

26th over: Australia 90–1 (Hayden 35, Ponting 29) Another lbw appeal from Flintoff after he beats Ponting for pace. Hawkeye says it would've knocked over the stumps – but Ponting's pad was just outside off stump. Superb stuff from Flintoff, who really deserves a wicket.

27th over: Australia 90–1 (Hayden 35, Ponting 29) Hayden is really struggling to counter Giles's spinners out of the rough (and yes, they are really spinning) – and one has just hit his pad and missed off stump by millimetres. "Re: Charles Heymann's keeping a pretence of work. I work in a sales office," says Shaun Rimmer. "We've changed the words from 'wicket' to 'sale' and 'boundary' to 'lost customer'. Our boss thinks we've had one big sale this morning and seven lost customers – don't know whether he's happy or worried!"

28th over: Australia 92–1 (Hayden 35, Ponting 30) Another England lbw appeal is turned down! Again it's Flintoff bowling to Hayden, who offers no stroke to one that comes back at him. Umpire Billy Bowden says it was going too high – Hawkeye showed he was right.

29th over: Australia 96–1 (Hayden 35, Ponting 34) Giles gives Ponting too much length and is cut for four – but next ball is quicker and straight and misses the edge – just. "Just nipped to the toilet to try and trigger an Aussie wicket, but was prevented by some militant cleaners who told me to wait 15 minutes," says Matt Brett. "Got back to my desk – no wicket. Theory proved! Do the cleaning staff of the nation realise they are preventing an England victory?"

WICKET! 30th over: Hayden b Flintoff 36 (Australia 97–2) Flintoff strikes after all! Freddie gets one to dart back in and uproots

Hayden's leg stump as he shuffles across. Listen to Old Trafford roar! Meanwhile this from a worried Edward Bannister. "Will pressing F5 non-stop make it more likely that my employer will be able to haul me over the coals for internet usage?"

31st over: Australia 97–2 (Ponting 35, Martyn 0) Brilliant fielding from Bell at forward short leg! In one movement he catches Martyn's full-blooded drive on the bounce and shies at the stumps. Martyn is miles out of his crease, but the throw misses the stumps and Geraint Jones.

32nd over: Australia 101–2 (Ponting 36, Martyn 2) Martyn brings up the 100 with a well-taken single. Flintoff is starting to tire – perhaps it's time for Simon Jones just before lunch? "We have the TV on in our office," says Russell Balkind. "It mysteriously turned off the ball before Flintoff got Hayden out and came back on of its own accord the ball afterwards. Very strange. I may be dealing with forces beyond my understanding, but it won't stop me turning the TV on and off repeatedly in order to precipitate an Aussie collapse."

33rd over: Australia 107–2 (Ponting 37, Martyn 7) Giles looks ineffective bowling to the right-handers and Martyn forces him away for his first boundary. "A toilet break followed by returning a call from my ex-girlfriend – I get back and there's been a wicket," says Ed Airey. "Can someone please re-assure me that it was the toilet break that did it, and that I am not going to have call my ex back eight times today – I fear it may send out the wrong idea."

34th over: Australia 112–2 (Ponting 37, Martyn 12) Simon 'first-ball wicket' Jones replaces Flintoff. To a loud "Ohhhhhhhhhh" from the Old Trafford crowd he steams in . . . and is hit through the covers for four. Jones then gets some reverse swing, appeals loudly for an lbw to Ponting, but finds umpire Billy Bowden unmoved.

35th over: Australia 116–2 (Ponting 37, Martyn 17) Giles again strays on to leg and is clipped away for four by Martyn, who's scored 17 off 16 deliveries. Giles is more King of Spain than King of Spin today. Meanwhile spare a thought for Ian Glover's office colleagues. "I just got back from the loo and a wicket had fallen," he writes. "Off to lunch soon, so I'll make sure I have the baked bean vindaloo with a very large helping of chillies to help bring some more wickets this afternoon."

36th over: Australia 117–2 (Ponting 37, Martyn 17) Unbelievable! The snickometer shows that Martyn got an edge from Jones's first delivery that over, yet no England bowler or fielder appealed. Bizarre. "Re: tips to help England win. Perhaps we could ask Kevin Keegan to declare that 'Only one team will go on to win this, and that team is Australia'," says David Maloney. "Plan B is to sneak Phil Neville on the pitch in a baggy green cap."

37th over: Australia 118–2 (Ponting 38, Martyn 17) Harmison replaces Giles as Vaughan strives for a third wicket. England deserve it – they've bowled pretty well this morning. Harmison's over is pedestrian until he thumps Martyn on the shoulder with an 88mph bouncer.

38th over: Australia 121–2 (Ponting 41, Martyn 17) Jones is getting some swing here – lots of sharp inswingers which Ponting has to jab down sharply on. But the Australian captain survives, and that's lunch.

Australia 302 and 121–2; England 444 and 280–6 dec

The afternoon session

BY SEAN INGLE

Preamble: The bookies now have it 6–4 England, 8–11 draw and Australia 18–1 – which isn't the worst bet in the world. As my over-by-over colleague Rob Smyth points out, they only need four an over from here. England should still fancy their chances – but they need at least three wickets this session." Surely the whole productivity/refreshing debate is a distraction," says Anthony Vigor. "The real threat to productivity is trying to come up with a witty email that you'll use. It's taken me until the fifth day of the third Test to build up the courage to send this in, wracking my brains every day in the process."

39th over: Australia 121–2 (Ponting 41, Martyn 17) Here we go again, Harmison to Ponting. A decent over, and another lbw appeal – Ponting pads up, but it was missing leg stump. Maiden. "I got a ticket!" cries Heather from Manchester. "I'm now home for lunch (a mile away). The crowd is raving over every ball and kids keep trying to climb these eight-foot fences. It's wacky fun, but they no longer sell newspapers in the ground. Boo. I think Simon Jones looks the most likely to do damage from my seat."

40th over: Australia 121–2 (Ponting 41, Martyn 17) Encouraging signs for England: Jones is getting some reverse swing. Maiden. "Whilst your English readers are nervously hoping for more wickets, I am stuck in a emotional quagmire," says Tristan Murphy. "As a patriotic Irishman and previously staunch opponent to the colonial/toff's game, I find myself attracted to crash of ball against wicket. And the even more heinous crime of cheering on the auld enemy against the dastardly Aussies. What am I to do? What if my friends find out? I fear, I might have to leave the country."

41st over: Australia 125–2 (Ponting 41, Martyn 19) Signs that Harmison is getting the bit between his teeth at last: he cracks Martyn on the helmet with a short one, before another lbw appeal – what's that this innings? 10? 11? – is rejected by umpire Bucknor. "Do I take it from the fact you are doing a second session on that trot that you have used your sports editor powers and arranged the rota so you get a whole day in what could be a very exciting hot seat?" asks James Peterson. "If so I admire the move – shows strong captaincy and a desire to lead from the front." And a lack of bodies in the office, James . . .

42nd over: Australia 125–2 (Ponting 45, Martyn 19) Another edge flies through the slips! It was too low to be caught, but England's frustration is growing. Next ball Jones launches into a *huge* lbw appeal, but it was turned down for missing leg. And the ball after that? Another rejected lbw appeal as Ponting pads up to one missing off stump. "Further to the tragically named Tristan Murphy's emotional bogside quagmire," says Alistair Connor. "As a New Zealander with French nationality, I might be presumed to be conflicted as to who to support. Hereditary enemies and all that. Fortunately the French don't play cricket so as a Kiwi I would obviously support Satan's XI against the Aussies – let's have some wickets!" Amen to that.

WICKET! 43rd over: Martyn lbw Harmison 19 (Australia 129–3) England get a huge slice of luck! Harmison raps Martyn on the pads in front of the stumps and, after a long, long delay, umpire Bucknor lifts the finger. However replays show it hit bat before pad and Ricky Ponting is not happy.

44th over: Australia 130–3 (Ponting 47, Katich 0) Jones is getting the ball to reverse swing like Elvis's hips circa 1956 and he immediately gets Katich swinging and missing. You can almost sense another wicket coming here. Meanwhile, more abuse for Irish England cricket fan Tristan Murphy. "I wouldn't have thought that anyone with a name like Tristan would ever have a problem with a colonial/toffs game," says Jason in Dublin. "I can see him now in the Pavillion Bar in Trinity College Dublin guffawing with his fellow students about the merits of silly mid-off while complaining about the ruffians who participate in the animalistic and unruly national sport!"

45th over: Australia 137–3 (Ponting 50, Katich 4) Ponting brings up his half-century with a flick through midwicket for three before a long-hop gets Katich off the mark". I've just got back from coaching the French Under 15s in the ECC championships in Rome," says Christophe Bartlett. "I'd like to see Alistair Connor tell the competition's leading run-scorer, a Frenchman who scored 99, 0, 103, 62, and 129 not out, that he can't play cricket."

46th over: Australia 144–3 (Ponting 53, Katich 8) Having seen Flintoff dismiss Katich bowling from around the wicket in the first innings, Jones is trying to repeat the trick. No luck so far – Jones strays on to leg stump and is clipped to fine leg for four. "I've no sympathy for Martyn at all," says Sam Blatherwick. "He should have walked earlier." Even though England didn't appeal, Sam?

47th over: Australia 154–3 (Ponting 63, Katich 8) Ashley Giles comes on and is immediately slog-swept twice to the boundary. Not the most inspired moment of captaincy in Michael Vaughan's career. "Re: the non-playing French. The first written trace of the word 'criquet' has been dated back to 1498 in the written defence of Quentin le Brasseur, who was accused of murdering another spectator at the Château de Liettres where 'men were playing criquet with a bat and a ball'," says Christophe in France. So now you know.

48th over: Australia 154–3 (Ponting 63, Katich 8) Umpires Bowden and Bucknor are conferring. Bowden's just asked, "What did he say?" It's pretty clear that they're talking about Ponting, who might yet face a disrepute charge come stumps. Meanwhile Flintoff is back and immediately gets Katich playing and missing twice at an outswinger. "Did French Kiwi Alistair Connor (42nd over) beat himself up over the *Rainbow Warrior* sinking?" asks Jamie Reeman, not unreasonably.

49th over: Australia 161–3 (Ponting 63, Katich 8) Ponting clatters Giles to the boundary again, this time cut through point. England now have three fielders on the boundary and a fairly defensive field, which is not what you need when you still need to take seven wickets. "Unlike us you are watching this Test," says John Edwards. "What would you give as marks out of ten for the five England bowlers?" So far today I'd give Flintoff 10, Jones eight, Harmison seven, Hoggard six and the *Guardian*'s Ashley Giles three.

WICKET! 50th over: Katich c Giles b Flintoff 12 (Australia 165–4) Katich – who's never looked comfortable – chases a wide one and edges to third slip, where Giles snags a smart catch. Flintoff then produces a 90mph first-ball snorter to Gilchrist, who does well to block. "Thought I'd share some fantastic news with you. My (previously entirely disinterested in cricket) wife has just called me at work to ask what an inside edge is, and why this should be relevant to whether or not the Aussie batsman is out lbw," says Nick Williamson, who's the envy of men across Britain.

51st over: Australia 171–4 (Ponting 69, Gilchrist 1) Giles stays on, a tactic that makes more sense seeing as the left-handed Gilchrist has some nasty rough outside his off stump. "Actually, the OED dates the first written trace of the word 'criquet' to 1478," says Mark Brenchley. "'Le suppliant arriva en ung lieu ou on jouoit a la boulle, pres d'une atache [vine-stake] ou criquet'. That's one hundred and twenty years before the first written trace of the word 'cricket' in England. Still, doesn't this mean that 'cricket' is about as English as loving a plate of frogs legs?"

52nd over: Australia 171–4 (Ponting 69, Gilchrist 1) More fast, fiery bowling from Flintoff. Gilchrist, who's not yet wafted at one outside off stump, is content to block. Drinks. "I've heard that criquet actually means 'the sound of a ball hitting wood'," says Phil Sawyer. "Can Cristophe (over 47) confirm this? I've always been impressed that the French had such an elegant word for it (presumably the English equivalent would be 'thunk')."

53rd over: Australia 175–4 (Ponting 75, Gilchrist 1) Ponting continues to take the fight to Giles, clouting him through square leg for four. Our *Guardian* colleague's figures? A stunningly average 0–64. "There are lots of female cricket fans out there," says Kat Knight (and others). "I've been going to matches whenever possible for 10 years, am keeping the lads in my office updated with the score thanks to an internet radio connection, go to the pub to catch an hour of play each lunchtime and am taking my boyfriend to the Saturday at The Oval in September. Is that enough?"

54th over: Australia 175–4 (Ponting 75, Gilchrist 1) Every time Flintoff runs in to bowl, Gilchrist looks as nervous as a crooked-teeth teen on her first date. But so far he's staying disciplined. Maiden. "I see Nick Williamson thinks it's good news that his wife is interested in cricket," says Sam Graham. "Is he mad? He's letting her in on one of the only pleasures he has left in life; watching cricket by himself. He's setting a dangerous precedent I tell you – before you know it she'll want to go fishing with him."

55th over: Australia 175–4 (Ponting 78, Gilchrist 1) Giles continues to probe, without actually threatening. "This Ashes seems to be like a football World Cup in that people who have never shown interest in cricket are getting into it," says Andrew Goldby. "A mate of mine was asking me about it the other day and he's always hated the game. So congratulations are in order for the ECB ensuring that next year's Tests aren't going to be on terrestrial. The short-sighted idiots."

56th over: Australia 181–4 (Ponting 79, Gilchrist 3) The crowd are trying to stir England, but it's slightly flat at the moment. Perhaps time for a change in the bowling? "Does it look like Michael Clarke will come out to bat this innings?" asks Geoff Maguire. "Hopefully housekeeping at the Australian team hotel changed his mattress for an extra soft one whilst he was trying to save the cause on Friday!" He will bat, Geoff, but because he's been away from the ground he can't come in before seven in the innings.

57th over: Australia 181–4 (Ponting 79, Gilchrist 4) Giles, who's still bowling over the wicket, is doing nothing to suggest he'll make the breakthrough. "Further to Nick Williamson's breakthrough in over 50, I was delighted when on Sunday my wife – forced to assume some interest as the cricket was on all day – asked me genuinely,

'That blond one is getting hit all the time, is he no good because he's fat? He doesn't look like a professional sportsman'," writes Ben Heywood. "Bless."

WICKET! 58th over: Gilchrist c Bell b Flintoff 5 (Australia 181–5) Flintoff strikes again! For the last three overs, he's been bowling short of a length to Gilchrist. But this one is pitched up, with a hint of outswing, and Gilchrist bites. A second later, Bell takes a straightforward catch in the slips and Old Trafford goes wild. Advantage England!

59th over: Australia 191–5 (Ponting 80, Clarke 8) Michael Clarke jogged to the crease, so perhaps his back is better? He certainly showed no signs of any spasms that over, smashing Michael Vaughan – on for Giles – twice to the boundary, before being beaten by a quicker one. "It is Andrew Goldby (55 over) who is the short-sighted one," insists Matt Knight. "Cricket on Sky next year means that we'll no longer have to lose playing time because, although the sun is shining, some housewife in Ealing wants to watch *Hollyoaks*."

60th over: Australia 194–5 (Ponting 80, Clarke 10) Flintoff, that weary warrior, continues for yet another over. He's tiring, though, and Ponting is hardly forced to play a shot. "My girlfriend is very much into the cricket," says Jon Casemore. "After both going to a couple of the Tests at the SCG and the WACA last series she really got interested. Now she spends her time at home with our 11–month-old daughter teaching her to signal fours and sixes. Only for England, mind. It's fantastic!"

61st over: Australia 200–5 (Ponting 87, Clarke 10) Vaughan continues to Ponting, who brings up the 200 by smashing him down the ground for four. I think England are missing a trick here – surely Simon Jones's reverse swing deserves another pop? Meanwhile Ian Simons wants to know how long Sky's ECB contract lasts. Until 2009, Ian, with highlights on Channel 5. Depressing, isn't it?

62nd over: Australia 206–5 (Ponting 89, Clarke 13) Flintoff, who must be shattered, continues for yet another over. "Re: Matt Knight and Andrew Goldby's spat over Sky coverage, while I'd much prefer it to stay with C4 I suspect that much of the World Cup atmosphere surrounding the series has been whipped up by the Murdoch papers to try to ensure maximum audiences when Sky takes over next year," suggests Stuart Anderson. Not sure about that Stuart, it is the Ashes after all . . .

63rd over: Australia 211–5 (Ponting 89, Clarke 18) Vaughan surprisingly turns to Hoggard, who serves up a juicy half-volley on leg for starters. Clarke, unsurprisingly, fills his boots. "Cricket highlights on Channel 5 'depressing'? Are you joking?" says Luke Shiach. "I can't wait to watch consummate broadcaster John Barnes say: 'Can Englandhold on. Towinagainst. All odds catch the action after. The. Break.'"

64th over: Australia 212–5 (Ponting 89, Clarke 19) Harmison replaces Flintoff, but he's still lacking the Tyson-esque menace that he displayed at Lord's. "Another disappointing thing about the cricket going to Sky is that their pictures will no longer be in sync with *Test Match Special* on the radio because of the extra satellite hop the signal has to take," says Tom Palmer. "So watching the cricket with the sound down and the radio won't be the same again."

65th over: Australia 212–5 (Ponting 89, Clarke 19) The *Guardian*'s Ashley Giles (0–68) comes back and has Clarke in all sorts of trouble with one that pitches on leg and spins sharply. Maiden. "It seems the Aussies now have half the runs they need, for the loss of half their wickets," says Pierre Burger from Zimbabwe. "Considering that their real batsmen (Warne, Gillespie) are still to come, I'd say England ought to be worried." The Aussies are 80–1 to win this, Pierre, and that's not being over-generous.

66th over: Australia 216–5 (Ponting 91, Clarke 20) Another huge lbw appeal from Harmison, who gets one to jigger-jagger back at Clarke. But Bucknor is again not for moving. That's tea.

Australia 302 and 216–5; England 444 and 280–6 dec

The evening session

BY JAMES DART

Preamble: England need five wickets in 42 overs.The bookies have it England 11–10, the draw 4–5 and Australia 40–1. Meanwhile John

Osbourne wants to know: "Why are pointless 'sports' for Pimms-drinking toffs such as the Boat Race, Wimbledon and probably some horse races protected by the Government and have to be shown on terrestrial television, while things of genuine importance and interest to everyone (ie Ashes Tests) are allowed to go to Sky." Well?

67th over: Australia 221–5 (Ponting 91, Clarke 24; 41 overs left) Ashley Giles kicks off this most crucial of sessions, with Michael Vaughan clearly unperturbed by the fact that 51 overs of spin have been bowled in the two second innings – with no wickets coming from them. The King of Spain immediately has a chance to change this, but puts down a caught-and-bowled chance off Clarke, one he'll feel he could have held, one-handed, low to his right. Clarke responds with a four down the ground. "Now then," starts Matt Howell. "I'm tense. Tight. Any tips from readers on how to calm the nerves during the final session?"

68th over: Australia 225–5 (Ponting 94, Clarke 25; 40 overs left) Less than 200 to win, at a mite under five runs an over. Could the Australians still pull this one off?

69th over: Australia 235–5 (Ponting 97, Clarke 29; 39 overs left) A major appeal from Giles is turned down against Ponting – it was just going down leg. Clarke is starting to play very positively, ending the over with a crack to the extra-cover ropes for four. Meanwhile, Ed Herman has some relaxation tips: "Matt Howell might find that logging onto this website www.punchaceleb.com with their excellent Ashes special helps to relieve a considerable amount of tension. Take that, Ricky. In your face, Glenn. Or something."

70th over: Australia 242–5 (Ponting 103, Clarke 29; 38 overs left) An elegant cover drive from Ponting registers his 23rd Test hundred – and his fifth against England. It's been an exquisite innings and has helped keep Australia alive and bring them within 181 runs of an improbable victory. "Isn't this all a little silly?" moans Richard Clarke. "Why not throw Hoggy and Jones on and get them to swing us to victory?" I agree with you, Richard, especially regarding Simon Jones, who has been massively underused in this second innings.

71st over: Australia 249–5 (Ponting 105, Clarke 34; 37 overs left) Clarke comes down the ground to Giles and effortlessly lofts him over mid-on and to the boundary. Ponting adds with two more and

Old Trafford is slowly losing its voice. Matt Howell's nerves are spreading. 174 to win.

72nd over: Australia 251–5 (Ponting 106, Clarke 35; 36 overs left, 172 to win) Harmison again fails to produce much from this ageing ball as the batsmen clip two singles down to fine leg. "Re 69th over – I'm tense too," says James Prestidge. "These last two games have not been good for my heart! I preferred it when England were rubbish so you only ever had to worry about how much they were going to lose by on the third day!"

73rd over: Australia 255–5 (Ponting 108, Clarke 36; 35 overs left, 168 to win) "FOR THE LOVE OF GOD GET JONES ON NOW!" yells Paul McKim, whose upper-case work underlines England's quandary. Matthew Hoggard has now come on with the old ball, but both Ponting and Clarke continue to comfortably add the singles – and maintain the run-rate. "I'm hoping, even wishing for the England win, but 40–1 against is worth a tenner," notes Olly Shore. "Not fussed if I lose it but the cash takes the sting out of our possible loss . . ." Shamefully, but possibly astutely, your OBO correspondent has also put a couple of quid on the Aussies at 40–1. Sorry, but they're 13–2 now.

74th over: Australia 260–5 (Ponting 110, Clarke 38; 34 overs left, 163 to win) Here's Simon Jones, albeit belatedly. I must admit I felt he must have been injured not to be bowling, but he's finally been given the ball. And it almost, *almost*, pays off; Clarke edges him through the absent second slip, with Marcus Trescothick's desperate dive unable to stop the ball.

75th over: Australia 263–5 (Ponting 111, Clarke 39; 33 overs left, 160 to win) Better bowling from Hoggard, spurred on by very vocal encouragement from his England team-mates. That's how they're dealing with their nerves – by shouting. Might not work in your office, mind.

WICKET! 76th over: Clarke b S Jones 39 (Australia 263–6) Got 'im! A cracker from Jones, who merely highlights the bewilderment at him not bowling sooner, jagging the ball back with some reverse swing and upending Clarke's off stump, after the batsman failed to even offer a stroke. Game on again!

WICKET! 77th over: Gillespie lbw b Hoggard 0 (Australia 264–7)

After a teasing couple of seconds from Steve Bucknor, his finger goes up to signify the end of Gillespie's innings and the cue for another eruption around Old Trafford – and GU Towers. Apart, that is, from an area of the Media section, where an Australian flag is quickly being lowered. A five-ball duck for Gillespie. "Do you think Warne has stayed in the pavilion because he's not talking to Ponting?" asks Damian Hebron, referring to the "erroneous" reports of disquiet between the pair.

78th over: Australia 269–7 (Ponting 117, Warne 0; 30 overs left, 154 to win) Having received an official warning for straying into the protected area of the pitch during his last over, Jones just strays down leg-side, enabling Ponting to clip him effortlessly to the square-leg boundary. "I'd just like to thank the dozens, nay, hundreds of office punters who put a couple of quid on an Aussie win at long odds, to 'soften the blow' if they should claim a world record victory," says a joyous Neil Goodall. "This now means that we've effectively paid off any hitches and England can go on to win!" I feel I've duly done my part, Neil.

79th over: Australia 270–7 (Ponting 117, Warne 0; 29 overs left, 153 to win) Just the one no-ball called against Hoggard in that over as Warne plays himself in. And both batsmen are talking to each other, just to answer those of you wondering (hoping) that the pair mightn't be communicating.

80th over: Australia 271–7 (Ponting 118, Warne 0; 28 overs left, 152 to win) Just the one run from that Simon Jones over, Ponting clipping him to square leg. The new ball is now available, but it'll be interesting to see, with Jones and Hoggard bowling so well with some clear reverse swing, whether Vaughan will immediately go for it.

81st over: Australia 274–7 (Ponting 118, Warne 3; 27 overs left, 149 to win) Two balls into the over, Hoggard takes the new ball. He doesn't get any swing with it, however, and Warne gets off the mark with a prod through midwicket. Surely it won't be long before Flintoff and Harmison are given a chance to rough Warne up here?

82nd over: Australia 281–7 (Ponting 125, Warne 3; 26 overs left, 142 to win) Jones takes the new ball for the first time, but his attempted slower ball results in a full toss which Ponting drives comfortably down to long-on for four. "I'm sitting in cowboy country Texas, pulling my hair out, wishing this country had a little more sense of playing cricket instead of that blasted baseball," moans Anirvan Chaudri. "If Australia manage to eke out a draw, Vaughan should shoulder the blame for not bringing on Jones and Hoggy and instead sticking on with the King of Spain's anodyne bowling!"

83rd over: Australia 287–7 (Ponting 126, Warne 8; 25 overs left, 136 to win) Harmison is brought back into the attack, but his over is costly, with Warne crashing him over the fielder at silly point and to the boundary. It surely can't be long until Mr Flintoff gets the nod from his skipper for another blast. Meanwhile, Ben Wrigley is another who's a bag of nerves. "This is definite P45 material at the moment," he says. "I am up against a tight deadline today and I cannot get anywhere with it as it is difficult to work a mouse with all 10 fingernails in your mouth at once. I live in Chicago and this all makes me thoroughly homesick."

84th over: Australia 293–7 (Ponting 127, Warne 13; 24 overs left, 130 to win) Flintoff is indeed brought back and his first two deliveries have Warne in all kinds of trouble. The first bounces just in front of first slip after a thickish edge and the second beats Warne all ends up outside off stump.

85th over: Australia 293–7 (Ponting 127, Warne 13; 23 overs left, 130 to win) Ponting sees this maiden over from Harmison off safely. "I'll name my first-born Fred (even if it's a girl) if he knocks 'em over," exclaims a delirious Craig Easterbrook, whose other half is sure to be delighted.

86th over: Australia 295–7 (Ponting 128, Warne 14; 22 overs left, 128 to win) A big, big lbw shout from Flintoff against Ponting, but the crooked finger isn't raised by umpire Bowden. Just a tad too high, but Fred really got to work out his vocal chords there.

87th over: Australia 297–7 (Ponting 128, Warne 15; 21 overs left, 126 to win) Harmison's turn to come agonisingly close to claiming Ponting's prized wicket, almost cutting him in half just over off stump. Exactly six runs an over required now, although survival is becoming more and more the likely escape route for Australia rather than chasing down the target.

88th over: Australia 298–7 (Ponting 128, Warne 16; 20 overs left, 125 to win) A fearsome over from Flintoff, who first makes Warne play right off the top of his bat, looping it, fortunately, to safety at silly point. He then beats him outside off stump, before a vicious bouncer rears up off the pitch, forcing Warne to take evasive action and prompting Geraint Jones into a good take behind the wicket.

89th over: Australia 298–7 (Ponting 128, Warne 16; 19 overs left, 125 to win) Ashley Giles gets the ball now in England's desperate search for these three remaining wickets. His over is tight and a maiden and almost makes me eat my words, catching Warne almost full toss on the toe – but it's inches short and umpire Bucknor's 'not out' decision is spot on.

90th over: Australia 301–7 (Ponting 128, Warne 19; 18 overs left, 122 to win) A nervous chip over gully from Warne sees the Australian all-rounder survive again, but only just. Ponting also escapes with a wild slash that he completely misses – but only by the smallest of margins.

91st over: Australia 309–7 (Ponting 129, Warne 26; 17 overs left, 114 to win) Five men are around the bat for Giles, with Vaughan able to commit far more aggressively now the run rate is becoming an afterthought. Warne still cracks a four to square, mind, after Giles comes up far too short outside off stump.

92nd over: Australia 313–7 (Ponting 129, Warne 30; 16 overs left, 110 to win) Simon Jones is recalled in place of Flintoff, but the stubborn Warne won't be denied. Kevin Pietersen, fielding at short midwicket, gets a diving opportunity off a full toss. It goes into the hands, but it comes straight back out.

93rd over: Australia 314–7 (Ponting 129, Warne 30; 15 overs left, 109 to win) As Hoggard returns to the attack, Pietersen is still glancing skywards in frustration at that miss in the last over. Five dropped catches – and no successful ones – in this series for Pietersen so far. If it proves costly, expect Warney to be texting his old mate with some thanks.

Drinks break: "I just can't bear this any more!" screams Ben Lowing. "Is it safe to say that we're not threatening, we won't get these last three wickets and that the Ashes are lost once again?" No, no and no, though Australia will surely take the biggest psychological lift from this game if they can hold on.

94th over: Australia 322–7 (Ponting 137, Warne 30; 14 overs left, 101 to win) "Just thought I'd let you know Gareth, my boyfriend, has gone off to the gym sulking having decided that it's a draw and he can't take any more," says Maria Turley. "I believe this to be a good sign as it probably means England will now do hugely exciting things and win. I'd like to say what hugely exciting things they'll do, but as a cricket novice I'd struggle frankly." They need all the help they can get, Maria.

95th over: Australia 330–7 (Ponting 140, Warne 34; 13 overs left, 93 to win) "If the situation was reversed, does anyone think England would have held on as long as this?" wonders Byron Cooper-Fogarty.

96th over: Australia 337–7 (Ponting 147, Warne 34; 12 overs left, 86 to win) Another look at the run-rate of just over seven an over may have one or two people worried again as Ponting first smashes Jones behind square, before nudging three more quick runs from the next two deliveries. Twenty-three runs from the last three overs.

97th over: Australia 338–7 (Ponting 148, Warne 34; 11 overs left, 85 to win) This must surely be Flintoff's final spell now, as he is given the ball by Vaughan. However, the field setting becomes a little more negative after a handful of England players could be seen in discussion at the end of that last over; probably wary of a rising Aussie run-rate. After a Ponting single, Freddie gets a shot at Warne, who plays and misses twice. "This is intense," says Robert Ellis. "I'm at the office and I can't leave until it's over. I'm an Aussie with a British passport and I'm praying that the Aussies hold on for a draw. It will be a fantastic escape. I've enjoyed seeing England do well in this series, but establishing a 2–1 lead would be worrying indeed – hold on, Warney!"

98th over: Australia 340–7 (Ponting 150, Warne 34; 10 overs left, 83 to win) Another landmark for Ponting with a prod towards cover for two; his imperious knock earns a rapturous standing ovation from English fans and Australians alike. It really has been a fantastic innings in the most pressurised of situations.

WICKET! 99th over: Warne c G Jones b Flintoff 34 (Australia 340–8)

Incredible scenes as Geraint Jones plays the hero again. Warne edges to Andrew Strauss at second slip, who completely misses the ball. It rebounds off his thigh towards the wicketkeeper, but looks like dropping short until Jones makes a stunning one-handed grab low to his right, just inches off the ground. Brett Lee comes to the crease with Old Trafford rocking again and Flintoff beats him outside off stump with his first delivery. Another unbelievable conclusion could still be on the cards! We're now reverting to ball-by-ball coverage.

100th over: Australia 341–8 (Ponting 151, Lee 0 – eight overs left)

First ball: Simon Jones's first effort tails away wide of off stump.

Second ball: A forward press from Ponting for no run.

Third ball: Another safe defensive stroke from the skipper.

Fourth ball: Ponting plays forward again for no run.

Fifth ball: He does get a single to short leg, to leave one ball for Lee to face.

Sixth ball: With Lee facing, Jones gets the ball to swing away, catch an edge and fly towards fourth slip. It lands agonisingly short.

101st over: Australia 341–8 (Ponting 151, Lee 0 – seven overs left)

First ball: Ponting continues to frustrate Flintoff with a forward defensive.

Second ball: A dive from Pietersen saves the single.

Third ball: Ponting clips to fine leg, but turns down the single.

Fourth ball: Flintoff beats the outside edge, but doesn't get any reward.

Fifth ball: Roared on by a fervent crowd, Flintoff gets Ponting tied up, but he prods it down to safety.

Sixth ball: Desperate to save the single, England get their wish as Ponting leaves a ball wide of off stump.

102nd over: Australia 349–8 (Ponting 152, Lee 5 – six overs left)

First ball: A delay with Simon Jones suffering from cramp – Harmison takes charge and demands the ball as Jones leaves the field to a roaring ovation. But the Durham quickie is pumped up and ready to take on Lee from the Stretford End. He strikes him on the arm first ball.

Second ball: Huge appeal from the England team for lbw, but umpire Bowden shakes his head. A very tight decision. Ponting's back on strike.

Third ball: Ponting leaves it well alone outside off stump.

Fourth ball: Two more leg byes down to fine leg.

Fifth ball: After Ponting delays Harmison on his first run-up, the bowler surges back in, but Ponting presses a quick single to silly mid-off. Sub fielder Stephen Peters has a shy at the stumps, but misses with Lee well out of his ground.

Sixth ball: A great yorker from Harmison, but Lee is equal to it, digging it out superbly and sending it through the fielders to the square leg ropes.

103rd over: Australia 349–8 (Ponting 152, Lee 5 – five overs left)

First ball: Flintoff beats Ponting all ends up, but it just misses the outside edge.

Second ball: Forward defensive to silly point for no run.

Third ball: Another defensive shot keeps Flintoff out.

Fourth ball: Ponting gets forward to nudge it safely to the fielder at silly mid-off – no run.

Fifth ball: An exact repeat dose of the previous delivery.

Sixth ball: Ponting leaves the final ball alone outside off stump again, giving Harmison another shot at Lee.

104th over: Australia 354–9 (Ponting 156, Lee 6 – four overs left)

First ball: This is England's biggest chance: bowling at Lee. Harmison steams in, but Lee defends it well.

Second ball: Lee digs another full-pitched ball out and collects a single.

Third ball: Majestic stroke to the midwicket boundary from Ponting.

Fourth ball: Not out! A very close call as England and the crowd appeal for lbw against Ponting.

Fifth ball: Forward defensive for no run from Ponting.

WICKET! 104th over, sixth ball: Ponting c G Jones b Harmison 156 (Australia 354–9)

Unbelievable repeat of the Mike Kasprowicz shot at Edgbaston. Ponting gets a short one in his ribs from Harmison and gloves it behind down leg, where Geraint Jones takes another impressive catch. Remarkable stuff with England just one wicket away!

105th over: Australia 358–9 (Lee 10, McGrath 0 – three overs left)

First ball: Flintoff v. Lee. One wicket will do. Incredibly, another tumultuous conclusion is upon us. In steams Freddie, with seven slips, but Lee plays and misses.

Second ball: Lee leaves the ball outside off stump.

Third ball: Forward defensive to silly point for no run.

Fourth ball: Ever so close for Flintoff, as Lee almost edges outside off stump, but misses – just.

Fifth ball: Flintoff has the ball swinging and it again beats Lee, wafting outside off.

Sixth ball: Lee times the ball a little too well, piercing the field, but reaching the ropes to keep McGrath on strike.

106th over: Australia 362–9 (Lee 10, McGrath 4 – two overs left)

First ball: Harmison faces McGrath, but his bouncer flies over the Aussie's head.

Second ball: Attempted yorker, but McGrath bravely digs it out.

Third ball: An inside edge on to his foot leaves McGrath in a state of anxiety – but the ball falls safe.

Fourth ball: Another good defensive stroke off McGrath's pads.

Fifth ball: Harmison goes full, but McGrath plays the full toss to the fine-leg boundary.

Sixth ball: Easy for McGrath to leave alone outside off stump. An impressive performance from him in that over.

107th over: Australia 366–9 (Lee 14, McGrath 4 – one over left)

First ball: Flintoff sees his opener played forward by Lee, back to the bowler.

Second ball: Good batting from Lee, who uses his feet well to get forward and defend.

Third ball: A massive lbw appeal, but umpire Bucknor is having none of it.

Fourth ball: Wide outside off and Lee can leave well alone.

Fifth ball: Back comes Flintoff but Lee defends well. No run.

Sixth ball: Lee plays neatly through midwicket and the ball, literally, trickles into the ropes and puts McGrath on strike against Harmison. Six balls remain.

108th over: Australia 371–9 (Lee 18, McGrath 5)

First ball: This is it! Wide down leg-side and Geraint Jones collects after McGrath misses.

Second ball: Inside the gate, but agonisingly wide of off stump.

Third ball: Single to short midwicket from McGrath as Lee returns to the strike.

Fourth ball: Another wasteful ball down leg-side again doesn't make the batsman play.

Fifth ball: Outside off stump and Lee leaves it alone.

Sixth ball: Here we go – the Test and possibly the series riding on one delivery . . . it's a full toss on leg stump from Harmison, but Lee cracks it away to the square-leg boundary. An incredible Test is over and Australia have survived manfully. Great credit must go to Ponting and the Australian tail and it's the tourists who are celebrating.

Postamble: And breathe. A hush has enveloped Old Trafford, with supporters apparently stunned by England's failure to win. But like Ponting and the Australian resistance, Vaughan's side still deserve great credit for this performance. Remember, were it not for the lost day's play, England would have been able to set Australia the best part of a day and a half to bat, if not more. And while the series scoreline remains 1–1, England will need to pick themselves up, safe in the knowledge that they still dominated the majority of this Test. So, two games to go. Trent Bridge is up next and neither team will be able to win the series before we all head off to The Oval.

Australia 302 and 371–9; England 444 and 280–6 dec; match is drawn

Fourth Test

Trent Bridge,
25–28 August 2005

First Day

The morning session

BY SEAN INGLE

Preamble: Good morning everyone, and welcome to the first day of the fourth Test at Trent Bridge (writes *Guardian* hack from his Farringdon bunker). The big news for England is that Glenn McGrath is out with a sore right elbow. Michael Vaughan has won the toss again, and, with even Ricky Ponting admitting it looks an "excellent wicket", it's no surprise that England will bat. Meanwhile Sean Fitzpatrick writes: "How is it possible that one can get so excited by watching a little desktop scorecard at 10am on a Thursday morning? I am shaking at my desk and people are beginning to stare."

1st over: England 0–0 (Trescothick 0, Strauss 0) Lee opens up with six looseners. "I take it that's not the ex-All Blacks hooker Sean Fitzpatrick who's shaking at his desk," says Matthew Maynard (not *the* Matthew Maynard, surely?). "On a rugby point why do the Aussies and England seem to prepare for a Test by playing rugby? You never see Jonny Wilkinson with a sturdy lump of wood in his hand before a rugby match – probably just as well." Anyone?

2nd over: England 1–0 (Trescothick 0, Strauss 1) Decent start from Kasprowicz, who's bowling at 81–83mph à la McGrath, and with his accuracy too. "I've got a meeting starting at 11am and running to 12pm," says Andrew Lyman. "How best to drop into the conversation that I intend leaving my desktop scorecard on throughout the meeting?"

3rd over: England 6–0 (Trescothick 0, Strauss 4) Two no-balls from Lee in an over that's as nasty as a U movie. "I think Matthew is exaggerating the level of pre-match rugby," suggests Jonathon Wood. "It's just a little throw-around to get reactions and movement up to speed. It's not as if you've got them practising line-outs, with Geraint Jones 'step-laddering' Harmy."

4th over: England 7–0 (Trescothick 0, Strauss 4) Kasprowicz gets some extra bounce which startles Strauss. He does well to control that.

5th over: England 11–0 (Trescothick 4, Strauss 4) Lee serves up a lollipop and Trescothick finally gets off the mark with a breezy flick off his pads. Shot! "I don't think England could risk Geraint Jones 'step-laddering' Harmy," suggests Mark Kirk. "It's bound to hurt being dropped from that height."

6th over: England 13–0 (Trescothick 4, Strauss 4) Maiden for Kasprowicz, but it's swinging even less than your great-grandfather's hips at a disco. "If Jonny Wilkinson spent eight years practising one drop-kick, how long would it take him to master the forward defensive?" asks Andrew Wheatley-Hubbard. "Ergo, he sticks to rugby."

7th over: England 18–0 (Trescothick 4, Strauss 8) After the crash, bang, wallop of the first three Tests, the first half an hour of the fourth Test has been more watchful.

8th over: England 26–0 (Trescothick 9, Strauss 12) England on the attack! First Trescothick clobbers Kasprowicz for three, then, next ball, Strauss pulls a no-ball to the boundary. "I'm not sure that cricket has captured the imagination of everyone," says Nick Sylvester. "I was in an Edinburgh bar during the Old Trafford Test and stupidly asked if they could put the cricket on. I was then almost beaten up by a neanderthal Scot, who took exception to a bunch of Welsh blokes in Scotland wanting to watch the cricket. What's that all about?"

9th over: England 26–0 (Trescothick 9, Strauss 12) Lee continues, but it's looking an easy pitch to bat on so far. Tom Paternoster says, worryingly: "Like Sean Fitzpatrick, I'm all a-quiver too. When I read that McGrath was out I wanted to kiss your pixellated outpourings. I fear I may be in danger of taking this too seriously and spending September feeling thoroughly miserable."

10th over: England 35–0 (Trescothick 16, Strauss 13) Huge slice of luck for England! Trescothick attempts to cut a wide one, but doesn't move his feet, and ends up chopping the ball. It misses his stumps by inches, before rolling away for four.

11th over: England 37–0 (Trescothick 16, Strauss 15) Shaun Tait replaces Lee. What you've heard about him is true: his action is very slingy and Jeff Thomson-like. "Apologies to Nick Sylvester (8th over) – some Scottish people have still got fairly offensive attitudes to all things perceived as English, including cricket," says Kenny Smith. "But lots of Scots are, like me, very excited about this series."

12th over: England 37–0 (Trescothick 16, Strauss 15) Kasprowicz is getting little help from a featherbed of a pitch. Maiden. "Mr Gee should have sympathy for Scotland's more neanderthal inhabitants," says Mark Leech. "Like our own bar-room bores, they can only bear to watch the sports in which they have a slim chance of success. They are currently being sustained solely by curling and featherweight boxing."

13th over: England 48–0 (Trescothick 25, Strauss 16) "I too am concerned about the emptiness of my life come September," says Emma Marchant. "The Ashes have taken over my life, but how will I avoid work come next month?"

14th over: England 53–0 (Trescothick 29, Strauss 16) "Does anyone like me feel similarly indebted to Microsoft for creating the Alt+Tab function to switch between windows instantly? It's a great tool against my evil boss whenever she walks past my computer," says Kurban Kassam. "I handily have a report that I am pretending to type up to avert her suspicion."

15th over: England 57–0 (Trescothick 29, Strauss 21) Tait isn't getting much out of this pitch, and he's smashed through midwicket by Strauss for another boundary. "As a Scot I feel I have to interject," says Gavin Templeton. "How a sport in which you can sit in a stadium and drink all day is not loved by all Scots is beyond me. At my first trip to The Oval I was told we were only allowed four cans each into the stadium. 'What, is there no bar?' I asked. 'The four cans are for the 40–odd minutes when the bar is closed at lunch.' Fantastic!" Nothing like perpetuating national stereotypes, eh, Gavin?

16th over: England 70–0 (Trescothick 34, Strauss 26) We've had more no-balls than a Eunuchs' convention this morning: three times Kasprowicz strays over the line – that's 12 in total (seven by Kasprowicz).

17th over: England 74–0 (Trescothick 35, Strauss 27) Tait continues to suffer on his Test debut and only two brilliant stops in the field prevent further runs.

18th over: England 76–0 (Trescothick 36, Strauss 28) Warne's first ball is slogged by Strauss through midwicket, but there's a man back. In fact, there are men back everywhere.

19th over: England 79–0 (Trescothick 38, Strauss 30) Trescothick and Strauss are (famous last words alert) surely looking as comfortable as any batsmen in history facing 92mph deliveries. "I too am shaking at my desk over here in Moscow," says Sky News's Laurence Lee. "I've even begun trying to teach cricket to our staff here, who are either Russian or Georgian. They don't understand why there aren't border guards on the boundary."

20th over: England 91–0 (Trescothick 47, Strauss 31) Brilliant stuff from Trescothick, who lifts Warne for six over long-on! Meanwhile, Joe Payne writes: "I have misguidedly booked my honeymoon in Sardinia during the fifth Test. I assumed that I'd be able to pick up *Test Match Special* on the World Service. But having just checked the schedules, it seems it's not on. Any tips for picking up the Test in far-flung places? I suppose I could try getting it through the web, but I doubt my (by then) Mrs would appreciate me leaving her by the pool on her honeymoon whilst I sit inside reading your commentary."

21st over: England 101–0 (Trescothick 55, Strauss 31) Trescothick brings up his fifty with an easy prod through midwicket. Andy Lyman (second over) is back. "The tone of this morning's meeting was set when my boss came into the office and said, 'We're batting – have you got that desktop scorecard on yet?' Result!"

WICKET! 22nd over: Strauss c Hayden b Warne 35 (England 105–1) Strauss extravagantly paddle-sweeps at a delivery, which goes from inside-edge on to foot, before ballooning to Matthew Hayden. "I'd suggest to Joe Payne that he considers investing in a new 'bluetooth radio headimplant'," says John Yates. "These ingenious devices enable you to log your brain into sports internet commentary from anywhere – without detection."

23rd over: England 110–1 (Trescothick 55, Vaughan 4) "I'm attending Joe Payne's wedding and am concerned that his marriage could hit the rocks when his wife sees him hunched over the internet, staring intently and uttering things such as 'bang it in' and 'nice googlies'," worries Alexander Brown.

24th over: England 110–1 (Trescothick 55, Vaughan 4) Warne smiles and then sledges Vaughan after producing a beaut of a delivery which just missed the inside edge. Meanwhile this from Tasmin Cox. "My Dad, a regular spectator at Nottinghamshire, says the team that bats first at Trent Bridge is the team most likely to lose; the pitch gets harder and faster as the match goes on, so England need to make 500 in this innings at least. On the other hand, Warne's already bowling . . . Ah, only noon on the first day and it's already balanced on a knife-edge!"

25th over: England 118–1 (Trescothick 61, Vaughan 4) "Sorry but you guys are amateurs when it comes to a cricket skive," says Chris from Ipswich. "I'm 'working from home to finish some reports without interruption' today. The reports in question were finished at 11pm last night and are being sent out at strategic intervals during today, creating the illusion of an industrious, productive day."

26th over: England 120–1 (Trescothick 61, Vaughan 6) Warne continues to aggravate Vaughan. Gilchrist continues to shout "Nicely bowled, Shane". "I work in housing on a project to renovate sheltered housing," says Kimberley Taylor. "Cheering at the desktop scorecard doesn't seem professional when I'm explaining to Mavis that she's going to get chucked out of her home."

27th over: England 120–1 (Trescothick 61, Vaughan 14) Shot of the morning from Michael Vaughan, who teases a fuller delivery from Lee through mid-off for four. Lunch.

England 129–1

The afternoon session

BY MIKE ADAMSON

Preamble: Another good opening session for England left them in a fairly strong position.

Then Adamson took up the over-by-over hot seat and the jinx struck again: rain, lots of it, forcing the groundsmen to bring the covers out to the middle. And so to an email while we wait: "For those of us in Australia," says Martin Lyons, "your OBO page currently shows an advert (presumably) from the Australian government saying 'There's never been a better time to become an Australian citizen.' Good sense of irony, eh?"

1.25pm: Play will resume at 2pm. Meanwhile, an email from Jeff Talbot: "We've been discussing David Boon's 52 cans of beer here at work. Does anyone know which beer it was and what size the cans were? Makes all the difference you know."

1.45pm: "According to Wikipedia, David Boon's effort was with 375ml-size cans," says Michael Chapman. "His entry also notes that Boon 'vomited on the hallowed Adelaide Oval turf in a WSC game in 1988 before a live nationwide TV audience of millions (he went on to make 122 and win Man of the Match)'. Lovely stuff from the big man." James Green adds: "Mike Tindall tried to beat it on England's flight home from the Rugby World Cup in 2003. Rumour is he got very close, mid to high 40s." While Mike Asquith notes: "November 14, 1996 was proclaimed David Boon Day in Tasmania, but was later overturned by the federal government as it was a ridiculous idea."

1.58pm: Play has been put back to 2.10pm. "This summer has introduced me to a novelty," says Thomas Whiteley. "We're playing the Aussies and actually praying it doesn't rain or stop. I think that tells you everything you need to know about this series."

28th over: England 132–1 (Trescothick 64, Vaughan 14) Michael Kasprowicz opens up after lunch, and immediately sends down the 19th no-ball of the day. "I'm going to guess at Fosters," says Edward Stone, trying to shed some light on David Boon's tipple of choice, "but how much more impressive it would have been if it was 13.5% extra free cans of Special Brew." And Ewan Dunnett chips in: "Don't know much about what Boony consumed, but to mark the event they once lowered the speed limit in Tasmania to 52mph to honour his achievement."

29th over: England 132–1 (Trescothick 63, Vaughan 14) Ricky Ponting throws the ball to Shaun Tait again after the debutant's disappointing (commentator language for "rubbish") first spell this morning. A maiden, though. "Fun as it was to read about other people's elaborate skiving cover-ups this morning," says Richard Frampton, before the inevitable "but" – "but have people thought that their bosses could also be nose-to-monitor, and that getting their story posted on the OBO could ultimately be their downfall?"

30th over: England 134–1 (Trescothick 65, Vaughan 15) "If they were to make a film of David Boon's life, who would you cast in the lead role?" asks Tom Newman. "Possibly a walrus."

Rain stops play: The players are trudging off again. Why do the same people who raise their umbrellas at the slightest drizzle then boo when rain stops play? "Surely the answer to the problem of your boss reading your email is to use a fake name," says Electrick Boycott-Prodde III.

2.30pm: The covers are on. No news on when play may resume. "Richard Frampton has a point," says Andy Smith, "but forgets that if your boss admits to reading your email on the OBO and tells you off for not working then he has clearly not been working either. It's a let's move on and say no more about it situation, while both grinning inanely about the state of the Aussie bowling attack."

2.50pm: "Can I just say what a snivelling, pointless simpleton my boss is?" says Paul Knapp courageously. "Just to check if he's reading the OBO, of course."

2.55pm: As I'm too lazy to look up the weather forecast, and nobody else is prepared to tell me, here's Stuart Parkin: "Trent Bridge seems to be getting the weather we've just had down the other end of the A52 in Derby – I appoint myself Chief Weather Watching Monkey and can tell you that we now have blue sky with a few fluffy white clouds so hopefully they'll be back out soon."

3pm: It would seem Stuart Parkin's weather assessment was correct because play is scheduled to recommence at 3.30pm. That's half an hour away for those whose arithmetic isn't the best.

3.10pm: "Surely the obvious candidate to play David Boon on the silver screen," says Jamie Russell, "would have been the great Oliver Reed but, as he is sadly no longer with us, what about George Best in a fat suit?" Good though your banter is, the cricket will begin again in 20 minutes.

England 134–1

The evening session

BY MIKE ADAMSON

Preamble: The heavens have opened again. Half the covers had been taken off when those umbrellas started going up again, and they had to be quickly rushed back on to the wicket once more. Further news will follow.

3.35pm: "As for all this 'what if my boss reads my name on the OBO' debate," says Steve Cajkler, "it's much more fun to impersonate one of your friends and hope that his boss is reading the OBO! So if anyone from Corus Caldicot is reading this: Matthew Rees is doing absolutely no work today." Sorry, Steve, I can't let you get away with that one.

3.50pm: The covers are off, and play is scheduled to resume in five minutes. Hopefully.

WICKET! 31st over: Trescothick b Tait 65 (England 137–2) Shaun Tait claims his first Test wicket in the first over of the session by pitching the ball up full. Trescothick tried to flick the ball through the leg-side, but simply missed it and it crashed into the stumps.

32nd over: England 139–2 (Vaughan 18, Bell 2) Bell is off the mark with a nice clip off his legs. A testing over from Kasprowicz, though. "Just wondering what workshy OBO readers recommend should the Ashes go down to the Monday of the Oval Test," says Mark Abbott. "Obviously you have to be there at about 6am, but can't chuck a sickie till approx 8.30am – assuming texting is no good – can you get some advice on how to drown out the 'Engerland' chants while palming your day's work off on the boss?" I'm afraid all tickets have been sold already, so you shouldn't have that problem.

33rd over: England 145–2 (Vaughan 23, Bell 3) It's incredible what a wicket can do for a young bowler. Tait suddenly looks like the demon bowler the Australian journalists have been telling us about. "Who is going to carry the can for this weather?" wonders Jonathan Harwood. "I blame the ECB, which might sound a bit harsh, but for the first time in a generation we've got Australia on the hop, yet all the Tests are scheduled at the end of the summer when the weather is worse, so they can accommodate Bangladesh and a load of pointless ODIs."

34th over: England 146–2 (Vaughan 23, Bell 3) "If there was ever a boss who wouldn't mind if his team did no more work for the rest of the afternoon," says James Hull, "surely it's Ricky Ponting."

WICKET! 35th over: Bell c Gilchrist b Tait 3 (England 146–3) And there's Tait's second Test wicket, a regulation catch for Gilchrist as Bell edges one that moves away a little.

35th over: England 152–3 (Vaughan 23, Pietersen 6) "Strewth," says Jon Mann, clearly not trying to hide his nationality. "You Poms fluke one Test match (by just two runs), now you think you can win the series! Not a chance mate – I reckon you guys have had one Fosters too many. And even rain won't save you this time, Bruce, because you need to win one of the remaining matches. Sorry guys I mentioned 'win' there, you Poms might need to look that word up."

36th over: England 154–3 (Vaughan 24, Pietersen 7) "We have a traditional 'Google question of the day' at work," says Thomas Whiteley. "Today's was: are there more rabbits than humans on this planet? Sadly, Google has not provided the answer. Does anyone out there know (btw, Australian batsmen don't count)?"

37th over: England 158–3 (Vaughan 24, Pietersen 11) A lovely shot from KP using his sub-continental-style wrists to whip the ball through midwicket for four. "Australian arrogance never ceases to amaze," says Tim Claremont, rising to the bait. "Has he been watching any of the cricket over the last two Tests? Reckon moment of the series so far was watching Glenn '5–0' McGrath celebrating scraping a draw to keep the series at 1–1."

38th over: England 161–3 (Vaughan 25, Pietersen 12) Kasprowicz almost takes Pietersen's wicket, the ball swinging viciously in these conditions between KP's bat and pad and missing off stump by a couple of inches.

39th over: England 167–3 (Vaughan 25, Pietersen 14) "What will the Aussies do now that they aren't the best in their favourite sports?" asks Jonny Martin. "I suggest they follow the American lead and invent new sports that only they play. We could have a World Series BBQ, or a NSL – a national sledging league."

40th over: England 169–3 (Vaughan 26, Pietersen 15) Kasprowicz drops Pietersen off his own bowling! "Not sure about the world," says Michael Knowles helpfully, "but there are about 300m rabbits in Australia alone, compared with just 19m people." So there you go.

41st over: England 174–3 (Vaughan 30, Pietersen 15) Lee replaces Tait, and Vaughan guides his first ball down to the boundary. "Yes, McGrath celebrating was a sign of the times for sure," says David Horn, "but underestimation of the series goes to Ricky Ponting who said that the gap between the two sides was 'quite vast' after the first Test."

42nd over: England 175–3 (Vaughan 31, Pietersen 15) Another catch put down by the Australians. This time it was Matthew Hayden at gully after Vaughan hit the ball to his left. By Test match standards it was a dolly. "One of my female friends who has just started watching cricket because of the Ashes texted me last night," begins Penny Glazzard in an effort to write a really long sentence, "saying that Jack (the hero) in Channel 4's *Lost* was the spitting image of 'the bloke who throws the ball really fast and got the short Australian out'. I think she means Steve Harmison. I can see where she is coming from, but Harmy is probably a bit leaner."

43rd over: England 179–3 (Vaughan 35, Pietersen 15) It really is raining hard, and it's surprising they're still out there. "No idea about the rabbits/humans saga," says Alec Stephens. "I do know, however, that Malta eats more rabbits per capita than any other European country."

44th over: England 180–3 (Vaughan 35, Pietersen 16) "Surely Jack's nose from *Lost* is more reminiscent of an absent Jason Gillespie's!" says Rowan Hillery.

45th over: England 187–3 (Vaughan 39, Pietersen 19) Vaughan plays the shot of the day, a perfect cover drive. Even Ponting looked tempted to applaud. "Australians don't like having it pointed out that once Michael Vaughan passes 50 against them his lowest score is 145," says Jonathan Harwood. Hang on, he's not there yet, Jonathan.

46th over: England 191–3 (Vaughan 39, Pietersen 23) The fickle weather is now producing glorious sunshine. And England are producing some glorious shots, Pietersen this time playing another wristy drive past midwicket. "Three hundred million rabbits?" exclaims Derrick East. "How old is that information as I make it that they double their population every three months, or an average of 2,289 per second, assuming that they breed like rabbits, of course."

47th over: England 196–3 (Vaughan 44, Pietersen 23) "Jonny Martin has suggested that the Aussies start making their own sports up to be the best in the world at," parps Neil Toolan. "Surely they started doing that some years ago with Aussie Rules Football. A sport that must have been born out of a David Boon-esque drinking session, as there appears to be elements of rugby, American football, basketball, football and even Gaelic football in it, and lord knows what you're supposed to do."

48th over: England 198–3 (Vaughan 45, Pietersen 23) "Given the pitch, weather forecast and the absence of McGrath, what's a good first-innings total?" asks Paul Graham. Before the rain, England would have been looking for 500 at least, but the downpours have changed how the pitch is playing, and England will just do well to get through to the end of play without the loss of any more wickets.

49th over: England 206–3 (Vaughan 53, Pietersen 23) Vaughan flies past 50, first clipping the ball to deep square leg, then timing the ball perfectly to add four more through the on-side. "In 2004 there were about 40 million rabbits in the UK," says Luke Pavey. "Also, there were 60,000 polecats, 275,000 badgers and 12,000 otters. Unfortunately, there were only 37,000 mink. I think it's fair to say there must be more rabbits in the world than people."

50th over: England 206–3 (Vaughan 53, Pietersen 23) The Aussies must be getting desperate: Ricky Ponting is on to bowl (no, seriously). "I don't watch *Lost*, but judging by Rowan Hillery's description I'm concluding that 'Jack's nose' is extremely hairy – is this integral to the plot?" asks Matthew Goodinson. Haven't the foggiest, Matthew. I don't watch it either. But enough of you are emailing in to inform me that he actually looks like Simon Jones.

51st over: England 207–3 (Vaughan 54, Pietersen 23)

52nd over: England 209–3 (Vaughan 55, Pietersen 24) Ponting is back with his dobbers. Pietersen continues to refuse to fall for the trap. "I've got to say, I think you're a touch pessimistic," says P Thompson. "If England keep chugging away as they have, they'll have 300 by the close. Even with one more down 500 is not out of reach and even with two more down, they'll want 420+."

53rd over: England 210–3 (Vaughan 55, Pietersen 25) "I feel I must point out to Luke Pavey that mink are an introduced species native to North America, and that they have a detrimental effect on the populations of endemic species such as otters," says Thomas Morris. "So it is in no way 'unfortunate' that there are only 37,000 of the blighters on the loose in our countryside."

54th over: England 210–3 (Vaughan 55, Pietersen 25) "When I was a student and had all the time in the world England had a bowling attack of the likes of Robert Croft, Mike Watkinson and Phil DeFreitas," says Thomas Atkins. "Now Harmison, Flintoff *et al* are sweeping all before them I have to follow it on an OBO. Not fair!"

55th over: England 213–3 (Vaughan 58, Pietersen 25) Tait replaces Lee. I wish someone would replace Ponting, whose tactic is deadly dull. "As a reluctant trivia bore," says Ben Dakin, hardly encouraging us to continue reading, "I have to point out that Australian Rules predates rugby and football, when it comes to formulation of rules and codes. It was invented to keep cricketers fit in the winter months – hence it being played on an oval!"

WICKET! 56th over: Vaughan c Gilchrist b Ponting 58 (England 213–4) The Australian captain takes the England captain's wicket. The ball moves ever-so-slightly off the seam away from Vaughan's bat, but the bat followed the ball and nicked it to the keeper. A crucial blow.

56th over: England 217–4 (Pietersen 25, Flintoff 4) Ponting has suddenly turned into McGrath. Bowling at a similar speed, with a similar line and length (admittedly without quite the same consistency), and moving both ways, he troubles Flintoff, whose first runs are a thick edge past the slip cordon.

57th over: England 222–4 (Pietersen 30, Flintoff 4) Pietersen flashes the ball to Ponting at gully, but it lands just in front of the Aussie skipper. "As a cricket nut in India, this Ashes has certainly got us hooked," says Akash Agarwal. "I must comment on the increasing chirpiness of your readers in England who are by now starting to dish out some good abuse. At the start of the series it was mainly about people telling how this was a nice series and had got them interested. Now they want blood and are willing to show emotion too."

58th over: England 223–4 (Pietersen 31, Flintoff 4) Flintoff is struggling to deal with Ponting, who is swinging the withered 58–over-old ball this way and that.

59th over: England 228–4 (Pietersen 32, Flintoff 8) A huge, ominous cloud has descended on Trent Bridge, which could either bring rain or bad light before too long. Flintoff doesn't seem to care, though, thrashing a wide Tait delivery through extra cover.

60th over: England 229–4 (Pietersen 33, Flintoff 8) In the decreasing light, Ponting has turned to Shane Warne. Quite why he wasn't on earlier when Ponting was bowling himself, I do not know. "I assume that the info on rabbits and badgers comes from some sort of census," says Andrew Donald. "How do they fill it in without opposable thumbs, let alone a postal address?"

Rain stopped play: The big black cloud has brought heavy rain with it, and the players have gone off. Though there has been no official word, it now seems certain there will be no more play tonight.

England 229–4

Second Day

The morning session

BY SEAN INGLE

Preamble: If Kevin Pietersen and Andy Flintoff can push on, they should reach 400. If not, we could be in for a traditional middle-order collapse. Once again it's another hugely important session. It's cloudy but dry at Trent Bridge, so play will start on time.

61st over: England 234–4 (Pietersen 38, Flintoff 8) After limbering up with a few 80s-style aerobic leg lifts (minus the Bjorn Borg headband, sadly) Brett Lee rolls in and bowls the mother of all looseners, which Pietersen flicks past leg stump for four.

62nd over: England 235–4 (Pietersen 39, Flintoff 8) Shane Warne gets an early whirl, but so far there's not much twirl. "What time do they finish today?" asks the superbly-monikered Jon Schnadhorst. "I finish at 5pm. Is it worth me skipping the pub, and running home to watch?" We're on till at least 6pm and possibly up to 6.30pm, Jon. So why not?

63rd over: England 239–4 (Pietersen 43, Flintoff 8) Shot from Pietersen, who hits a front-foot cut for four. "How long can the Aussie batsmen continue not fulfilling their potential?" ponders Michael Girling. "Their world-beating Test averages would suggest they're due to score big at some point." Hasn't happened so far this series, though, Michael.

64th over: England 239–4 (Pietersen 45, Flintoff 8) First huge bellowing appeal from Warne, who reckons he's got Flintoff out lbw. Warne screams and screams and screams some more, but umpire Bucknor rightly judges that the delivery was missing leg stump. "I think KP (we're close) is getting too chatty with the

Aussies," claims Craig Easterbrook. "At Old Trafford he was in mid-conversation with Warne just before Lee bounced him out. Head down, son." He's looking good so far, Craig.

WICKET! 65th over: Pietersen c Gilchrist b Lee 45 (England 241–5)
Er, what was I saying? First ball of the over, Lee pitches one up fuller, it gets a hint of outswing, and Pietersen edges one behind. "Stop being gloomy, please!" asks Nina Blakesley. "I'm having a rubbish day already and the thought of a good result is the only thing keeping me from having a cry in the loos."

66th over: England 252–5 (Flintoff 17, G Jones 2) An exquisite cover drive from Flintoff brings up the 250. "I went into the pub here in Dublin after work yesterday evening to find a load of lads watching the cricket – guy in a thick Dublin brogue goes, 'Once Vaughan goes past fifty he usually goes on to get a big hundred,'" says Brian Aherne. "Wrong he may have been, but worrying for the future of my country nonetheless."

67th over: England 252–5 (Flintoff 18, G Jones 2) Flintoff takes an early single and then Jones blocks. "Craig Easterbrook makes a good point about hob-nobbing with the Aussies (over 64). Aggers was saying the same thing last night – he was interviewing Simon Jones when Gilchrist came up and gave him a high-five (Jones, that is, not Aggers. BBC cricket correspondents don't do high-fives)," says Jonathon Swan. "Anyway, a bit of camaraderie is one thing, but come on chaps, remember – they ARE the enemy." Disagree, Jonathon – Nasser Hussain's England players were in awe of the Aussies: by drinking and socialising with them, England's players will realise they're only human.

68th over: England 257–5 (Flintoff 22, G Jones 2) Flintoff takes on Warne! It's a slight mishit, but it takes one bounce before going into the stands.

69th over: England 264–5 (Flintoff 22, G Jones 7) Biggest shock of the morning? It's taken eight overs for the first no-ball. "It's all very well scoring centuries against the shoddy attacks of New Zealand, West Indies, Zimbabwe and Bangladesh. But when is the last time these Australians actually faced top-quality pace bowling other than in their own nets?" asks Peter Williams.

70th over: England 265–5 (Flintoff 24, G Jones 7) Warne continues to probe, and has Jones playing and missing with a fizzing leggie. For once Gilchrist's repeated cry of "Bowling Warney!" rings true. "In the last Test they discussed the merits of Green Day, now Aggers is talking about the Stranglers and the delights of piercings," splutters Matthew Cobb. "Vic Marks isn't partial to either, it appears. I kid you not. What are they putting in their cakes?"

71st over: England 270–5 (Flintoff 29, G Jones 7) Flintoff jabs at one down leg-side, it hits his glove, and flies past Gilchrist's diving glove by inches. Good first over for Kasprowicz, who has replaced Brett Lee. "Cheer up Nina (over 65)," cries Stuart Suffolk. "It's a Bank Holiday weekend. Besides, you can't follow the over-by-over reports in the toilet."

72nd over: England 272–5 (Flintoff 30, G Jones 8) "I think Peter Williams (over 69) is spot-on," says P Thompson. "The Aussies are – as encapsulated by Hayden – a bunch of flat-track bullies. The exception is clearly Ponting, who showed last Test how good he really is. England's bowlers just prod away at their weaknesses and force them to play differently – not the aggressive dominant way they like to. This is why we will win the Ashes."

73rd over: England 276–5 (Flintoff 31, G Jones 10) "I am currently watching the cricket via Sky Satellite, listening via digital radio and reading your page on my laptop, via my Wi-Fi broadband connection," says Oliver Bridges. "Can anyone beat this? I am also, currently (ahem), working from home."

74th over: England 281–5 (Flintoff 33, G Jones 13) "There are downsides to being an Aussie," says Neil Stork-Brett from Brisbane. "Such as lifelong exposure to sunshine, cold beer and deadly animals. But I'm actually enjoying watching our blokes struggle. They've had it too easy for too long – forget Bradman's Invincibles – the current Australian side aren't even as good as our Ian Chappell-led sides of the 70s."

75th over: England 286–5 (Flintoff 39, G Jones 13) Pietersen's dismissal apart, it's been a sedate first hour: the pitch looks more scoring-friendly than an 18–30 holiday. Drinks. "It's not a bank holiday for us Brits here in Moscow," sobs Alek Sang. "On a more positive side, we're three hours ahead, so it's a good excuse to stay late in the office following the OBO. The boss is impressed."

76th over: England 292–5 (Flintoff 44, G Jones 13) More good stuff from Flintoff, who rocks back before cracking Warne through the covers for another boundary. "England should change their name to Great Britain, if only to help Welshmen like me have easier lives," says Chris Mason. "It's so tedious explaining to work colleagues how I can support 'England' in cricket and England's opposition in rugby and football."

77th over: England 297–5 (Flintoff 44, G Jones 17) Andrew Snowball has a dilemma. "I have to go to my gran's 80th birthday party tomorrow afternoon, which is messing with my plans to watch the cricket all day," he writes. "Can OBO readers help with any excuses to avoid the do?" What about the inheritance, Andrew?

78th over: England 300–5 (Flintoff 45, G Jones 19) "I would bet my house on us losing a wicket within three overs of the drinks break," suggests Tim Vogel. "It's the curse of the stoppage." You've just lost your house, Tim, although it was a close-run thing: half-way through that over, Warne got some extra bounce, Jones got a low nick, and it bounced just in front of Hayden at first slip.

79th over: England 303–5 (Flintoff 45, G Jones 22) Jones continues to essay the cut, and continues to score runs from it. "I would say you will beat all records of hits on your site today," suggests Jason in Dublin. "It has taken me nearly an hour to get in (on and off), very frustrating when you are denied dossing at work."

80th over: England 313–5 (Flintoff 54, G Jones 23) Warne strays on to leg stump, Flintoff can resist no longer and slog-sweeps him over midwicket for six! Meanwhile suggestions for Andrew Snowball on how to avoid his gran's 80th birthday party: "Tell her you've got flu and don't want to give it to her – works every time," chuckles David Bowerman.

81st over: England 318–5 (Flintoff 54, G Jones 27) Shaun Tait takes the new ball, thunders in, and sees Jones clout it past him for four. Shot! "Andrew Snowball could tell his gran his gout's giving him gip. At least she'll identify with that," suggests Paul Jackson.

82nd over: England 323–5 (Flintoff 58, G Jones 28) Good first over from Lee, who – unlike yesterday – is getting the ball to swing. Flintoff's response? An almost feathery push-drive, straight down the ground for four. "If Andrew Snowball poisons his grandmother at some point overnight, he might get away with receiving the inheritance and watching the cricket all day all in one go, thus killing two birds with one stone," suggests someone who refers to remain anonymous. "It's the perfect crime."

83rd over: England 336–5 (Flintoff 70, G Jones 28) Superb from Flintoff! First he pulls Tait over midwicket for four, then, next ball, he smashes him straight down the ground. Two balls later, another pull shot flies to the boundary! "I think that everyone is underestimating Andrew's gran," suggests Jacqueline Anne Woodward-Smith. "She's probably watching the cricket even now, over a nice cup of a tea and some Battenburg. How does Andrew know that she wouldn't rather that everyone left her alone to watch the cricket tomorrow?"

84th over: England 336–5 (Flintoff 70, G Jones 29) Lee is making the new ball sing: he unleashes an inswinger which goes between Jones's bat and pad . . . and over the stumps. "Given his nan's age and no doubt her inability to catch a ball, she'll probably get called up to the Australian side to provide some much needed youth," suggests Andy Smith. "On top of this she'll get free tickets so he'll be able to be with her on her birthday, while drinking heavily in the stands and watching the cricket. Everyone's a winner."

84th over: England 341–5 (Flintoff 72, G Jones 32) The 100 partnership comes up off 126 balls. England are in the box seat. "Not wishing to perpetuate any stereotypes or anything, but maybe if you can come up with some bingo-related game based on the cricket, you can watch the cricket with your gran at the party AND follow the ups and downs of the game," suggests Paul Haynes.

85th over: England 342–5 (Flintoff 73, G Jones 32) "Anon's suggestion in over 82 would almost certainly lead to granny's funeral during the all-important decider at The Oval, no?" suggests Michael Darbyshire, not unreasonably.

86th over: England 342–5 (Flintoff 73, G Jones 32) Kasprowicz replaces Tait, and immediately launches into a huge lbw appeal against Flintoff. Umpire Aleem Dar is rightly unimpressed. "Owners of the fine Ashes guide issued free with the *Guardian* at the beginning of the series will already possess a cricketing TV-related bingo game," points out Neil Wallington (and others).

87th over: England 343–5 (Flintoff 73, G Jones 33) Beavis and Butthead Lee continues to give Jones a working over, which only ends when the England batsman just gets a bat on to a nasty yorker.

88th over: England 344–5 (Flintoff 73, G Jones 34) Flintoff sees off Kasprowicz and England leave the field to a standing ovation. It's justfied too: 114 runs came off 29 overs, with just one wicket. Meanwile Mark Cleland has the final word of the morning. "Valid point from Mr Darbyshire in over 85, but if Andrew Snowball can convince his family that gran was an avid cricket fan, there's the perfect and somewhat ironic solution of scattering her ashes at The Oval in the Ashes decider," says Mark Cleland. "That way he and all his family get a pitch-side view of the match too."

England 344–5

The afternoon session

BY MIKE ADAMSON

Preamble: Freddie Flintoff's batting average has at long last clambered above that of his bowling, a statistic he fully deserves after his imperious performances over the last two years or so. If he can go out after lunch and score a big hundred, England will be in a dominant position.

90th over: England 353–5 (Flintoff 74, G Jones 42) Brett Lee throws down a 77mph slower ball first up after lunch, and a huge appeal for caught behind follows. Steve Bucknor shakes his head as it was hard to decipher whether the noise was the bat hitting the ground or the ball. My erstwhile colleague Rob Smyth writes: "Does anyone know what Shaun Tait's favourite TV show is?" I'm sure you do, Smyth.

91st over: England 362–5 (Flintoff 78, G Jones 43) A sloppy start from Kasprowicz, whose first few deliveries all drift on to leg stump, allowing Flintoff some easy runs. Kim Whatley chuckles in response to the previous over's question: "Tait the high road?" Dear, dear.

92nd over: England 368–5 (Flintoff 79, G Jones 48) Jones nurdles Lee around while Channel 4's Analyst suggests that the England keeper was not out when the Aussies appealed for caught behind in the first over of the session. "For the good of us all, please don't write things like 'If he can go out after lunch and score a big hundred England will be in a dominant position' given England's propensity for losing wickets at the beginning of a session," says an angry Tom Ellis-Jones. Point taken.

93rd over: England 382–5 (Flintoff 92, G Jones 48) Two powerful hits from Flintoff – one through the leg-side, one through the off – yield eight runs, then a wonderfully timed back-foot drive off another Kasprowicz no-ball adds another five to the total. Warren Nicolas chips in with "Tait half hot mum", while John Whiting adds, "Is his favourite show *The Catherine Tate Show*? His bowling would be a welcome comic addition to that laugh-free phoned-in junk." Thankfully only a couple of you have seen the ulterior motive of Smyth mentioning this, but I'm afraid the show will not be mentioned here today, Robert.

94th over: England 385–5 (Flintoff 93, G Jones 50) Lee almost traps Flintoff plumb in front of his stumps, but an inside edge saves the big Lancastrian. "Just been reading *Small Talk*'s interview with Tait where he mentions his favourite biscuit is a TimTam," says Steve Smith. "Not being unaware of the charms of a TimTam myself from my time Down Under, I happen to know that, when I last checked anyways, Safeway & Tesco stock the whole range."

95th over: England 391–5 (Flintoff 94, G Jones 54) "For the benefit of us nouveaux cricket fans unused to the technical terminology, could you explain what 'to nurdle' means (over 91)? It's a great word and I'd like to see if I could use it in everyday conversation." Well, Fran Turner, it means to nudge the ball around into areas devoid of fielders for ones and twos. There must surely be ways of using it in conversation, but I'll leave that up to you lot as I'm a bit pushed for time.

96th over: England 395–5 (Flintoff 94, G Jones 59) "Steve Smith should find it easy to assess the charms of Tim Tams given that they are in fact just re-branded Penguins," says Jon Chapman. "The biscuits, obviously."

97th over: England 400–5 (Flintoff 98, G Jones 60) "Conversations can be nurdled," says Tim Hinton. "Just interject with a well-timed 'yeah', 'mmm' or 'it's like that last time isn't it?' every now and then to keep the conversation chugging along (and hopefully the other half happy). Perfecting this is particularly useful when trying to watch the cricket."

98th over: England 405–5 (Flintoff 99, G Jones 64) "I'm currently 'nurdling' papers around my desk in the pretence of working, as, I'm sure, is everyone else reading this," says Jamie Reeman.

99th over: England 405–5 (Flintoff 99, G Jones 64) Ponting chooses not to bring the field up to make it more difficult for Flintoff to reach his hundred. Flintoff tries to cut a shortish Warne delivery but plays and misses to gasps from the Aussie fielders. He remains on 99. "Surely it has been used in playground football when picking sides and you get to the last two," chortles Nigel Owen. "'That nurdle do,' announces the captain."

100th over: England 405–5 (Flintoff 99, G Jones 64) Another maiden, this time from Tait. "I wouldn't touch anything called a TimTam with a bargepole," says Jon Hawkins. "Certainly not from a man who imagines dinosaurs were the unfortunate victims of the earth's surface suddenly giving way under their weight."

101st over: England 406–5 (Flintoff 100, G Jones 64) And there it is! Flintoff scores his fifth Test match century and his first against Australia. A great performance, and my colleague James Dart is pretty chuffed too – he placed a bet on Freddie to win the BBC Sports Personality of the Year award at the start of the year at 7–1.

102nd over: England 414–5 (Flintoff 102, G Jones 65) The game is starting to slip away from Australia here. We've had 70 runs already this session, and none of the bowlers are really troubling the batsmen. "One of my pals emigrated to Oz, but came back for my wedding," says Jonathan Gardner. "We undertook a controlled experiment, Tim Tam v Penguin, which had two elements: Guess the Penguin and proffer an opinion as to your favoured biscuit/tea improver. Despite the blindfolds, the majority (7 of 9) incorrectly identified the Penguin. Furthermore, Tim Tam won hands down on the taste and consistency front."

103rd over: England 418–5 (Flintoff 102, G Jones 69) Warne drags one short and Jones knocks it out to Langer on the off-side boundary. Langer, though, to the delight of the Trent Bridge crowd, overran the ball, slipped and the ball trundled past him. John Sims writes: "My 18–month-old daughter also uses 'nurdle' in conversation with her twin brother: 'Nurdle, nurdle, nurdle, nurdle?' To which his response is usually, 'Gah!'"

WICKET! 104th over: Flintoff lbw b Tait 102 (England 418–6) Having reached his hundred, Flintoff tries to hoick one too many to cow corner and is caught on the knee-roll in front of his stumps. An easy decision for umpire Bucknor. It was a great innings, but this breakthrough has thrown Australia a glimmer of hope.

105th over: England 421–6 (G Jones 72, Giles 0) With Flintoff back in the pavilion, Warne has turned to attack, bowling over the wicket. And he looks far more dangerous. "Just went to the pub for our lunch-break, and the pub in question had the cricket on a screen about five yards wide, and we left as Freddie picked up his hundred," says Jonathan. "Needless to say there were a lot of men in the pub and a large cheer as the century came. Two women then walked out of the pub, one turning to the other saying, 'It's very busy, is there rugby on or something?'"

106th over: England 426–6 (G Jones 73, Giles 4) Jones's aggression almost proves his undoing as he tries to hook Tait. His mistimed shot bloops the ball into the air but the onrushing mid-on just fails to reach it. "Being from Newcastle I can confirm, categorically, that 'nurdles' can be purchased in chicken, prawn or beef variety from my local Chinese take-away," says Ally Mogg.

107th over: England 428–6 (G Jones 74, Giles 5) In the absence of Flintoff, Jones is continuing to take the game to Australia, but Warne is bowling better now that he has changed his approach to over the wicket. That's my waffly way of admitting that I missed the majority of that over. "Jonathan Gardner really knows how to organise a cracking wedding doesn't he?" says Andrew Goldby rather cheekily. "All right then, lads, who's up for some biscuit tasting? I've got a blindfold."

108th over: England 428–6 (G Jones 74, Giles 5) A maiden from Tait. "Given that more rain is likely, is a declaration on the agenda at some stage in order to give the lads the time to take 20 wickets?" asks Ian Macintyre. "Or do they just grind on and try to score 650 and put the game completely safe? Me, I'd look to declare. Sends a very big message."

109th over: England 429–6 (G Jones 75, Giles 5) Just one off the over, Jones working Kasprowicz through cover. "I can't wait till you lot come to Australia next time on your next futile effort to win the Ashes," says Burt Bosma, just stirring things up a little. "Then you'll realise that on real cricket grounds most of the shots by your so-called big hitters turn out to be catches two-thirds of the way to the boundary. As happened to Beefy when he got off your toy English ovals."

110th over: England 432–6 (G Jones 77, Giles 5) "Having just flown in from a US work trip my girlfriend has messengered me at work to reassure herself that '422 is quite a big score isn't it?'" says Monty Menon, "thus proving that not all women are oblivious to cricket and also reassuring me that I could quite easily spend the rest of my life with her." Ahhh.

111th over: England 444–6 (G Jones 85, Giles 10) Freddie Flintoff is spied on the pavilion balcony staring at his laptop, maybe at the OBO report. If so Freddie, drop us a line. "Given her propensity to nurdle, and following Thorpe's retirement," says Matt Dolman, "could John Sims's daughter (103rd over) usefully be called up in place of Ian Bell?"

112th over: England 448–6 (G Jones 85, Giles 14) An excellent over from Warne, varying his pace to Giles, is ruined when Giles swipes cross-batted at the last ball and drags it for four. "Is Burt Bosma suggesting the groundsmen sneak out to move the ropes between innings?" asks Jason Boissiere. "I've only been listening on the radio, so I might have missed that."

WICKET! 113th over: G Jones c & b Kasprowicz 85 (England 450–7) Jones's excellent knock comes to an end as he tries to smack Kasprowicz over midwicket but instead inside-edges the ball on to his pad and into the air. The alert bowler quickly rushed forward and took a good diving catch. "Maybe the smaller English ovals account for the laughable amount of no-balls by the tourists," says Neil Mckie. "They aren't afforded the room for the full run-up."

WICKET! 114th over: Giles lbw b Warne 15 (England 450–8) Oh dear. Giles attempts to sweep Warne, but the ball goes straight on and even umpire Bucknor doesn't take too long to make his mind up over that one. "Over 110: Is that a marriage proposal?" wonders David Horn. "If so, is that a first for OBO? Can S Ingle officiate?"

115th over: England 454–8 (Hoggard 2, Harmison 2) Hoggard plays his one defensive shot (the forward defence) a few times against Kasprowicz, then exhibits his one attacking shot (the front-foot cover drive) to pick up two runs. "Just checked eBay for tickets to the Oval Test on the very off chance and was offered two for a paltry £640," says Daniel Pimlott. "Who knows what the touts are charging? Was it only last summer that I got two to see the Oval Test against the West Indies for £20 quid a pop off a tout, less than half the cover price?"

WICKET! 116th over: Harmison st Gilchrist b Warne 2 (England 454–9) Warne tosses the ball up and Harmison can't resist trying to hit the ball to us here in Farringdon. Sadly his confidence was misplaced, and Gilchrist was left with a simple stumping as Harmison toppled over on to his backside. Let's hope England don't regret this late-order collapse just before tea.

117th over: England 462–9 (Hoggard 3, S Jones 7) A cracking shot from Jones sees the ball hurtling down to the cover boundary. And then he lofts the ball to mid-on for another couple. Oh, and for those who are asking, tea has been delayed until the fall of the final wicket. "I too have a girlfriend who appears to know a little about cricket," says Robert Wickes, "but insisting I get out of bed at seven in the morning to analyse her forward defensive is taking it a little too far, I think." And that'll do on that subject.

118th over: England 470–9 (Hoggard 3, S Jones 15) Jones adds eight more to his name with two thrilling shots: first, taking Warne on and hitting him down the ground, then somehow digging out a yorker at great speed through the off-side. Why is this man at No. 11?

119th over: England 471–9 (Hoggard 4, S Jones 15) Hoggard plays his one attacking shot (cf. over 115) to give Jones the strike, but the Welshman is more respectful to Lee than he was to Warne. "Hi there, what's the last time a team scored three consecutive 400+ first-innings totals in Tests against the Aussies?" asks Ed Barlow. "Please can you check your *Wisden*, or put it to the masses?"

120th over: England 471–9 (Hoggard 4, S Jones 15) With regards to the earlier possible marriage proposal, Anton Lawrence writes, "Vow-by-vow commentary? Now there is an idea."

121st over: England 471–9 (Hoggard 4, S Jones 15) Remarkable. Brett Lee strikes Jones on the shoulder, the ball bounces and then hits the stumps six inches up. Hard. Incredibly the bails were not dislodged. Then Jones nonchalantly boots the ball away, and the unlucky bowler can but smile. That's one run from the last three overs. If Shep was umpiring, surely we'd be at tea by now.

122nd over: England 476–9 (Hoggard 9, S Jones 15) An eventful over as Hoggard first square cuts Warne for four, then the Aussie spinner is up in arms as Bucknor turns down another lbw appeal. The ball pitched just outside leg stump. "I've got ten tickets together for the Oval on Sunday," boasts Thomas Hopkins. "Looks like I've got a straight choice between going with my mates or putting a deposit down on a house. Simple choice really."

123rd over: England 477–9 (Hoggard 10, S Jones 15) Hoggard may not be the most exciting England batsman to watch but he's doing well here as these two put on 23 valuable runs. "Why is this man at No. 11?" says Mark Harris, before answering his own question. "Maybe to minimise the chance of commentators and fans becoming confused by both batsman having the same name?"

WICKET! 124th over: Hoggard c Gilchrist b Warne 10 (England 477 all out) Hoggard plays his customary shot to Warne's first ball of the over, but this time nicks it for a regulation catch for Gilchrist. That's tea.

England 477 all out

The evening session

BY MIKE ADAMSON

Preamble: When England set out yesterday morning they would probably have been looking for between 450 and 500, given the gentle nature of the pitch, so they'll be satisfied with the position they're in. Now it's up to the bowlers to turn the score into a big advantage.

1st over: Australia 0–0 (Langer 0, Hayden 0) A massive appeal from Harmison for lbw against Langer is quickly rejected by Steve Bucknor. But it's a maiden to start. Craig Burley (surely not the former Chelsea player?) writes: "India were the last team to score three consecutive 400+ first-innings totals against Australia: 501 in 3rd Test at Chennai, 2000/01, 409 in 1st Test at Brisbane, 2003/04; 523 in 2nd Test at Adelaide, 2003/04." Wear that anorak with pride, Craig.

2nd over: Australia 4–0 (Langer 0, Hayden 4) As if the stattos weren't being tested enough today, here's another from Tony Wellby: "When, if ever, have all the batsmen been out in the order that they appear on the scorecard? No. 11 excepted of course?"

3rd over: Australia 11–0 (Langer 6, Hayden 4) Langer rides his luck as his attempted cut off a ball that wasn't that short from Harmison is almost chopped on to his stumps. He atones for his error by playing the shot to perfection next ball, beating the diving Pietersen at point. "Have you noticed during all this wonderful cricket from Trent Bridge," says Andy Breakell, "that the English women look like they are going to beat the Sheilas by a very large amount and if they do it will be the Test series for England?"

4th over: Australia 13–0 (Langer 6, Hayden 2) A loose last delivery spoils a tight Hoggard over, gifting Hayden two runs to square leg. "As well as being a gap-toothed one-time box-to-box donkey," says Rob Smyth, about to tell us an interesting stat no doubt, "Craig Burley is (in a sense) wrong: the last team to get three consecutive 400+ scores in the first (match, rather than team) innings of a Test against these Aussies was . . . actually nobody has done it before. Ever. And yes, I am wearing my frankly majestic brown Penguin anorak."

5th over: Australia 19–0 (Langer 11, Hayden 6) It's a strangely subdued atmosphere given the importance of this session to the entire series. Harmison is yet to really find his rhythm. "Considering the potential for rain, all talk of anoraks should be banned lest the Adamson curse strikes," says Charlie Taylor.

6th over: Australia 19–0 (Langer 11, Hayden 6) A big appeal from

Hoggard for lbw against Langer. Alim Dar shakes his head, but the ball was swinging back towards the stumps and would have hit middle-and-off. "Is there any swing out there?" asks Peter Lovell. "I have a tenner on Hoggard to be man of the match." The latest entry should have answered your question, Peter.

7th over: Australia 19–0 (Langer 11, Hayden 6) Simon Jones replaces Harmison. He said before this Test he was keen to be handed the new ball so he could show he can do more than just use reverse swing. Well here's his chance, and his first over is a good one.

8th over: Australia 19–0 (Langer 11, Hayden 6) A third maiden in a row, and a second for Hoggard. The Australians are being noticeably watchful at the start of the innings. "Re: Rob Smyth in the 4th over," begins Alan Synnott, cleverly mixing two earlier riffs. "Could he tell the difference between a Penguin anorak and a Tim Tam anorak if he was blindfolded? At a wedding?"

9th over: Australia 20–0 (Langer 11, Hayden 7) This is really good stuff from Simon Jones, who is bowling a perfect line and length. Hayden is looking very tentative, as if he is unusually concerned about the chance of getting out should he play an aggressive shot.

WICKET! 10th over: Hayden lbw b Hoggard 7 (Australia 20–1) After one lbw appeal is turned down because of an inside edge, Hoggard produces an identical inswinger, Hayden completely misses it this time, and umpire Dar raises his finger. Peter Lovell (over 6), your bet looks good. "What is the OBO view on group fancy dress at Test matches?" asks James Bogue. "There are ten of us going on Saturday at The Oval and at the moment '80s Sporting Legends' is the firm favourite."

WICKET! 11th over: Ponting lbw b S Jones 1 (Australia 21–2) It's always important to try to get Ponting out before he settles, and England have done it. The ball was going on to hit half-way up middle stump, but Ponting's reaction suggests there may have been some bat involved. Looking at the replay, it was pad first. A good decision.

WICKET! 12th over: Martyn lbw b Hoggard 1 (Australia 22–3) My goodness! Three lbw decisions in three overs. Martyn certainly got an inside edge on that one, but umpire Dar didn't notice it, so Australia are three down and in disarray. That "gentle" pitch isn't looking so harmless now. "Can I suggest that James Bogue goes as Fatima Whitbread?" asks John Larn. Of course you can, John. "It's a challenge and it'll give those of us at home something to look out for during the drinks breaks."

13th over: Australia 30–3 (Langer 15, Clarke 4) Hoggard and Jones are swinging the ball a long way, and the Australian batsmen are struggling to cope. Langer ends up on his knees as he plays and misses.

14th over: Australia 31–3 (Langer 15, Clarke 5) Hoggard moves the ball away from Clarke and into Langer with devilish accuracy. "Eas-eh! Eas-eh! Eas-eh!" sings G Clews. "Can we have some communal OBO virtual chanting please, I feel like I'm missing out." That's certainly the sound emanating from the Trent Bridge crowd.

15th over: Australia 37–3 (Langer 19, Clarke 6) "I'm assuming one of those ten is going to have Eddie 'the Eagle' Edwards covered," says an anonymous emailer anxiously. "Please, just put my mind at rest, will you."

16th over: Australia 43–3 (Langer 25, Clarke 7) A streaky shot to open the over from Langer, but the ball was so wide and full from Hoggard that it deserved to go where it did – the boundary. "A former colleague met his future wife while dressed as the Pink Panther at a Test match," says John Hogan. "Now he has to ask permission for a couple of beers after work."

17th over: Australia 47–3 (Langer 25, Clarke 11) Flintoff replaces Jones at the Radcliffe Road End and is on the spot just outside off stump straightaway. "So it's far too early to mention it but I'm going to anyway," whispers Rob Hoare. "Follow-on anybody?" Not if Clarke continues in this vein of form.

18th over: Australia 55–3 (Langer 26, Clarke 17) Hoggard finds the edge of Clarke's bat but the slip cordon is a yard or so too far back and the ball doesn't carry to Marcus Trescothick. "In answer to the fancy dress question why don't you dress up as the current England team," asks Alix Young, who wants it to be observed that she is a women. "It means you stand a chance of getting chatted up in the pub afterwards – after all, isn't there a flood of women suddenly interested in cricket?"

19th over: Australia 58–3 (Langer 27, Clarke 18) Pietersen excites the crowd by pretending to have caught a bump ball, then Flintoff rattles Langer's helmet with a ball that wasn't that short; Langer's rather shaken up. "It does appear that Australia are getting the worse of the umpiring decisions in this series," says David Horn. "Dear, oh dear, oh dear. I do feel bad for them." Don't we all, David.

WICKET! 20th over: Langer c Bell b Hoggard 27 (Australia 58–4) It's not the reverse swing that's bothering the Australians today, it's good old-fashioned Matthew Hoggard swing. The ball popped up a bit, struck Langer's glove, then his pad, and looped into the hands of Bell at short leg.

21st over: Australia 60–4 (Clarke 20, Katich 0) A quiet over from Flintoff. He's done his bit for the day, and has passed the limelight on to Hoggard. "I'm not sure I should say such things for fear of being blamed for the potentially horrific repercussions," says Simon Denn, setting himself up for a fall, "but for the first time I actually truly believe we can win the Ashes!"

22nd over: Australia 66–4 (Clarke 20, Katich 6) Katich is off the mark, this time clipping the ball off his hips past Bell at short leg. "Maybe the Aussies are regretting dropping Gillespie," says an emailer whose name I have accidentally deleted (sorry). "Who's going to keep Warne company when he's batting?"

23rd over: Australia 67–4 (Clarke 20, Katich 7) Flintoff fires down a vicious bouncer straight at Clarke's head. The Australian does well to evade it. "I don't know about anyone else," says Stephen Long, "and it may be heresy to say it, but I just hope that the next Ashes series is at least competitive: it's so dull when cricket gets so one-sided and if Australia can show some spirit and some fight then they just might make a contest of it."

24th over: Australia 67–4 (Clarke 20, Katich 7) Simon Jones replaces Hoggard, but the last over before drinks is another quiet one as Australia look to take the sting out of the England attack. "Dressing as Fatima Whitbread isn't really much of a challenge," says Benjamin Fitzpatrick. "A leotard, a fake comedy moustache and an appropriately placed pair of size 11 football socks is all anyone would need."

25th over: Australia 77–4 (Clarke 24, Katich 10) Clarke picks up three runs as Flintoff strays on to his pads. "As a bored American cricket fan hoping for a Glazer-like takeover of this fine sport," says Daniel Reilly, but bear with him, "I am currently sitting in my windowless office in Washington DC, desperately trying to understand/follow this so-called Ashes. I need you to liven things up for me. Are the Steve Harmison dancers scantily-clad on the sidelines, waiting to erupt at the next wicket? When is the half-time show? Will Janet Jackson come out and drink tea? Has Shane Warne been tested for steroids? If the Australia Superkangaroos win this, will they declare themselves 'world champions'?" Yes, between innings, no, yes, they already do.

26th over: Australia 77–4 (Clarke 24, Katich 10) A maiden from Jones, notable only for a ridiculous appeal for leg-before – ridiculous because of the huge inside-edge from Katich's bat. "I think it should be a rule that Peter Lovell should enquire about swing during the first ten overs of every Australian innings," says Neil Taylor, who is clearly chuffed with the progress England have made this evening. "Likewise, you'll have to put a tenner on Hoggy every match from now on."

27th over: Australia 81–4 (Clarke 28, Katich 10) An email which escaped my notice was received just after 3pm from "Fred Flintoff": "Well I haven't had it that easy since my gran used to make me Lancashire Hot Pot for me tea. Looking forward to whacking a few of those Ozi's out later on and bringing t'Ashes back to where they belong!" Hmm.

28th over: Australia 86–4 (Clarke 28, Katich 15) "I must say that this series has warmed the cockles of my heart, after years and years of pain, whether we win or lose it is brilliant to see England playing the way they are! Freddie Flintoff for Prime Minister!" proclaims James Green. "And while we are at it let's make him King as well!"

29th over: Australia 90–4 (Clarke 28, Katich 19) A gorgeous straight drive from Simon Katich puts another four on Autralia's total. "I've just turned the TV off in disgust," says David Mayo. "I can't bear to watch the humiliating demise of a once-great team. Short of a miracle – and we're running out of miracle makers – the Poms have the Ashes in the bag. A shocking admission from an Aussie, I know."

30th over: Australia 95–4 (Clarke 32, Katich 20) Jones is still getting a prodigious amount of swing, but the two batsmen look well set and are picking it up easier now. "Remarkable lack of 'how do I keep it from my boss that I am following the OBO' emails today," notes David Keech. "Is it because, being Friday, all the workers spent the afternoon in the pub so nobody was expecting much anyway?"

WICKET! 31st over: Clarke lbw b Harmison 36 (Australia 99–5) Harmison darts one back into him and Clarke's plumb in front of the stumps. It's been a wonderful day for England.

Australia 99–5; England 477

Third Day

The morning session

BY ROB SMYTH

Preamble: Morning. Well this is quite a thing isn't it: Australia 378 behind with only five wickets left. They are up a creek, and I can't see too many paddles.

31st over: Australia 100–5 (Katich 20, Gilchrist 1) "Can anyone help me?" asks Rosamund Surtees. Probably not. Next. "Due to poor holiday planning I am going to be out of the country for the last day of the 4th Test and the first three days of the 5th Test. Does anyone know anywhere in Salzburg or Prague where I can watch the cricket live or whether I can get LW radio?"

32nd over: Australia 103–5 (Katich 22, Gilchrist 2) Some early shape for Hoggard, who beats Gilchrist's crooked force outside off stump. "Don't want to seem too pessimistic," begins Alan Parsons, lining up a "but" with chilling purpose, "but, in 1994 I was at Headingley watching England play South Africa, England scored 477 and had SA at 105 for five on Saturday morning. Then both Kirstens got centuries and SA scored 447. The match was drawn."

33rd over: Australia 109–5 (Katich 22, Gilchrist 6) Flintoff comes on straightaway around the wicket to Gilchrist. It's all teasing, tantalising stuff – slightly wide and inviting him to reach for one. "Morning," winces Sarah Robinson. "My head hurts. And I've got two hours to do the work I didn't do yesterday, find a 70s costume, pack for the weekend, and watch as much of the cricket as possible. Maybe radio is a good compromise?" Whatever.

34th over: Australia 112–5 (Katich 23, Gilchrist 8) I guess emails will be quieter than usual this weekend: a) because I'm on, b) because I'm on and c) because it's Bank Holiday weekend. But don't be shy. Meanwhile, Hoggard curves a cracker past Gilchrist's forward push. Nicely bowled.

35th over: Australia 116–5 (Katich 24, Gilchrist 11) Gilchrist works Flintoff through wide mid-off for three more, and England seem just a fraction flat here – as they often do the morning after the night before. (This, of course, is not meant to imply that they were caning Bombay Sapphire with Diane Keaton and that fella from Babylon Zoo till the small hours; rather that they sometimes take a while to shake off their slumber in the field when they have had an outstanding evening the night before).

36th over: Australia 138–5 (Katich 33, Gilchrist 22) A quiet over: just 22 from it. It began with a remarkable little assault from Gilchrist. First ball from Hoggard he picks up and hoicks over midwicket for four; second ball is swatted majestically down the ground for six. I think it's fair to say Gilchrist has got his eye in.

37th over: Australia 147–5 (Katich 41, Gilchrist 22) Contrary to popular opinion and the impression I'm obviously giving, I'm in a good mood today, chiefly because I'm *not* hungover. At all. Some of us were too busy fumbling our words on 5Live last night to be out on the sauce like you lot. Mug's game. I sincerely, genuinely hope you all feel bloody awful this morning.

38th over: Australia 157–5 (Katich 45, Gilchrist 27) Katich and Gilchrist have form for match-turning counter-attacks – there was an absolute ripper in New Zealand earlier this year – and they really have doused what little fire England came out with this morning. It's been brilliant stuff so far, and there's so much good cricket that I barely have time to talk about myself let alone print your emails.

39th over: Australia 157–5 (Katich 45, Gilchrist 27) Subtle change of tactics from Flintoff, who bowls much wider to Gilchrist in the hope of getting him to chase one. He does, kitchen sink and all, and misses. A maiden, and I'd get Simon Jones on at the other end now. "Babylon Zoo were one-hit wonders," says Dan Rowley. "Kinda like Ian Bell." That's it? That's your whole dog and pony show? Get out.

WICKET! 40th over: Katich c Strauss b Jones 45 (Australia 157–6) How's that?! Jones *does* come on, and strikes with his second ball.

In truth it was a rancid delivery, a wide half-volley, but Katich chased it and sliced straight to gully. I'm claiming that.

WICKET! 40th over: Warne c Bell b S Jones 0 (Australia 157–7)
Simon Jones is on a hat-trick! He turned Shane Warne round first ball, and the leading edge looped nicely to Ian Bell at cover. It is amazing how many wickets he has taken in the first over of a spell in this series.

40th over: Australia 158–7 (Gilchrist 27, Lee 1) Brett Lee gets nicely forward to repel the hat-trick ball. "Why do England keep letting Australia back into this series?" says Nick Watson. "It is somewhat worrying that Australia haven't been playing very well at all in the series since Lord's and they are still level in the series and coming back rapidly in this match." Agreed. It's a sickener. I think it's time for Fletcher and Vaughan to go, to be honest. Bring in Beefy as coach and Aftab Habib as skipper.

41st over: Australia 163–7 (Gilchrist 27, Lee 6) Brett Lee flashes Flintoff supremely past point for four; Flintoff responds by thundering a short one into the bit of the arm where you had those horrible Tetanus jabs as school. I hated those.

42nd over: Australia 163–7 (Gilchrist 27, Lee 6) Lee is beaten by an absolute snorter from Jones, that lifted and whistled past him from absolutely nowhere. A maiden, and a fine one.

WICKET! 43rd over: Gilchrist c Strauss b Flintoff 27 (Australia 163–8)
Take a bow, Andrew Strauss: that was a truly sensational catch to get rid of Gilchrist. Flintoff got one to pop off the pitch and Gilchrist steered it wide of second slip, where Strauss dived to his left to take a magnificent one-handed catch, right at the end of his fingers and at the full extent of his dive.

43rd over: Australia 175–8 (Lee 9, Kasprowicz 5) It's the burning question: why aren't I married? But as this page can only store a maximum of 400,000 words, here's an alternative: should England enforce the follow-on? While I think they will, it must be quite tempting not to: they could ramp their lead up to 550 – enforcing the follow-on is soooo 1990s, don't you know – and have two days to bowl Australia out.

WICKET! 44th over: Kasprowicz b S Jones 5 (Australia 175–9) Any of you nouveau cricket fans who want to know what 'bowled neck and crop means', put on Channel 4 now. That was wonderful from Jones, a booming full-length outswinger that beat the bat by a mile and clattered into middle stump.

44th over: Australia 180–9 (Lee 13, Tait 1) "If we get the chance we have to take the follow-on," says Kieran Taylor. "If weather does come into play we can't afford to be cautious and build up an unassailable lead. What have we got to fear by putting their batsmen in again anyway?" Headingley 81? No, I've revised my frankly nonsensical opinion: England have to enforce the follow-on here.

45th over: Australia 188–9 (Lee 20, Tait 1) Brett Lee responds to the shambles with a truly astonishing shot, smearing Harmison miles over midwicket and out of the ground. I've seen everything now. I've seen it all. Meanwhile, anyone know of anything good going on in the Camden Lock/Chalk Farm area tomorrow evening? Smyth needs something to do with his guests.

46th over: Australia 200–9 (Lee 31, Tait 1) More fun from Brett Lee: first he sweet-spots Jones thrillingly over midwicket for six, then he scythes one over the slips for four.

47th over: Australia 206–9 (Lee 37, Tait 1) Some amusing cat and mouse between Harmison and Lee which I would describe but I honestly can't be bothered. "The follow-on," begins Jeremy Bullock. "It's a bit like taking a puppy when he's done something on your carpet, and pushing his nose in it – it kind of emphasises the point. This is what we need to do to the Aussies – make them clear on the situation."

48th over: Australia 210–9 (Lee 40, Tait 2) Tait, backing away like a lady who has a Scottish Austin Powers character grinding his derriere into her on a dance floor, steers Jones just short of second slip, and then he gets a single off the third ball. Then Lee gets one off the last ball to keep the strike.

49th over: Australia 218–9 (Lee 47, Tait 2) Another simply monstrous hit from Lee, clobbering Harmison square on the leg-side and out of the ground. Lee does have such a good eye when he's at the crease. When he nails it, it stays nailed. Now that the lead is moving down towards 250, I think England should bat again. If Australia get 450 –

not exactly inconceivable – England could have problems chasing 200 against Warne on a last-day pitch.

WICKET! 50th over: Lee c Bell b S Jones 47 (Australia 218 all out) Brett Lee uppercuts Jones to third man, where Ian Bell takes a good catch to end a superb cameo. Five wickets for Jones, who is quietly having a storming series, and a lead of 259 for England. "Ah Jesus, Smyth," begins my colleague Mike Adamson, although I'm not sure he needed the comma there. "I am not in a good state. The Roadhouse produces evil drinks." Mug's game. "But what a catch, eh? The Radley boy done good. OK, back to bed. PS That incredibly uninspiring email took me about 45 minutes to type."

England have enforced the follow–on Meanwhile, a quiz question: which of England's bowlers currently – right here, right now – has the lowest bowling average? Harmison? Wrong. Freddie? Good one. The answer is, of course, Simon Jones. 27.98, and he averages nearly 16 with the bat as well, which is a minor miracle given his technique.

Australia second innings

1st over: Australia 6–0 (trail by 259 on first innings; Langer 6, Hayden 0) The last time Australia followed on in a Test, in Pakistan in 1988, I was a spotty, four-eyed socially inept geek with the propensity for mumbling, racked by insecurity and self-doubt and forever wondering if I'd meet 'The One'. I'll let you finish the gag, eh? Langer starts and nearly finishes his innings by slashing Hoggard's second ball through the vacant fourth-slip area for four.

2nd over: Australia 10–0 (Langer 6, Hayden 4) Simon Jones really has gone up in the world: he's been given the new ball, I reckon for the first time in his Test career. He is pulled crisply for four by the former world-class batsman known as Matthew Hayden, and England's half-decent change pair of Flintoff and Harmison wait in the wings. "Result!" exclaims Sarah Robinson. "Andy (the driver) is still faffing at home and we're not leaving til at least 1. Except now I have a very anti-cricket Becca in my house to placate. I just tried to explain follow-on to her and was met with a very blank, yet almost hostile, look. On the upside, she lives in Camden and says go to Barfly tomorrow."

3rd over: Australia 10–0 (Langer 6, Hayden 4) Maiden from England's shaggy Hogg (doesn't work, does it?) to Langer. At the risk of sounding like, well, me, I really don't think England should have enforced the follow-on here. If Australia bat well and bat properly – and let's be honest, they're due – they could easily get 450 here. Imagine chasing 200 against Warner on the last day!

4th over: Australia 14–0 (Langer 9, Hayden 5) That's lunch. "If I wanted to read the word 'propensity' every few lines I'd read one of the economics textbooks propping up my bed," wah-wahs Alec Gregory. "Stop it, please." Propensity propensity propensity. There, I've said it.

Australia 218 and 14–0; England 477

The afternoon session

BY ROB SMYTH

Preamble: Afternoon. Australia have followed on for the first time since Robin Beck was in the charts, and they took lunch on 14–0, a deficit of 245.

So bad he sent it four times, and he still can't spell Buchanan "Morning, Mr Smyth," says Al. "Since a certain Mr Buchannan seems to regard Simon Jones as a rabbit, perhaps Mr J should put on some ears, offer him a carrot and inquire, 'Eeerrrr, what's up Doc?' Salad for the Aussie lunch then?"

5th over: Australia 19–0 (trail by 259 on first innings; Langer 10, Hayden 9) Hayden drives Hoggard gunbarrel straight for four. Terrific, no-nonsense shot.

6th over: Australia 23–0 (Langer 14, Hayden 9) Fairly cautious field for Harmison's first over: two slips, no short leg and nobody to stop Langer creaming a wide one through the covers for four.

7th over: Australia 24–0 (Langer 14, Hayden 10) "Do you know if the teams have lunch together, or whether there is one happy room and one somewhat rueful room?" asks Brian Woolcock. No. "In the absence of any hard evidence, I am going to imagine one big room, a bit like the dining room at school, where, for the first time in years, it's the English with all the banter, and the Aussies pushing their food round the plate." You like your commas, don't you Brian?

8th over: Australia 31–0 (Langer 18, Hayden 13) Simon Jones is moving more than a little gingerly in the field, which is not good. Obviously. It could be Freddie time.

9th over: Australia 35–0 (Langer 21, Hayden 14) Langer survives a biggish lbw appeal to a Hoggard inswinger; rightly so, as it was *just* sliding down leg. Or not: Hawkeye has it shaving leg stump, which paradoxically justifies Steve Bucknor's decision. I haven't had an email since lunch so, y'know, thanks for nothing.

10th over: Australia 36–0 (Langer 21, Hayden 14) "Thank God for free wireless internet," says Adrian Goldman. "I can sit in my conference in Florence and follow your OBO, which is probably better than following your BO. The conference is full of Australians with glum faces. There, you have an email now, and after lunch. Happy?" Never. Never satisfied.

11th over: Australia 37–0 (Langer 21, Hayden 14) "Can't think of anything to say," says James Green, saying plenty. "Feeling a bit nervy. Kinda like a bloke who has just asked the girl of his dreams out, only for her to say yes, and now in the excitement he is not quite sure whether he can go through with it." Blimey, you've obviously been dreaming long and hard about her if you've got cold feet already.

12th over: Australia 41–0 (Langer 22, Hayden 17) These Aussie openers look pretty comfortable at the moment. "I'm alternating between your commentary and reading a thesis about fungi," says George Tew. "Weird combination." And yet strangely compatible.

13th over: Australia 50–0 (Langer 22, Hayden 26) England need a pick-us-up here, as the warning signs are just starting to contemplate the merest flicker. "Best excuses for pulling a sickie to watch the cricket," begins Neil Stork-Brett. "What about a sudden attack of 'lycanthropy of the buttocks' – the more hirsute man will know what I mean."

WICKET! 14th over: Hayden c Giles b Flintoff 26 (Australia 50–1)

Quite frankly, I'm on fire. I called Jones earlier in the day and he got two wickets in his first over, and now Flintoff strikes in his first over. It was a decent delivery, angling away from around the wicket, and hapless Hayden snicked a drive – the ball was probably too short for the shot – straight to Giles at gully/fifth slip.

14th over: Australia 50–1 (Langer 22, Ponting 0) "Fungi thesis?" says Katy Robinson. "Very impressive. I'm just watching the cricket and reading the OBO – all in all, there's not mushroom for anything else (sorry)." You will be. So will you, Duncan James. And the rest of you who sent that shocker in.

15th over: Australia 56–1 (Langer 28, Ponting 0) Simon Jones, sans niggle it seems, is brought into the attack for Ponting; England seem to have a go-to bowler for almost every Aussie batsman.

16th over: Australia 56–1 (Langer 28, Ponting 0) No more fungi jokes. Please. Fun guy, mush room, Mungo Jerry – whatever it is, I don't wanna hear it. More important, Flintoff bowls a probing but ultimately harmless maiden to Ponting. "Afternoon," says Keele University's (I used to go there, of course) Emma Brooker. "As for the thesis about fungi . . . I'm writing a dissertation about American vice-presidents. At the moment, Australia are Dan Quayle." Very droll.

17th over: Australia 57–1 (Langer 29, Ponting 0) Brilliant stop from Pietersen saves four when Langer drives at Jones, and NOW THEY'RE GOING TO FUGGIN NEWMARKET FOR THE RACING! NOW TELL ME THIS: WHAT THE FUGG IS GOING TO GET MORE VIEWERS; THE 2.40 AT CHEPSTOW, OR WHATEVER THE BEJEESUS IT IS, OR THE GREATEST TEST SERIES IN ENGLAND'S MODERN HISTORY? I'LL TELL YOU WHO WINS: A BLEEDIN' HORSE! FE£@!*&$%£*!$&£!

18th over: Australia 58–1 (Langer 29, Ponting 0) "As it's so quiet in your inbox, maybe it's my chance for fame," says Aidan Byrne, who's clearly big on self-esteem. "I should be finishing my PhD, but instead I'm trawling round odd cricket sites. Can we have a shout-out to the Men's Thinking Society CC, currently storming the Finnish Cricket Association League? Much love, Aidan." Much love? Much love?!

19th over: Australia 63–1 (Langer 33, Ponting 1) Harmison returns to the attack, and Langer coaxes him through the covers for two more. He looks in good nick, as he has all series without really going on, and here's the omnipresent James Green. "I don't know any mushroom jokes but I know a joke that seems quite apt as 90% of the Australian population is of, shall we say, a fair hair colour. 'What do you call a clever blond? A golden retriever!' I won 200 quid at the pub quiz for that one." What, as medical compensation for the shoeing it inspired from the pub residents?

20th over: Australia 68–1 (Langer 37, Ponting 2) I can't lie to you: I didn't see that over because of the racing. But Flintoff has figures of 4–2–6–1 now, which sounds like something Ted Rogers would do after one turboshandy too many. Here's James Green again. "Possibly the only bonus with Sky getting the cricket is that we don't have to watch the racing! However that is far outweighed by the fact that we have to sit through days of 'Mr Personality' David Gower!" Actually I'm glad you mentioned that as it segues nicely into a subject I've been thinking a lot about recently. Sack these 'best commentator' polls; which Sky/C4 commentator would be best in the sack? My money's on Tony Greig. No-nonsense.

21st over: Australia 78–1 (Langer 37, Ponting 10) Ponting hits consecutive boundaries off the listless Harmison, whose series average has disappointingly edged past 30.

22nd over: Australia 80–1 (Langer 38, Ponting 11) A bad drop from Andrew Strauss, who took a scorcher earlier but grasses a relative sitter here at second slip when Langer skews a drive off Flintoff. Gah.

23rd over: Australia 81–1 (Langer 39, Ponting 11) With England's top guns of Flintoff and Harmison on, this is a rugged, tough passage of play, no quarter asked, given, or handed over reluctantly to a persistent beggar on Camden High Street.

24th over: Australia 90–1 (Langer 40, Ponting 17) Flintoff beats Langer, outside off stump rather than about the person, but his no-ball problems persist: two there in an otherwise terrific, bat-jarring over – at least until Ponting picks up the last ball and swivel-pulls it stunningly for six. "Who the chuff is doing the commentary on BBC 5Live?" wonders Richard Peel. "The mike sounds like it's half-way up one of 'em's larynx, with every breath relayed to the world." Has Gerald Sinstadt moved into cricket?

25th over: Australia 93–1 (Langer 42, Ponting 18) "Are you secretly Australian?" asks Katy Robinson. Not at all cobber, I mean Pommy. Dude. Sorry, I meant chav, sport. Mate.

26th over: Australia 99–1 (Langer 47, Ponting 20) Flintoff beats Ponting with an awesome lifting leg-cutter, but later in the over Langer carts another four through extra cover.

27th over: Australia 100–1 (trail by 259 on first innings; Langer 47, Ponting 21) Big lbw shout from Harmison against Langer but don't bother getting excited – it pitched miles outside leg. Not even Steve Bucknor could get that wrong. "Hello again," says Emma Brooker. "I felt compelled to add my thoughts on the "best in the sack" poll. If you need anyone to judge Mark Nicholas's performance, I'll happily volunteer. For purely scientific reasons, I could also compare him to Michael Slater if that would be any help?" You're too kind.

28th over: Australia 104–1 (Langer 47, Ponting 24) I'm starting to worry now; England shouldn't have enforced the follow-on, and I shouldn't have gone up for coffee. I wish. Meanwhile, Giles gets his first bowl of the match.

29th over: Australia 106–1 (Langer 48, Ponting 25) Here's Matthew Cobb with an alarming and sordid little tale. "On *TMS* Blowers is talking about 'sucking Manx knobs' – some are big, some are small, he says, but whatever, he loves sucking those knobs. Sadly, I think they are talking about the sweets in the attached tin." Subliminal.

30th over: Australia 108–1 (Langer 49, Ponting 26) "Did I see that you used to go to Keele University? I always thought Guardian Unlimited was dominated by public school-educated Oxbridge types," says Chris Martin. "Well done on bucking the trend." Anyone else out there, feel free to patronise me as and when the mood takes. It gets me going.

31th over: Australia 115–1 (trail by 259 on first innings; Langer 53, Ponting 29) Justin Langer brings up a gritty half-century with a dab to third man off Harmison, and this is just starting to get interesting now. So it's a good time to take a break. That's tea.

Australia 218 and 115–1; England 477

The evening session

BY ROB SMYTH

Preamble: Evening. This is starting to get interesting: Australia, following on, are 115 for 1 in their second innings, a manageable deficit of 144. Ricky Ponting is playing very well, and Justin Langer is at his most dogged. It's a bit early to say England have problems, but the prospect of chasing 200 in the fourth innings is not a particularly pleasant one. And now I'm boring myself, so somebody please send an email about something other than cricket.

32nd over: Australia 120–1 (Langer 56, Ponting 31) Quiet first over after tea from Giles. Bad news comes with the fact that Simon Jones is off the pitch with the niggle that troubled him earlier. Hmm. "Re: the follow-on," says Eleanor Ward, kindly sending an E.E. Cummingsian email and leaving me to cap up the relevant bits. Cheers. "I fear you may have been right. For once. I hope that's not the case though, and that normal service will be resumed." Honk! I refer the honourable lassie to my suggestions that Jones and Flintoff should bowl earlier in the day, and the consequences thereof.

33rd over: Australia 128–1 (Langer 61, Ponting 34) I don't mean this in a lame, come-on-then-fate-what-do-you-make-of-this-tempter way, but it's hard to see how England are going to get a wicket at the moment. . .

WICKET! 34th over: Langer c Bell b Giles 61 (Australia 129–2) Gilo has done it, with Justin Langer caught at short leg for the second time in the match. He pushed forward tentatively to a nothing delivery and, after the ball looped up off glove then pad, Ian Bell took a good catch diving forward. That's a really big wicket for England.

34th over: Australia 129–2 (Ponting 35, Martyn 0) Here's Richard Hatton. "There I was happily nodding off at my desk when a pigeon flies with a massive crash straight into the window. After I crawled back out from under my desk assured World War III wasn't starting I just wondered: has anyone seen a bigger bird fly into a house? Without wanting to sound sadistic I would love to see the bemused expression on a swan's face after a close-up with the glass."

35th over: Australia 129–2 (Ponting 35, Martyn 0) Simon Jones is officially off the field with "discomfort in his right ankle", and Hoggard has just bowled a maiden to Ponting. "In Murmansk in 1993 I saw an albatross fly into the Russian Naval Command building," says Richard Jones.

36th over: Australia 130–2 (Ponting 35, Martyn 1) Giles rips a replica of his ball of the century/month/day/over to Damien Martyn at Old Trafford past Martyn's outside edge. A jaffa.

37th over: Australia 130–2 (Ponting 35, Martyn 1) Hoggard. Martyn. Maiden. Tense times. Right, as there's no particularly interesting riffs for this evening's OBO – the bird one was inevitably ruined by the Vanessa Feltz gags that poured forth – the riff can be: what should the riff be? Brilliant. My suggestion? Seth Cohen one-liners.

38th over: Australia 133–2 (Ponting 36, Martyn 3) "I have to say that there is a deterioration in the quality of the musings sent in by readers of the OBO coverage at the weekend," says John Springford, covering himself in glory with that rip-snorter of an intro. "Is this because only financial people in the City are working – and they don't have much of a sense of humour? Or they're too busy making their millions? How much do you earn working for the *Guardian*, then?" Definitely, maybe, and a lot less than you think.

39th over: Australia 133–2 (Ponting 36, Martyn 3) Ponting gets over the top of an attempted pull off Hoggard. That ball didn't really get up. "Seth Cohen one-liners?" says Shehzad Charania. "I think somebody has beaten you to that one."

40th over: Australia 139–2 (Ponting 41, Martyn 4) There are 37 overs left after this one, in which Ponting drives Giles sumptuously inside-out for four.

41st over: Australia 141–2 (Ponting 42, Martyn 4) In the absence of much swing, Hoggard is sweeping the shop floor assiduously at the moment.

42nd over: Australia 147–2 (Ponting 47, Martyn 5) "Mr Smyth, Sir," says Hannah Rowe. "The genius that is Seth Cohen has many wonderful one-liners, but I think one the Australians may find comforting now is: 'One day we are all going to laugh about this. I know that day feels far off, but comedy is just tragedy plus time'."

43rd over: Australia 148–2 (Ponting 47, Martyn 6) Hoggard beats the outside edge of a tentative Martyn, and here's David Keech. "Talking of birds, did any of you ever see that baseball pitch from Randy Johnson, at close to 100 mph, that hit and annihilated a bird in mid-flight with a suicide bomber-like explosion of white feathers? Most incredible thing I ever saw watching sports." Even more incredible than David Pleat's comedy dance round Maine Road?

44th over: Australia 155–2 (Ponting 48, Martyn 12) "How exactly is it that you know who Seth Cohen is, Rob?" asks Jeins. "Surely only teenage girls watch the OC?" Obviously not Jeins. Next!

WICKET! 45th over: Ponting run out 48 (Australia 155–3) What a moment for Gary Pratt, the young substitute from Durham! Martyn played tip and run to cover, and Pratt charged in and threw down the stumps superbly with Ponting just short. It went to the third umpire, but everyone knew it was out. The introduction of Flintoff brings the wicket, though not how we expected, and what a wicket – Ponting had been playing very impressively. That really was an outstanding piece of fielding on the run.

45th over: Australia 159–3 (Martyn 12, Clarke 4) Ponting was swearing violently at the England balcony when he went off, presumably to do with the fact that England had a sub fielder on. It looked like sour grapes; in fairness England's fast bowlers have gone on and off the field a lot in this series – they have certainly bent the rules, though not broken them – but the simple fact is that Simon Jones is injured, and so a sub is on, who happens to be a pretty useful fielder. "At the current run-rate Oz will just about have caught up with England's 447 by the close," smirks Richard Jones just about a split-second before Ponting was run out.

46th over: Australia 161–3 (Martyn 13, Clarke 4) Interesting – Ian Bell comes on, presumably in the hope that the ball might curve around a gentler pace as it did for Ricky Ponting on day one, and to test Michael Clarke's inconsiderable patience. For now Clarke contents himself with some respectful forward defensives.

WICKET! 47th over: Martyn c G Jones b Flintoff 13 (Australia 161–4) Another failure for Damien Martyn, but no dodgy umpiring this time – just a poor shot and a decent delivery from the marvellous

Flintoff. England are well on top now; I told you they were right to enforce the follow-on.

47th over: Australia 161–4 (Clarke 4, Katich 0) "One thing you've gotta do," says Tony Greig imperiously on Channel 4. "When Aussies get upset make them more upset." And so England do – mini-Jonty Trevor Penney, 74, is on for the injured (sic) Steve Harmison. It's like American football with all these specialists sneaking on, and if you're reading Ricky it's a great loophole isn't it?

48th over: Australia 169–4 (Clarke 5, Katich 5) Ian Bell continues, which confirms the assumption that he is on primarily to bowl at the impetuous Clarke. That said he nearly gets Katich, who flaps one tantalisingly over extra cover for four.

49th over: Australia 171–4 (Clarke 6, Katich 5) "Smudger," begins Duncan Steer of SPIN 4magazine. "Penney is only 37! How can that be true? He looks 50! D'ya think Matthew Maynard will be on the field next? But more importantly, isn't Penney Zimbabwean? Will the whole series be declared void if England field an illegal?" Nah, he was born in Zimbabwe but he qualified to be England's specialist 13th man and Aussie-riler ages ago. Look in the book, son.

50th over: Australia 172–4 (Clarke 7, Katich 5) It looks like Ian Bell is just getting a little bit of reverse swing. Chuck in his numerous catches, and someone could already be lining up that godawful gag about how he'd be an all-rounder if only he could bat.

51st over: Australia 172–4 (Clarke 7, Katich 5) Harmison replaces Flintoff. A maiden. And yes, as many of you have said, if any lipreaders out there care to translate Punter's invective to the England balcony, I'll happily chuckle at what he said and then not print it on 'family website' grounds.

52nd over: Australia 175–4 (Clarke 7, Katich 8) Giles replaces his Warwickshire buddy Bell, and – sorry – just got the typing yips for a split second then: I couldn't finish the word 'Warwickshire', no matter what I tried. Finally, after all these years, I know what it feels like to be Keith Medlycott.

53rd over: Australia 180–4 (Clarke 11, Katich 10) Clarke cuts Harmison with considerable elan for four. "But Rob," begins John

Hall. "Does the *Guardian*'s style guide not allow swearing in context when it's 'absolutely necessary to the facts of a piece, or to portray a character in an article'. I think it's your duty to print what Ponting said." Sure; if someone tells me, I will. I definitely read an 'eff'.

54th over: Australia 182–4 (Clarke 12, Katich 11) Giles has a silly point, a short cover and the silliest of mid-offs for Clarke, but nothing much happens. Sorry.

55th over: Australia 183–4 (Clarke 13, Katich 11) Here's John Bone, a happy soul. "I don't understand why Ch4, which you are apparently watching rather than being ar$ed to get yourself up to Trent Bridge, haven't introduced lip-reading technology." Absolutely. Does my head in. I mean, why don't they just put the stump mics on full blast and all the new eight-year-old converts to the game can hear all the pretty eulogies that are shared out in the middle?

56th over: Australia 184–4 (Clarke 14, Katich 11) Simon Jones has gone to hospital for tests on his injured ankle. Giles bowls another nondescript over.

57th over: Australia 187–4 (Clarke 17, Katich 11) Nothing doing, and it's another quiet little passage of play. "I think Ponting said, 'Cheating f****ng c***s' (and that's not 'cakes')," says Katy Robinson. "Made me laugh though! And I cannot believe Penney is on. I can remember him from my youth, and I'm 59." It's OK – Harmison's back on so he's gone off now to feed a few Werther's Originals to his grandson.

58th over: Australia 190–4 (Clarke 18, Katich 13) I missed that Gilo over for a toilet break, but I don't think anything happened.

59th over: Australia 193–4 (Clarke 20, Katich 14) Hoggard returns to replace Harmison, and I presume England will rotate their three remaining seamers at one end for the rest of the day, with Flintoff given a final burst at the death. "I bet Cyril Poole's in the crowd if they need him," says Richard Jones. "He's a local. England now one wicket away from cautious optimism." Exactly. I sincerely couldn't agree more.

60th over: Australia 195–4 (Clarke 21, Katich 15) Giles almost does Clarke with the quicker ball for the second time in the series. That was beautifully bowled and it *just* missed the outside edge.

61st over: Australia 200–4 (Clarke 25, Katich 16) The consensus on the GU desk is that England could do with one more tonight. If Australia get into the black with four down, and Gilchrist primed, a few bums may start to squeak around the country.

62nd over: Australia 202–4 (Clarke 26, Katich 17) My presumption of over 59 proved amusingly inept: Flintoff is on for Giles, and he starts with a quiet over.

63rd over: Australia 212–4 (Clarke 35, Katich 18) Geraint Jones has bungled a straightforward stumping chance. Clarke advanced down the wicket at Giles and missed a whip to leg, but Jones couldn't take the ball cleanly. An absolute sitter.

64th over: Australia 213–4 (Clarke 35, Katich 19) "Am I the only one wondering what England's recent record on chasing targets is, and having a slight fear that it's not that good," says Joe Stead. Fear not, it's pretty good: they chased in excess of 250 against New Zealand twice last year, and they haven't lost chasing under 300 since that dark Sunday at The Oval in 1999. "Also have become aware that, especially when wearing a helmet, Vaughan bears more than a passing resemblance to Miranda from Sex and the City." That, however, is something we should all be worried about, especially as she was always my favourite.

65th over: Australia 213–4 (Clarke 35, Katich 19) Maiden from Giles to Katich. No action and no emails. Come on!

66th over: Australia 214–4 (Clarke 36, Katich 19) Flintoff is trying to summon one last push as the day moves towards its end. I, by contrast, have long since closed the book on such an absurd ambition, so this is all you're getting for this over.

67th over: Australia 222–4 (trailed by 259 on first innings; Clarke 38, Katich 24) "Australia remind me of a spider I once tried to kill," says Fin. "I gathered the creature up in some toilet paper and flushed it down the toilet. However, about half an hour later it was back and as sparky as you like – almost mocking me in the way it moved. Even deep in a hole, the Aussies are still keeping us very, very uneasy. A bit like that spider. As our emailers have said: we need one more tonight." True that.

Bad light stops play Oh well, that looks like that for the day:

Australia's batsmen are offered the light and they take it. Probably not a bad thing for England either, who are looking slightly leg weary.

Australia 218 and 222–4; England 477

Fourth Day

The morning session

BY ROB SMYTH

Important things about the day's play that I'm too sluggish to put into a coherent paragraph as I've only just woken up after sitting up till 3.00am watching *Deadwood* and *Seinfeld*

The new ball is due in 13 overs' time

Simon Jones won't be bowling

Adam Gilchrist is due

Michael Clarke is in great nick

The pitch is pretty flat

England got a standing ovation coming *on*to the pitch

How exciting is this?

England could be 2–1 up by tonight!

68th over: Australia 224–4 (trail by 259 on first innings; Clarke 39, Katich 25) Inevitably Flintoff begins, bowling over the wicket to Katich this time, and promptly beats him with a beautiful, trampolining leg-cutter.

69th over: Australia 228–4 (Clarke 42, Katich 26) Clarke greets Harmison with a crunching straight drive for two. "We don't have to worry about the pitch," chirps Nick Frost. "As long as England bowl as they have done, the Aussies will play injudicious shots and we'll win. It's all very well saying Gilchrist etc are due an innings, but there's a reason why they haven't got big scores – poor batting." Controversial.

70th over: Australia 228–4 (Clarke 42, Katich 26) Maiden from Flintoff to Clarke. Not much sign of swing and wotnot, but then it is a very old ball.

71st over: Australia 232–4 (Clarke 43, Katich 28) Just singles in that Harmison over. "Just wondering if you can set the scene of today's play," says Giles Anderson. "You know, just how packed is GU Towers, size of TV screen, size of GU hack's desperation at lack of emails . . ." Well, you couldn't cut the atmosphere with a Samurai sword here – I'm the only person on the entire floor, the TV screen is one of those little, Ron Jeremy-size Hitachi ones (15 inches tops), and I couldn't give a stuff whether I get a single email all day because my iPod is working again, the cricket is fascinatingly poised and I'm not hungover. I'm benign contentment personified, with strawberry blond hair.

72nd over: Australia 234–4 (Clarke 43, Katich 29) It's the calm before the new-ball storm, though how England will juggle their three seamers to get Harmison and Hoggard with the new ball, I'm not sure.

73rd over: Australia 235–4 (Clarke 43, Katich 30) Ah, that's how they'll juggle the bowlers: Giles is on for Harmison, and he almost strikes straight away.

74th over: Australia 236–4 (Clarke 43, Katich 31) "Hello," says Abby Robinson. "I'm an Australian who doesn't really care if they lose the Ashes (I hope no one I know is reading this) but there's a bit of chicken-counting going on over there that makes me nervous – not you, but others." I agree: the English (fans, not players) have been dreadful winners this summer: smug, annoying and fearfully unfunny. And we haven't even won anything yet!

75th over: Australia 240–4 (Clarke 46, Katich 32) Pretty good stuff from both sides so far. That said, Clarke is living on the edge as always – here he cuts at Giles and the edge flashes between keeper and slip.

76th over: Australia 242–4 (Clarke 48, Katich 32) Great stuff from Flintoff, who bangs two successive short ones in to young Clarke (I've done it. For the first time in my life, at the age of 29, I've prefaced someone's surname with 'young'. I'm finished.) This is really good, hard-boiled Test cricket you're inexplicably reading about rather than watching just now.

77th over: Australia 242–4 (Clarke 48, Katich 32) Clarke is itching for action like a 16–year-old on his first visit to Chasers. He sets off then for an absurd single and is sent back, and if the bowler Giles's throw had hit he would have been home by the merest fraction.

78th over: Australia 242–4 (Clarke 48, Katich 32) As if to legitimise Duncan Fletcher's argument over sub fielders, I had to take an urgent call of nature then. OBO reporters are allowed seven minutes; any longer than that and you can't OBO for a certain length of time. Anyway, don't think you missed much.

79th over: Australia 243–4 (Clarke 48, Katich 33) Big shout for lbw against Clarke from Giles. It pitched outside leg, but I'm here to tell you Steve Bucknor thought long and hard about that.

80th over: Australia 244–4 (Clarke 48, Katich 34) "I'm the temptress, can you resist me?" says Mark Nicholas, although sadly he was talking about Ian Bell's deliberately wide deliveries to hyperactive young Clarke.

81st over: Australia 244–4 (Clarke 48, Katich 34) England don't take the new ball – chiefly because Matthew Hoggard is off the field. Like waking up next to Hetty Wainthrop after the mother of all benders, that really is not good.

82nd over: Australia 244–4 (Clarke 48, Katich 34) Bell continues with a maiden to Clarke, and Hoggard is back on the field, munching furiously on something.

83rd over: Australia 247–4 (Clarke 50, Katich 35) Clarke just about gets to the pitch in order to swat Giles through midwicket for two to bring up his half-century. This is intense, old-school Test cricket.

84th over: Australia 248–4 (Clarke 50, Katich 36) Stephen Harmison (is it Stephen? Steve? Steven? Ste?) returns, new ball and all, and England could really do with something from him here: he's taken only five wickets since that storming performance at Lord's. This is such an important passage of play now. In the meantime, it's drinks. Who would have thought Messrs McGrath and Gillespie would be the waiters?

85th over: Australia 249–4 (Clarke 50, Katich 37) No real sign of swing for Hoggard in his first over with the new ball.

86th over: Australia 249–4 (Clarke 50, Katich 37) This game has a similar feel to the Oval 1991 Test against the West Indies, only with an even bigger prize. England had a nervy run-chase then, and it's looking ever more likely that they'll have one here.

87th over: Australia 253–4 (Clarke 54, Katich 37) Nice delivery from Hoggard first up, just moving away a fraction, and Clarke edges it down to third man for four. England could really, really do with a wicket here – this partnership has been going more than 40 overs now.

88th over: Australia 254–4 (Clarke 54, Katich 38) "I'm sure your reader (very droll – Smyth) will be delighted to know that later on today I will be emailing off the manuscript of my pop sci book on 17th-century science, which has delighted the readers of GU OBO and footie commentaries over the last year or so, in particular my old adversary, Richard Jones, who sometimes claims to be a Professor at Geneva University," says Matthew Cobb in the longest sentence I've read since that John King book *Headhunters* almost ten years ago. "That explains why I'm reading you rather than watching C4 downstairs." Good excuse, but what's everybody else's? This stuff about living in places where they don't show the cricket, like Finland/America/Belgium/Greenland/Grimsby – I'm not buying it.

89th over: Australia 254–4 (Clarke 54, Katich 38) Still no real sign of much happening with the new ball, although England are bowling with good discipline. A maiden from Hoggard.

90th over: Australia 255–4 (Clarke 55, Katich 38) Clarke continues to show impressive patience outside off stump – these two have played excellently, and increasingly responsibly – and England are going to have to work bloody hard for this next wicket you feel.

91st over: Australia 257–4 (Clarke 55, Katich 38) I've been reduced to pathetic attempts to goad fate, such as preparing the morning session document for the OBO archive and putting Australia's score as 2xx-4. I really am a very sad man, but the ease with which these two are playing is starting to get a little bit worrying. That said, Steve Bucknor thought long and hard and then some more over a huge lbw shout by Hoggard against Clarke, who was on the walk, before turning it down. It wasn't plumb but it was out.

92nd over: Australia 258–4 (Clarke 55, Katich 39) It is indeed Freddie time, immediately around the wicket to Katich. Nothing doing.

93rd over: Australia 261–4 (Clarke 56, Katich 41) Clarke drives Australia into the lead. Tense times. "The significant thing is that every run now counts double," says Tony Greig. I didn't realise cricket had introduced a European football-style away-runs-but-only-when-you-follow-on-then-take-the-lead rule. That said, there is the same nervous we've-done-the-hard-yards-but-what-if-we-lose-now tension in the Trent Bridge crowd that you get at Old Trafford when United have drawn the away leg 0–0 (see Monaco 1998 and Madrid 2000). And rather ominously, United usually – nay, always – lose in such circumstances.

94th over: Australia 261–4 (Clarke 56, Katich 41) That was a big chance for England. Katich was sent back by Clarke and was comfortably short of his crease, but the bowler Flintoff missed the stumps. Gah! A maiden.

WICKET! 95th over: Clarke c G Jones b Hoggard 56 (Australia 261–5) That's the breakthrough! Hoggard, who has bowled really well today, finally, finally tempts Clarke to fiddle unnecessarily outside off stump at an away-swinger, and Jones takes a straightforward catch.

95th over: Australia 262–5 (Katich 41, Gilchrist 1) "Perhaps we are witnessing the next stage of the Australian Masterplan," opines Duncan James. "They have lulled us into a false sense of security. Now they will bat out this match, McGrath will stop pretending to limp and they will win the last match by a world record innings and 673 runs." I'm more worried about them winning here. If they do, the match at The Oval will be the biggest anti-climax since David Brent's blind date.

96th over AKA Flintoff v. Gilchrist: Australia 270–5 (Katich 41, Gilchrist 9) Two slips and two gullies for Flintoff to Gilchrist, who seems to have adopted the strange Pietersen get-the-bat-miles-behind-your-back leave. Not that he used it too often: Flintoff pitches one up, and Gilchrist simply slams it through the covers for four. Then he pulls the next one for four. For the first time in this series, he has looked like the real Adam Gilchrist in this match. But there wasn't much he could do against a cracker that zipped past the outside edge off the penultimate ball of the over. And that's lunch.

Australia 218 and 270–5; England 477

The afternoon session

BY ROB SMYTH

Preamble Hello. I spent my lunchtime eating an apple and listening to Death Cab's 'The Sound of Settling' on loop. Not particularly or even remotely interesting, but I have to write something, so . . .

97th over: Australia 275–5 (trailed by 259 on first innings; Katich 44, Gilchrist 11) Katich slices the first ball after lunch, from Hoggard, agonisingly over the head of Giles at gully. "England need to help Gilchrist hit and hit himself OUT," says Richard Jones. Anybody out there who speaks Richard Jones and could translate?

98th over: Australia 276–5 (Katich 45, Gilchrist 11) Flintoff v. Gilchrist, the resumption, and Gilchrist is beaten all ends up by a quite delightful swinging leg-cutter from around the wicket.

WICKET! 99th over: Gilchrist lbw b Hoggard 11 (Australia 277–6) Steve Bucknor has had a shocker there I reckon, but who cares? Actually no he didn't – it pitched *right* on leg stump and straightened as Gilchrist walked across his stumps so that it would have hit leg stump. That is a simply massive moment, and I apologise to Mr Bucknor, Sir – that was a fine decision, and a brave one as well because those usually aren't given on the (often erroneous) assumption that the ball will swing down leg.

99th over: Australia 278–6 (Katich 46, Warne 0) Apparently that is the first time in his Test career that Gilchrist has been lbw to a seamer, which is a truly remarkable statistic.

100th over: Australia 280–6 (lead by 21; Katich 47, Warne 0) More shabby running ends with Katich miles out of his ground when Trevor Penney's throw from square leg misses the stumps.

101st over: Australia 284–6 (lead by 25; Katich 51, Warne 0) A typically economical nudge brings Katich his first boundary of the day – and also his fifty.

102nd over: Australia 290–6 (lead by 31; Katich 51, Warne 6) Warne uppercuts Flintoff deliberately for four; he doesn't look in the mood to hang around either.

103rd over: Australia 291–6 (lead by 32; Katich 52, Warne 6) "I think I'm in love with you but you must get a lot of that," says Madeline Swarbick. "Always nice to hear though, eh?" First time for everything. "Listening/reading in Abu Dhabi so no worries about stalking." What a coincidence – I'm going there for my summer holidays this very week.

104th over: Australia 293–6 (lead by 34; Katich 53, Warne 6) Flintoff is bowling really well at the moment, from over and around the wicket, asking Katich pretty much every difficult question you can imagine with the possible exception of: 'What's the capital of Borneo?'

105th over: Australia 299–6 (lead by 40; Katich 58, Warne 7) "Help," says Jess Harris. "Can someone out there suggest a plan/ploy for a suitable first-date venue for this afternoon? It has to be suitable enough to impress, but devious enough to be in touch with the day's final session." Sadly Wetherspoons, my first-date venue of choice, don't have TVs, so you'll have to really push the boat out and go to a Hogshead or a Yates's instead. Or you could sack the date off. Face it, it'll only end in tears. Yours prob'ly.

106th over: Australia 311–6 (lead by 52; Katich 58, Warne 19) Good shot from Warne, flogging a pull off Flintoff for four. And then he squeezes the next one behind point for four. And then he smears a slower ball superbly through extra cover for another boundary. Here's Aaron Richardson, who made me snigger for the first time today (it says more about me than him, as you'll see). "Hello Madeline (103rd over), I'm in Dubai, which is close, and I'm also sat next to post-rock apologist Benedict Fisher, so you may have stalking issues of your own to deal with in the not too distant future . . ."

107th over: Australia 313–6 (lead by 54; Katich 59, Warne 20) I keep forgetting to update the "lead by" bit, which is starting to annoy me. As is Australia's lead. Here's Jane Clemetson. "This lawyer, who is, alas, at the office on this fine afternoon, albeit with access to the OBO and with the TV on in the corner of her office, feels that if you number amongst your acquaintances many people who refer to themselves as 'one' then you probably mix with too many lawyers (or Dowager Duchesses) and need to get out more – proposed visits to the movies notwithstanding – or start working for the yellow press."

WICKET! 108th over: Katich lbw b Harmison 59 (Australia 314–7)
Huge breakthrough for England, and another controversial lbw decision, this time from Aleem Dar. It pitched well outside leg from over the wicket *and* it was going over the top. Katich, who has laid down his life out there, is justifiably extremely peeved, and yet another England bowler – this time Steve Harmison – has a wicket in the first over a new spell.

108th over: Australia 314–7 (lead by 55; Warne 21, Lee 0) Jones, diving in front of first slip, drops a thick edge from Brett Lee! He had every right to go for it but, had he not, Trescothick at first slip would probably have taken it comfortably.

109th over: Australia 325–7 (lead by 66; Warne 32, Lee 0) A double bowling change, as Giles replaces Hoggard. Giles to Warne is a risky tactic here, although England don't have much choice now that they're down to a four-man bowling attack. England still should have taken a wicket off the last ball, but Geraint Jones knocked both bails off just before Strauss's throw hit the stumps with Brett Lee out of this ground. A shocker from Jones, I'm afraid, and a good time for a breather: it's drinks.

110th over: Australia 330–7 (lead by 71; Warne 32, Lee 4) Brett Lee is having real problems against Harmison. If I was him, I'd play my natural game – especially given how far he tonked Harmison on more than one occasion yesterday. "I'm very pleased I made you snigger Rob," says Aaron Richardson, "but in all seriousness Madeline, where do you work? What's the exact address?" This dead horse doesn't need any more flogging, Richardson. Let it go.

111th over: Australia 333–7 (lead by 74; Warne 35, Lee 4) "Is Jess (105th over) a boy or a girl?" asks Katy Robinson. "In fact, stuff that – doesn't matter. (S)he should suggest a nice afternoon watching the cricket. Perfect first-date material and no mistake – and no deviousness required."

112nd over: Australia 334–7 (lead by 75; Warne 37, Lee 4) Only one slip for Warne, who edges Harmison low to third man for a single.

WICKET! 113th over: Warne st G Jones b Giles 45 (Australia 342–8) Another mighty hit from Warne off Giles, down the track and over midwicket. Even if it means Ian Bell bowling, Giles has got to come out of the attack here. Now. But not just yet, eh? Moments after I typed that, Warne came again, but Giles ripped one past his attempted slog and Jones did the rest.

113th over: Australia 348–8 (lead by 89; Lee 5, Kasprowicz 5) "Is it wrong to suggest I hate Geraint Jones right now?" asks Thomas Hopkins. "He's cost us at least 100 runs this innings." Hate is wrong, Thomas, it's a negative emotion – but if we lose this game because of that effing Papua New Guinean &£!@OWZAT! Great stumping! Is it wrong to suggest I love Geraint Jones right now?

114th over: Australia 352–8 (lead by 93; Lee 6, Kasprowicz 8) I'm sure I've seen these two hold England up with the bat somewhere before. "Cautious optimism, me boy," says Richard Jones. "Cautious optimism." That'll be the use of the word "maybe", then. Next!

115th over: Australia 356–8 (lead by 97; Lee 7, Kasprowicz 11) So. England are now entering banana-skin territory, but on this pitch it would still be utterly criminal to lose chasing 150 or under. "For the anoraks," begins Peter Moran. "Is that the first time an English spinner has got an Aussie spinner out at Trent Bridge in the 112nd over? Just wondering." Actually, no: in 1472, my ancestor Aubrey Surgeon-Smyth, a leggie by trade, dismissed Aussie blacksmith Lou Carpenter in similar circumstances.

116th over: Australia 359–8 (lead by 100; Lee 10, Kasprowicz 11) England will now need to chase three figures to win, as news reached us that Simon Jones has gone back to hospital. That's pretty worrying with a view to the Oval Test as I wouldn't fancy Chris Tremlett or Jimmy Anderson in the heat of such an important contest. It couldn't mean a recall for Andy Caddick or even Darren Gough. Could it?

117th over: Australia 363–8 (lead by 104; Lee 12, Kasprowicz 13)

Twenty-five minutes to tea, and if Flintoff has anything in the tank I'd get him on now. More likely is that he and Hoggard will come on straight after tea. "Hi Rob," says Pete. "My colleagues Vicky, Lisa and myself are all working in a law office today . . . though we don't have a TV and are relying on your idiosyncratic but nonetheless enjoyable service for our updates. None of us have ever used the term 'one' though we do work in the North West and this sort of talk would be greatly frowned upon." True that, which is why I still want to live there, so if anybody has any journalism jobs up North, or dustman's for that matter, I'm free.

118th over: Australia 369–8 (lead by 110; Lee 15, Kasprowicz 16) All of the Aussie team have got to double figures in this innings without anyone getting to 70, which is eerily reminiscent of their back-from-the-dead victory in not dissimilar circumstances in Sri Lanka (total 471; top score 68) in August 1992. I'm just stating the facts here.

119th over: Australia 373–8 (lead by 114; Lee 16, Kasprowicz 19) Flintoff does return, and Kevin Pietersen drops another catch! Number six of his Test career, and a relatively easy one. Surely that famous self-belief of his isn't wavering, is it?

WICKET! 120th over: Australia 373–9 (Kasprowicz c G Jones b Harmison 19) Kevin Pietersen is reprieved by the one man who knows how he feels – Geraint Jones. A full away-swinger from Harmison, and a straightforward edge through to Jones as Kasprowicz attempted to drive.

120th over: Australia 373–9 (lead by 114; Lee 16, Tait 0) Shaun Tait takes guard somewhere around Nottingham town centre to Harmison – go to The Social, son, it's a great bar – but he survives the rest of the over.

121st over: Australia 374–9 (lead by 115; Lee 17, Tait 0) A couple of brilliant yorkers from Flintoff, the second of which knocks Brett Lee comically off his feet. Meanwhile, I'm getting mildly narked with the weary oh-so-English emails saying that we have let Australia off the hook in the last two Tests due to a lack of killer instinct. Do you think dethroning the best team in the world is easy? That they might not consider putting up a real fight once or twice? England have done bloody well to chip away at a very strong batting line-up on a very good pitch, and despite some very bad and demoralising dropped catches, and with a weakened bowling attack, and now they are in a position where, 24 times out of 25, they will win. As Chris Martin once sang, reducing me to tears in the process, "Nobody said it was easy".

122nd over: Australia 383–9 (lead by 124; Lee 22, Tait 4) Brett Lee has the grandfather of all yahoos at Harmison and slices over the slips for four, and then Tait fences a snorter past a diving Flintoff at second slip for four more.

123rd over: Australia 387–9 (lead by 128; Lee 26, Tait 4) For the umpteenth time in this series, the stumps have been hit without the bails coming off. That was amazing – a full-pitch delivery from Flintoff, that didn't lose any pace off bat or pad, clanked against leg stump but the bails stayed on. England actually appealed for a caught behind, such was the woody noise. Unlike me being unmarried at 29, that defies all logic.

WICKET! 124th over: Tait b Harmison 4 (Australia 387 all out) Truly dreadful batting from Shaun Tait, who walks miles across his stumps off the last ball of the Harmison over and is bowled all over the shop. England will need 129 to win after tea.

Australia 218 and 387; England 477

The evening session

BY ROB SMYTH

Preamble: 129 to win. A doddle, right? Wrong! Not if the series so far is anything to go by, anyway. And 129 is only one less than Australia needed at Headingley in 1981 – the last time an Ashes Test was won by a team following on. But the pitches then and now could not be more different. That was a minefield, fast and nasty; this is slow and benign and, if Australia are to win this, it will take a career-defining bowling performance or an era-defining bottle job.

1st over: England 1–0 (chasing 129 to win; Trescothick 1, Strauss 0) Good early pace from Brett Lee, and Trescothick leaves one that goes very close to his off pole. Then Strauss, driving first ball, is beaten by a glorious inswinger that somehow misses his inside edge and his off stump. "OK Rob, here's a real question," says Matthew Cobb. "Why did *Nathan Barley* attract so little attention? Nobody watched it apparently, and I don't think there will be another series. But it was brilliantly funny. What went on?" No idea – I thought it was gloriously funny. Two possible factors: it was shown on a Friday night, when the very goons who would have appreciated it were probably out in Shoreditch (I know I was), and maybe it satirised a milieu that is only amusing if you've been part of it. But then I guess your email contradicts that second point.

2nd over: England 8–0 (Trescothick 8, Strauss 0) Kasprowicz shares the new ball, which has to be the right decision – Tait could lose the game in four overs with the new ball, even if he is a potent threat.

3rd over: England 15–0 (Trescothick 13, Strauss 0) Brett Lee rampages in and Trescothick – who has been England's unsung hero in this series, having played quite beautifully at times, and set a crucial tone on the first morning of the second Test – pushes him deliciously back down the ground for four. Comfortable progress so far. So far.

4th over: England 27–0 (Trescothick 24, Strauss 1) Kasprowicz starts that over with a disgusting long-hop that Trescothick simply carts square on the off-side for four, and already there is a sweeper out. Sweeper or no sweeper, Trescothick clouts Kasprowicz over cover, and England are going at seven an over.

5th over: England 32–0 (Trescothick 27, Strauss 1) Imitation, flattery, etc. No, people aren't colouring their hair ginger – sorry, strawberry blond – all round Farringdon, but rather Australia have adopted the extremely silly mid-off position for Andrew Strauss that England have been using for Matt Hayden. "Hi," says Mark Echezarreta Murphy. "I am in Mexico . . . enjoying the cricket . . . but in a very non-cricket country . . . any suggestions on how to explain my Mexican girlfriend what an LBW is?" I have a horrible feeling the readers may have a few.

WICKET! 6th over: Trescothick c Ponting b Warne 27 (England 32–1) No surprise that Shane Warne is on already, because Kasprowicz bowled a load of rubbish. Only Warne's personality can win this game now – and he strikes with his first ball! Trescothick pushed forward and gave a textbook pad-bat catch to silly point, straightforward as you like. Now then.

6th over: England 32–1 (chasing 129 to win; Strauss 1, Vaughan 0) "Noooice Shane," chirps Adam Gilchrist, and Australia know they have just a sniff now. I remember seeing England struggle to chase 74 in Sri Lanka when the heat was on, so I'm ruling nothing out just yet.

7th over: England 36–1 (Strauss 5, Vaughan 0) After nudging one fine for four, Strauss has an unseemly waft at a sharp delivery from Lee, who has only one slip and a gully.

WICKET! 8th over: Vaughan c Hayden b Warne 0 (England 36–2) Blimey. Shane Warne has 2 for 0. Michael Vaughan played against the spin to the invitingly vacant midwicket area, and the resulting leading edge flew to Hayden at slip. Splendid thinking, splendid bowling – and given that Ian Bell is next, this is officially squeaky bum time.

8th over: England 37–2 (chasing 129 to win; Strauss 5, Bell 1) Mark Nicholas makes the valid point that, when it comes to a mental battle – which this emphatically is now – Warne will fancy himself every time. Has there ever been a mentally tougher or smarter cricketer?

9th over: England 39–2 (Strauss 5, Bell 3) Two runs to Bell off Brett Lee, but this is all about what goes on at the other end now: it's Strauss against his old pal Shane Warne. "We will win this match," says Kieran Taylor. "Effing hell Rob it's only two wickets. You should be enjoying this. Don't bother getting wed; you will only be thinking about the divorce on the happy day." Yeah, and I'll be right an' all.

10th over: England 40–2 (Strauss 6, Bell 3) Warne beats Bell with a ripper that drifts in, and then spins and kicks off middle stump to beat the outside edge. Warne is getting a lot of drift here.

11th over: England 51–2 (Strauss 17, Bell 3) Strauss, looking to pull Brett Lee, French cuts fortuitiously past leg stump and away for two, then he slices a cut up and over for four. Meanwhile, the emails have gone very quiet. I hear ya.

12th over: England 56–2 (Strauss 22, Bell 3) Nice shot from Strauss, cutting Warne crisply for four against the spin, but then he works a big-spinning delivery in the air past short leg.

13th over: England 57–2 (Strauss 23, Bell 3) A superb yorker from Lee swings and beats Strauss outside off stump. "I just had a bottle of Australian wine," says Ingar. "Is that wrong of me?" Absolutely – I'd have caned at least three by now with tension like this. Talking of which, it's drinks.

WICKET! 14th over: Strauss c Clarke b Warne 23 (England 57–3) Problems here – Andrew Strauss has gone. He worked one round the corner to leg slip and, after a referral to third umpire, the decision was given.

14th over: England 57–3 (chasing 129 to win; Bell 3, Pietersen 0) This is pure magnetic personality from Shane Warne, as the pitch is a long way from a minefield, even if there are the inevitable foot holes. We're about to find out a hell of a lot about Kevin Pietersen's temperament.

WICKET! 15th over: Bell c Kasprowicz b Lee 3 (England 57–4) Ian Bell has played a disgusting shot, hooking straight down long leg's throat, and we really do have a game now.

15th over: England 64–4 (chasing 129 to win; Pietersen 1, Flintoff 5) Zoinks. Flintoff carves his second ball in the air through the vacant gully area for four, and then digs out a splendid yorker, albeit it a no-ball. And then he almost gives me a coronary by hooking . . . nice and safe to square leg for one. "Your stiff upper lip is quivering," goads Manish Khanduri. "All that bravado took two balls from the Fat Boy to vanish, eh? Don't worry, I give England a win by four wickets." How munificent of you.

16th over: England 65–4 (Pietersen 2, Flintoff 5) Clammy hands are everywhere, not least in Farringdon, as the second ball rips back and hits pad and elbow as Pietersen, desperately trying to get his gloves out the way, hilariously follows through to clout himself on the helmet. The big difference here, as Richie Benaud observes, is that Australia have two bites at this cherry, England just one. If England lose, the Ashes are gone; if Australia lose they know that victory at The Oval would be enough to retain the Ashes. I hate this.

The tension is enough here; if I was in the middle I'd bottle it completely.

17th over: England 73–4 (Pietersen 8, Flintoff 7) Now this really is interesting – Shaun Tait is coming on. The words "death", "or" and "glory" spring to mind, as do "special" and "brew", come to that.

18th over: England 78–4 (Pietersen 8, Flintoff 12) This is how big this game is: if Scarlett Johansson walked in now cooing huskily she'd get the only rejection of her life. On the TV I am watching, Flintoff drives Warne airily but emphatically past the man at short cover for four.

19th over: England 81–4 (Pietersen 10, Flintoff 13) The target is under 50 now. "Re: your lack of bottle," says Peter Richards. "If you were England captain and the score was 100 for 5 with seven overs left and you were offered the light, what would you do?" Phone a friend.

20th over: England 82–4 (Pietersen 10, Flintoff 14) A wonderful diving stop from Ponting at short cover saves four runs.

21st over: England 89–4 (Pietersen 16, Flintoff 15) No slips now for Shaun Tait – it's all about Warne – and a storming piece of running from Pietersen brings two to fine leg when he only had a right to one. Then he works one even finer for four. I think Ponting should bring himself on here; he's the most likely to keep it tight at the non-Warne end.

22nd over: England 95–4 (Pietersen 16, Flintoff 21) Warne has a big shout for lbw against Flintoff, and when Alim Dar says no he appeals some more. It was pad first and, though Flintoff got a huge stride in, it was a very decent shout. Flintoff's response is majestic, a sweet drive over midwicket next ball for four.

23rd over: England 102–4 (Pietersen 22, Flintoff 21) Tom Cochrane makes a very good, if lengthy and humourless point. "If there was ever any doubt as to who are the big players in the England dressing-room they are being answered now. Australia made ground because they have, in Shane Warne, someone who relishes being put in a match-saving or match-winning situation, which very few people genuinely enjoy. And now we are seeing that Pietersen and Flintoff are made in a similar mould." Flintoff has oozed certainty today.

24th over: England 103–4 (Pietersen 23, Flintoff 21) A really lucky escape for England. Warne continued into the rough to Pietersen, who tried to clip a ball that came across him and somehow watched the leading edge plop safely on the off-side. "A thought," begins Bob O'Hara. "We've been waiting all summer for a big Flintoff–Pietersen partnership. No, we never expected it to be like this, did we?" No, we expected it to be like the one on the first day at Edgbaston. Next!

WICKET! 25th over: Pietersen c Gilchrist b Lee 23 (England 103–5) The heroic Brett Lee returns to the attack for the last onslaught – and he strikes first ball! It moved away just a touch and found the edge as Pietersen looked to flail through the off-side. Adam Gilchrist, diving to his right, did the rest one-handed with the minimum of fuss. Ironically, an accomplished piece of glovework brings Geraint Jones to the crease.

26th over: England 108–5 (21 to win; Flintoff 24, G Jones 1) Flintoff works Warne into the leg-side for a single, then Jones gets on top of a lifter for another. Flintoff then drives two more; 21 to go.

WICKET! 27th over: Flintoff b Lee 26 (England 111–6; 18 to win) The heroic Brett Lee has bowled Flintoff with an unbelievable delivery! It was shortish, swung in a long way from outside off stump and just clipped the top of the off. I think Flintoff was done for pace there.

27th over: England 114–6 (15 to win; G Jones 2, Giles 2) Giles digs out a brilliant yorker, although it was again a no-ball, and then works a couple to leg: 15 to win and don't bother emailing as I'm nowhere near competent enough to cope with this thriller, my nerves *and* your emails. Here's the last one. "Four wickets," says Manish Kandhuri smugly, although in fairness he said so before, and now he's saying it again. "I said so before, and I'm saying it again. England win by four wickets, and the resultant celebrations are muted, thereby satisfying the English national character of never really being *happy*." If England win this, come and find me by Camden Lock around 11 tonight. See those muted celebrations.

WICKET! 28th over: G Jones c Kasprowicz b Warne 3 (England 116–7; 13 to win) An outrageously poor shot from Geraint Jones, trying to dump Warne over the top – the field was up, inviting the shot – and instead slicing high, high, high to mid-off.

28.1 overs: England 116–7 (13 to win; Giles 3, Hoggard 0) Hoggard digs out a hot one. Yikes, I can't take this.

28.2 overs: England 118–7 (11 to win; Giles 3, Hoggard 2) Forcing shot from Hoggard brings two. Camera cuts to Andrew Strauss in the dressing-room smiling. *What the hell are you smiling about?*

28.3 overs: England 118–7 (11 to win; Giles 3, Hoggard 2) Short one left alone outside off. Camera cuts to Michael Vaughan on balcony. He isn't smiling.

28.4 overs: England 118–7 (11 to win; Giles 3, Hoggard 2) Huge lbw appeal turned down by Bucknor. It was the yorker, and it was going miles down leg. Good decision. The heroic Brett Lee's frenzied appeal was the most disproportionate in the history of Test cricket, but we'll let him off in the circumstances.

28.4 overs: England 119–7 (10 to win; Giles 3, Hoggard 2) No-ball! A no-ball!

28.5 overs: England 119–7 (10 to win; Giles 3, Hoggard 2) Left alone outside off, and rightly so.

29 overs: England 119–7 (10 to win; Giles 3, Hoggard 2) Dot ball, full and straight and coolly played. It's Warner time again.

29.1 overs: England 119–7 (10 to win; Giles 3, Hoggard 2) Ten runs, AKA Everest. Giles begins with a confident defensive drive.

29.2 overs: England 119–7 (10 to win; Giles 3, Hoggard 2) Left alone outside off.

29.3 overs: England 121–7 (8 to win; Giles 5, Hoggard 2) Nicely played by Giles, into the leg-side for two.

29.4 overs: England 121–7 (8 to win; Giles 5, Hoggard 2) Harmison on the balcony looks absolutely *terrified*. Giles repels the slider.

29.5 overs: England 121–7 (8 to win; Giles 5, Hoggard 2) Nice and solid in defence again from Giles, the fiercest concentration written all over that face of his.

30 overs: England 121–7 (8 to win; Giles 5, Hoggard 2) Another defensive stroke; another dot ball.

30.1 overs: England 121–7 (8 to win; Giles 5, Hoggard 2) What would you give for the champions' champion, Glenn McGrath, right now? Me: diddly squat, obviously, as we'd be gone and forgotten if he was playing. Anyway, Hoggard manages to get out the way of a snorting 91mph bouncer. Don't try it at home.

30.2 overs: England 121–7 (8 to win; Giles 5, Hoggard 2) If a song sums up how I feel now, it's The Smiths's "Please, Please, Please Let Me Get What I Want". I'm sorry Scarlett – in the world of top trumps, a three-wicket Ashes win beats you every time. Another short one from Lee, left alone. He's setting him up . . .

30.3 overs: England 121–7 (8 to win; Giles 5, Hoggard 2) . . . for the fuller ball, which is jabbed to gully.

30.4 overs: England 125–7 (4 to win; Giles 5, Hoggard 6) Full toss, and clubbed through the covers for four! It was the attempted yorker, and it went just a fraction wrong.

30.5 overs: England 125–7 (4 to win; Giles 5, Hoggard 6) Steve Harmison looks like he's having a nervous breakdown on the balcony. That ball is defended to point by Hoggard.

31 overs: England 127–7 (2 to win; Giles 5, Hoggard 8) Worked away to leg for two more by Hoggard. Really well played. One to tie!

31.1 overs: England 127–7 (2 to win; Giles 5, Hoggard 8) Flipped behind square by Giles and no run. "COME ON WARNEYYYYYY!" yelps Adam Gilchrist.

31.2 overs: England 127–7 (2 to win; Giles 5, Hoggard 8) Forward prop from Giles, and an assured defensive stroke.

31.3 overs: England 127–7 (2 to win; Giles 5, Hoggard 8) A full toss is whipped savagely and straight at Simon Katich at short leg. Michael Vaughan was off and celebrating then – until he realised it had gone straight into Katich.

31.4 overs: England 127–7 (2 to win; Giles 5, Hoggard 8) Warne sneaks a slider right between bat and pad, and the merest fraction away from off stump. Amazing.

ENGLAND WIN BY 3 WICKETS! That's it! England have won another unbelievable game of cricket, despite a truly heroic performance from Shane Warne and Brett Lee. Ashley Giles hits the winning runs, and I'm in need of a breather. Once again, it's been absolutely epic.

England 477 and 129–7; Australia 218 and 387

Fifth Test

The Oval,
8–12 September 2005

First Day

The morning session

BY SEAN INGLE

Preamble: Good morning, everyone, and welcome to the decider. As expected, it's Paul Collingwood who will replace the injured Simon Jones in the England XI. Australia are as predicted, with an unchanged top seven and a four-man attack of two tearaways, Brett Lee and Shaun Tait, and two champions, Glenn McGrath and Shane Warne. "Is it cowardly to pray for rain?" asks Jon Hoare. "I think the answer is probably yes, but it's the patriotic thing to do." Wouldn't bank on rain saving England, Jon, they have to win this. The toss will be huge . . .

Speaking of which . . . : Michael Vaughan flicks, Ricky Ponting calls heads – and it's tails! The Oval launches into perhaps the loudest cheer ever heard for a toss as Vaughan, who sports a huge smile, announces that England will bat.

"Just wondered if anyone else was getting irritated as I am by people with no interest in cricket who have managed to get tickets for The Oval?" splutters Martin Cruise. "My brother's girlfriend is going and admits she knows nothing about what she's watching, but as she knows I go to the cricket 'could I explain what would be happening.' Grr."

A dilemma: "You might remember that before the first Test, I called for your series prediction," says Alan Synott. "You went for 2–2, a remarkable shout, and one which could pay for a trip to the next Ashes if you invested in it. Did you? And do you still stand by it?" Not sure, Alan. Ended up backing England to win the Ashes after they lost the first Test at 11–1. So here's a dilemma: do I lay it off to win around £100, or hold firm to win £150?

Jerusalem rings around The Oval . . . The weather is sunny, the pitch looks a belter, the desktop scorecard is working again, and we'll be getting under way very shortly. "Can somebody please explain why it is that 'Jerusalem' has been adopted by the Last Night of the Proms brigade as this triumphalist English anthem?" asks Darren Lee. "Call me overly precious, but I can't see how Blake's doomy lament about the aesthetic distastefulness of the industrial revolution is an appropriate theme to celebrate our great national achievements? Surely 'Made in England' by Elton John would be more fitting?"

1st over: England 1–0 (Trescothick 1, Strauss 0) McGrath rolls in, that ridiculous mullet surely taking a few mphs off his run-up, and bowls a nasty first-ball bouncer at Trescothick, which is well left. McGrath continues to probe at 85mph – quicker than he has been for a while – before Trescothick gets off the mark with a prod through mid-off. "Hold firm with your bet," says Matthew Porter. "Win your £150 and then head to London to spend it in pubs where 90% of the people serving your drinks will be Australian. That would seem to me to be the perfect way to maximise the enjoyment of your money."

2nd over: England 5–0 (Trescothick 5, Strauss 0) First boundary of the Test from Trescothick! A scrappy start from the Aussies. "Apart from a rousing tune, 'Jerusalem' is on a par with the 'Marseillaise' as a revolutionary anthem," points out Tony Warner. "A violent attack on the established church (not on industrialisation) and the rotten aristocratic society that it supports." Which is one of the reasons why it'd make a much better national anthem than "God Save the Queen", no?

3rd over: England 7–0 (Trescothick 5, Strauss 2) Another probing, metronomic over from McGrath – just like his last 11,078, then. Meanwhile Daniel Walker isn't happy. "I've had enough of these quiche eaters who get corporate tickets and have no idea what is going on. Where were they during the Jason Gallian years?" he splutters. "Where were they when Craig White was hailed as the new Botham?" Probably laughing at Baddiel and Skinner and listening to Oasis, Tony.

4th over: England 7–0 (Trescothick 5, Strauss 2) Big shout from Lee for lbw – but none of his team-mates seem convinced. Nor, more importantly, does umpire Bowden.

5th over: England 11–0 (Trescothick 5, Strauss 2) McGrath gets some *enormous* movement off the seam – it pitches short, on middle stump, and curves wildly between Gilchrist and Warne at first slip, before racing for four byes. "Surely the main problem with our national anthem is that it's not actually about our nation – it's about one spoiled old German biddy who happens to live here," says Mike Hopkin.

6th over: England 20–0 (Trescothick 13, Strauss 2) A very comfortable start for England. Meanwhile, more mullet talk. "Surely the aerodynamic properties of the Aussie mullet can never be underestimated?" ponders Graham Pepper. "Sleek, greasy, thinning hair is worth a good 5mph with a following wind."

7th over: England 21–0 (Trescothick 13, Strauss 3) Much better from McGrath – who's fuller and straighter than his previous three overs. He ends with a beauty which beats Trescothick all ends up and nearly snags the edge. "I'm not sure that all this effing and fuming about newbie cricket fans is justified," suggests Thomas Whiteley. "Shouldn't we rather rejoice in cricket's new popularity? I have no sympathy for elitist, grumpy old sports fans harking back to the old days. It is so much more fun to have so many people you can talk cricket to."

8th over: England 29–0 (Trescothick 13, Strauss 11) Lee, all Beavis and Butthead snarl, continues to struggle. "I know it's too early to get carried away, but where is the OBO Ashes celebration party going to be held?" asks Ian Hamilton. "How about an OBO parade from Australia House down to Temple Walkabout?" Steady Ian, long way to go yet.

9th over: England 38–0 (Trescothick 14, Strauss 19) Shot! McGrath over-pitches and Strauss hits a Goweresque cover drive for another boundary. Meanwhile, more "Jerusalem" talk. "There is a religious sect that believes Blake's vision of Jerusalem will be realised in the Victorian back streets of Bedford," says Dan Levene. "They've been holding out there for the second coming for about two centuries now. Proof, if needed, that a diet featuring too many artichokes is not a good thing."

10th over: England 40–0 (Trescothick 15, Strauss 19) Tait replaces Lee and immediately gets one to swing back. It raps Trescothick, who (over-by-over reporter dons anorak) hasn't been out lbw in his last 66 Test innings, but it was going down leg-side.

11th over: England 44–0 (Trescothick 19, Strauss 19) McGrath continues, and so does the punishment, with Trescothick hooking a bouncer down to fine leg for four. "At least Jerusalem is more fitting than the Aussie's unofficial national anthem Waltzing Matilda – a song about a drunken tramp who's stolen a sheep and is trying to cook it in a knackered pan," says Ben Moore.

12th over: England 57–0 (Trescothick 29, Strauss 20) England are beginning to accelerate like a champion racehorse in the final furlong, and both Strauss and Trescothick are looking set. "Newbie cricket fans are all well and good, but can you really be bothered having to chat cricket pleasantries with old ladies in the supermarket queue?" says Andrew Tait. "This has become an all too familiar and tedious occurrence recently."

13th over: England 61–0 (Trescothick 33, Strauss 20) As a murderous straight drive from Trescothick races away to the boundary, McGrath shakes his head like a sulky teenager. Meanwhile this from Andrew Snowball: "Can I just say thanks to all the OBO readers who offered excuses to get me out of my gran's birthday party (fourth Test, day two)," he says. "I didn't need to use any in the end, because after two glasses of champagne she was happy to slump in front of the TV and babble on about 'that nice Alan Flintoff'."

14th over: England 65–0 (Trescothick 37, Strauss 21) Warne on for Tait, but will he get much turn on a first-day pitch? It's certainly a decent start – Strauss nearly edges the slider before a genuine nibble flies past Hayden at first slip. Meanwhile this from Bob O'Hara: "Ben Moore (and others) might be amused to know that Waltzing Matilda came close to being the official Aussie national anthem, in a National Song Poll in 1977. It came second."

15th over: England 74–0 (Trescothick 37, Strauss 29) Tait is back, but he starts with a full toss which Strauss guides through midwicket for four. The Aussies are looking ragged. "How's this for a totally insane conspiracy theory?" says Steve Gaythorpe. "1) England are doing well, increasing interest in the real beautiful game. 2) Cricket is going to Sky next year. 3) Sky is owned by an Australian. Is it totally beyond the realms of possibility that Rupert Murdoch nobbled his fellow countrymen to increase subscriptions?" Yes, Steve, it is. Isn't it?

16th over: England 78–0 (Trescothick 41, Strauss 29) Interesting bowling from Warne, who's deliberately straying outside off stump, encouraging the batsmen to take him on. It nearly works as Trescothick takes an almighty hoick at one, misses, and is nearly stumped.

17th over: England 81–0 (Trescothick 43, Strauss 30) Tait continues to huff and puff, but like Lee earlier he hasn't found much line or length. "I find it's a great boost for one's ego being constantly consulted by these 'newbie cricket fans' about various laws of the game," says Alastair Baird. "During the last Test I was sitting in a pub and had three girls hanging off my every comment as I feigned a role as the Oracle."

WICKET! 18th over: Trescothick c Hayden b Warne 43 (England 82–1) Warne strikes! Trescothick jabs at a wide one and Hayden takes a splendid diving catch at first slip. Game on! "If we had a vote for National Anthem, Crazy Frog would win, wouldn't it?" argues Andrew Goldby. "The Government would probably think in its dad-dancing way that making it a text vote would be 'like really cool eh, kids?' On the plus side, a drunken rendition by the Burberry Cap brigade before internationals would be fun."

19th over: England 84–1 (Strauss 31, Vaughan 2) McGrath returns. He's as predictable as a Stereophonics riff, and Vaughan takes just the one single from the over. "All this new interest is all well and good, but am I the only one who thinks it's a bit much when Richard & Judy do a feature on the Fifth Test?" asks Teresa Hourihan. Suspect not, Teresa.

20th over: England 92–1 (Strauss 31, Vaughan 11) Vaughan on the charge! First he goes after a wide one and *pulls* Warne through midwicket for four. Then, shades of 2003, he plays an absolutely glorious cover drive for another four. "A group of us have had the same seats for the first day of the Oval Test every day for the last 11 years, and have had to suffer very poor England teams," says Mark Doig. "This year, non-members' tickets were allocated on a free-for-all-ballot and we didn't get a sniff. What's the betting that, as soon as the excitement dies down, these new supporters will never be seen again?"

21st over: England 93–1 (Strauss 32, Vaughan 11) Another steady over from McGrath. "If any of you sourpusses would like to get away from these new cricket fans, then come to Beijing, no one gives a jot here," says Tom Herbert, Beijing Number 12 High School. "However, if England do win the Ashes then there will be many confused Chinese children given a 50–minute lesson on the virtues of cricket next week."

22nd over: England 96–1 (Strauss 32, Vaughan 11) Warne continues to tease and torment Strauss. He's the only Australian bowler who looks dangerous at the moment. "Will OBO be adopting a new format for the final day of the Test?" asks Joshua Hardie. "What's the internet equivalent of 'not a broadsheet, not a tabloid, but a Berliner?' Perhaps it's an opportunity to solve the still problematic refreshing and scrolling issue? I struggle to think of a more fitting way to mark the rebirth of cricket and the England team." Steady, Joshua – one redesign at a time.

23rd over: England 102–1 (Strauss 38, Vaughan 11) Strauss rocks back before cutting McGrath impeccably through gully to bring up the 100. The run-rate is 4.33, and England are progressing nicely.

WICKET! 24th over: Vaughan c Clarke b Warne 11 (England 102–2) Dear, oh dear, oh dear. A terrible shot from Vaughan, who rocks back and lofts a topspinner towards midwicket. Unlike earlier, there's someone there, and Clarke takes a simple catch. "Re Richard & Judy. It was particularly cringe-worthy when they showed a clip of the studio guest Richie Benaud from his playing days and Richard said 'Look at the buns on that'," remembers Oliver Shepherd. "Richie looked about as happy as he would listening to the Twelfth Man."

25th over: England 103–2 (Strauss 40, Bell 0) Bell isn't the most expansive shot maker at the best of times, and with lunch approaching he's more obdurate than ever.

WICKET! 26th over: Bell lbw b Warne 0 (England 104–3) Strauss, who hitherto this series has played Warne with all the confidence of an England football manager facing a posse of tabloid hacks following a defeat in Belfast, is looking assured. He blocks comfortably, before taking a single. That brings on Bell, who's beaten by a quicker straight one, and goes for a duck. Oh dearee me. The ball isn't turning, yet Warne's figures are now 7–1–27–3. "All the new interest in cricket is very welcome," insists John Everington. "The automatic assumption that we are going to reclaim the Ashes just by turning up most definitely is not. It fosters an arrogant complacency that every side in the world will be queuing up to puncture, and could well lead to delusions of grandeur similar to those of the England rugby team since November 2003."

27th over: England 115–3 (Strauss 40, Pietersen 10) Pietersen comes in, and immediately Tait serves him up a juicy full toss, which is splayed through the covers for four. Another one follows, this time on leg stump, and Pietersen again picks up another easy boundary. That's lunch.

England 115–3

The afternoon session

BY ROB SMYTH

Grossly outsized preamble: What superlative can you find to do justice to Shane Warne? And, no, "fat" isn't the answer. He was wonderful this morning; Australia were getting slaughtered when he came on, and in the blink of an eye he took 3 for 27 – on a flat pitch, offering negligible turn – to change the complexion of the match completely. Make no mistake, this is a 400+ pitch, and England could need all of those eight batsmen they have so inexplicably and negatively chosen. I'm a big fan of Paul Collingwood – he's strawberry blond, for a start – but he has about as much in common with Simon Jones as Radiohead do with Boyz II Men. It should have been like for like. Anyway, I'll let it go.

28th over: England 117–3 (Strauss 44, Pietersen 10) The first ball after lunch, from Warne, snakes past Strauss's expansive drive. One more wicket now and England are right in it. "Now Paul Collingwood is in the team it would be an apt time to discuss the worst ever England 'all-rounder'," deigns Chris Paul. "Shaun Udal gets my vote. You can almost hear Ray Illingworth saying 'Good county player, spins the ball a *bit*, can bat a *bit* . . .'. I don't mean to be cruel."

29th over: England 120–3 (Strauss 44, Pietersen 13) Brett Lee returns and Pietersen works him away for two to square leg as I prepare to mount a defence of Ian Bell and Jimmy Anderson. "This afternoon's riff," says Robbie Lambert. "I always like the one at the start of 'Money for Nothing' by Dire Straits, what do u reckon?" Ugh.

30th over: England 120–3 (Strauss 44, Pietersen 13) The Anderson/Collingwood debate will have to wait for a rainy day, or until tea, when I can be bothered to articulate why it was so wrong to pick Collingwood. Meanwhile, Warne bowls a maiden to his old mate Pietersen, who you can almost see visibly itching to welt one to cow corner.

31st over: England 121–3 (Strauss 45, Pietersen 13) A fusillade of short stuff from Lee to Strauss, who watches it all go past his body until dropping the last ball for a single. Both sides are waiting for the other to make their move here.

32nd over: England 124–3 (Strauss 48, Pietersen 13) Warne beats Strauss, who drives the next ball pleasantly and pragmatically through cover for three. "The predictability of Stereophonics riffs was mentioned during this morning's session," says Nathan Smith. "This may be so, but they also wrote 'The Bartender and the Thief' – surely a contender for an alternative Aussie national anthem." First person to mail in mentioning a song called 'The Convict' gets a happy-slapping.

33rd over: England 131–3 (Strauss 53, Pietersen 14) Strauss back-cuts Lee for four to reach his first first-innings fifty of the series. "C'mon," says James Guppy. "Paul Collingwood has more in common with Simon Jones than James Anderson, at least Collingwood can swing the bat . . ."

WICKET! 34th over: Pietersen b Warne 14 (England 131–4) Shane Warne bowls Kevin Pietersen with a fine delivery, and England are in huge trouble. Pietersen looked to play that cross-court tennis whip of his to a ball pitching on leg stump, but it span back – it may have done him for pace a little – and then went from pad on to off stump as Pietersen wafted across the line. Warne has 4 for 32 and he has been quite magnificent.

34th over: England 133–4 (Strauss 53, Flintoff 2) Looks like we'll need another miracle from you then, Freddie. "I don't think Giles's record stands up in this series," says Antony Melvin. "Can we drop him a couple of months ago as well?"

35th over: England 138–4 (Strauss 54, Flintoff 2) Lee greets his new best friend Flintoff with a rasping bouncer, which flies for four leg byes off Flintoff's helmet. We'll do the gags here. Meanwhile, here are your rubbish all-rounder nominations: Chris Cowdrey, Mike Watkinson, Mark Ealham, Robert Croft (all-rounder! Good one), Ian Greig, Ian effing Greig. And *loads* of Derek Pringles.

36th over: England 141–4 (Strauss 57, Flintoff 2) Shane Warne bowls a googly! For those who know cricket – not you oooh-what's-a-doosra Johnny Come Latelys – that is actually quite unusual, the first one he's bowled for about six years. As if he wasn't good enough! "Darren Gough," says Michael Collins. "Do you know any reason why he wasn't considered as a stopgap for Jones. He has a skiddy action and can reverse it. Is he injured?" No, but he *is* useless and aged about 44.

37th over: England 146–4 (Strauss 58, Flintoff 6) Amid the Warne-inspired maelstrom, Andrew Strauss is serenity personified. I hope that isn't tempting fate. Meanwhile, am I the only person who listened to Boyz II Men's *End of the Road* on the way to work today? Anyone else have any similarly guilty pleasures? Anyone for Wilson Phillips? The Cranberries? 99 Red Balloons?

38th over: England 147–4 (Strauss 59, Flintoff 6) Strauss will get a ton today. There, I said it. Back in the real world, Warne beats Flintoff with a total jaffa – drifting on to leg, then spitting past the outside edge. This is a masterclass. "Bell replaced by Colly and Anderson would have been the best choice," says Richard Jones. Thank you. Exactly.

39th over: England 153–4 (Strauss 60, Flintoff 11) Let's think about this: nags at Doncaster or the biggest cricket match ever? You guessed it – Channel 4 are going to the racing soon. F*!&'$ sake. Meanwhile, Freddie thick-edges Brett Lee to third man for four. "I love Foreigner," says Gareth Radford. "'I Want To Know What Love Is', the video is genius and it makes me want to cry. Err, better not print that in case any of my cricket team are reading." Err, too late. Anyway, it's "I *Wanna Know What Love Is*". Philistine.

40th over: England 156–4 (Strauss 62, Flintoff 12) "C'mon Darryl," drawls Shane Warne, in reference to his one-time bunny Darryl Cullinan (if you don't know the story, it's hilarious. Well, vaguely amusing. OK, it made me laugh) and his part-time bunny Strauss. "This morning's drive to work was highlighted by 'Nothing's Gonna Stop Us Now', by Starship," chuckles Steve Mahoney. You sick, sick man.

41st over: England 161–4 (Strauss 66, Flintoff 13) McGrath back in the attack again – just what England need – and Strauss clips him crisply to the midwicket fence. And now they're off to the effing racing! "I listened to the Backstreet Boys's 'The One' on the way to work," says Chris McMahon. "As probably the only Australian working in Slough, it's about as good as my workday normally gets."

42nd over: England 161–4 (Strauss 66, Flintoff 13) A horse won a race, and while I had the displeasure of watching it, not much happened at The Oval. "'Especially for You' by Kylie Minogue and Jason Donovan," says Sunil Gossain. "I wanted to play this as our first dance at my wedding, but my wife wouldn't let me." Did she file before or after the honeymoon?

43rd over: England 163–4 (Strauss 68, Flintoff 13) "I saw Phil Collins's 'Two Hearts' video on VH1 this morning and realised that Outkast's recent 'Hey Ya' video is a complete rip off," says Stuart Miller. "Phil Collins was a visionary."

44th over: England 165–4 (Strauss 69, Flintoff 14) Strauss looks to be cocooned in a lovely zone of concentration at the moment. "Would we all agree that the equivalent of the offside rule in football is the lbw law in cricket?" says Matt Jones. "Has anyone had to explain it yet with salt and pepper pots?! Incidentally, a sport with laws has to be superior to one with rules, doesn't it?" You're right. That *is* incidental.

45th over: England 168–4 (Strauss 70, Flintoff 16) In most contexts, 168 for 4 is an OK score. So why does it feel so bad? "I got David

Brent's 'Freelove Freeway' on my shuffle," says Lawrence Barber with an unfortunate turn of phrase. "I got it off a dodgy site for a joke, but I actually quite enjoy it." Me too. Guilty.

46th over: England 174–4 (Strauss 76, Flintoff 16) Warne is still causing plenty of mischief; in that over, Flintoff props forward and under-edges past his leg stump for a single. "My iTunes threw Geri Halliwell at me yesterday," says Olly Wehring. That doesn't mean you couldn't have thrown it straight back. "As Microsoft Messenger shows people what you're listening to at the time, I fear I'm yet to hear the end of it from my work colleagues. Although I do secretly think 'Look at Me' is quite a decent pop choon." The best-kept secret, eh?

47th over: England 180–4 (Strauss 77, Flintoff 21) McGrath isn't really at the races, although Channel 4 will be in a minute no doubt. Sorry, that was pitiful. Pathetic. Here's Charles Walford. "I get frowned upon by all and sundry for owning Five's Greatest Hits. Admittedly only a handful of the songs could lay claim to the title of 'great' but it's well worth an airing to raise the spirits." So is a warm bottle of Lambrini in the morning, but that doesn't make it right.

48th over: England 185–4 (Strauss 78, Flintoff 25) A sumptuous shot from Flintoff, easing the Warne slider through extra cover for four. There is so much more to his game than brute strength.

49th over: England 186–4 (Strauss 79, Flintoff 25) This is so tantalisingly poised that it almost makes me want to do some impromptu, thrusting star jumps in GU Towers. The Wayward but Hugely Promising Shaun Tait returns to the attack in place of McGrath, and does nothing.

50th over: England 193–4 (Strauss 86, Flintoff 25) Warne gives that sore shoulder of his a rest to end a majestic spell of 18–3–55–4. In his place come the chinamen of Simon Katich, whose quicker ball is slashed for four by Strauss. "Surely," begins Nick Watson, "any top sportspeople should have the melody of 'Simply The Best' by Tina Turner ringing in their ears."

51st over: England 198–4 (Strauss 87, Flintoff 29) Plenty of bristle and bluster from Tait, but this is just a beautiful batting surface and Flintoff clunks a gunbarrel-straight drive for four. Primeval. "Charles

Walford said he is frowned upon for owning Five's Greatest Hits,"
says Lee Calvert. "My best mate Lars Joyce was once chucked out of
a Hard House club for requesting Five from the DJ for a 40-minute
period before becoming aggressive at said lack of Five and being
forcibly ejected." It's thugs like that who ruin society. Now if it'd
been a Five *Star* song he was after . . .

52nd over: England 201–4 (Strauss 89, Flintoff 30) "So very, very
true," affirms Ben Hawkins. I agree: Paul Collingwood *is* strawberry
bl- "Phil Collins is a musical genius of contemporary times. Easily
adapting from his one-dimensional role as a percussionist in Genesis
to a lyrical master of pop music."

53rd over: England 203–4 (Strauss 90, Flintoff 31) Strauss chases a
wide one from Tait and misses. "Are you embarrassed or not?" asks
Shane Warne, who really has taken exception to Strauss for some
reason. "185 for 4 feels bad cuz it's TBCME (the biggest cricket
match ever) and it's a scoring pitch," fumes Cathy Anderton. "Do
we girlies have to explain everything?" Ooooh, get you. Anyway
they're 203 for 4 now, so . . .

54th over: England 207–4 (Strauss 91, Flintoff 34) Two overs to tea,
and if England lose a wicket now it'll be bloody annoying. Flintoff
could have lost his there, mowing across the line horribly at Katich,
but it scoots away for two.

55th over: England 213–4 (Strauss 92, Flintoff 39) Flintoff guides
Tait deliciously through extra cover for four – no power, no brute
strength, just marvellous technique and timing. That's tea.

England 213–4

The evening session

BY ROB SMYTH

Preamble: Evening. "Why so very belligerent today, Smyth?" asks
Dan Jones. "It's as if you're having to sit in a hot Farringdon office
fielding emails from internet freaks about Graham Thorpe. Ah,
right. On another note, I know the PR who does the, erm, PR for

Fish Fingers. Go on, drool away. I hear those oblong slivers of crumbed cod really jog your pulse."

56th over: England 217–4 (Strauss 92, Flintoff 43) The return of the Warne, as some wag points out that Australia need 13 to avoid the follow-on. If you're going to essay a gag, Peter James, a) make it funny and b) get your facts right (they need 14. Actually it's 18 now, as Flintoff has just driven Warne over midwicket for a one-bounce four). That aside, well played, Sir. "Why do rappers love Phil Collins?" asks someone. "Perhaps the greatest mystery of all concerning the beloved now-living-in-tax-exile sticksman – why does he garner such approbation from the hip-hop 'community'?" Anyone?

57th over: England 223–4 (Strauss 97, Flintoff 44) Tait makes way for Lee, and the trademark Strauss back-cut takes him to 97. "So what's better then, Dan Jones?" begins Chris Gibbons. "Being an internet freak writing emails about Graham Thorpe, or writing emails about internet freaks writing emails about Graham Thorpe? Or writing emails about writing emails about internet freaks writing emails about Graham Thorpe?" No idea, but I suspect all of the above are better than having the surname "Gibbons".

58th over: England 235–4 (Strauss 97, Flintoff 56) Successive swept fours from Flintoff off Warne bring Flintoff a very mature half-century, and he makes it three in a row with an exquisite on-drive. Brilliant.

59th over: England 240–4 (Strauss 102, Flintoff 56) Andrew Strauss reaches his century! He got there with a clipped four through midwicket off Brett Lee, and it's been a cracking innings. "My step-brother once wasted money on me by buying me some 'posh' salt from Selfridges," says Mark Foster. "Essentially it was salt, just salt."

60th over: England 243–4 (Strauss 105, Flintoff 56) I still say Strauss has had a slump this summer: one 50+ score in the first four Tests, and the most indeterminate displays of his Test career to-date. Anyway.

61st over: England 243–4 (Strauss 105, Flintoff 56) Australia could really use a wicket here, but you can't always get what you want in life, eh? To prove the point, Channel 4 go to the effing racing again.

62nd over: England 248–4 (Strauss 109, Flintoff 57) FAO all you idiots who have belittled my suggestions that Strauss was in a slump prior to this match: there is more to cricket than statistics, suckers: Strauss's one 50+ score was in a declaration-march freebie. He has been miles short of his outstanding best, as he has shown by displaying said best today. Next!

63rd over: England 256–4 (Strauss 109, Flintoff 65) Flintoff *just* reaches a very wide delivery from Lee and *just* gets it over point, albeit at such speed that even Colin Bland wouldn't have got it. Who's Colin Bland you say? Get out, JCL. Then Flintoff plays possibly the shot of the day, a scrumptiously timed cover drive off Lee.

64th over: England 261–4 (Strauss 114, Flintoff 65) The runs are coming pretty easily at the moment; there Strauss sweeps Warne very precisely for four. "I'm enjoying your idiosyncratic coverage," says Michael Paterson. "However, it poses me a problem. I work in the HR department at *Guardian* headquarters. I formulate policy on matters such as what constitutes excessive internet usage on company time. I have spent so much time following your coverage today that I will have to sack myself – obviously not until close of play."

65th over: England 261–4 (Strauss 114, Flintoff 65) Strauss has previous for low hundreds – he has seven, but none have reached 150 – so here's hoping he can go on to at least 211 today. Blimey, Lee went up big-time for a caught behind as Strauss chased a wide swinger, but Gilchrist et al barely appealed and Rudi Koertzen said no. There was a huge noise; it may have been bat on ground, but I'm 92% certain it was edge of bat on ball. Make that 100%. Gilchrist didn't even appeal! What an idiot!

66th over: England 267–4 (Strauss 114, Flintoff 71) More spine-tingling fare from Freddie Flintoff, who drives Warne imperiously over long-on for his first six of the day.

67th over: England 268–4 (Strauss 115, Flintoff 71) All of a sudden, England are on top: 2–1 up in an Ashes series and 268–4 in the final Test with a blond colossus playing brilliantly.

68th over: England 269–4 (Strauss 116, Flintoff 71) An unbelievably good slider from Warne beats Strauss, and then he thought he'd bowled Flintoff round his legs, started whirring his arms like David

Brent on the dancefloor, then realised he hadn't. Dignity was always overrated anyway.

69th over: England 273–4 (Strauss 120, Flintoff 71) Glenn McGrath is back for another spell, on a pitch that has given the seamers less than nothing all day. To prove the point, Strauss nails yet another back-cut thrillingly for four more.

70th over: England 274–4 (Strauss 120, Flintoff 72) Strauss is almost yorked, the ball just going past the outside edge and off stump. Warne responds by flinging the next ball angrily past Strauss's head to Adam Gilchrist. The name Darryl isn't mentioned.

WICKET! 71st over: Flintoff c Warne b McGrath 72 (England 274–5) Freddie has gone! He was looking to force McGrath off the back foot, but it was too tight to his body for the shot and he simply chopped it to Warne at slip, who clasped it smartly.

71st over: England 274–5 (Strauss 120, Collingwood 0) Glenn McGrath to Paul Collingwood, playing his first Test innings in England, and *there's only one slip*? McGrath tries to set Colly up with the slower ball. He doesn't fall for it.

72nd over: England 282–5 (Strauss 125, Collingwood 3) This is an immensely significant passage of play. The difference between a close score of, say, 340 for 5 and 310 for 8 is enormous. Warne draws Collingwood forward only to spit one past his outside edge. Beautiful bowling. Then Collingwood gets off the mark with a little dabble to third man.

73rd over: England 282–5 (Strauss 125, Collingwood 3) A maiden from McGrath to Collingwood, which I missed due to a prior engagement with some unfunny emails.

74th over: England 288–5 (Strauss 126, Collingwood 7) Collingwood, with nothing more than a short-arm jab, times Warne wonderfully through midwicket for his first boundary.

75th over: England 289–5 (Strauss 126, Collingwood 7) Shaun Tait is brought back, with McGrath resting for one last push with the second new ball. It's quite the dullest over I've seen for many a moon, with just a tantalising hint of reverse swing to keep you JCLs interested.

76th over: England 289–5 (Strauss 126, Collingwood 7) Strauss fresh-airs an attempted slog-hoick at Warne, who then has an lbw appeal turned down next ball – Hawkeye has it missing leg stump.

WICKET! 77th over: Collingwood lbw b Tait 7 (England 289–6) Great decision to pick Paul Collingwood, eh? In fairness he was triggered by Rudi Koertzen there – hit on the toe outside the line by an admittedly terrific reverse-swinging yorker from Shaun Tait, who was brought back into the attack for just that purpose. It looked out live at full speed, but it wasn't. An erroneous and possibly crucial decision, because 450 is a par score here and England are, well, 161 away from that.

77th over: England 289–6 (Strauss 126, G Jones 0) "I have to say that you are being rather nasty to all the people who take the time to email you and make the OBO a little more interesting," says Diana Ingrey. "Without all these people we would just have to listen to you all day; try appreciating them a little more." Yes, you're right – I'm sorry. I smile all the time really.

78th over: England 291–6 (Strauss 128, G Jones 0) Shane Warne's 30th over of the day; erm, yeah, that's about it.

79th over: England 295–6 (Strauss 128, G Jones 4) Geraint Jones gets off the mark in very classy fashion, skimming a cover drive against the Tait reverse swing for four. That one shot is enough to bring in a cover sweeper, and make it just one slip for the new batsman, the No. 8 at that. Attacking defensive fields, for want of a less ostensibly oxymoronic expression, have been one of the features of this series. I reckon it's the beginning of an indelible shift in the way we view orthodox (sic) fields in cricket, but I'm paid by the word so I may have just made that up in an attempt to sound profound and secure an extra thing of Polos.

WICKET! 80th over: Strauss c Katich b Warne 128 (England 297–7) Five wickets for the magnificent Shane Warne, and the end of Andrew Strauss's splendid innings. He prodded wearily forward, and the ball went from pad on to bat and up in the air. Simon Katich, diving forward on to the pitch from silly point, did the rest with an outstanding one-handed catch. England are up a certain creek here.

80th over: England 297–7 (G Jones 5, Giles 0) After all that Phil

Collins nonsense, Ed Britton mercifully rediscovers a more highbrow and typically *Guardian* tone: "If Bez and Pete Doherty were to set upon each other in comedy sumo suits, who would win?"

81st over: England 301–7 (G Jones 9, Giles 0) The new ball is available, but there's no chance of it being taken in this mood. Jones, meanwhile, brings up the 300 by shanking Tait over the solitary slip. There is generous applause, but I suspect that's from the people who don't know what they're talking about. England don't have nearly enough runs yet.

82nd over: England 303–7 (G Jones 10, Giles 1) Suddenly the prospect of trying to bowl Australia out in these conditions with four bowlers tomorrow doesn't seem so clever. "Bez obviously would win," says Averil Dourado. Is the right answer. "He's Northern for a start (and so much harder than a shandy-drinking Southerner) and besides Doherty would probably start to cry and start quoting Byron if you gave him a little shove."

83rd over: England 305–7 (G Jones 11, Giles 1) "This has been annoying me all series," begins Tif A. "Why is it on the desktop scorecard that with all players in the England team you have their initials then surname (eg AJ Strauss). Yet with Geraint Jones it is GO Jones, GO. Is this a message to the man to do something useful?" Are you for real?

84th over: England 309–7 (G Jones 16, Giles 1) Here's Jim Denvir. "Why oh why oh why did you make that comment about 310–8 (72nd over). If that's the score at the close, you'll be the one to blame." A little thing I like to call "doing my job". It's hardly my fault I was right.

85th over: England 313–7 (G Jones 20, Giles 1) Jones unfurls that picturebook cover drive of his, and sends it spinning delightfully to the fence. "Doom and gloom re: the runs," says Gareth Sherratt. Yeah, well, you're not the one who got given a barely-cooked keb– "Australia haven't posted enough throughout the series; good pitch or not. Why should this change now? England's bowlers can get amongst them as per usual." Oh, you mean England's *four* bowlers? There was me thinking they usually operate with five.

86th over: England 315–7 (G Jones 21, Giles 2) "Stop worrying about England having four bowlers," says David Bailey. "It'll rain tomorrow and we can all light cigars and sit back and enjoy victory." I don't smoke.

87th over: England 315–7 (G Jones 21, Giles 2) The new ball is taken, and it's put straight into those surgical hands of Glenn McGrath. Ricky Ponting is so excited that he puts two whole slips in, and it's a maiden. It's a sign of how far England have come that a score of 315 for 7 against Australia is a tad disappointing.

88th over: England 319–7 (G Jones 21, Giles 5) That's the end of another absolutely fantastic day's play. England will hope to sneak up to somewhere near 400 tomorrow to give their poor besieged four-man attack something to bowl at.

England 319–7

Second Day

The morning session

BY SEAN INGLE

Preamble: Another hugely important morning for England. "I am doing a rain dance on my desk as we speak," says James Green. It's not working, James. It's 25 degrees and sunny at The Oval.

Meanwhile your predictions are flying in. "England to struggle to 350 today, Australia will post 450, Pom second innings no more than 250, Aussies to get the runs five wickets down early on Monday," predicts Neil Stork-Brett from Brisbane. "Not to worry though – what's wrong with a drawn series?" Er, the Aussies retaining the Ashes, Neil?

89th over: England 320–7 (G Jones 21, Giles 6) McGrath opens with a slowish bouncer, and has Giles playing and missing with his second delivery, but otherwise it's a sedate start. "Can you explain how on a pitch that's not supposed to be turning, Warney can get so many wickets?" asks a bemused Philip Smith. Flight, change of pace, and more cunning than a fox that's graduated with honours from the school of cunning, Phillip.

WICKET! 90th over: G Jones b Lee 25 (England 325–8) Jones is undone by a lightning quick outswinger that takes out his off stump. "What are the odds for Flintoff being BBC Sports Personality of the Year?" asks Mark Greenwood. "And has it ever been awarded to a non-Brit?" He was evens the last time I looked, Mark – and, no, it's never been snagged by a non-Brit. Unless you consider 1971 winner Princess Anne being of German extraction, of course.

91th over: England 326–8 (Giles 8, Hoggard 0) Hoggard is content to look and leave. "Can we not move these important games for England up to Scotland where we have ample rain to force a draw?" asks Brian Donnelly. "It's chucking it down as I type." It's also raining in Dublin, Durham, Luxembourg and Wagga Wagga, according to various email correspondents. Thanks to one and all.

92nd over: England 326–8 (Giles 9, Hoggard 0) Lee, who's made a bright start, has Giles ducking and weaving more than Muhummad Ali in the Rumble in the Jungle. "Re: the BBC's sports personality of the year award. It's unlikely ever to be won by a non-Brit as they have the overseas sports personality of the year award for people who aren't British," harrumphs Chris Powell (and several hundred others).

93rd over: England 330–8 (Giles 12, Hoggard 0) Giles keeps the scoreboard ticking. Hoggard, meanwhile, is at his obdurate best. "In 1985 Barry McGuigan won the above award," says Seamus McCann. "McGuigan was born in Clones in Co Monaghan in the Republic of Ireland – he acquired a British passport at some stage but he's really not a Brit." Thanks to all of you who've pointed out that Canada's Greg Rusedski and Lennox Lewis both won the award too.

94th over: England 331–8 (Giles 13, Hoggard 0) Interesting, very interesting. Lee is getting some genuine outswing here, and beats Hoggard all ends up with an absolute pearler.

95th over: England 336–8 (Giles 18, Hoggard 0) Shot from Giles! McGrath bounces one in short, and Giles hooks him – think Botham Headingley 81 – for four down to fine leg. "Over a quarter of your 'English' cricket team is made up of non-Brits, so why couldn't they win the sports personality of the year award?" asks Raymond Logan, chucking a Molotov cocktail into the debate.

96th over: England 337–8 (Giles 19, Hoggard 0) "If Princess Anne won, who had less personality than her?" poses Pat Lockley. "Seems, to coin a phrase, like it was a bad year for sports personalities."

97th over: England 338–8 (Giles 20, Hoggard 0) "Raymond Logan has forgotten to include the 43 subs England will be using during this Test which brings the Brit average up significantly," points out Neil Jones.

98th over: England 341–8 (Giles 23, Hoggard 0) Twelve overs into the new ball and already Brett Lee is getting some reverse swing. "Please encourage everyone to vote for Freddie in the sports personality of the year award – we can't let Ellen MacArthur win on the grounds that sailing on your own, without any opposition, is not a sport."

99th over: England 343–8 (Giles 24, Hoggard 0) Hoggard is frustrating the hell out of McGrath here. Finally, he does get an edge – and Ricky Ponting at second slip puts a difficult catch down! Then, last ball of the over, the Aussies reckon Hoggard gets an edge to Gilchrist – but Koertzen says "Not out!" Replays show Hoggard definitely got a nick. "Why are people praying for rain?" asks Jeremy Hillman. "What lack of justice to the series would rain be? Victory or death for both sides – a draw would be the biggest let-down of the millennium thus far."

100th over: England 345–8 (Giles 24, Hoggard 1) Warne replaces Lee and already he's getting the ball to samba-dance this way and that. "Do you reckon Hoggy told Punter: 'You've just dropped the Ashes, mate'," suggests my colleague Rob Smyth.

WICKET! 101st over: Hoggard c Martyn b McGrath 2 (England 345–9) McGrath chucks in a slower one (74mph) and induces the false stroke: Hoggard finds Martyn at mid-off and The Oval goes silent. Shortly afterwards, Harmison nearly goes first ball – he defensively pulls it towards short midwicket, just out of reach of the diving Katich. Meanwhile this from Alistair Moffat: "Just thought you might like to know that the bowling figures after 5.1 overs for a certain JM Anderson for Lancs at Chelmsford read 2–17."

102nd over: England 353–9 (Giles 27, Harmison 6) Harmison somehow survives a whole Warne over without swinging his bat like Arnold Schwarzenegger in *Conan the Barbarian* and getting bowled/stumped. "Re: Jeremy Hillman (over 99). Where's the justice in Australia winning and returning home with the Ashes even though the series will have been drawn when they have been out-bowled (maybe one exception!), out-batted and generally outplayed?" asks David Glover.

103rd over: England 358–9 (Giles 31, Harmison 8) Both batsmen are going after McGrath here – lots of inside edges, mishit shots and singles turned into twos. England survive, but for how long? "Pick Jimmy Anderson just because he's got rid of Jefferson (who?) and

Flower?" fumes Karl Bates. "Not quite the same thing as playing Australia in the most important Test match for years."

104th over: England 360–9 (Giles 31, Harmison 8) "In response to Jeremy Hillman – a rain-induced draw would in no way be unjust," says Andrew Epps. "We drew the Old Trafford Test due to bad weather. Let the Aussies feel the frustration of having a team on the ropes only for the weather to come to the rescue."

105th over: England 373–9 (Giles 32, Harmison 20) Brilliant from Harmison, who smashes three fours off that over! "With Warne making hay, surely we should have dropped Bell, ignored both Collingwood and Anderson, moved wheelie bin up to bat at four and gone in with an all-spin attack consisting of Giles, Vaughan, Salisbury and Min Patel," writes Tony Hodson. Playing an extra spinner might not be a bad idea on this pitch, Tony – it certainly looks very dry.

WICKET! 106th over: Giles lbw Warne 32 (England 373 all out) Warne appeals after rapping Giles on the pads and Bowden gives it – even though Hawkeye shows it was missing off stump. It's hard to say without seeing Australia bat, but England will be a touch disappointed with 373. Still, at 131–4 and 301–7 it could've been a whole lot worse.

Australia first innings

1st over: Australia 1–0 (Langer 1, Hayden 0) Patchy start from Harmison, who opens with a snarling bouncer before Langer gets off the mark with a misshit pull shot. Australia's top first-innings score this series is just 308; I think England would certainly settle for that. "What is all this weak-kneed talk of rain?" asks Tom Joyce. "Does no one else recall the previous four Tests, in which the Aussie top order batted as if they'd just left the iron on?"

2nd over: Australia 2–0 (Langer 2, Hayden 0) Immediately Hoggard gets some swing – first he tempts Langer to play a calypso shot at an outswinger and then nearly attracts a Hayden edge with one that doesn't swing.

3rd over: Australia 4–0 (Langer 4, Hayden 0) Harmison still hasn't got his line right yet; there's none of the confident hostility of Lord's yet.

4th over: Australia 6–0 (Langer 4, Hayden 1) Hayden has been trying to bully Hoggard without success. Indeed he's beaten by an absolute beaut that moves in the air then jack-in-a-boxes off the pitch. "My boyfriend is doing my head in with his persistent negativity," says Kate Fordham. "The latest is he thinks Michael Vaughan is showing signs of bird flu, and that a nest of dragons is about to become active again under the Oval pitch and devour everybody, thus ensuring that the Ashes will return Down Under. Please tell him somebody."

5th over: Australia 6–0 (Langer 4, Hayden 1) A half-hearted lbw appeal from Harmison is immediately rejected by umpire Koertzen. "Why, when things get exciting, does streaming radio from the BBC always go down," fumes Dr Ewan Main. "Cricinfo and your commentary are the only things between me and heading home for proper radio/TV." And that's a good thing, Ewan?

6th over: Australia 14–0 (Langer 12, Hayden 1) Langer looks to be getting the measure of Hoggard. First, he clouts him through the covers, then eases him through mid-off for another boundary. "I'm no expert on the laws of cricket, but were a nest of dragons to devour The Oval and all in it (Kate Fordham, 4th over) would it not result in a draw and thus ensure that the Aussies' tight grasp on the urn is released?" asks David MacDonald.

7th over: Australia 19–0 (Langer 16, Hayden 2) Harmison looks to be getting into his groove. He whacked Langer on the elbow in his previous over, now he has him playing and missing at a teasing outswinger. But then he serves up a juicy half-volley which Langer feasts on. "In my defence, I was very tired whilst watching the end of *Reign of Fire* last night, and I did take Kate to the Lord's Test match," says Rob Burley (Kate's boyfriend, 4th over). "Some gratitude. Oh, and by the way, if any OBO readers dropped a £20 note on the second day of the first Test, see Kate. She picked it up, procrastinated for 20 minutes about whether to hand it to a steward or give it to charity, then neatly pocketed it." Meanwhile, that's lunch.

England 373 all out; Australia 19–0

The afternoon session

BY MIKE ADAMSON

Preamble: So what would make this upcoming session a good one for England? Two, maybe three wickets? With the weather forecast constantly changing – and currently suggesting sunshine for all five days – England certainly can't rely on the rain to help them force a draw.

8th over: Australia 19–0 (Langer 16, Hayden 2) Matthew Hoggard bowls the first over after lunch, and a tidy one it is too. A maiden in fact. "What with all the increasing hullabaloo about umpiring fallibility," writes Richard Marsden, "it occurred to me that there's one very simple measure that could be taken to clear up the problem of whether the ball pitches / hits the batsman in line. Why don't the groundsmen just paint Channel 4's red zone, or something equivalent to it, on the pitch as an umpiring aid? That would certainly have saved Simon Katich a few quid – and possibly Paul Collingwood's Test career."

9th over: Australia 25–0 (Langer 21, Hayden 3) "Anyone see the photos of England players when they were kids in yesterday's *Metro*?" asks Denby Dale. "Best ball I've ever seen from Michael Vaughan. And the photo of Banger when he was younger proved that he must have loved sausages, and pies, and lots of food in general."

10th over: Australia 29–0 (Langer 21, Hayden 7) Matthew Hayden is being noticeably watchful at the start of this innings, presumably aware that two more failures and an Ashes series defeat could spell the end of his Test career. "The problem with the red zone on the pitch is that it would give batsmen an unfair advantage so that they knew where their off stump was," says Chris Langmead, "and this would deprive us of the comedy when Michael Clarke shoulders arms only to see his furniture re-arranged."

11th over: Australia 36–0 (Langer 26, Hayden 7) Freddie's on – Harmison obviously didn't impress Vaughan too much with his one post-lunch over. "On the general subject of Tresco's teenage lardiness," says Dave Voss on a subject which will always be welcome here, "apparently he didn't eat steak until he was 27, which is a bit odd for someone who appears so fond of his tucker."

12th over: Australia 37–0 (Langer 26, Hayden 8) There's no swing for Hoggard at the moment, therefore he's not troubling the Australians in any way. "My prediction is Oz to post 390–420 by tea tomorrow, leaving a session and two clear days for England to work their magic wonder," says Richard Hutchinson. "And what is it with these clouds and predictions of rain anyway – are there competing tribes of Oz and English shamans manically either praying for rain or clear skies? Personally, I want to see it go all the way to the final day – now all I need to do is start dreaming up excuses to get off work on Monday." Yeah, there could be a lot of sick people in England on Monday.

13th over: Australia 37–0 (Langer 26, Hayden 8) "Beetles taste like apples," says Will Cooper cryptically, "wasps like pine nuts, and worms like fried bacon. I wonder if Tresco's love of food would stretch this far?"

14th over: Australia 42–0 (Langer 31, Hayden 8) Gary Pratt (the substitute who ran out Ponting in the last Test) is on, presumably in an attept to rile the Australians. He watches on as Hayden sends the ball flying through the gully area for four. "What Dave Voss (over 11) missed in the statement about Tresco not eating steak until he was 27," says Andy McLellan, "was that it was referring to months, not years."

15th over: Australia 45–0 (Langer 34, Hayden 8) Flintoff steams in again, but there is no-ball deviation either in the air or off the pitch. This is looking a little worrying. "A bunch of Aussies and English are sitting here in Switzerland with no TV, no BBC radio, and therefore no idea about whether it's going to bucket down or not at The Oval," says H Gandhi. "Care to post a few words on whether it is about to rain or not over there?" Of course. Well, when I took over the hot seat, there was barely a cloud in the sky above The Oval, but as the corporate folk begin to return to their seats after a Marcus Trescothick-sized lunch, so too are clouds starting to appear. The prediction is that there will be thunderstorms at some stage today, though probably not until after the end of play.

16th over: Australia 46–0 (Langer 35, Hayden 8) Harmison returns to the attack from the Vauxhall End, but it's fairly ineffective fare once again. Oh for Simon Jones. "The good burghers of Zurich, in their infinite wisdom, have this year chosen next Monday to celebrate their Knabenschiessen public holiday – Knabenschiessen can be literally translated as 'adolescent-shooting'," says Colin Huxtable. "Rather than picking off teenaged hoodies on Bahnhofstrasse I'll be comfortably ensconced on my sofa watching the cricket on my illegally imported satellite TV. It just doesn't get much better."

17th over: Australia 48–0 (Langer 36, Hayden 9) "I've taken Monday off already, so no worries there, but I'm at a wedding tomorrow," says Tamsin Cox. "Any ideas for subtly keeping tabs on the score whilst the happy couple say their vows? Honestly, you'd think they could have checked the Test schedule first."

18th over: Australia 52–0 (Langer 36, Hayden 13) "In response to the comment that there could potentially be a lot of sick people on Monday – apparently one in seven people who are off ill today and Monday will actually be off just to watch the cricket," says Marie Thomas. "I'm sure one of your more mathematically-minded fans could calculate the loss to businesses." Come on then, any boffins out there.

19th over: Australia 66–0 (Langer 50, Hayden 13) An enormous six from Langer – Ashley Giles, the new bowler, sees his second ball go hurtling straight back over his head and endangering some snoozy people in the crowd. And another huge maximum – this time hoicking the ball over midwicket. An inauspicious start for Giles, who England really need to perform well here. "In response to Tamsin Cox (17th over), have a word with the vicar and see if he'll use the board normally reserved for putting up hymn numbers as a makeshift scoreboard," says Nick Pettigrew.

20th over: Australia 69–0 (Langer 51, Hayden 13) Harmison is still working hard from the Vauxhall End, but there really is little on offer for him at the moment. "Having been at weddings for most weekends of the summer, I can confirm that the only way to get away with keeping tabs on the cricket is to WAP throughout the service," says Alex Pinhey, deviously. "Hymns usually provide some cover for any stifled celebrations."

21st over: Australia 72–0 (Langer 52, Hayden 15) No cricket briefly, as Channel 4 consider the DBS St Leger Yearling Stakes (Class Two) for two-year-olds far more important. The early leader is Imperial Sword, but he (or she, not sure which) is chased down by Princess Cleo for a clear victory. "Don't go for sickness on Monday," advises Martin Cruise. "There needs to be a build-up of coughing and sneezing etc to be convincing. Go for a domestic emergency such as the washing machine flooding the kitchen. Unavoidable and no tricky questions afterwards."

22nd over: Australia 73–0 (Langer 53, Hayden 15) Giles returns to the attack after a change of ends, and bowls a much tighter over. "The loss to business as so accurately forecast by the CBI would be £300,000 p/h," says Hugh Sowerby, rising to the boffin bait, "thus suggesting running its full course would stretch to over 19 million. However – should it rain, the party could continue to Tuesday, financially crippling the country, but at least we'll have the Ashes."

23rd over: Australia 78–0 (Langer 58, Hayden 15) A ball which beat the bat! Hooray! And then Collingwood teases an edge out of Langer, but Trescothick chooses to go with just one hand to his right, and palms the ball over the bar for four rather than clinging on to it. "As the only person in the office with internet access, I'd be lynched if I dared not come in, otherwise I wouldn't be able to keep everyone up to date," says David Leach. "My manager saw me checking the cricket – instead of a telling-off he asked for the scores! I've never been so important."

24th over: Australia 85–0 (Langer 64, Hayden 16) "You keep getting stymied every time C4 goes racing," says Stephen Russell. "While it's a pain in the backside for everyone, can you confirm that your employers at the *Guardian*, despite the vast numbers of people who read the OBO, are far too tight to invest in some way that you could skip to FilmFour? What does this mean for OBO next year when not only will they have to provide a digital connection but also Sky Sports subscription? Is this, like Richie's, your farewell match? I think we should be told." Sadly our connection to FilmFour is down at the moment (honest).

25th over: Australia 87–0 (Langer 65, Hayden 17) "I can't believe all these people writing in about enjoying watching the cricket," says

Roland Langebein anxiously. "It's much too important to be enjoying it. I thought I would be more nervous when England were batting, but since lunch I've actually started feeling physically sick." Haven't we all.

26th over: Australia 88–0 (Langer 65, Hayden 18) Giles races through another over without troubling the two Aussie openers, but also just conceding a single to mid-on. "When listening to the cricket via an ear-piece during a wedding ceremony, don't jump up and celebrate an Australian wicket after the vicar has asked 'are there any objections,'" chuckles Jamie Singer.

27th over: Australia 95–0 (Langer 66, Hayden 24) Hayden is playing like a man who knows his career is on the line, not taking any risks, but putting the bad ball (such as Collingwood's first of this over) away. "People at work who don't follow the cricket but have started now England are good: (a) Don't walk past my TV at lunch and ask 'What's the score?' when it's clearly displayed. (b) Don't ask 'Is it going to be a draw then?' when we're half-way through day two and I DON'T KNOW. (c) Don't ask me anything. Ever." So says an angry Joe Neate.

28th over: Australia 96–0 (Langer 66, Hayden 25) Ashley Giles has a big (and valid) appeal for lbw turned down by Bowden. Langer lucky to survive. "Was anyone else as disturbed as I was by the talk of open-topped buses and booking Trafalgar Square for 'we win the Ashes' celebrations?" asks Andrew Bethell. "I reckoned it would goad Warne into an extra five wickets and the Aussie top order to score an extra 300 runs. I was right about Warne (and that's just the first innings) and watching these two settling in rather drives home the premonition."

29th over: Australia 96–0 (Langer 66, Hayden 25) An outrageous appeal from Flintoff (the ball pitched about a foot and a half outside leg stump) is laughed off by umpire Koertzen.

30th over: Australia 101–0 (Langer 71, Hayden 25) A top-edged Hayden sweep draws an ambitious shout of "catch it" from Geraint Jones, but the ball lands safely in the gap.

31st over: Australia 103–0 (Langer 72, Hayden 26) As most of you emailing in seem more concerned by the weather than the cricket, here's an update: the clouds are now hovering above The Oval, and looking menacing. Rain is not due until the close of play, but it doesn't look too far away to this observer.

32nd over: Australia 105–0 (Langer 73, Hayden 27) Umpire Bowden has a word with Ashley Giles to tell him to keep off the wicket, which, in truth, he may also be told by his captain too unless his bowling becomes more threatening. "It's hammering down in Isleworth – everyone's going outside to try to blow the clouds towards The Oval," says Kate Higham.

33rd over: Australia 112–0 (Langer 75, Hayden 32) "Is it not raining in Vauxhall yet?" asks Chris Harrison. "We're getting drenched in Kingston. Could it be the gods are conspiring against us?" It's just started spitting at The Oval, but the play has come to a halt anyway because the players and umpires need to have some tea.

Australia 112–0; England 373

The evening session

BY SEAN INGLE

Preamble: The skies are looking apocalyptic over London, so this might not last long. Indeed, the umpires are already debating whether to offer Australia the light.

3.30pm: The light is offered . . . and Langer and Hayden have accepted! Wouldn't it be funny if this cost them the Ashes on Monday night? "I am 'working' at The Oval," writes my boss Emily Bell, via BlackBerry. "I would like to report that I have been given directions by Ian Botham, met Richie Benaud and can confirm that the Channel 4 commentary team eat Maynard's Wine Gums." So now you know.

3.40pm: Umpire Koertzen is explaining why he offered Australia the light. Umpire Billy Bowden follows up by pointing out that "it has to be fair contest between bat and ball, and Australia have every right to walk off the pitch". The skies are darkening by the minute, and thunder can be heard across London.

3.50pm: Just in case you didn't believe my comments re: the London weather, here's Martin Dow. "I can report that the view from the 24th floor in the City of London this afternoon is glorious: thick, black cloud and lightning rolling over south London . . . enough to bring a tear to the eye," he sobs.

4.15pm: Apparently we were about to restart a few minutes ago, but then the umpires took another light reading which revealed the light had "got considerably worse".

4.25pm: It's still not raining at The Oval, which means the Aussies have lost an hour's play. "I can also report that it is raining in Victoria and Balham," says Sian Jones, who seems to be in two places at once. "What we need is some weather control to ensure the rain reaches The Oval. Where's Paul McCartney when you need him? If he zapped a few clouds for a stupid concert he can certainly do the same when there is sporting glory at stake."

4.56pm: Rain has started to fall, but it's light drizzle at most. And the light isn't bad either. So the Aussies could certainly bat in this. Meanwhile this from Channel 4's Louise Peake: "My sister in Perth, WA, has told me that school kids are starting to use the phrase 'Nice one, Shane' as a response to anything good," she writes. "Stump mics are a wonderful thing."

5.18pm: Still no sign of play. There's little wind, and I'm guessing that'll be it for the night. "I bet David Shepherd is glad they nicked that last single before tea. He'd have fallen over by now for sure," says David Smale.

5.25pm: It's raining at The Oval, which is now three-quarters empty. It's only a matter of time before the umpires call play off for the day. "I reckon Australia are screwed," says Nick Warbuton. "You know what it's like in this country. You sit all day in the office with the sun beaming outside and soon as it hits 5pm on a Friday and you look forward to a weekend of great weather, the rain comes down and the break from work is a washout. That leaves the Australians only Monday from roughly 9am to do something." Let's hope so, Nick.

Australia 112–0; England 373

Third Day

The morning session

BY ROB SMYTH

Preamble: Morning. Play will begin at 11am after early-morning rain.

First email of the day: "That is the shortest preamble I have ever seen," says James Green. It's called a hangover.

Moment of the morning: Sky News reporting live outside The Oval as Paul Collingwood strolls in. "Morning Geraint, how are you?" says reporter. "Name's Paul mate," says Colly. Walks off in disgust. Priceless.

34th over: Australia 116–0 (Langer 78, Hayden 33) Hoggard has a huge lbw shout turned down first ball! Langer fell over – literally – a sharp inswinger and although my instinct was out – I even said 'out' to nobody in particular, making a complete idiot of myself in the process – Richie Benaud was absolutely convinced it wasn't out. And he was wrong, according to Hawkeye.

35th over: Australia 116–0 (Langer 78, Hayden 33) A sensible move, I think, to begin with Flintoff rather than Harmison given that the ball should zip around in the air. Here's the genuinely and mercifully inimitable Richard Jones. "A day of many interruptions – rain, light – none longer than 30 minutes will leave the following EOD score: Australia 292 for 7 off 60–odd overs. Collingwood and Flintoff will have done the damage."

36th over: Australia 123–0 (Langer 81, Hayden 37) Good over from Hoggard again.

37th over: Australia 123–0 (Langer 81, Hayden 37) Another big shout for lbw as Langer again falls over an inducker – seam rather than swing this time, and Flintoff rather than Hoggard. My instinct was that it pitched outside leg, and in a rare development I was right. "Have you seen the Betfair market on Richie's last words?" says Dan Hare. "Unbelievable."

38th over: Australia 128–0 (Langer 81, Hayden 42) Hayden glances Hoggard fine for four, then Hoggard has a big lbw shout turned down – it was pad first, and a very decent shout. Here's Katy Allen. "Somewhere in Guardian Towers should be a big brown envelope containing cakes specifically for the OBO team. Make sure you lot get it and someone else hasn't sneakily snaffled it. I always think cake is perfect for a hangover. Starchy carb and it tastes nice, goes perfectly with a brew."

39th over: Australia 128–0 (Langer 81, Hayden 42) Three overs this morning, three maidens for the man Tony Greig calls Flintorf.

40th over: Australia 138–0 (Langer 86, Hayden 47) Yet another let-off for these Aussies this morning: Hayden drives loosely at Hoggard and the edge flies just wide of Strauss at second slip for four.

41st over: Australia 138–0 (Langer 86, Hayden 47) The umbrellas are going up. We'll have some of that! The umpires succumb to the inevitable, and the players are going off.

11.45am No change in the conditions. "Does faux-virginal mean prissy?" asks Richard Jones. "Or is it an out-of-tune medieval musical instrument?

Play will restart at 12.05pm

41st over: Australia 139–0 (Langer 86, Hayden 48) "Never mind the cricket," says Matthew Cobb. "It's let's provoke the strawberry-blond faux-Mancunian time. How many goals will Cole score against United today?" I thought Arsenal were playing Middlesbrough?

42nd over: Australia 140–0 (Langer 86, Hayden 49) "If England don't win the Ashes, will the media crucify them, or praise them for playing a huge part in the greatest Test series of all time?" says James Green. The latter, surely. "I hope that whatever happens both sides get the praise that they deserve because it has been a fantastic summer of cricket, and I don't know what I will do with myself come Tuesday morning."

43rd over: Australia 144–0 (Langer 88, Hayden 50) Catharsis of sorts for Hayden, who reaches fifty in his final Test match.

44th over: Australia 145–0 (Langer 88, Hayden 51) A quiet over from Hoggard to Hayden, the sort which no amount of artistic licence could enable me to make interesting. "Am currently travelling westwards on the train from London to Bath, following your commentary on my crackberry (love the modern world) and it's been raining from Reading to Didcot," says Lawrence Aggleton. "Huzzah!" And, indeed, huzzah!

45th over: Australia 150–0 (Langer 88, Hayden 56) Harmison comes on, and his half-tracker loosener is pulled with a healthy clump to the fence by Hayden. There is an air of resignation around the ground now; Australia are blatantly going to get 550 here.

46th over: Australia 154–0 (Langer 88, Hayden 60) Wide filth from Hoggard first up, and Hayden lambasts it through the covers for four – that was the Hayden of 2001–04.

47th over: Australia 157–0 (Langer 91, Hayden 60) That's lunch, after a truncated morning session in which Australia firmed their grip on this contest.

Australia 157–0; England 373

The afternoon session

BY ROB SMYTH

Preamble: A sly pint of Star at lunchtime made me feel better for a couple of minutes, before the hangover and concurrent self-loathing came storming back. Meanwhile, the sporting action on Channel 4 is being affected by rain. Sadly it's the effing racing in Doncaster, a distraction we may have to endure for the afternoon. Yes I know it's on FilmFour; yes I know that's free; yes I also know we can't get it in GU Towers. What I don't know is why.

48th over: Australia 161–0 (Langer 93, Hayden 62) Ashley Giles gets his first bowl of the day and is milked effortlessly by Langer and Hayden – how's that for an enduring image? – for four singles.

49th over: Australia 162–0 (Langer 93, Hayden 63) In the last four Tests at The Oval, seven of the eight first innings have been in excess of 400, and it's easy to see why: this pitch is just an absolute belter. I think England are really struggling here; yes I know I'm the sort of person who doesn't see the glass half empty so much as smashed to smithereens, but this has got Warne 7 for 61 and 2–2 written all over it. We might as well pack up now to be honest.

50th over: Australia 167–0 (Langer 97, Hayden 64) There is plenty of rough for Giles, but I always think he's a better bowler when there's no significant expectation on him – he wears the underdog skin well. "Fear, Loathing and Cricket in Fakenham," says Andrew Goldsby. I think he meant Farringdon. "Well at least you've got the name of your 'bio sorted." I was going to call it "The Inherent Absurdity of Nostalgia, Victor. In Fakenham".

51st over: Australia 168–0 (Langer 97, Hayden 65) Pretty anodyne stuff from Harmison, who just hasn't fired since that blistering first morning at Lord's. That was only eight weeks ago. Feels like about eight years.

52nd over: Australia 174–0 (Langer 97, Hayden 70) Hayden drives Giles for a one-bounce four, which Flintoff at long-on didn't clap sight on at all.

WICKET! 53rd over: Langer b Harmison 105 (Australia 185–1) Justin Langer gets on top of a Harmison lifter, guiding it to third man to complete a really admirable century. I thought Langer was a bit of a prat before this series, but everything he has done on and off the pitch has really impressed me. I'm sure he'll be thrilled. But then he falls, dragging on a rapid delivery to end a really fiery over from Harmison. Boy, did England need that wicket.

Rain stops play! Two in a minute for England – the wicket of Langer, and then the covers come on before Ricky Ponting can be booed to the wicket.

2.05pm update nicked straight from Channel 4 The rain is a lot heavier than anybody had anticipated, and already puddles are forming on the pitch. "We've got real problems," says Mark Nicholas, fair-minded as ever, but I'm sure most of you won't be too bothered.

A very good point from Ken Abbott Which I myself was going to make but couldn't (be bothered to) articulate properly. "Am I the only Englishman out there who is starting to believe that the rain, whilst obviously hampering Australia in a practical sense, is having just as much a negative effect physiologically on England? The more they start to believe that the rain is going to get them the draw they need, the worse they seem to be playing. Australia still have plenty of time to win this match even if the rest of today is lost. What England need to do is wake up to that fact, rain or no rain!" I think it's too late: England's mindset, erm, gearstick is, erm, stuck now.

That's tea The evening session theoretically begins at 3.30pm, though I suspect we won't get play till 4 at the earliest.

Australia 185–1; England 373

The evening session

BY ROB SMYTH

Preamble: Afternoon. No time has yet been set for play to resume; when there is, you'll hear it here eighth.

Emails, while you wait "What are you gonna do for the rest of the day if it keeps raining?" asks Ben Reynolds. "Presumably you're contracted to stay at work till about 6pm." The Man does indeed have possession of my cojones until 6pm, so if it rains I'll do what I'm doing now – following United's game on a rival site, listening to some Arcade Fire, and sifting through literally *tens* of emails.

Play will resume at 3.30pm And, weather-permitting, it'll be a three-and-a-half-hour session. "I know all about hangovers and self-loathing," says Karen Steele, which is an introduction to get any boy excited. "I have just done an internet search to find out what happened in the new series of *The OC* last week in the US. And now I'm gutted that I've ruined the suspense. Anyway, let me know if you want to know what happens." Go on then.

53rd over: Australia 185–1 (Hayden 70, Ponting 0) Harmison completes his over, although there's nothing to report as Channel 4 are at the racing.

54th over: Australia 186–1 (Hayden 70, Ponting 0) England bring Flintoff back into the attack, unsurprisingly, and not much happens. It looks pretty pleasant at The Oval, weather-wise.

55th over: Australia 190–1 (Hayden 74, Ponting 0) Harmison has a bit of a spring in his step at the moment, hitting the bat very hard in that over, but Hayden helps a short one on its way to fine leg for four.

56th over: Australia 192–1 (Hayden 74, Ponting 1) "Get over that hangover and give us some sparkling prose," says Rob Linham, who seems to have misunderstood this over-by-over arrangement. "I'm in work on a Saturday afternoon confronting an epic in-tray, and in a deserted office you're all that's standing between me and going gently out of my mind."

57th over: Australia 198–1 (Hayden 75, Ponting 6) Ponting gets in a real lather against a well-directed Harmison bouncer, shaping to pull but then just checking his shot in the air through square leg. He gets it bang on later in the over, swivelling smoothly to pull low through midwicket and to the fence.

58th over: Australia 203–1 (Hayden 77, Ponting 9) Giles is surprisingly brought on instead of Flintoff, and Ponting forces him through the covers off the back foot.

59th over: Australia 203–1 (Hayden 77, Ponting 9) Harmison has a biggish shout for lbw turned down against Hayden, who thrust his pad at a ball that was too high and missing off. There was a better shout next ball, but instinct suggested it pitched outside leg. And so it did.

60th over: Australia 211–1 (Hayden 78, Ponting 12) As happy news reaches me of "biblical" thunderstorms in east London, Hayden fresh-airs a slog-sweep at Paul Collingwood and the ball flies over wicketkeeper Geraint Jones's right shoulder for four byes.

61st over: Australia 218–1 (Hayden 84, Ponting 13) Hayden, slowly rediscovering something resembling his old authority, pulls Harmison meatily in front of square for four.

62nd over: Australia 223–1 (Hayden 88, Ponting 13) An urgent call of nature there, and looking at the replays it seems Giles should have had Ponting given out caught at silly point. Billy Bowden said no.

63rd over: Australia 226–1 (Hayden 90, Ponting 14) Flintoff on for Harmison, but there's very little happening at the moment – no sign of reverse swing, and even fewer signs of seam movement.

64th over: Australia 231–1 (Hayden 91, Ponting 18) A marvellous shot from Ponting, who rocks back to belabour a Giles long-hop through the covers off the back foot. That was a pretty filthy piece of bowling.

65th over: Australia 241–1 (Hayden 100, Ponting 19) Hayden crunches Flintoff back down the ground for four, and then works four more to long-on to bring up a fighting century, which prompts a grin of almost child-like relief.

Rain stops play! "I still don't rate him," chuckles Cricinfo's Andrew Miller of Hayden, as the rain returns to The Oval and the players dash off. It's absolutely punting it down. "I've got a feeling that he may go on, weather permitting, to get a really big score now," says Chris Hewitt. "How anaemic has our attack been, that we can allow a batsman as chronically out of form as Hayden to get a century? Grr, argh, snarl, etc."

4.35pm Hear those sweet thunderclaps.

Rain report "It's now raining so heavily in south London I've got a flood in my back garden," says Simon. "Is not looking good for any more play today."

The covers are off And play will resume at 5.30pm.

66th over: Australia 244–1 (Hayden 101, Ponting 21) Right, there are 18 overs left of play tonight. Giles completes his unfinished 15th over; I'd be surprised if he continued in the attack – England will surely bowl Harmison and Flintoff.

67th over: Australia 251–1 (Hayden 104, Ponting 25) It is Stephen Harmison, with just one slip, and Ponting clips him firmly through midwicket for three. Anyone still out there?

68th over: Australia 253–1 (Hayden 104, Ponting 26) Giles does continue from the Vauxhall End; two off an uneventful over.

69th over: Australia 257–1 (Hayden 105, Ponting 29) These two have taken a lot of quick singles in this short passage of play – a deliberate ploy to move the innings up a gear, presumably.

70th over: Australia 258–1 (Hayden 105, Ponting 30) Giles and pals go up for lbw when Hayden misses a slog-sweep, but it hit him outside the line.

71st over: Australia 263–1 (Hayden 105, Ponting 35) Too short from Harmison, and Ponting pulls for four with a regal swivel. "How do the bookies see this then, Mr Smyth?" asks David Booth. Good question. Any bloodsucking bookies out there?

72nd over: Australia 264–1 (Hayden 105, Ponting 36)

WICKET! 73rd over: Ponting c Strauss b Flintoff 36 (Australia 264–2) Andrew Flintoff returns to the attack and strikes straight away. It was a good delivery, popping a little off the pitch, and Strauss at gully took a really good low catch diving forward.

73rd over: Australia 268–2 (Hayden 105, Martyn 4) "Bowlers win matches, batsmen lose them," says Jeremy James. "And should England lose, I hate to say it but one or two English batsmen are going to have some very difficult questions to ask themselves."

76th over: Australia 274–2 (Hayden 108, Martyn 8) Sorry about that – a few technical problems. "Current best prices on Betfair are approximately: 4/6 Draw, 7/4 Australia, 20/1 England." Cheers to Rory McQueen for that.

77th over: Australia 275–2 (Hayden 109, Martyn 8) One off the over from Giles, who has been pretty impressive in this little passage of play.

Bad light stops play With five overs left, Australia have taken the offer of the light – it is pretty dark out there, the new ball is due, so you can kind of understand this more than yesterday's decision. That will be that for the day.

Australia 277–2; England 373

Fourth Day

The morning session

BY ROB SMYTH

Preamble: Hello, and welcome to the fourth day of the final Ashes Test at the Kennington Oval in Farringdon. It's gloomy but not raining; another stop-start day is predicted. Tense times: the pathetically *British* comedy rain dancing has tended to obscure the fact that England are in a bit of a mess here. It all points to having to bat 90–odd overs on the final day against Shane Warne, a man for whom the highest tension is as invigorating as a freshly opened can of Red Bull.

An email "No hangover?" asks Richard Coopey. "You're very chipper this morning Rob . . . no hangover today? Are the OBO team letting drinking standards slip, or just trying to maintain peak professional form for such a crucial day of cricket?" It's merely a reflection of the rampant professionalism you've come to expect and indeed love from the OBO team.

79th over: Australia 278–2 (Hayden 110, Martyn 9) Flintoff bowls the last two balls of his half-finished over, and a no-ball as well. One over to the second new ball, and I'm sure it'll be taken immediately. "Have you noticed all the JCL talk about England either winning or losing the Ashes?" asks Simon Ward. "One ought perhaps explain that England may 'fail to regain' the Ashes. And isn't this Test exactly how you imagined the summer to be: England getting not enough runs, Aussies piling on a massive total. I've been quite amazed how the bowlers have got them out of a hole every time." Yep. It's been a weird match. A combination of things – rain, only four bowlers, the need for only a draw, fatalism – meant that England seemed resigned to being under the gun for the rest of the Test once they didn't take an early wicket, so now Australia will be able to bat pretty much as they please.

80th over: Australia 280–2 (Hayden 111, Martyn 10) In that Giles over, a good one, Martyn drives into the ground and Collingwood's excellent parry at cover brings a rush of oohs and aaahs.

WICKET! 81st over: Martyn c Collingwood b Flintoff 10 (Australia 281–3) Just the start England wanted. Flintoff, with the old ball no less, gets some really nasty bounce and Martyn, done for pace and late on the pull stroke, spoons a simple catch to square leg from high on the bat. For such an elegant player, that was a seriously ugly stroke.

81st over: Australia 282–3 (Hayden 112, Clarke 0) What happens with the new ball could be crucial. If England, say, bowl these Aussies out for about 450, that time/runs equation will become so much tighter. If Australia blast off to 600, England will need 227 just to engage that time/runs equation.

82nd over: Australia 282–3 (Hayden 112, Clarke 0) A maiden from Giles (his first of the innings), and he varied his place cleverly there to keep Hayden honest. "For all the thousands upon thousands upon thousands of words the pundits have written before, during, and no doubt after this series, it all comes down to this: the only real difference between the two sides is Shane Warne," says Neil Stork-Brett. "Discuss." And McGrath. Had he not got injured I think Australia would be 3–1, maybe 4–0 up.

83rd over: Australia 286–3 (Hayden 113, Clarke 3) Flintoff takes the second new ball in those bucket hands of his, and has a big shout for lbw turned down after Hayden jams down on an inswinging yorker. In other news, JCL means Johnny Come Lately, for those who were wondering, though anyone who thinks Tim Lovejoy wearing a Ramones T-shirt on his excellent and generation-defining Allstars show makes him a Johnny Come Bloody Lately is being harsh on the great man.

84th over: Australia 287–3 (Hayden 114, Clarke 3) Matthew Hoggard shares the new ball, which he might have done even if Steve Harmison was on the field. He isn't, but silver fox Trevor

Penney is. Hoggard gets one to really kick off a good length and almost whack Clarke under the armpit.

85th over: Australia 287–3 (Hayden 114, Clarke 3) Australia are offered the light but, unsurprisingly, don't take it, and Hayden is beaten when he chases a wide one from Flintoff. A maiden, and it's getting more and more gloomy at The Oval.

86th over: Australia 296–3 (Hayden 122, Clarke 4) A rare display of mortality from Flintoff at second slip, who drops an absolute sitter when Clarke flails outside off stump at a Hoggard away-swinger. England were bowling for just that dismissal, and they should have got it.

87th over: Australia 301–3 (Hayden 122, Clarke 9) Australia have conspicuously upped the tempo here: in that over, Clarke eased Flintoff classily to the cover fence off the back foot. The problem Australia have is this: the moment they declare, England will be off for bad light. I think they might be better served to bat all day and rattle up a monster of a total and hope for the predicted better weather and a full day's Pommie-bashing tomorrow. "Loved Flintoff's remark to the umpire when the Aussies were offered the light," says David Hope. "'Can you put some lights on the bails, I can't see what I'm bowling at!' You can't buy that sort of class."

88th over: Australia 307–3 (Hayden 127, Clarke 10) The umpires are still nattering over the light, though I don't get why – Australia want to stay on. End of story.

89th over: Australia 308–3 (Hayden 128, Clarke 10) In fading light, Flintoff wisely sticks a few short ones up Michael Clarke, and Steve Harmison is warming up to do exactly the same. "So, Smyth," begins Rob Linham. "In the office ready for 10.30 on a Sunday morning. What is it: double time, the hope of promotion, or the lingering threat of a disciplinary interview from last year's Christmas party? I think we should be told." As much as I'd love to claim some kind of lusty farrago from last year's Christmas party, particularly if it involved (insert name of GU crush here), it's just a very geeky excitement: if you'd told me when I was some spotty, virginal, illiterate 14–year-old that I'd be covering an Ashes decider for the *Guardian*, I'd have bitten your zits off.

90th over: Australia 317–3 (Hayden 135, Clarke 11) Harmison it is to make some sweet chin music, and Hayden – aided by the fact that Hoggard at fine leg couldn't see the ball at all – lap-pulls him for four. And no, to answer your emails, the umpires can't force a batting side to take the light. I don't think.

91st over: Australia 319–3 (Hayden 137, Clarke 11) "What the hell planet is Neil Stork-Brett on?" thunders Simon Green. "And worse – you seem to be agreeing with him! 'If McGrath had played throughout the Tests England would be 3–1 down'? Tosh. Australia's batting has been incapable of getting big runs. That's where this series has been won and lost. Not sure McGrath would have added a great deal in this department." He might the way he plays these days but, more to the point, he wouldn't have allowed England to get the first-innings totals that have pressured Australia's top order into making mistakes. Besides, I predicted 5–0 at the start of the summer so I have to justify getting it so spectacularly wrong somehow.

92nd over: Australia 323–3 (Hayden 138, Clarke 14) England are having real trouble sighting the ball in the field – in that over Clarke carved Harmison over gully, where Giles ducked out of the way. Shades of Usman Afzaal (remember him?) in New Zealand in 2002.

WICKET! 93rd over: Hayden lbw b Flintoff 138 (Australia 323–4) Andrew Flintoff strikes again, with the aid of the slowest lbw decision I've ever seen from Rudi Koertzen. It was a really good off-cutter to the left-hander, pitching on middle and jagging back a long way to trap Hayden in front. The end of a cathartic and career-saving innings, and a nice "Well bowled, mate" from Hayden to Flintoff as he walked off.

93rd over: Australia 323–4 (Clarke 14, Katich 0) "I'm a nerd," announces Bob O'Hara, with feeling. "The umpires can force the batsmen to take the light. Law 3, section 9, sub-section d: If at any time the umpires together agree that the conditions of ground, weather or light are so bad that there is obvious and forseeable risk to the safety of any player or umpire, so that it would be unreasonable or dangerous for play to take place . . . they shall immediately suspend play, or not allow play to commence or to restart."

94th over: Australia 329–4 (Clarke 19, Katich 1) With the ball zipping around in the air it's a sensible move to bring Hoggard back for Harmison, I think, and it almost yields first ball. Clarke sliced a drive up and over, and had Bell on the point boundary been able to sight it properly he would have caught it. He didn't, and didn't.

WICKET! 95th over: Katich lbw b Flintoff 1 (Australia 329–5) Freddie is on fire! That was a lovely inducker to Katich, trapping him in front as he flailed across his front pad. Beautiful bowling, and maybe Australia won't get 600 after all. Oh, here comes Adam Gilchrist.

96th over: Australia 338–5 (Clarke 20, Gilchrist 8) Hoggard beats Gilchrist first up with a real jaffa. Gilchrist's response is to time one thrillingly through square leg for four, and then to pull another majestically over midwicket. Shot! I wish I could be in bad nick like Gilchrist.

97th over: Australia 343–5 (Clarke 21, Gilchrist 12) An inside edge saves Clarke from what would have been a pretty adjacent lbw shout.

98th over: Australia 351–5 (Clarke 23, Gilchrist 18) Gilchrist has another dart outside off stump and edges Hoggard wide of the diving Strauss for four: he has 18 off 11 balls now.

99th over: Australia 352–5 (Clarke 23, Gilchrist 19) Flintoff switches to around the wicket for Gilchrist, who diligently watches a few go past his off stump before taking a single. Then Flintoff has a big lbw shout against Clarke turned down – missing leg, I reckon. He is bowling marvellously here.

100th over: Australia 353–5 (Clarke 23, Gilchrist 20) Hoggard goes up wildly for a catch down the leg-side. There was definitely a noise of some description as the ball passed Gilchrist's bat, although replays justified Billy Bowden's decision.

101st over: Australia 356–5 (Clarke 23, Gilchrist 23) Another big shout against Gilchrist, this time when a nasty lifter beats his roundhouse cut, but there didn't appear to be any nick.

WICKET! 101st over: Gilchrist lbw b Hoggard 23 (Australia 356–6) Gilchrist has gone to the last ball before lunch. It pitched on and, though it swung back a long way, Hawkeye had it hitting leg stump. That is a huge wicket for England, and I'm off for some Lucozade.

Australia 356–6; England 373

The afternoon session

BY ROB SMYTH

Preamble: "Can I just point out that that is massive," says Andrew Miller of Cricinfo fame. I think and sincerely hope he was referring to the wicket of Gilchrist.

102nd over: Australia 358–6 (Clarke 24, Warne 0) Hoggard completes the over he began before lunch, and is given a second warning by umpire Bowden for encroaching on the wicket. And then he has Clarke dropped by Geraint Jones! He went a long way in front of first slip, and actually dived too far across so that the ball hit him on the wrist. Gah!

103rd over: Australia 359–6 (Clarke 25, Warne 0) Shane Warne chips one back tantalisingly close to the bowler Flintoff as he follows through. Another fine over from the indefatigable Freddie. "So hungover it's untrue," winces Sarah Robinson. As if it was someone else's fault! "But, every time my eyes close through pain we take a wicket, so I feel like I'm unconsciously doing my bit."

WICKET! 104th over: Clarke lbw b Hoggard 25 (Australia 359–7) With the light improving, the unpalatable prospect of England trying to fend off GD McGrath on a juiced-up track – it is doing plenty, in the air and off the pitch – moves ever closer. But they'll take this for now: Clarke, on the walk, plays around a straight one from Hoggard that came back a fraction.

104th over: Australia 362–7 (Warne 0, Lee 3) "After two weeks of pure hedonism," begins Kevin Taylor, "and cricket, my parents have returned from holiday just as I was settling down on their couch to watch the afternoon session. Dad walks in and turns TV over straightaway to the effing motor racing. Pah."

WICKET! 105th over: Warne c Vaughan b Flintoff 0 (Australia 363–8)
A mesmeric over from Flintoff gets its reward with his first Ashes
five-for and his first in a Test in England. Warne was beaten three
times in a row by two outswingers and a rip-snorter of a lifter, and
in an attempt to hit his way out of trouble he pulled the next ball
straight up in the air, where Michael Vaughan held on to an
absolute dolly at the second attempt. Flintoff has bowled
outrageously well today.

**WICKET! 106th over: McGrath c Strauss b Hoggard 0 (Australia
363–9)** Now we have seen everything in this series – Glenn McGrath
has been dismissed. Textbook outswinger and he just edged a drive
to second slip. To be honest, I'm more concerned about what he'll
do in 15 minutes' time on this pitch. England could get rolled for
120 here – Australia are 86 for 7 today – and then Australia would
knock off the runs in sunshine tomorrow.

106th over: Australia 363–9 (Lee 3, Tait 0) "Could you also tell the
OBO followers that the term JCL comes from the world-famous Red
Issue website that the *Guardian* is so fond of," says Rik Butler. So
what's the cricket equivalent of ABUs anyway? ABAs? ABMs?

107th over: Australia 367–9 (Lee 6, Tait 1) Tait, desperate to get
away from Flintoff's bat-jarrers, takes a risky single and would
probably have been run out had Collingwood hit from cover. Then
Lee does likewise and gets away with it.

WICKET! 107th over: Lee c Giles b Hoggard 6 (Australia 367 all out)
Who'd have thought it: England take a first-innings lead. Lee had a
big yahoo at Hoggard and Giles at deep midwicket took a brilliant
running catch. England lead by six runs, and now things could get
really interesting.

Innings break thoughts At the risk of sounding like, well, me, I
think this may just be a blessing in disguise for Australia: if they are
to chase, they will get to chase in much better conditions for
batting tomorrow. As for today, McGrath on a sweaty is not an
appealing prospect when the Ashes are at stake. Remember the
damage he did when it was going sideways at Lord's? Anyway.
"Freddie Flintoff for PM," says Duncan Cameron. No argument
here.

England second innings

1st over: England 1–0 (led by 6 runs on first innings; Trescothick 1, Strauss 0) As Kelis once sultrily sang: "This is it". The decisive point of the summer, and I'm very nervous. I've never seen, with the openers in, a dot ball being cheered on behalf of the *batting* side before. I have now. The atmosphere is astonishing. "We haven't quite had yet everything in this series," writes Sean Ingle. "What price a Pietersen catch at 6.30pm tomorrow to win the Test and the Ashes?"

2nd over: England 1–0 (led by 6 runs on first innings; Trescothick 1, Strauss 0) Little sign of swing for Lee in his first over, although he does beat Trescothick with one that jagged away late off the pitch.

The umpires have a look at the light! But they're playing on, and they get booed for their trouble.

3rd over: England 2–0 (led by 6 runs on first innings; Trescothick 1, Strauss 1) Trescothick is beaten by McGrath, and Shane Warne is warming up – Billy Bowden, it seems, has told Ricky Ponting that the light will be offered if the seamers stay on. "I have a stomach-churning feeling that that six-run lead could prove vital," says Sean Moore. "Here we go again." You didn't think this series would go quietly did you?

WICKET! 4th over: Strauss c Katich b Warne 1 (England 2–1) Warne it is. What has he got for us this time? What do you think – a wicket fourth ball! It was just a routine bat-pad catch to short leg as Strauss prodded forward, and the tension has been ramped up a notch or 50. "Do any of the readers know what the record Fourth innings score at The Oval to win is?" asks Nicholas Stone. England's 263–9 against Australia in 1902. Next!

5th over: England 6–1 (Trescothick 2, Vaughan 3) McGrath does continue, slightly surprisingly, and immediately sticks a quick and beautifully directed short one up Vaughan, who takes evasive action at the last minute. The next ball is inside-edged to fine leg for one, and Vaughan is clearly unhappy with the light. Who'd be an umpire? Billy Bowden, who has just told Ponting he has to bowl a spinner at both ends now. "Why the relentless negativity??" says Steve Anthony. "I mean at least you're consistently negative, I'll give you that, but do you think your readers really need to hear another doom prediction? Time to get behind England! Come off it, lighten up for once. An Australian win is not gonna happen, it's in the bag for us, or I will eat my modem." I hope you're hungry.

Bad light stops play! I'm surprised at that, given that Warne is bowling, but the light is offered and the roar is like St James's Park when Alan Shearer bangs one in from 30 yards. Shane Warne looks pretty naffed off, and it's easy to see why: there is no physical danger facing Shane Warne in this light. He might force you to have a nervous breakdown with a couple of zooters, but that's a different matter.

2.50pm An early tea has been taken, and I'll be back in 20 minutes.

Australia 367; England 373 and 6–1

The evening session

BY ROB SMYTH

Play will resume at 3.10pm Ooh, I feel all nervous again. There are 61.3 overs to be bowled, potentially, in this session, which can go until 7.00. Sixty-one overs! Four hours!

6th over: England 9–1 (led by 6 on first innings; Trescothick 3, Vaughan 5) The entire Australian team – except Matt Hayden, not that he's in any way humourless – have come on to the field wearing sunglasses. Brilliant. When the action begins, Warne's first ball is driven well by Trescothick and brilliantly fielded by Brett Lee at mid-off.

7th over: England 17–1 (Trescothick 3, Vaughan 13) It is Glenn McGrath, and it's sobering to think that – weather permitting – there are still nearly *160* overs left in this game. That's a lot of overs. In that one, Vaughan rocks back and cuts McGrath crisply for four. And he does it again next ball, in front of square this time.

8th over: England 21–1 (Trescothick 6, Vaughan 14) It's fascinating watching Warne always manoeuvring his field; he really is cricket's great lost captain. Three off the over, including a nasty lifter that took the gloves of Vaughan before bobbing away safely. Promising signs for Australia.

9th over: England 22–1 (Trescothick 6, Vaughan 15) That over from McGrath is a good one – on the money and with just a hint of returning rhythm.

10th over: England 24–1 (Trescothick 6, Vaughan 17) Beautiful stuff from Warne, who draws Vaughan forward and then spins one violently past his outside edge. These are tense times, because rarely has the adage "one wicket brings two" been more apposite than when Ian Bell is the next man in and Shane Warne is on song.

11th over: England 25–1 (Trescothick 7, Vaughan 17) The light has deteriorated, and so Michael Clarke (SLA) comes on for Glenn McGrath (RFM). And, backed up by some comedy hyperbole from Gilchrist and Warne ("That's the natural variation, Pup!"), he causes some mild unease as Trescothick misses an attempted sweep.

12th over: England 28–1 (Trescothick 9, Vaughan 18) Typically mischievous over from Warne, but no alarms for England.

13th over: England 33–1 (Trescothick 13, Vaughan 19) A quarter chance for Katich, as Trescothick middles one right between Katich's legs at short leg. Sometimes they stick.

Bad light stops play again! "What are they doing?" thunders Geoff Boycott, and Ricky Ponting, in conversation with Billy Bowden, looks *seriously* hacked off. "When England have won, I'm sure the box set of the Ashes series will be out soon after to keep you amused forever," says Chris Beavis. "Of course the obligatory 'Bonus Disc' will be included – with special highlights of rain and bad light!!" Er-herr, Beavis, er-herr.

5.10pm It's got a bit gloomier, and it looks ever more likely that there will be no more play today. That would mean 98 overs tomorrow, when the forecast is much better, so it's not time to celebrate the return of the urn just yet.

Play abandoned for the day That's it. Umpires Bowden and Koertzen have surrendered to the inevitable. England close on 34 for 1, a lead of 40, and after all the stunning drama of the summer it now comes down to this: one day, one decent batting performance and the Ashes will be coming home. Blimey.

Australia 367; England 373 and 34–1

Fifth Day

The morning session

BY SEAN INGLE

Preamble: So, here we go. After 21 days, four Tests and more snakish twists and turns than Peter Mandelson on the Pepsi Max Big One, England are just 98 overs from winning the Ashes.

Latest odds, from Betfair: Australia 6–1, England 20–1, the draw 1–5. Meanwhile this from Paul Scott: "I'd be interested in my fellow OBO followers' thoughts on the behaviour of the England supporters at recent Tests," says Paul Scott. "Most of it has been great, but there's an element that's become *Sun*-esque, with more bile and hatred directed at the Aussies. Let's hope we win the Ashes, but we shouldn't forget the Aussies' contribution to such a fantastic cricketing summer. Let's be good, grown-up winners. Or am I just a snob?" No, think that's fair, Paul. Anyone else?

14th over: England 39–1 (Trescothick 14, Vaughan 23) Shane Warne steps in to finish his over. The first ball has a hint of turn – there's more oohing and arrhing than a West Country farming convention after Vaughan nearly bat-pads it to silly point – but the England captain then clouts Warne down the ground for four. Shot! "If England get away with a draw today then I think it is only fair that they award man of the match to their star player this weekend: English Weather," says Andrew Patton, a hopeful Aussie.

15th over: England 38–1 (Trescothick 14, Vaughan 23) Steady first over by McGrath. "I've said it before, owing to the lack of success of our national football team, the football element is all too quick to jump on to the back of our other sporting successes," says David Glover. "Where were they in the previous Ashes Tests and rugby World Cups? No doubt fighting with rival Burberry Cap Brigades."

16th over: England 44–1 (Trescothick 15, Vaughan 28) Lee comes on for Warne and he's already bristling with snarling intent. "At the start of the Ashes series, I hated Brett Lee," says James Townrow. "Now I think he's great – he has a crack with the crowd and plays the game in the right spirit, hard but fair. He is no longer the arrogant, sneering prat of a few years ago. Maybe Wayne Rooney will one day be the same?" Maybe, James. And maybe not.

17th over: England 50–1 (Trescothick 16, Vaughan 33) Another lowish Vaughan edge squirts between fourth slip and gully and races away for four, before another easy cover drive brings up the 50. Meanwhile this from Tim Denning. "I'm glad cricket is going to Sky," he writes. "Not because I have any particular fondness of the Murdoch Dynasty but because no other broadcaster has been prepared to stump up the cash for overseas cricket coverage. Sky have done as much for the popularity of English cricket as any other broadcaster." Really Tim? Let's see how much cricket's popularity grows in the next four years, when 250,000 (at most) are watching the home Tests.

18th over: England 52–1 (Trescothick 17, Vaughan 35) "I'm probably woefully behind on this one, having spent the second and third Tests holed up in a vineyard in Portugal," hurrahs Nick Vivian. "But answer me this: when was the last time that Australia retained the Ashes whilst fielding a team including no moustachioed member whatsoever? The dropping of Jason Gillespie may now seem a little rash."

19th over: England 57–1 (Trescothick 17, Vaughan 41) It's heartening to report that there's no weak-kneed defensiveness from England so far: an effortless cover drive, reminiscent of Vaughan at his 2002 best, races to the boundary and a pull shot takes him into the 40s. Meanwhile, more Sky talk. "Can you see Sky interrupting the Ashes to go to horse racing?" asks John Andre. Can you see eight million people paying £480 a year to watch Sky Sports 1, John?

20th over: England 60–1 (Trescothick 18, Vaughan 41) Not before time, Warne comes on, and immediately there's drama. Warne gets one to spit out of the rough, it hits Trescothick's pad and bat and drops millimetres from Ricky Ponting's hands. "Can anyone shed any light on why Shane Warne wears flares to play cricket?" asks Lewis Holmes.

21st over: England 62–1 (Trescothick 18, Vaughan 42) We haven't seen much of the McGrath of Lord's so far today, but with the last ball of the over he produces an absolute beaut which jigs this way and that before missing Trescothick's outside edge. "The Aussie fans and team have been brilliant," writes Shane (who I'm guessing sports a peroxide-hued mullet). "I was there Saturday and experienced the last Ashes tour in Oz and each time the sportmanship has astounded me. I love the way the Aussies came out wearing shades yesterday – still having a laugh in the most important Test ever, genius."

22nd over: England 67–1 (Trescothick 21, Vaughan 45) Warne is definitely getting some turn here, but both batsmen look easy-chair comfortable against him. "The BBC is not blameless in the coverage of cricket debate," points out James Scowen. "They didn't bother to bid for the rights to the TV coverage, and their radio coverage, while excellent, is relegated to the terrible sound of long wave. Many people don't have long-wave radio access these days."

WICKET! 22nd over: Vaughan c Gilchrist b McGrath 45 (England 67–2) Brilliant catch from Gilchrist! McGrath gets the tiniest amount of outswing, Vaughan gets the nick and Gilchrist takes a diving catch with one hand. Game on! "Re: Shane Warne's flared pants. As anyone who watches Trinny and Susannah would know, flares have a slimming effect on anyone with a sturdy girth," says Paul Scott (and several hundred others).

WICKET! 23rd over: Bell c Warne b McGrath 0 (England 67–3) Bell goes first ball! McGrath produces an identikit delivery and Bell edges it behind to Warne at first slip. This is squeaky bum time for England. "Isn't this day made for Graham Thorpe?" asks Habib Butt, not unreasonably.

23rd over: England 67–3 (Trescothick 21, Pietersen 0) McGrath, on a hat-trick, bounces Pietersen – it hits something and loops behind to

Ponting, but umpire Bowden spots that it clattered into shoulder not glove.

24th over: England 67–3 (Trescothick 21, Pietersen 0) Pietersen is dropped! Warne gets the ball to turn sideways, Pietersen nicks it behind – Gilchrist gets a touch and it hits Hayden on the knee. Has Gilchrist just dropped the Ashes?

25th over: England 73–3 (Trescothick 25, Pietersen 2) More probing from McGrath, who – after a month of searching for it – has found his nagging just-outside-off-stump length. "Given Bell's abysmal performances throughout this series would it not be even more remarkable if we won the Ashes when we have effectively played with only 10 men?" asks Alex Bowes.

26th over: England 75–3 (Trescothick 26, Pietersen 3) A HUGE appeal from Warne! He pitches it at least three foot outside off stump and – unbelievably – it jags back and raps Trescothick just outside off stump. Umpire Koertzen hesitates before correctly deciding: not out.

27th over: England 79–3 (Trescothick 26, Pietersen 7) Shot from Pietersen! McGrath tries to bounce him, Pietersen's response is a crashing pull shot that dances to the boundary. Still, these are tense times at The Oval. "Is there a bigger over-by-over idiot than me?" asks Rich Rowe. "Back earlier in the year I went on to the Oval site when the fifth-day tickets went on sale. I even clicked buy now, but had second thoughts and decided it would be a depressing experience with nothing to play for. Idiot. I only have myself to blame and am now stuck in the office for the day." Anyone got any worse tales?

28th over: England 81–3 (Trescothick 27, Pietersen 8) Warne is making the ball sing. Pietesen plays and misses at another textbook leggie before scrambling a single off another inside edge.

29th over: England 82–3 (Trescothick 27, Pietersen 9) McGrath continues to probe, Pietersen and Trescothick to block. "Here's a bad luck story for you," writes Tim Ward. "On the day the tickets went on sale I had ten tickets for the Friday and another ten for the Monday of the final Test selected in the form on my computer screen all ready to be paid for. I then entered my credit card details, pressed send – and the Oval's website crashed. I spent the next few hours trying to get back onto the site to no avail. When I finally got in the tickets had all gone – bah!"

30th over: England 89–3 (Trescothick 32, Pietersen 11) Lucky escape for Pietersen, who attempts a run to Michael Clarke. Clarke hits the stumps, but Pietersen is in . . . just. "Surely it was somewhat premature of the ECB to book Trafalgar Square for a victory celebration," writes Stuart Wigley. "If the Aussies do retain the Ashes perhaps we could hang Ian Bell from Nelson's Column and the crowd can pelt him with cricket balls?"

31st over: England 93–3 (Trescothick 32, Pietersen 15) Unbelievable! Warne has just dropped an absolute dolly after Pietersen edged a fullish one off Lee. Both bowler and catcher are shaking their heads in disbelief: Pietersen has now been dropped twice, and England get another huge let-off. "Musings – this is more stressful than either the birth of my children (Sam and George) or the time when learning to drive that I went the wrong way down a dual carriageway," writes Stuart Ashead, who I'm betting is not alone.

32nd over: England 106–3 (Trescothick 32, Pietersen 28) More jaw-dropping stuff: Pietersen has just slog-swept Warne TWICE for six over deep midwicket. However, in between, he swung and missed at one outside off stump and was nearly stumped.

33rd over: England 109–3 (Trescothick 33, Pietersen 30) Suddenly the sun is out and England are looking slightly steadier. Another good over from Lee, though, including a toe-breaking yorker which Pietersen only just dug out. "I'm sure you're aware, but your sports website server must be taking a monster hit right now, because it's almost impossible to get through to it," writes Mark Hatton. "I reckon nine out of 10 requests to refresh the page are timing out. Quick! Beef up the servers! Don't deny me my cricket fix in the office! Not now!"

WICKET! 33rd over: Trescothick lbw Warne 33 (England 109–4) Er, what was I saying? Warne gets prodigious turn, it stays low and Trescothick is hit in front of off stump. Umpire Koertzen rightly decides it was hitting off: Out! "At 8.10 this morning my two-year-old son, unprompted, raised his hands in the air and shouted 'Freddie Flintoff'," writes Crispin Heath. "My wife almost had a hernia laughing, I shed but a single tear."

34th over: England 110–4 (Pietersen 30, Flintoff 1) Flintoff comes in to huge cheers and then is beaten by an absolute jaffa, before a fine cut gets him off the mark.

35th over: England 112–4 (Pietersen 31, Flintoff 2) Amazingly, the draw is still a too-short 4–11, with the Aussies 5–1 and England 14–1. Lee continues to test Pietersen until he strays on to leg stump and is brushed away down to fine leg.

36th over: England 112–4 (Pietersen 31, Flintoff 2) Another HUGE appeal against Pietersen after Warne thwacks him on the pads. Umpire Koertzen mulls it over in his mind and says not out. Hawkeye, however, reckons it would've hit off stump. Pietersen's third escape of the morning. "Re: idiotic cricket misjudgements. I had a ticket for Sunday at Edgbaston but decided it wasn't worth the journey to Birmingham for the last two wickets – does that count?" asks Tom Flynn. Rather think it does, Tom.

37th over: England 122–4 (Pietersen 34, Flintoff 4) Some customary looseness from Lee, whose radar deserts him as he sends down four byes. Meanwhile England are content to nibble and nurdle. "We have the cricket on TV at work, and I am currently being given tactics advice by a lady who was taught the rules yesterday by her boyfriend," fumes David Penney. "Hold me back."

WICKET! 38th over: Flintoff c and b Warne 8 (England 122–5) This is what we came for: Warne v. Flintoff. You sense that whoever wins this duel could win the Ashes – and no sooner than I write about an exquisite Flintoff cut, he drives one straight back at Warne who takes an excellent catch at ankle height. "Re: the Guardian Berliner. Where do I find the new hamburger-sized OBO? And can I get chips with it?" asks Tim Richmond.

39th over: England 122–5 (Pietersen 34, Collingwood 0) Pietersen's just been whacked on the ribs, so there's a short break while he gets treatment. Next ball back KP fails to pick up another bouncer which hits him again. And then Lee nails him with another bouncer, which hits his gloves . . . and loops over third slip. Great stuff from the Aussies. That's lunch. I'm just going to get my breath back.

Australia 367; England 373 and 122–5

The afternoon session

BY SEAN INGLE

Preamble: Judging from my inbox, the doom-mongers are already fearing the worst, but if England can bat past tea they should be at least 220 in front with around 45–odd overs left, which will surely give them the edge. "I've been feeling ropey all morning, but when I read Flintoff being out had to go and be sick," says Jim Carpenter. "Anyone else suffering physically just from reading a website?"

40th over: England 130–5 (Pietersen 38, Collingwood 0) Ominous first delivery from Warne, which shoots low and is only just dug out by Pietersen. But England are continuing to play aggressively: Pietersen takes a sharp second and then steals a single. "England should declare now," says Paul Hannaford. "Australia are notoriously bad at chasing 130–ish. Declare now and they will crumble. Get them chasing 180–200 and they will cruise it!"

41st over: England 141–5 (Pietersen 49, Collingwood 0) Lee bounces Pietersen – who hooks him for six over fine leg! Listen to those boozy post-lunch roars and, if I'm not mistaken, the first chant of "Barmy Army". Later in the over Lee gets some reverse swing and nearly yorks Collingwood. "I just realised that if Australia win today we'll have a palindromic Test series: Aus win, Eng win, draw, Eng win, Aus win," says Brendan Jones, from Australia. "Wouldn't that be nice?"

42nd over: England 144–5 (Pietersen 52, Collingwood 0) Pietersen brings up an adventurous, if slightly lucky 50, with a prod through mid-off. Collingwood then sees out the over with Tavare-esque defence. Meanwhile this from one of our Australian readers: "We are still the No. 1 one-day team in the world," writes Jesse Noakes from Perth. "The law of probabilities says Gilchrist, with a better average than any Pom since probably Sutcliffe, needs to come good at some stage – where better than with the Aussies needing 230 to win off 30 overs?"

43rd over: England 160–5 (Pietersen 68, Collingwood 0) There's a fine line between genius and foolhardiness – and at the moment Pietersen's an absolute genius. First he slogs Lee for six then, next ball, he repeats the trick only to miscue it towards Tait, who drops a difficult one-handed diving catch. Still Pietersen goes after Lee, and another four to fine leg follows – off a 97mph bouncer – and England's fans are going wild. "I think I may be suffering from RSI from pressing F5," says Jonathan Carter. "I know it refreshes but I'm too nervous to wait.

44th over: England 162–5 (Pietersen 68, Collingwood 1) Warne continues to wile and beguile. Collingwood is struggling, until Warne bowls too short and he gets off the mark. "Just came from the pub," writes James LeMaurier. "I had to leave after two overs because the guy sat next to me was one of these fancy Johnny Come Latelys, season ticket at Chelsea types. He asked me how long it had taken England to 'shoot' their first 130 runs. 'Three or four hours?' I wished 10,000 deaths upon him, especially when he started clapping and cheering at Pietersen's six off Lee. I almost prayed for an Aussie win, just to keep his sort out of my way. The upshot, I came back to the office to sit in righteous indignation in front of the OBO."

45th over: England 171–5 (Pietersen 76, Collingwood 2) Lee is bowling seriously quickly – consistently around 95mph – and looks to have trapped Collingwood lbw. Only for Bowden to rule, wrongly, that Lee had no-balled. Oh dear, oh dear, Bowden is having a shocker. Collingwood dabs a single, and then Pietersen twice thumps Lee straight down the ground. Incredible cricket! "I've put £100 on Australia to win in the same way I did for the Rugby World Cup final," says James Peterson. "It matters so much that we win that I want some financial compensation to drown my sorrows if we lose. Anyone else have some better ways of reducing the pain of such sporting events?"

46th over: England 173–5 (Pietersen 77, Collingwood 3) What a turnaround since lunch: we've had only six overs, but England have smashed nearly 50 runs. There's a carnival atmosphere at The Oval, and bookies have responded by pushing the Aussies out to 6–1 – but, remember, there are still 66 overs left today.

47th over: England 176–5 (Pietersen 77, Collingwood 4) Big moment in the game, this. McGrath is on for Lee, and the Australians desperately need a wicket. Collingwood, who's scored just four off 32 balls, refuses to oblige. "I'd give man of the series to Shane

Warne regardless of what happens today," says a generous Tim Jones. "Although Flintoff has been excellent, Warne has just been so dangerous whenever he has the ball. Has there ever been a more dangerous bowler on any surface? Also he's made important runs."

48th over: England 181–5 (Pietersen 78, Collingwood 5) Pietersen slogs Warne on to his boot, and it balloons to Hayden, who appeals a catch – the umpires confer before agreeing the shot also hit the ground as well as boot. "I agree with Tim Jones," says Richard Foxton. "Would the Aussies be in with even the slightest sniff of the Ashes if it wasn't for Shane Warne? You could compare him to Diego Maradona at the 1986 World Cup."

49th over: England 181–5 (Pietersen 78, Collingwood 5) Great over from McGrath, tight and straight. Maiden. Meanwhile this from Richard Moore: "Apparently my wife's boss, who only learned the rules of cricket yesterday from her young son, has announced in a conference call with the Sydney office that 'Shane Warne is a perfect sporting example' for her young son, and that 'she hopes he grows up just like him'. There was an obvious guffaw from Sydney, closely followed by the sound of my wife's head hitting the desk due to a sudden dizzy spell."

50th over: England 181–5 (Pietersen 78, Collingwood 5) Another big lbw appeal as Warne hits Pietersen on the foot. Umpire Koertzen correctly spots that Pietersen's foot was outside leg stump, however, "When the Aussies are in, what's to stop us bowling a ridiculously slow over rate?" asks Adam Horridge. "Get Gilo trotting in from the boundary. I know we'd be fined but what price for the Ashes? Four overs an hour would do nicely." Hardly good sportsmanship, is it, Adam?

51st over: England 182–5 (Pietersen 78, Collingwood 5) McGrath is keeping it tight, but (famous last words alert) he's not look like taking a wicket. That's drinks, and England surely have one hand on the Ashes. "Let's not be too hard on the JCLs," says Christopher Price. "Over the weekend I have finally explained the basic laws of cricket to my French, and female, housemate. After a summer of confusion we had a moment of *My Fair Lady*-like clarity, and by Jove she's got it. While I am suffering at work she is watching the cricket on her own. I feel like a proud father who has just taught his child how to ride a bike."

WICKET! 52nd over: Collingwood c Ponting b Warne 10 (England 186–6) Just when England look home and hosed, Collingwood dabs one to Ponting, who takes a desperate catch at silly point. Game on! "Will you stop," growls Toni Garcia. "Whenever you say something extremely positive we lose another wicket."

53rd over: England 187–6 (Pietersen 79, G Jones 1) Jones gets off the mark with a confident drive through the covers. England now lead by 194.

54th over: England 188–6 (Pietersen 79, G Jones 1) Warne gives Jones the verbals after he leaves one that spins out of the rough and misses his off stump by inches. "We started with a Twenty20 game, and we're going to finish with one too," predicts Alex Fleetwood. "What was it we set the Aussies to make in the very first game of the summer? 200–odd off 20 overs? Collingwood taking an unbelievable catch to finish Hayden? It's all going to happen again, mark my words. Except they'll get a lot closer this time."

55th over: England 189–6 (Pietersen 80, G Jones 1) The runs have dried up, and the heady, calypso atmosphere of earlier has gone too. McGrath ekes out another tight over, Jones gets an edge to one delivery, but it falls short of Warne at first slip. "Are the Betfair adverts now annoying everyone as much as me?" asks Ross Bell. You mean they haven't annoyed you before, Ross?

56th over: England 190–6 (Pietersen 81, G Jones 1) Warne is still trying to bamboozle Pietersen, without any success so far. Just the one run off the over, but England won't mind: there are only 56 overs left today. "Twenty20?!" splutters the extravagantly-monikered Alan May Estebaranz. "This is more like Stick Cricket."

57th over: England 199–6 (Pietersen 90, G Jones 1) Another gamble from Ponting: Tait replaces McGrath. He could easily go for 30 off three overs, here – indeed his first two deliveries have gone for eight runs.

WICKET! 57th over: G Jones b Tait 1 (England 199–7) Unbelievable. Tait produces an absolute Exocet which rips out Jones's off stump and sends it tumbling ten yards behind the wicket. Suddenly it's game on again.

58th over: England 201–7 (Pietersen 90, Giles 2) Warne continues to tease and torment: when one raps Giles's pads there are shouts of

"Catch it! catch it!", but Giles is able to survive. "Re: those comments about being sick with tension. Get a grip, you big girl's blouses, it's a game of bloody cricket!" says Jason Wilshaw.

59th over: England 209–7 (Pietersen 95, Giles 5) To huge cheers, Giles picks up three after a flick off his pads. Then Pietersen, who changes bats mid-over, clobbers a boundary through midwicket to move on to 95. We now have 53 overs left. "You don't need to remind us after each wicket that it's game on," says Joshua Davis. "From the burning in our stomachs and the residual taste of vomit in our throats, I think we all know!"

60th over: England 211–7 (Pietersen 96, Giles 5) "In response to Adam Horridge's question about bowling a ludicrously slow over rate (50th over), would it not be cruel and unsportsmanlike, but nonetheless effective, to bowl everything at the Australians under-arm?" suggests Dennis O'Neil. "After all, they have form themselves with that technique."

61st over: England 212–7 (Pietersen 97, Giles 5) After Pietersen takes a single off the first ball, Tait has five deliveries at the *Guardian*'s Ashley Giles, who blocks and evades them all, without much discomfort. Meanwhile this from Anthony Kerr. "My wife's cat was cremated in June and its remains are in a box in our living-room," he writes. "I plan to run round with it above my head and emulate the 1953 commentator by shouting 'It's the Ashes!' at the close tonight. Who's good in your legal department?"

62nd over: England 213–7 (Pietersen 98, Giles 5) Again Pietersen takes an early single, again Giles sees out the rest of the over. Time is running out and Australia desperately need another wicket. "Under-arm bowling is now illegal," points out Jonathon Kirk. "Rule was probably brought in due to the unsporting Aussies in that game against New Zealand in the 80s."

63rd over: England 219–7 (Pietersen 104, Giles 5) Biggest roar of the day as Pietersen reaches his maiden Test hundred with a glorious shot through the covers. He jumps up, punches the air, and goes "Yeah!" Meanwhile, the cries of "England, England!" ring round The Oval. That's tea.

Australia 367; England 373 and 219–7

The evening session

BY ROB SMYTH

Preamble: Afternoon, and welcome to the tension-free evening session at The Oval. This is that brilliant scene in *Out of Sight* with Jennifer Lopez and George Clooney in the bar, the bit where you're in the taxi with the girl/boy of your dreams on a Friday night. The deal is done, and this is that lovely window between unspoken confirmation and orgiastic actuality. So sit back, enjoy it – even send a funny email if you've got it in you – because after 16 years of 'Bowled Warner', Karl Kennedy, and Jim Robinson popping up in *The OC*, THE FRIGGIN' ASHES ARE COMING HOME!*

64th over: England 222–7 (add 6 for their lead to save me doing it every over; Pietersen 105, Giles 7) No lumps in the fat lady's throat in that Warne over – my *Guardian* colleague Giles survives with some meticulous forward thrusts. "Is it possible that Josh Schwartz (*OC* creator, for the grossly uninitiated) could have played his own part in the soon-to-be-realised Ashes success?" says Stuart Youngs. "By killing off Jim Robinson in the tail-end of season two I think the psychological hold of the man over the entire British nation was broken and thus our boys in white were free to go on and wrestle back that pesky urn." He certainly did more than Ian Bell . . .

65th over: England 226–7 (Pietersen 105, Giles 11) A really nasty, last-chance-saloon over of short stuff from the admirable Brett Lee – it only took them 70+ years to copy our Bodyline, eh? "One of my co-workers said that cricket lovers were naturally anally retentive," says Dave Penney, carefully setting himself up for a gag that is nowhere near as good as he thinks it is, if I'm honest, though I'm sure he's still a decent person so we shouldn't judge him really. "I told him to shut up and to never use my tea mug for coffee again."

66th over: England 229–7 (Pietersen 108, Giles 11) Warne has a biggish shout for lbw turned down. Pitched outside leg. "The

---

*Guardian Unlimited does not in any way endorse the premature chicken-counting of a deranged fool and would like to stress that, if Shane Warne were to take a hat-trick straight after tea, Australia would need an eminently gettable 228 in 46 overs.

sitting-in-the-back-of-a-taxi scenario is an apt comparison with the present situation," says Thomas Morris, "because in my experience it is usually followed by the young lady suddenly remembering a boyfriend who had previously slipped her mind, or the realisation that she's got an early start the next morning and would I mind awfully if she let me out when we passed the nearest tube?" Relax: it's over. So much so that I'm taking nominations for the inevitable (and unfunny) "Your boys took one hell of a beating, mate" speech that will surely follow come 6.30 tonight.

67th over (45 left, minus two for change of innings): England 232–7 (add 6 for their lead; Pietersen 109, Giles 13) As Lee's over passes without incident, a boozy crowd is counting chickens and pints with giddy abandon. "Statistical question for you Rob," says Rick Eyre, whose cricket blog you should google if you get a minute. "Is Kevin Pietersen the first person ever to score a Test century with a dead skunk under his helmet?" He's the first South African-born one, for sure.

68th over (44 left, minus two for change of innings): England 236–7 (add 6 for their lead; Pietersen 112, Giles 14) Another soft-handed edge from Pietersen off Warne brings two, and time is running out for Australia.

69th over (43 left, minus two for change of innings): England 236–7 (add 6 for their lead; Pietersen 112, Giles 14) Australia's required rate is now up to about six an over. It's all over, Red Rover! In that over, Lee gives it absolutely everything to Giles, who sensibly ducks and weaves at every opportunity.

70th over (42 left, minus two for change of innings): England 239–7 (add 6 for their lead; Pietersen 113, Giles 16) Another over, another Shaun Tait misfield, and no alarms for Pietersen and my colleague Gilo. "Are there any plans to release the collected OBOs of this Ashes?" says Laura Stuart. "Whatever the outcome, it would be a fantastic chronicle record of collective office-bound nervousness and attempts by terrified people to distract themselves from gnawing their hands off. And a worthless Christmas stocking-filler to boot." "Whatever the outcome". Good one.

71st over (41 left, minus two for change of innings): England 245–7 (add 6 for their lead; Pietersen 119, Giles 16) The admirable Brett Lee has given everything and more in this series, but he is still tearing in at well over 90mph, and Pietersen pops a nasty lifter over the vacant silly-point area. Pietersen's response is to pull a majestic six; the party is officially under way, which means Pietersen is in just the position he likes: national hero.

72nd over (40 left, minus two for change of innings): England 257–7 (add 6 for their lead; Pietersen 130, Giles 17) Pietersen is icing the cake now – in that Warne over he drives sweet and straight for a regal six, his sixth of the innings. Then he welts four more down the ground for good measure. He'll be dining out on this innings for years. "Good to see you in a better mood than last week," says Tim Ward. "I reckon the tension must have been getting to you, which is understandable."

73rd over (39 left, minus two for change of innings): England 258–7 (add 6 for their lead; Pietersen 131, Giles 17) More sinew-straining short stuff from Brett Lee, but Giles has got his eye in now. Here's Jeremy James. "CMJ on *TMS* thinks Vaughan ought to declare 'in the spirit of the game, to give the other side a chance'!!! Do you think he will?" No idea, but has anyone seen any marbles?

74th over (38 left, minus two for change of innings): England 258–7 (add 6 for their lead; Pietersen 131, Giles 17) "Who fancies declaring?" ask about 400 of you. Sack that – let's have some Pietersenian entertainment to finish things off.

75th over (37 left, minus two for change of innings): England 262–7 (add 6 for their lead; Pietersen 132, Giles 23) The last throw of the dice, aka Glenn McGrath, and Giles scythes him past point for three. Anyone out there biting their nails, don't. A) it's minging; B) it's bad for you, and C) it's unnecessary.

76th over (36 left, minus two for change of innings): England 272–7 (add 6 for their lead; Pietersen 138, Giles 27) Even Warne's body language betrays imminent defeat now, which is as sure a sign as you'll ever get. In that over, Pietersen cuts him thrillingly for four. "I think a good test for a JCL is whether they know what CMJ on TMS means," says Howard Miller. True that. And indeed OBO which, for those asking, means Over By Over.

77th over (35 left, minus two for change of innings): England 277–7 (add 6 for their lead; Pietersen 142, Giles 25) Camera cuts to Ron Howard of *Happy Days* fame talking to Stuart MacGill on the Aussie balcony, but not even The Fonz could save this one. "Now the Ashes are almost won, it's time to honour our gallant opponents for the part they've played in this series," says David Russell. "I've particularly admired the contribution of Shane Warne and Mattie Hayden today, as they've literally handed us the Ashes by dropping KP. Thanks boys!" Go back to your Hackett store, you fool.

78th over (34 left, minus two for change of innings): England 278–7 (add 6 for their lead; Pietersen 142, Giles 26) Wonder who the man of the match will be? I'd still go for Flintoff – it'd complete a hat-trick of MOTM awards, officially making it Freddie's Ashes, and his heroism yesterday (not to mention an absolutely vital innings on the first day) was unlike anything I've ever seen.

79th over (33 left, minus two for change of innings): England 286–7 (add 6 for their lead; Pietersen 142, Giles 34) Giles cuts McGrath for four – will his late bid for the Man of the Series get its just reward? He edges four more to give the judges a real dilemma.

80th over (32 left, minus two for change of innings): England 298–7 (add 6 for their lead; Pietersen 153, Giles 35) Make that an Ashes-record seven sixes in an innings for Pietersen, this one a free-and-easy drive over long-on off his old mate Warne. The next ball is cut for four to bring up an Ashes-winning 150. You don't need Pink (or an idiot like me) to tell you that the party has started, big-time. "So let's get this right," begins Paul Store. "After 16 years we have finally defeated, at cricket, a country with only a third of our population, with the help of bad weather. Why is this worth a celebration? Am I missing something?" Serotonin?

81st over (31 left, minus two for change of innings): England 299–7 (add 6 for their lead; Pietersen 153, Giles 36) The new red cherry is taken, which makes me think of Gareth's rhyme in *The Office*. "Continuing the *Out of Sight* analogy," says Daniel Way. "Aren't we through the front door and being led up the stairs by the hand?" Yes, Sir, yes we are. "We're possibly fiddling with a prophylactic." So why is there a fat lady clearing her throat?

82nd over: England 304–7 (Pietersen 154, Giles 39) Just to repeat for those of you who have been stuck in a dark room with some funky cheese since July 20: England have regained the Ashes. So all ears turn to Richie Benaud's last words. I'm tipping "Bugger", but the 3–1 favourite is "Goodbye". "This must mean so much more for those who remember Nasser being booed on the balcony after we lost to NZ six years ago," says Dave Forrest.

WICKET! 83rd over: Pietersen b McGrath 158 (England 308–8) McGrath cleans up England's Ashes-winner with a full, leg-cutting jaffa that knocks his off pole over. The end of a marvellous innings – sketchy at first, epic thereafter.

83rd over: England 309–8 (Giles 39, Hoggard 1) Richie has gone, and I was so preoccupied that I missed his final words. Gah! Sean Ingle thinks it was "Greig". "Off to the pub to catch the last few overs," says Chris Gibbons. "Thanks for the commentary over the last few weeks, even if you did take the piss out of my surname when you were in full-on tetchy mode on Friday." Thursday actually, you miserable piece of . . . Just kidding, Clive.

84th over: England 309–8 (Giles 39, Hoggard 1) So how does it feel, this Ashes-winning lark? It's pretty good, isn't it? But I reckon it'll feel a whole lot better at 2am tomorrow morning. "I'm going to be heretical," says Joy Clancy, at which point I skipped to the next email. Nothing personal, but we do get a lot.

85th over: England 310–8 (Giles 40, Hoggard 1) "Am angling for an acknowledgement of the two Brits who have been stuck in an internet café in Cuba since absurdly early this morning coping with non-existent air-conditioning, bad internet connection and lots of pesky locals (just like the office at home then)," says Stuart McInnes. "On the plus side we'll be celebrating with Mojitos and Cohibas tonight!" A plain old 12 pints of Stella will do most people over here, I suspect.

86th over: England 313–8 (Giles 41, Hoggard 1) Brett Lee is still steaming in, even though it's long gone, still peppering England with short stuff. Where does he get the pride from?

87th over: England 325–8 (Giles 50, Hoggard 4) Giles pulls away at the last minute but McGrath follows through to knock his off pole over anyway, before wheeling away Ian Rush style in a comedy celebration. Then Giles clouts him through extra cover off the back foot for four, and smears him down the ground to reach his fifty. "The Aussies," says Kieran Blackburn. "It's time to salute one of the greatest sports teams ever, and a good bunch of blokes too. Well played, mates."

88th over: England 325–8 (Giles 50, Hoggard 4) Brett Lee is still seriously fired up – 94mph and then some, teeth gritted angrily, giving it absolutely everything. Let it go, son! It's over!

89th over: England 330–8 (Giles 55, Hoggard 4) Ashley Giles carts McGrath to midwicket for four more, and it's just a matter of when the action gets called off now. To my mild chagrin, the drunken idiots at The Oval are chanting: "Are you Scotland in disguise?" No, they're Australia, one of the greatest cricket teams in history and – just an idea – why don't you celebrate the fact we've been good enough to beat them rather than go to the xenophobia autopilot, eh?

90th over: England 334–8 (Giles 59, Hoggard 4) The game can't finish for another eight overs (when the final hour begins) and 20 minutes. In the meantime, Giles tonks Warne through the covers off the back foot for four. He can't get a ton, surely?

91st over: England 335–8 (Giles 59, Hoggard 4) Shaun Tait relieves Glenn McGrath at the Pavilion End – we'll do the gags here – and McGrath gets a really good ovation as he goes to field on the boundary. It's one big love-in! "You've gotta love Warney," says Gavin Monks. "He'll still be getting rat-arsed at the end of the day." We've got a lot in common.

WICKET! 92nd over: Giles b Warne 59 (England 335–9) How's that for a parting gesture from Shane Warne? For the umpteenth and one last time on English soil, he bowls a Pom around his legs with an absolute jaffa that drifted out and ripped back in. It ends the biggest and best innings of the *Guardian*'s Ashley Giles's Test career, and gives Warne one last five-for. What a legend.

WICKET! 92nd over: Harmison c Hayden b Warne 0 (England 335 all out) Hayden at slip takes a wonderful catch to give Warne his sixth wicket (40 for the series), and he and Glenn McGrath embrace warmly on the way off before saying their final farewells to Test cricket in England. For the incessant torture of the last 12 years, cheers fellas.

Bad light stops play! Australia are offered the light in Steve Harmison's first over, and Hayden and Langer are toddling off. It hasn't been confirmed yet, but trust me, all I need are your bank detai— sorry, I meant that it's all over! In fact, the umpires Bowden and Koertzen made a complete effing a mess of that; nobody seemed to know what was going on, so now England are walking off fairly sheepishly. But who cares?

Two minutes later The England heroes and Ian Bell are looking a bit confused on the balcony – basically they're waiting for confirmation that the game has been called off, but before that happens some nugget has to leaf through all 742,013 pages of the laws of cricket to make sure he won't get fired for allowing England to do what everyone already knows they've done. It's bureaucracy gone mad. Get it sorted! "Only cricket can make a moment like this so confusing and messed up," says Dave Forrest. "COMMON SENSE please."

After all the faffing, it's official: ENGLAND HAVE WON THE ASHES! Umpire Bowden – never one to miss a moment of ceremony – marches out to the middle with that other umpire and symbolically removes the bails. It's over! We've effing done it!

Australia 367 and 4–0; England 373 and 335

Postamble

It was epic from start to finish. It had the lot: skill, derring-do, a new set of national heroes, unprecedented sportsmanship, a truly abominable haircut, a comical foul-mouthed rant that nobody will ever forget, and some of the most spectacular drinking sessions seen in English sport since Tony Adams learned to play the piano. But enough about the summer's over-by-overs – you saw that lamentable excuse for a gag coming a mile off, didn't you? – the event that they were covering, the Ashes 2005, was one to remember.

It was quite simply, and without risk of hyperbole, The Greatest Test Series Ever Until The Next Time England Win The Ashes™. It produced the most unlikely national obsession since some be-Stetsoned Texan oil tycoon got plugged (it was Kristin Sheperd you know), and from July 21 to September 12 it was the only thing anyone worth talking to was talking about. Apart from themselves, obviously.

Depending on which funky cheese you were eating, cricket became the new brown, the new football, the new rock'n'roll or even the new black.

Whatever: the key thing was that it was no longer the old beige. Even though half the country had no idea what was going on, it WAS STILL SO EXCITING! As the drama mushroomed almost like a mushroom, literally tens of hooked office-bound Guardian Unlimited readers knew there was only one place to follow it: in the pub, quaffing warm Lambrini until they could no longer feel their legs. But with that not an option, the over-by-over became the zeitgeisty reason to do less than zero at work.

Much of the reason for that was the emails, whose compelling inanity made them as fundamental to the OBO experience as Freddie's bouncer and Warney's slider. Even the rubbish ones: goons writing in saying they had a bet on who'd get mentioned first and they weren't in any way sad and could we please publish theirs; goons writing in saying they had nothing to say except COME ON ENGLAND and could we please publish theirs. Actually no, not the rubbish ones. But a few really made it all worthwhile, like this from Tom Paternoster on the morning of the first day of the fourth Test: "When I read that McGrath was out I wanted to kiss your pixellated outpourings." Quite. We'd hope you agree: it's been defiantly chronological.

Rob Smyth